The Winding Trail

EDITED BY ROGER SMITH

The Winding Trail

with cartoons by Sheridan Anderson

DIADEM BOOKS LTD LONDON

First published in 1981 by
Diadem Books Limited, London

All trade enquiries to:
Cordee, 249 Knighton Church Road,
Leicester

Copyright © 1981 by Roger Smith

The Winding trail
  1. Great Britain — Description and travel —
  1981 —
  I. Smith, Roger
  914.1'04'867   DA632

ISBN 0-906371-75-9

Printed in Great Britain by
R. J. Acford, London and Chichester

Contents

Part 1: Old Trails

Part 2: Trails Through History

Part 3: Classic Trails

6 CONTENTS

Part 4: Epic Trails

Part 5: Fair Summer Trails

Part 6: Hard Winter Trails

8   CONTENTS

List of Plates

Jacket illustration:
  Descent from An Teallach. *Photo: Gordon Gadsby*

30. Camp near Loch Coruisk, Skye, on the Camasunary to Glen Brittle path. *Photo: John Allen*
31. Winter trekking across the Tarmachans in the Southern Highlands of Scotland. *Photo: Ken Andrew*
32. The ridge leading to Stoney Hill in Alaska's Mt. McKinley National Park. *Photo: Kevin White*
33-55. George Borrow, John Muir, Michael Tobias, E. F. Knight, Alasdair Borthwick, Peter Kelemen, Brian Atkin, Hamish Brown, John Hay, Phillip Gribbon, Frances Slade, Kev Reynolds, W. H. Murray, Malcolm Gwyn Thomas, Ray Shepherd, Dianne Bullard, Dick Crawshaw, John T. K. Barr, Malcolm Arney, George B. Schaller, Hugh Westacott, Dewi Jones, Laura and Guy Waterman.

Maps and Cartoons in the Text

12   LIST OF PLATES

Foreword

JOHN HILLABY

One difficulty about writing a foreword to such a rich collection of recalled experiences, is that it is all too easy to slip into the beguiling style of the authors who, with one possible exception (my own), have disclosed what lies most close to their hearts. I shall therefore start with one who is otherwise unrepresented.

A wise man, King Solomon, said a long time ago that no man can find out the world from beginning to end because the world lies in his own heart and in his understanding of it; likewise, I might add, a man may live in his dreams and yet be wholly unprepared for their realisation. This came home to me with curious force some years ago in the city of Metz where, after walking for 34 consecutive days on my own winding trail around canals, across plains and over mountains from the North Sea to the Mediterranean, I pitched down, gratefully, in the house of a rich and hospitable young man who was also one of the saddest fellows I have ever met. A down-at-soul chap. He said he wanted to travel alone, as I did, but somehow he could never make up his mind to begin. How did one do it?

Tired as I was that night, really dog tired, I lolled back in one of his huge leather chairs, put my feet up, sipped glass after glass of some old stuff and answered his questions, determined to get down to the fundamentals of travel on foot. Obviously he was well off. What was his health like? I can't tell you exactly what he said because his English was nearly as bad as my French, but it came out that he was in pretty good nick. He played squash two or three times a week. Had he any dependents? He shrugged his shoulders. There was, it seems, a girl somewhere, partly dependent on him, but he indicated that it would do her no harm to fend for herself. Might be good for her — and him, too, he thought. Exactly, said I in one of those generalisations you are ashamed of afterwards. Travel on foot was the very essence of independence. Alone, with a pack on your back, you can set off at any time, anywhere and change your plans on the way if you want to. It depended, of course, on what one did for a living. Could he get away for a few weeks? He shook his head sadly. Very difficult, he said. He ran a travel agency.

A travel agency. One of those hundreds and hundreds of places where tickets for transport and accommodation are as easily available as oysters on the open shell. They merely cost money. We are moving towards Instant Travel. The difference is that nowadays it costs more and takes greater ingenuity, imagination and enterprise to work out and endure travel risks on off-beat routes than it once took to avoid them. And I take it for a demonstrable fact that confinement to a city for long periods takes a man out of the truth of himself.

The next morning, a morning for song, as I swung through the handsomely named woods of Ars-Laquenexy, I wondered what, if anything, would have convinced that sorry fellow that, day by day, he was throwing away his liberty as surely as if he'd locked himself up in a tower. Many are already old before they are through their teens but, as Stevenson puts it, to travel deliberately through one's ages is to get the best out of a liberal education. To know what you like and to know fairly clearly what you *don't* know is, surely, the beginning of wisdom.

What you are about to read is a substantial book, a book to be dipped into at any time, anywhere. It has durability. It covers a variety of trails from the High Sierras to the Himalayas. But in it there are not words enough to express more than a fraction of what you will *experience* in an hour or two of good going when the less privileged are just thinking about getting out of bed. Let me try to give you an example. The other day, at prime, on my way back to my moorland cottage, I had switched over from normal cruising speed to what I call 'Ambulatory Overdrive', an almost supercharged form of motion known to long-distance solitaries, a gliding movement in which you are scarcely conscious of your feet touching the ground. It allows the mind free range, especially in high places. Apart from mentioning that one ridge after another caught the first light of the morning, I shall not attempt to describe the sunrise. To do so is always perilous.

As I strode along with that dragon-slaying feeling of distance done, I tried to reconstruct the scenery as it was before the hills were thrust up by mighty forces from below, that time when North Yorkshire was the delta of the great Jurassic river. At the same time I kept my eyes open for a beautiful little plant like a Lilliputian lily, the Eyebright which is an indicator of limestone. I noted several patches. Strange to find them there on acid soils. There were sounds to be thought about, too. Above the heart-touching calls of curlew and golden plover, spaced out at intervals of about half a mile, I heard the cascading love calls of tree pipits, which is no less strange when you consider that the moors have not been clothed in native pine for thousands of years. All this and more, including thoughts of bacon, eggs and grilled kidneys for breakfast, occupied my imagination in less time than it has taken to write it down.

Allow me to end on some personal matters, the first of which is an old story. It concerns the slave girl Scheherezade who, in an effort to divert the attentions of her cruel and amorous master, told tale after tale which have been set down in *The Thousand and One Nights.* One of them was about a man who, when he felt himself to be in love, tied a small bell to his foot so that women might know he was dangerous. For many years now I have been such a man, a wanderer with no particular place to come back home to. A solitary by instinct and obligation. But all is now changed. Girl Friday was waiting in the cottage, and together we often walk as one. And what do we read at night? Such books as this.

As you take your pleasure from the pages that follow, I suggest you try reading some passages aloud, because writing which is worth reading reflects the sound of the author's voice, and something of his character. It's as if he were talking to you and to you alone. There is dignity, almost majesty in the voice of John Muir which, as I understand it, exactly fits the stature of that great mountaineer and trail-blazer.

It has been said of that braggart Belloc that he used his religion like a supporter's rattle at a football match, constantly gibing at those not of his persuasion. I never could understand how he managed to get through the high passes of the Alps without maps, wearing an old cotton suit and why, throughout that long journey, he never saw a single flower, bird, animal, even a butterfly worth mentioning. But, God knows, he could write like an angel.

George Borrow is a bit of a mystery, too. A fussy fellow, one feels, a bit too fond of his knowledge of Romany, Basque, Welsh and other tongues. But what a walker! And who could paint portraits more deftly of those he met on the way? That donkey-driver, Robert Louis Stevenson, I love as dearly as you can love anyone you have never met. Here he has to say what must surely be about himself:

> You should have heard him speak of what he loved; of the tent pitched beside the talking water; of the stars overhead at night; of the blest return of the morning, the peep of day over the moors, the awakening of birds among the birches; how he abhorred the long winter shut in cities; and with what delight at the return of the spring, he once more pitched his camp in the living out-of-doors.

Introduction

I got the idea for this book after reading Ken Wilson's climbing anthology, *The Games Climbers Play*. Was it not time that someone did the same service for walking? Surely there must be rich seams of material to be quarried; it should not be too difficult to put together a collection of about eighty articles, representing the ethos of the walker and backpacker?

The simplicity of this idea turned into a task far harder than I had anticipated. There *was* a lot of material, but only a small proportion of it seemed suited to an anthology. This led me to reflect on the difference in approach between the climber and the walker.

Climbing, particularly at its more severe levels of difficulty, is a mixture of euphoria, terror and boredom. For long periods you may be unable to move, waiting for your companion to get up the next pitch. The end of a climb really does take you 'over the top' in a climax that can be almost brutal in its suddenness.

Walking rarely encompasses these extremes, and the difference is reflected in the way walkers write. The pace is generally more gentle, less staccato, and there is little of the self-mockery that is used to such effect by the better mountaineering writers. This dichotomy of approach is typified in Walt Unsworth's *Rough Shoot,* a comic tale of a group of climbers who decide to go walking and get themselves into all kinds of trouble.

Wild country walkers, in Britain and elsewhere, are generally well prepared. More often than not they have planned their route before setting out, and are competent in the use of map and compass. Exceptions to this approach, at least as far as the literature of walking is concerned, seem to be few, and confessions of ill-preparedness do not abound. Graham Newson's article *Coarse Walking* and Alasdair

Borthwick's *Hunger March* are unusual in this respect. In fact, we've all had our coarse walks and our hunger marches, but most of us prefer not to spill the beans by writing about them.

The breadth of this book comes, therefore, not from the actual approach of its contributors as much as from their enormously diverse geographical and temporal backgrounds. We travel with William Wordsworth — something of a coarse walker himself, though his sister usually kept him in hand — with the great individualists and pioneers of the nineteenth century, such as George Borrow, John Muir and Robert Louis Stevenson, and with the walkers of our own time, with their designated trails and waymarked paths.

One result of its temporal span is that the book reflects the way in which the whole philosophy of walking has changed over the past two hundred years, and is still changing. In the eighteenth and nineteenth centuries, people walked because they had to. They walked in their everyday clothes, and they walked long distances as commonplace.

The enjoyment and perception of the landscape and its flora and fauna, evident in the writings of Wordsworth, Borrow and others, seems acute to us now. Our ignorance of things natural would, I fear, seem quite astonishing to them.

The first great upsurge of walking as a pastime rather than a necessity came in Europe generally, and Britain in particular, in the 1920s and 1930s. With the beginnings of the Youth Hostelling movement, and in a period of increasing unemployment, large numbers of people — not all of them young — took to the roads and the wild country as an escape from the depressing atmosphere of the large towns.

This movement was notably strong in Scotland, and is celebrated in Borthwick's writing. Showell Styles' *Lament for the Roadside Fire* also harks back to this era, with its hint of 'roughing it' through force of circumstance *and* through a very real sense of enjoyment, and ends with the wistful hope that those times might return.

At the same time, in England, walkers were fighting for the right of access to open country, notably in the Peak district of Derbyshire, an area largely given over to grouse shooting.

The climax of the battle is described in *The Kinder Scout Trespasses;* several of the main protagonists were sent to prison, and the public outcry that followed this harsh sentence can now be seen as the beginning of the movement that led eventually to the setting up of National Parks in England and Wales and the definition and enshrinement in law of rights of way.

In the past 30 years, the scene has changed even more rapidly. In Britain, Europe and the USA, the phenomenon of waymarked long-distance trails has grown at an astonishing rate. Organisations exist throughout these areas to protect and maintain the network of rights of way and footpaths. The Appalachian Trail, which runs for over 2,000 miles through 14 eastern States of the USA, has become famous as the world's longest waymarked trail. That does not make it an easy stroll, as will be seen from reading those contributions to the anthology which stem from experiences on the trail.

Equipment has progressed from simple adaptations of household items to the products of a highly sophisticated technological industry, using mainly synthetic materials. There is still a strong body of opinion that prefers natural fibres and informality in dress, but the benefits of lighter weight and greater weather protection are gratefully accepted by most walkers and backpackers.

In all this change, something has been lost and something gained. It can seem hard to sustain a spirit of free adventure when the trail is waymarked, your map, compass and guide-book lead you unerringly, and your gear gives you the confidence of knowing you can cope in all weathers.

How do walkers today regard their pastime? Apparently in as many different ways as there are different landscapes and seasons. World travel is now the norm, and the adventurous walker can take his pleasure in Britain this year, America next, and Nepal the year after. We follow this trend; you can read about the gentleness of England's South Downs Way in summer, the Alps in winter, the stark topography of the Sinai Desert (in a fascinating piece of pyrotechnic writing by Michael Tobias), and the grandeur of the Himalayas.

But I must not anticipate too many of your pleasures. Any

selection of this kind is invariably eclectic and bends to a greater or lesser degree to the editor's whim. Despite my apprehensions, I believe this anthology should give pleasure to anyone who enjoys the simple pastime of travelling on foot. I present it to you without apology.

ROGER SMITH

Glasgow
  January 1981

PART 1

Old Trails

These pieces all have historical or literary associations going back through nearly two hundred years of writing — and walking.

One should not forget that men such as William Wordsworth and Thomas de Quincey, best known to us as writers, walked a great deal, both because they had to and because they derived enjoyment and inspiration from walking.

Apart from de Quincey, who seems to have been something of an innovator in lightweight tent design, their walking was done in everyday clothes. If they got wet, it was accepted as nothing out of the way, and that went for the ladies of the day, too. Wordsworth's devoted sister, Dorothy, accompanied him on many of his walks, and thought nothing of travelling 15 or 20 miles merely to collect the post or visit friends for tea, even in winter.

If there is an odd man out, it is John Muir, the Scot who did so much both to open up the Californian interior and to guarantee the preservation of the wilderness in National Parks. Nevertheless, I would venture to suggest that the spirit of his writing is very similar to that of his fellows in this section. In a way, that is a compliment both to him and to them.

Vision of the Alps

HILAIRE BELLOC

Just as I came to the end of the rise, after perhaps an hour, perhaps two, of that great curtain of forest which had held the mountainside, the trees fell away to brushwood, there was a gate, and then the path was lost upon a fine open sward which was the very top of the Jura and the coping of that multiple wall which defends the Swiss Plain. I had crossed it straight from edge to edge, never turning out of my way.

It was too marshy to lie down on it, so I stood a moment to breathe and look about me.

It was evident that nothing higher remained, for though a new line of wood — firs and beeches — stood before me, yet nothing appeared above them, and I knew that they must be the fringe of the descent. I approached this edge of wood, and saw that it had a rough fence of post and rails bounding it, and as I was looking for the entry of a path (for my original path was lost, as such tracks are, in the damp grass of the little down) there came to me one of those great revelations which betray to us suddenly the higher things and stand afterwards firm in our minds.

There, on this upper meadow, where so far I had felt nothing but the ordinary gladness of The Summit, I had a vision.

What was it I saw? If you think I saw this or that, and if you think I am inventing the words, you know nothing of men.

I saw between the branches of the trees in front of me a sight in the sky that made me stop breathing, just as great danger at sea, or great surprise in love, or a great deliverance will make a man stop breathing. I saw something I had known in the West as a boy, something I had never seen so grandly discovered as was this. In between the branches of the trees was a great promise of unexpected lights beyond.

I pushed left and right along that edge of the forest and

25

along the fence that bound it, until I found a place where the pine-trees stopped, leaving a gap, and where on the right, beyond the gap, was a tree whose leaves had failed; there the ground broke away steeply below me, and the beeches fell, one below the other, like a vast cascade, towards the limestone cliffs that dipped down still further, beyond my sight. I looked through this framing hollow and praised God. For there below me, thousands of feet below me, was what seemed an illimitable plain; at the end of that world was an horizon, and the dim bluish sky that overhangs an horizon.

There was brume in it and thickness. One saw the sky beyond the edge of the world getting purer as the vault rose. But right up — a belt in that empyrean — ran peak and field and needle of intense ice, remote from the world. Sky beneath them and sky above them, a steadfast legion, they glittered as though with the armour of the immovable armies of Heaven. Two days' march, three days' march away, they stood up like the walls of Eden. I say it again, they stopped my breath. I had seen them.

So, little we are, we men; so much are we immersed in our muddy and immediate interests that we think, by numbers and recitals, to comprehend distance or time, or any of our limiting infinities. Here were those magnificent creatures of God, I mean the Alps, which now for the first time I saw from the height of the Jura; and because they were 50 or 60 miles away, and because they were a mile or two high, they were become something different from us others, and could strike one motionless with the awe of supernatural things. Up there in the sky, to which only clouds belong and birds and the last trembling colours of pure light, they stood fast and hard; not moving as do the things of the sky. They were as distant as the little upper clouds of summer, as fine and tenuous; but in their reflection and in their quality as it were of weapons (like spears and shields of an unknown array) they occupied the sky with a sublime invasion: and the things proper to the sky were forgotten by me in their presence as I gazed.

To what emotion shall I compare this astonishment? So, in first love one finds that *this* can belong to *me*.

Their sharp steadfastness and their clean uplifted lines compelled my adoration. Up there, the sky above and below them, part of the sky, but part of us, the great peaks made communion between that homing creeping part of me which loves vineyards and dances and a slow movement along pastures, and that other part which is only properly at home in Heaven. I say that this kind of description is useless, and that it is better to address prayers to such things than to attempt to interpret them for others.

These, the great Alps, seen thus, link one in some way to one's immortality. Nor is it possible to convey, or even to suggest, those few 50 miles, and those few thousand feet; there is something more. Let me put it thus: that from the height of Weissenstein I saw, as it were, my religion. I mean, humility, the fear of death, the terror of height and of distance, the glory of God, the infinite potentiality of reception whence springs that divine thirst of the soul; my aspiration also towards completion, and my confidence in the dual destiny. For I know that we laughers have a gross cousinship with the most high, and it is this contrast and perpetual quarrel which feeds a spring of merriment in the soul of a sane man.

Since I could not see such a wonder and it could work such things in my mind, therefore, some day I should be part of it. That is what I felt.

This it is also which leads some men to climb mountaintops but not me, for I am afraid of slipping down.

from THE PATH TO ROME *1933*

The Ascent of Snowdon

GEORGE BORROW

After staying about an hour at Caernarvon we started for Llanberis, a few miles to the east. Llanberis is a small village situated in a valley, and takes its name from Peris, a British saint of the sixth century, son of Helig ab Glanog. The valley extends from west to east, having the great mountain of Snowdon on its south, and a range of immense hills on its northern side. We entered this valley by a pass called Nant y Glo or the ravine of the coal, and passing a lake on our left, on which I observed a solitary coracle, with a fisherman in it, were presently at the village. Here we got down at a small inn, and having engaged a young lad to serve as guide, I set out with Henrietta to ascend the hill, my wife remaining behind, not deeming herself sufficiently strong to encounter the fatigue of the expedition.

Pointing with my finger to the head of Snowdon towering a long way from us in the direction of the east, I said to Henrietta: "Dacw Eryri, yonder is Snowdon. Let us try to get to the top. The Welsh have a proverb: 'it is easy to say yonder is Snowdon; but not so easy to ascend it.' Therefore I would advise you to brace up your nerves and sinews for the attempt."

We then commenced the ascent, arm in arm, followed by the lad, I singing at the stretch of my voice a celebrated Welsh stanza, in which the proverb about Snowdon is given, embellished with a fine moral, and which may thus be rendered:

> "Easy to say, 'Behold Eryri,'
> But difficult to reach its head;
> Easy for him whose hopes are cheery
> To bid the wretch be comforted."

We were far from being the only visitors to the hill this day; groups of people, or single individuals, might be seen going up or descending the path as far as the eye could reach. The path was remarkably good, and for some way the ascent was anything but steep. On our left was the vale of Llanberis, and on our other side a broad hollow, or valley of Snowdon, beyond which were two huge hills forming part of the body of the grand mountain, the lowermost of which our guide told me was called Moel Elia, and the uppermost Moel y Cynghorion. On we went until we had passed both these hills, and come to the neighbourhood of a great wall of rocks constituting the upper region of Snowdon, and where the real difficulty of the ascent commences. Feeling now rather out of breath we sat down on a little knoll with our faces to the south, having a small lake near us, on our left hand, which lay dark and deep, just under the great wall.

Here we sat for some time resting and surveying the scene which presented itself to us, the principal object of which was the north-eastern side of the mighty Moel y Cynghorion, across the wide hollow or valley, which it overhangs in the shape of a sheer precipice some 500ft. in depth. Struck by the name of Moel y Cynghorion, which in English signifies the hill of the counsellors, I inquired of our guide why the hill was so called, but as he could afford me no information on the point I presumed that it was either called the hill of the counsellors from the Druids having held high consultation on its top, in time of old, or from the unfortunate Llewelyn having consulted there with his chieftains, while his army lay encamped in the vale below.

Getting up we set about surmounting what remained of the ascent. The path was now winding and much more steep than it had hitherto been. I was at one time apprehensive that my gentle companion would be obliged to give over the attempt; the gallant girl, however, persevered, and in little more than twenty minutes from the time when we arose from our resting-place under the crags, we stood, safe and sound, though panting, upon the very top of Snowdon, the far-famed Wyddfa*.

The Wyddfa is about 30ft. in diameter and is surrounded on three sides by a low wall. In the middle of it is a rude cabin, in which refreshments are sold, and in which a person resides throughout the year, though there are few or no visitors to the hill's top, except during the months of summer. Below on all sides are frightful precipices except on the side of the west. Towards the east it looks perpendicularly into the dyffrin or vale nearly a mile below, from which to the gazer it is at all times an object of admiration, of wonder and almost

* It will not be amiss to observe that the original term is gwyddfa; but gwyddfa being a feminine noun or compound commencing with g, which is a mutable consonant, loses the initial letter before y the definite article — you say Gwyddfa a tumulus, but not y gwyddfa *the* tumulus.

of fear.

There we stood on the Wyddfa, in a cold bracing atmosphere, though the day was almost stiflingly hot in the regions from which we had ascended. There we stood enjoying a scene inexpressibly grand, comprehending a considerable part of the main land of Wales, the whole of Anglesey, a faint glimpse of part of Cumberland; the Irish Channel, and what might be either a misty creation or the shadowy outline of the hills of Ireland. Peaks and pinnacles and huge moels stood up here and there, about us and below us, partly in glorious light, partly in deep shade. Manifold were the objects which we saw from the brow of Snowdon, but of all the objects which we saw, those which filled us with most delight and admiration, were numerous lakes and lagoons, which, like sheets of ice or polished silver, lay reflecting the rays of the sun in the deep valleys at his feet.

"Here," said I to Henrietta, "you are on the top crag of Snowdon, which the Welsh consider, and perhaps with justice, to be the most remarkable crag in the world; which is mentioned in many of their old wild romantic tales, and some of the noblest of their poems, amongst others in the *Day of Judgment* by the illustrious Goronwy Owen, where it is brought forward in the following manner:

> Ail i'r ar ael Eryri,
> Cyfartal hoewal a hi.

'The brow of Snowdon shall be levelled with the ground, and the eddying waters shall murmur round it'."

"You are now on the top crag of Snowdon, generally termed Y Wyddfa, which means a conspicuous place or tumulus, and which is generally in winter covered with snow; about which snow there are in the Welsh language two curious englynion or stanzas consisting entirely of vowels with the exception of one consonant, namely the letter R.

> Oer yw'r Eira ar Eryri, — o'ryw
> Ar awyr i rewi;
> Oer yw'r ia ar riw 'r ri,
> A'r Eira oer yw 'Ryri

O Ri y'Ryri yw'r oera, — o'r ar,
Ar oror wir arwa;
O'r awyr a yr Eira,
O'i ryw i roi rew a'r ia.

Cold is the snow on Snowdon's brow,
It makes the air so chill;
For cold, I trow, there is no snow
Like that of Snowdon's hill.

A hill most chill is Snowdon's hill,
And wintry is his brow;
From Snowdon's hill the breezes chill
Can freeze the very snow.

Such was the harangue which I uttered on the top of Snowdon; to which Henrietta listened with attention; three or four English, who stood nigh, with grinning scorn, and a Welsh gentleman with considerable interest. The latter coming forward shook me by the hand exclaiming:

"Wyt ti Lydaueg?"

"I am not a Llydauan," said I; "I wish I was, or anything but what I am, one of a nation amongst whom any knowledge save what relates to money-making and over-reaching is looked upon as a disgrace. I am ashamed to say that I am an Englishman."

I then returned his shake of the hand; and bidding Henrietta and the guide follow me, went into the cabin, where Henrietta had some excellent coffee, and myself and the guide a bottle of tolerable ale; very much refreshed we set out on our return.

from WILD WALES *1862*

A Dartmoor Mist

WILLIAM CROSSING

One of the dangers to which the Dartmoor wanderer is liable is the sudden arising of those thick mists, so frequent there and enveloping every object in so impenetrable a shroud, that unless he be well acquainted with the moor, it is impossible for him to find his way. And even if the moor is known to him there is often great difficulty in accomplishing this, for he is apt to be misled by the strange appearance that even familiar objects seem to wear, so distorted do they become. It is only when his knowledge is sufficient to enable him to tell where he is by observing the formation of the ground over which he is passing that there is any chance of making his way through it.

Strangers who have never experienced a real Dartmoor mist are apt to imagine that a map and a compass are all that are required to enable one to make one's way across the trackless waste. These, it is true, are accompaniments which no one unacquainted with the moor should neglect to be provided with when venturing to explore its more remote parts, and certainly by pursuing as straight a course as is possible with their aid the confines of the moor may be reached. But it is equally sure that after having gained them he will not find himself at the place which he hoped to arrive at. Bogs, mires, turf-ties, and other impediments to a straight course are constantly presenting themselves, compelling the traveller to frequently turn aside, so it must not be thought that a map and compass will enable one to make a bee-line over the moor.

But to one who knows the moor so thoroughly as to be able to ascertain his whereabouts in a mist by noticing the nature of the ground around him, that which might prove an impediment and a stumbling-block to the stranger, is as a beacon light, serving to let him know his exact position, and though the way may yet be not easy (so thick are these mists that everything around is concealed from view), still he can be in no danger of losing himself entirely.

I have known many instances of people, well acquainted with certain parts of the moor, losing their way in a mist and wandering about in it for hours in the vain endeavour to find their path. To such, a compass (presuming they know the use of it, which it is scarcely necessary to say but few of the Dartmoor people do) would have proved a ready means of setting them in the right track. The wife of Mr. Hooper, who lives at the little farm at Nun's Cross, went out one evening about 6 p.m. to fetch in their cows to be milked, and a mist quickly enveloping her, when at no distance from the house, she wandered on the moor until 4 a.m. the next morning, reaching home in a drenched condition for the driving mists quickly soak one to the skin. By her statement to me she could not have gone far from her house — not more than a mile or two — but in vain endeavoured to find her way to it. She got into the valley of the Plym, and came more than once upon the ruins at Eylesbarrow Mine, and appears to have been wandering in a circle, which is usual with persons lost in a mist. Most people after walking about on the moor a whole night would be glad enough to go to rest without delay on gaining their home, but Mrs. Hooper had purposed going to Loddiswell, near Kingsbridge, the next morning, to see her son, so on arriving at her home she, without loss of time, proceeded to make her butter, as usual, and at 6 a.m. it being then clear weather, she set out to walk to Brent across the moor. On arriving at that place and finding she was too late for the train, she walked the extra two miles to Kingsbridge Road, to take the coach to her destination.

Her husband not long afterwards lost himself in a somewhat similar manner, but by following the Plym reached Cadaford Bridge, near which he was able to obtain shelter till the morning.

This plan of following a stream is the very best that anyone who has any doubt about his way, when lost in a mist, can adopt; and though, perhaps, conducting him far from his desired destination, will yet enable him to reach the roads on the confines of the moor.

It is surprising how distorted objects will become in these Dartmoor mists, and how confusing is the appearance to the traveller. Small objects, close at hand (and only such as are near can be seen at all) look like large ones beheld at a distance. They will sometimes burst upon the sight with almost startling suddenness, and with bewildering effect. I have seen sheep that when first perceived looked like beasts as large as bulls, and with their woolly coats reminded one of the mammoths of old, which on getting but a few steps nearer to them at once assumed their natural appearance. I remember on one occasion, when riding slowly in a dense mist down the Abbots' Way near Red Lake, being startled by coming suddenly upon what at first sight appeared to be some huge black Newfoundland dogs but what the nearer approach of a few yards showed me to be several rough and shaggy calves of the black Scotch cattle, kept on Harford and Ugborough Moors, and immediately afterwards the cows they were following came into view.

I have had many — very many — experiences of Dartmoor mists, but the most curious illusion I ever remember to have met with happened to me once near Glascombe Bottom, some short distance to the northward of the Eastern Beacon on Ugborough Moor. I was making my way along the slope with a companion, the mist being so thick that one could see but a very short distance, and so penetrating that we were wet through, and feeling cold and chilled, when suddenly I saw looming up through the dull mist what I supposed to be a cottage with several fir trees growing close to it, and my companion also saw it at the same time. I stopped bewildered, not being able to understand where I had got to. I knew how very easy it was to deviate from one's course in such weather, and to gradually swerve round to quite an opposite direction to the one intended to be pursued, and at first thought that I must have done this. But even if such were the case, I could not understand for the life of me where I was, for I knew every inch of the ground, and was positive that there was no such thing as a cottage on the moor anywhere near. Besides, the ground I was treading made me feel sure I had not wandered out of my track, but was descending towards the

Glaze, according to the route I had decided upon taking when the mist first came on. Yet, there in front of me appeared a cottage as plain as ever I saw anything in my life. My companion, as soon as he sighted it, suggested that we should make towards it, and after looking around me in wonder, I acquiesced. We stepped briskly forward along the slope with this intention, when, lo! as if by the effects of enchantment, the cottage, trees and all, vanished from our sight, and in their place a granite block, not above two feet high, with a straight side and a sloping top, with a tuft of rushes growing beside it, was all that there was to be seen. It could not have been more than about a score of yards distant from us when first we saw it, but looked to us over a hundred. No illusion could be more complete; the walls, the roof, and the trees, all appeared perfectly plain, and had we been strangers to that part, and by any chance passed on our way, it is quite certain we should have believed that we had seen a habitation.

There is not much doubt that natural illusions of this kind have given rise to many of the tales of witchery and enchantment related in connection with the pixies of the moor. These little elves are credited with having performed the most wonderful things, although it is true that the Dartmoor peasant of today has somewhat lost faith in their ability to accomplish all that they have been credited with, and can only say that he has 'heerd tell' that such was the case. The stories of the stone circles having been seen dancing at noon have been considered to owe their origin to a purely natural cause. Objects that are seen through the agitated waves of air arising from the heated surface of the ground assume a quivering motion, and it is this which has doubtless given rise to these superstitions.

The Will-o'-the-Wisp, too, has, no doubt, had a hand in originating some of our Dartmoor superstitions, that which science easily explains having been set down as supernatural.

Towards the close of the year 1878, I remember meeting with a very unpleasant adventure in a mist on the moor. I had left Hexworthy in the forenoon, which was bright and pleasant, and climbed up the hill to Aune Head, from whence, by way of Whitaburrow, I had made for Brent. Here

I stayed until about 6 p.m., when I set out on my return journey across the moor, though not by the same route as I had chosen in the morning. I now took one which is always used by the farmers and moor-men around Dartmeet, Dunnabridge or Hexworthy, when crossing to Brent, and with which I was perfectly well acquainted. This enters the moor at Dockwell Gate, about 2½ miles from the town of Brent, and passing over a small portion of Brent Moor, crosses Dean, Buckfastleigh and Holne Moors, and meeting the road close by Cumsdon Tor, enters upon the forest at Saddle Bridge. There is no actual path, but here and there certain natural objects which serve to denote the route.

It was drawing towards dusk when I reached Dockwell Gate, and slightly misty, but only sufficiently so to obscure objects at some distance off. I pushed on over Brent Moor, where for a little way we have a green track among the heather, and which I have many a time made my way over at all hours of the day and night, and in about half-an-hour reached a little ford on Dean Moor, from near which a track-line leads direct to the summit of a hill to the northward called Pupers. This track-line, like the others upon the moor — and there are many — consists of a bank of earth and stones, four or five feet in height, and five or six feet in width. Some are much wider than this, and have been termed trackways and regarded as roads, but, I cannot help thinking in error. The moormen always term them 'reaves', and look upon them as ancient boundaries, which in all probability they are. It is not unlikely that many of them were bounds set up by the tinners of the moor, the question of properly defining the extent of the ground over which each tinner, or company of tinners, had a right to labour, being one that received a great amount of attention, as the laws made by them at their parliament at Crockern Tor, and which are still extant, attest.

I had now the ascent of the hill before me, which, however, is only gradual, the distance to the top from the little ford referred to being about a mile. Pupers possesses two tors upon its summit. On its western slope, amid the rocks with which the hill is strewn, there is another small tor. The two principal tors, although of no great size, are rather prominent objects, and render Pupers an easily recognisable hill from a great distance around, and more particularly from the south and east. Being a border hill the view from it is varied and extensive, and the ground surrounding it being mostly of a good hard character, it is easily accessible.

It was growing dark as I descended the opposite side of this hill, but as yet the mist had only slightly increased. Between this hill and another, known on the moor as Snowdon, there is a rocky gully called by the moormen Snowdon Hole, in front of which rises a small rivulet, which trickling down into a hollow forms a mire extending for some distance down the slope. When riding it is necessary to know how to cross this spot, which can only be done at one place — the entrance to the gully — where a little path, not much more than a foot in width, and oftener than not covered with water, affords the means of passing. Below, the miry ground prevents a passage being made with a horse, and above, the rock-strewn hole is equally an obstacle. To the traveller on foot it is not of so much importance about striking the exact spot, for so long as he keeps high enough he will avoid the mire, and if he should not strike the path, he will, at the worst, only be put to the trouble of clambering over the stones.

However, the ground was well-known to me, and though it was now nearly dark, I made my way to the little path and gained the further side of Snowdon Hole all right. Here, the course is along the side of the hill, care being taken not to sink too much toward the bottom. Suddenly the mist, which had hitherto been hanging around the hill tops, descended, and wrapped everything in an impenetrable veil, which added to the darkness, warned me to exercise caution. In less than ten minutes I found I had got too low. I knew there was a large patch of ferns growing on the hillside, and the proper route to pursue was above these, while I found myself in the midst of them. To correct this error by turning slightly up the hill again was soon done, but I utterly failed to discover one or two well-known landmarks, in the shape of tiny fording places over little rivulets that drain from the boggy ground above. However, I made nothing of this, for I knew I could not be more than a score or two of yards out of my way, but proceeded carefully on through the mist, which was now so thick about me that it was impossible for me to see more than a few steps in advance.

At some short distance further on I had to cross a very wide bottom, with extremely precipitous sides, and through which courses a stream that runs by Combe, a hamlet near Scoriton, and falls into the Dart below Buckfastleigh. This combe, like Snowdon Hole, can only be conveniently crossed by horses at one spot, a fording place known on the moor as Hapstead Ford, leading to which a pathway, worn by the ponies of moormen and farmers, runs down the bank on each side. My aim now was to strike the top of this pathway, so as to descend the steep bank in safety, but the thick mist, combined with the growing darkness, made it a matter of impossibility for me to do other than guess at its position. I had to be exceedingly careful, too, where I trod, because I knew the bank to be so steep — in some places almost perpendicular — that if I approached too near, a single false step might precipitate me down it.

My only assurance that I was going towards it was my thorough knowledge of the ground. Though I could see nothing whatever, I knew I was proceeding in the direction of the combe, but whether I should be fortunate enough to hit upon the pathway to the ford was quite uncertain. I did not, however, feel much anxiety about that, as being on foot it would be easy enough to cross it at any point by exercising care in climbing down the bank; at the same time I wished to strike it if I could, as by so doing I should, of course, know exactly my whereabouts, and be better able to shape my course over Holne Moor, which I had yet to cross before reaching the forest bounds.

Making my way carefully onward I at length reached the edge of the deep combe, but no signs of the pathway could I discover. I stood still for a few moments to consider my position, and at length came to the conclusion that I had kept rather too low down the hill, and that if I made my way with caution along the top of the bank in an upward direction, I should at length strike the path. This I did, walking along for some distance, but without finding what I was in search of. I stopped again, but any examination of my surroundings was quite out of the question. I had gained the combe and that was all I knew, but whether I was above or below the pathway I could not determine. It now seemed to me that if I had been below it when I first gained the edge of the gully I should have come to the pathway by this time, so thinking I had been mistaken and that I was above it after all, I was determined to try the bank downwards, which I did for some distance, but with no success.

Rain now began to fall, but the mist continued as thick as ever. As I proceeded slowly through it down the edge of the bank, a sudden thought struck me. The combe at some distance below where I had aimed at reaching it, I knew turned to the right rather sharply, and a fear lest I had arrived at this portion of it took possession of me, for I was aware that if I had, and tried to cross it there, I should be going away from home instead of towards it, and I stood still undecided what to do. It was now that a compass would have been of service to me, for by its aid I might have discovered at once whether I really was by this lower portion of the gully or not, but I had none with me. By following the stream that ran through the combe I might have got off the moor, of course, but this was not what I wanted to do, my destination lying quite in the opposite direction. Even this though in the mist and darkness would not have been quite so easy as it may seem, for the stream would have been invisible, and I should have had to feel my way along its banks.

However, I was able to relieve my perplexity by a little reflection. I could only dimly perceive the nature of the bank, it was true, but nevertheless saw enough of it to convince me I had not got to the spot I feared. At the place where the ford is situated, the side of the combe for some distance is high and steep, and by climbing partly down it, and making a careful scrutiny I discovered that it was so at the spot where I was standing. This reassured me, so giving up all thought of looking for the path, I cautiously clambered down the remaining portion of the steep side, and reached the bottom. Feeling my way in the darkness, a very few steps brought me to the little stream, which is of no great width, so not staying to search for a convenient spot to cross it, I walked through it, and then making across the bottom of the gully, gained its opposite side, which is not so high as the one I had just descended. Scrambling up this I looked about me for a moment, and then deciding upon my course, struck out, with a hope that I might be able to keep to it, up the ascent before me.

The rain now descended in torrents, blowing into my face, and causing me to keep my head well down. I have sometimes when in a mist on the moor steered by observing the direction the wind is blowing from, which, if it were not liable to shift, might be a good plan enough, but as one, of course, can never be sure about this condition, it is not a safe one. In the present instance it was not even possible for me to adopt this course, so I endeavoured to go as straight as I could without such aid, and at first imagined I was doing so, though it was not very long before I discovered my mistake.

It was now intensely dark, and a most miserable, wretched night. I was drenched to the skin, and as I wandered on through the darkness I tried to cheer myself with the belief that I should shortly see the bright, cosy peat fire on the hearth at home. But soon this hope grew fainter and fainter. I felt convinced I was going in the wrong direction, or I should ere this have hit upon landmarks which I knew. For a long, long time I moved on; where I wandered I cannot tell, but I found it quite impossible to make any real headway.

I stopped at last bewildered, and began to feel weary and weak, and wished that I had made my way to the in-country before crossing the gully. This, however, was worse than useless, so I determined to keep moving, and hoped that I might yet chance upon some object which would enable me to learn my position. Several times I saw what looked like a wide valley before me, the slope of the opposite hill seeming to loom through the mist and darkness, and when first beheld I thought I was looking across the valley of the Wobrook to the hill known as Down Ridge. But this was only an illusion; a small hillock, on rather higher ground, sometimes but a few yards distant, being the object to which this treacherous mist had given the appearance of a hill.

Still the rain beat fast upon me, and the mist and darkness shut out everything around me, as I plodded wearily on, knowing that my only chance was to keep moving. Suddenly the ground seemed to sink beneath my step! and I fell out into the darkness, and went rolling down, down a steep bank, falling breathless upon my back at the bottom. Luckily the bank was overgrown with heather, which broke my fall, so that I sustained no hurt beyond a severe shaking. Laying for a brief space I gradually recovered myself, and then perceived I was at the bottom of a narrow gully. I thought little of my accident then; in fact I may say I almost congratulated myself upon it, for it was the means of showing me where I was. I now knew I was in an old mine working known as Ringleshutts Girt, near to which I should have passed had I been able to have kept to my proper track, for I was aware there were no other such trenches in that part of the moor.

Climbing up out of this pit, on the side opposite to which I had fallen, I sat down on the bank to rest, raining as it was. I felt it would be madness to leave this gully, and strike out over the moor. Cumsdon Tor, where I should touch the road, was my next point, but I saw at once that it would be far better to abandon any attempt at making a direct course, and to follow these workings. They would lead me to some ruined mine buildings, where a little stream, called Wennaford Brook — a tributary of the Dart — takes its rise, and which I could follow. But I felt exhausted, and almost sleepy, and a feeling came over me that I must yet rest awhile before I could pursue my way. Groping about I discovered some thick tufts of heather growing over a little hollow on the edge of the bank, and creeping under them, I laid myself down, and had the rain not been falling I believe I should have stayed there, so weary did I feel. I closed my eyes, but quickly found that to remain there in the pitiless rain, which the heather but very imperfectly shielded me from, would be sheer madness, so pulling myself together, I felt my way once more to the bottom of the girt, and climbed up the other side again, knowing I should have better ground there. I had to feel my way along its edge, for to see anything was quite impossible, and so slowly made my way down by it towards the mine.

On a sudden something white appeared before me. This I found to be a gravelly path, and knew that I had come upon an old track. It is called Sandyway, and is to be seen here and there in its course from Holne Moor to Fox Tor Mire. This raised my spirits, but soon I lost the track, and the mist so bewildered me that I scarcely knew what to think. However, I kept on by the edge of the workings, and at last I saw to my great joy the tall chimney shaft of old Ringleshutts rising up before me.

I was all right now, though I had still several miles to go before I could reach home. But I did not mind that, for I knew I was saved from having to wander about the moor through the pitiless night. I stopped at the little stream and quenched my thirst, and then debated with myself whether I should follow it to Wennaford Bridge, or whether I should walk back towards Holne Moor Gate by the old mine road, which is a very good, plain track. The former would have been very much the shortest, but I felt that it would be likely to take me quite as long to perform, for it would be no easy task to follow the stream down the rough bottom in the darkness, so I chose the latter. I had to walk almost back to Holne Moor Gate before getting into the road to Hexworthy, but by stepping briskly out, which the knowledge that I was now in a fair way of reaching home encouraged me to do, I soon gained it. Here I stopped by the roadside and pulled off my boots; and emptied them of the water which they contained, after which I set out as quickly as I could for the little settlement, for I had still between three and four miles to go.

I had now a good road across the moor, so had no further difficulties to encounter, though my weary state and the rain and mist combined to make the walk anything but a pleasant journey. But it was all over at last; Hexworthy was reached and I was once more beneath the hospitable roof of the Forest Inn. I need scarcely tell with what gusto I sat down to the meal which was hastily prepared for me — not staying to take off my wet garments, so hungry was I, but making good work at my trencher, and then getting off speedily to bed.

Of course, I was not expected. As I had not arrived in the evening it was thought that the weather had deterred me from returning, and it was with surprise that my wife and our good host and hostess found me come back in the night. Most unpleasant was my experience, but 'all's well that ends well', and if one will be a rambler upon the old moor, why one must of course take it in all its humours, and must not expect but that he will, at some time or other, get overtaken by a Dartmoor mist.

from AMID DEVONIA'S ALPS *1889*

A Night among the Pines

ROBERT LOUIS STEVENSON

From Bleymard after dinner, although it was already late, I set out to scale a portion of the Lozère. An ill-marked stony drove-road guided me forward; and I met nearly half a dozen bullock-carts descending from the woods, each laden with a whole pine-tree for the winter's firing. At the top of the woods, which do not climb very high upon this cold ridge, I struck leftward by a path among the pines, until I hit on a dell of green turf, where a streamlet made a little spout over some stones to serve me for a water-tap. 'In a more sacred or sequestered bower . . . . nor nymph nor faunus haunted.' The trees were not old, but they grew thickly round the glade: there was no outlook, except north-eastward upon distant hilltops, or straight upward to the sky; and the encampment felt secure and private like a room. By the time I had made my arrangements and fed Modestine, the day was already beginning to decline. I buckled myself to the knees into my sack and made a hearty meal; and as soon as the sun went down, I pulled my cap over my eyes and fell asleep.

Night is a dead monotonous period under a roof; but in the open world it passes lightly, with its stars and dews and perfumes, and the hours are marked by changes in the face of Nature. What seems a kind of temporal death to people choked between walls and curtains is only a light and living slumber to the man who sleeps afield. All night long he can hear Nature breathing deeply and freely; even as she takes her rest, she turns and smiles; and there is one stirring hour unknown to those who dwell in houses, when a wakeful influence goes abroad over the sleeping hemisphere, and all the outdoor world are on their feet. It is then that the cock first crows, not this time to announce the dawn, like a cheerful watchman speeding the course of night. Cattle awake on the meadows; sheep break their fast on dewy hillsides, and change to a new lair among the ferns; and houseless men, who have lain down with the fowls, open their dim eyes and behold the beauty of the night.

At what inaudible summons, at what gentle touch of nature, are all these sleepers thus recalled in the same hour to life? Do the stars rain down an influence, or do we share some thrill of mother earth below our resting bodies? Even shepherds and old country-folk, who are the deepest read in these arcana, have not a guess as to the means or purpose of this nightly resurrection. Towards two in the morning they declare the thing takes place; and neither know nor inquire further. And at least it is a pleasant incident. We are disturbed in our slumber only, like the luxurious Montaigne, 'that we may the better and more sensibly relish it'. We have a moment to look upon the stars. And there is a special pleasure for some minds in the reflection that we share the impulse with all outdoor creatures in our neighbourhood, that we have escaped out of the Bastille of civilisation, and are become, for the time being, a mere kindly animal and a sheep of Nature's flock.

When that hour came to me among the pines, I wakened thirsty. My tin was standing by me half full of water. I emptied it at a draught; and feeling broad awake after this internal cold aspersion, sat upright to make a cigarette. The stars were clear, coloured, and jewel-like, but not frosty. A faint silvery vapour stood for the Milky Way. All around me the black fir-points stood upright and stock-still. By the whiteness of the pack-saddle, I could see Modestine walking round and round at the length of her tether; I could hear her steadily munching at the sward; but there was not another sound, save the indescribable quiet talk of the runnel over the stones. I lay lazily smoking and studying the colour of the sky as we call the void of space, from where it showed a reddish grey behind the pines to where it showed a glossy blue-black between the stars. As if to be more like a pedlar, I wear a silver ring. This I could see faintly shining as I raised or lowered the cigarette; and at each whiff the inside of my hand was illuminated, and became for a second the highest light in the landscape.

A faint wind, more like a moving coolness than a stream of

air, passed down the glade from time to time; so that even in my great chamber the air was being renewed all night long. I thought with horror of the inn at Chasseradès and the congregated nightcaps; with horror of the nocturnal prowesses of clerks and students, of hot theatres and pass-keys and close rooms. I have not often enjoyed a more serene possession of myself, nor felt more independent of material aids. The outer world, from which we cower into our houses, seemed after all a gentle habitable place, and night after night a man's bed, it seemed, was laid and waiting for him in the fields, where God keeps an open house. I thought I had rediscovered one of those truths which are revealed to savages and hid from political economists: at the least, I had discovered a new pleasure for myself. And yet even while I was exulting in my solitude I became aware of a strange lack. I wished a companion to lie near me in the starlight, silent and not moving, but ever within touch. For there is a fellow-ship more quiet even than solitude, and which, rightly understood, is solitude made perfect. And to live out of doors with the woman a man loves is of all lives the most complete and free.

As I thus lay, between content and longing, a faint noise stole towards me through the pines. I thought, at first, it was the crowing of cocks or the barking of dogs at some very distant farm; but steadily and gradually it took articulate shape in my ears, until I became aware that a passenger was going by upon the high-road in the valley, and singing loudly as he went. There was more of goodwill than grace in his performance; but he trolled with ample lungs; and the sound of his voice took hold upon the hillside and set the air shaking in the leafy glens. I have heard people passing by night in sleeping cities; some of them sang; one, I remember, played loudly on the bagpipes. I have heard the rattle of a cart or carriage spring up suddenly after hours of stillness, and pass, for some minutes, within the range of my hearing as I lay abed. There is a romance about all who are abroad in the black hours, and with something of a thrill we try to guess their business. But here the romance was double; first, this glad passenger, lit internally with wine, who sent up his voice in music through the night; and then I, on the other hand, buckled into my sack, and smoking alone in the pine-woods between four and five thousand feet towards the stars.

When I awoke again (Sunday 29th September), many of the stars had disappeared; only the stronger companions of the night still burned visibly overhead; and away towards the east I saw a faint haze of light upon the horizon, such as had been the Milky Way when I was last awake. Day was at hand. I lit my lantern, and by its glow-worm light put on my boots and gaiters; then I broke up some bread for Modestine, filled my can at the water-tap, and lit my spirit-lamp to boil myself some chocolate. The blue darkness lay long in the glade where I had so sweetly slumbered, but soon there was a broad streak of orange melting into the gold along the mountain-tops of Vivarais. A solemn glee possessed my mind at this gradual and lovely coming in of day. I heard the runnel with delight; I looked round me for something beautiful and unexpected; but the still black pine-trees, the hollow glade, the munching ass, remained unchanged in figure. Nothing had altered but the light, and that, indeed, shed over all a spirit of life and of breathing peace, and moved me to a strange exhilaration.

I drank my water-chocolate, which was hot if it was not rich, and strolled here and there, and up and down about the glade. While I was thus delaying, a gush of steady wind, as long as a heavy sigh, poured direct out of the quarter of the morning. It was cold, and set me sneezing. The trees near at hand tossed their black plumes in its passage; and I could see the thin distant spires of pine along the edge of the hill rock slightly to and fro against the golden east. Ten minutes after, the sunlight spread at a gallop along the hillside, scattering shadows and sparkles, and the day had come completely.

I hastened to prepare my pack, and tackle the steep ascent that lay before me, but I had something on my mind. It was only a fancy: yet a fancy will sometimes be importunate. I had been most hospitably received and punctually served in my green caravanserai. The room was airy, the water excellent, and the dawn had called me to a moment. I say nothing of the tapestries or the inimitable ceiling, nor yet of the view which I commanded from the windows; but I felt I was in someone's debt for all this liberal entertainment. And so it pleased me, in a half-laughing way, to leave pieces of money on the turf as I went along, until I had left enough for my night's lodging. I trust they did not fall to some rich and churlish drover.

from TRAVELS WITH A DONKEY *1879*

A Walk to Hardraw Force

WILLIAM WORDSWORTH

We were now in Wensley dale and D and I set off side by side to foot it as far as Kendal. A little before sunset we reached one of the waterfalls of which I read you a short description in Mr. Taylor's tour. I meant to have attempted to give you a picture of it but I feel myself too lazy to execute the task. Tis a singular scene; such a performance as you might have expected from some giant gardiner employed by one of Queen Elizabeth's Courtiers, if this same giant gardiner had consulted with Spenser and they two had finish'd the work together. By this you will understand that with something of vastness or grandeur it is at once formal and wild. We reach'd the town of Askrigg, 12 miles, about six in the evening, having walked the last three miles in the dark and two of them over hard-frozen road to the great annoyance of our feet and ankles. Next morning the earth was thinly covered with snow, enough to make the road soft and prevent its being slippery. On leaving Askrigg we turned aside to see another waterfall — 'twas a beautiful morning with driving snow-showers that disappeared by fits, and unveiled the east which was all one delicious pale orange colour. After walking through two fields we came to a mill which we pass'd and in a moment a sweet little valley opened before us, with an area of grassy ground, and a stream dashing over various lamina of black rocks close under a bank covered with firs. The bank and stream on our left, another woody bank on our right, and the flat meadow in front, from which, as at Buttermere, the stream had retired as it were to hide itself under the shade. As we walked up this delightful valley we were tempted to look back perpetually on the brook which reflected the orange light of the morning among the gloomy rocks with a brightness varying according to the agitation of the current. The steeple of Askrigg was between us and the east, at the bottom of the valley; it was not a quarter of a mile distant, but oh! how far we were from it. The two banks seemed to join before us with a facing of rock common to them both, when we reached this point the valley opened out again, two rocky banks on each side, which, hung with ivy and moss and fringed luxuriantly with brushwood, ran directly parallel to each other and then approaching with a gentle curve, at their point of union presented a lofty waterfall, the termination of the valley. Twas a keen frosty morning, showers of snow threatening us but the sun bright and active; we had a task of twenty one miles to perform in a short winter's day, all this put our minds in such a state of excitation that we were no unworthy spectators of this delightful scene. On a nearer approach the water seemed to fall down a tall arch or rather nitch which had shaped itself by insensible moulderings in the wall of an old castle. We left this spot with reluctance but highly exhilarated. When we had walked about a mile and a half we overtook two men with a string of ponies and some empty carts. I recommended to D to avail herself of this opportunity of husbanding her strength, we rode with them more than two miles, twas bitter cold, the wind driving the snow behind us in the best stile of a mountain storm. We soon reached an inn at a place called Hardraw, and descending from our vehicles, after warming ourselves by the cottage fire we walked up the brook side to take a view of a third waterfall. We had not gone above a few hundred yards between two winding rocky banks before we came full upon it. It appeared to throw itself in a narrow line from a lofty wall of rock; the water which shot manifestly to some distance from the rock seeming from the extreme height of the fall to be dispersed before it reached the bason, into a thin shower of snow that was toss'd about like snow blown from the roof of a house. We were disappointed in the cascade though the introductory and accompanying banks were a noble mixture of grandeur and beauty. We walked up to the fall and what would I not give if I could convey to you the images and feelings which were then communicated to me. After cautiously sounding our way over stones of all colours and sizes encased in the clearest ice formed by the spray of the waterfall, we found the rock which before had seemed a perpendicular wall extending itself over us like the ceiling of a huge cave; from the summit of which the water shot directly over our heads into a bason and among fragments of rock wrinkled over with masses of ice, white as snow, or rather as D says like congealed froth. The water fell at least ten yards from us and we stood directly behind it, the excavation not so deep in the rock as to impress any feeling of darkness, but lofty and magnificent, and in connection with the adjoining banks excluding as much of the sky as could well be spared from a scene so exquisitely beautiful. The spot where we stood was as dry as the chamber in which I am now sitting, and the incumbent rock of which the groundwork was limestone veined and dappled with colours which melted into each other in every possible variety. On the summit of the cave were three festoons or rather wrinkles in the rock which ran parallel to each other like the folds of a curtain when it is drawn up; each of them was hung with icicles of various length, and nearly in the middle of the festoons in the deepest valley made by their waving line the stream shot from between the rows of icicles in irregular fits of strength and with a body of water that momently varied. Sometimes it threw itself into the bason in one continued curve, sometimes it was interrupted almost midway in its fall and, being blown towards us, part of the water fell at no great distance from our feet like the heaviest thunder shower. In such a situation you have at every moment a feeling of the presence of the sky. Above the highest point of the waterfall large fleecy clouds drove over our heads and the sky appeared of a blue more than usually brilliant. The rocks on each side, which, joining with the sides of the cave, formed the vista of the brook were checquered with three diminutive waterfalls or rather veins of water each of which was a miniature of all that summer and winter can produce of a delicate beauty. The rock in the centre of these falls where the water was most abundant, deep black, the adjoining parts yellow white purple violet and dovecolour'd; or covered with water-plants of the most vivid green, and hung with streams and fountains of ice and icicles that in some places seemed to conceal the verdure of the plants and the variegated colours of the rocks and in some places to render their hues more splendid. I cannot express to you the enchanted effect produced by this Arabian scene of colour as the wind blew aside the great waterfall behind which we stood and hid and revealed each of these faery cataracts in irregular succession or displayed them with various gradations of distinctness, as the intervening spray was thickened or dispersed. — In the luxury of our imaginations we could not help feeding on the pleasure which in the heat of a July noon this cavern would spread through a frame exquisitely sensible. That huge rock of ivy on the right, the bank winding round on the left with all its living foliage, and the breeze stealing up the valley and bedewing the cavern with the faintest imaginable spray. And then the murmur of the water, the quiet, the seclusions, and a long summer day to dream in! — Have I not tired you? With difficulty we tore ourselves away, and on returning to the cottage we found we had been absent an hour. Twas a short one to us, we were in high spirits, and off we drove, and will you believe me when I tell you that we walked the next ten miles, by the watch over a high mountain road, thanks to the wind that drove behind us and the good road, in two hours and a quarter, a marvellous feat of which D will long tell. Well! we rested in a tempting inn, close by Garsdale chapel, a lowly house of prayer in a charming little valley, here we stopp'd a quarter of an hour and then off to Sedbergh, seven miles farther, in an hour and thirty-five minutes, the wind was still at our backs and the road delightful. I must hurry on, next morning we walked to Kendal, 11 miles, a terrible up and down road, in three hours, and after buying and ordering furniture, the next day by half past four we reached Grasmere in a post chaise. So ends my long story. God bless you,   WILLIAM WORDSWORTH

LETTER TO SAMUEL TAYLOR COLERIDGE
Christmas Eve 1799

The Passes of the High Sierra

JOHN MUIR

We will now endeavour to see the Mono Pass in more detail, since it may, I think, be regarded as a good example of the higher passes accessible to the ordinary traveller in search of exhilarating scenery and adventure. The greater portion of it is formed by Bloody Canyon, which heads on the summit of the range, and extends in a general east-north-easterly direction to the edge of the Mono Plain. Long before its discovery by the whites, this wonderful canyon was known as a pass by the Indians of the neighbourhood, as is shown by their many old trails leading into it from every direction. But little have they marked the grand canyon itself, hardly more than the birds have in flying through its shadows. No stone tells a word of wild foray or raid. Storm-winds and avalanches keep it swept fresh and clean.

The first white men that forced a way through its sombre depths with pack-animals were companies of eager adventurous miners; men who would build a trail down the throat of the darkest inferno on their way to gold. The name Bloody Canyon may have been derived from the red colour of the metamorphic slates in which it is in great part eroded; or more probably from the bloodstains made by the unfortunate animals that were compelled to slide and shuffle awkwardly over the rough cutting edges of the rocks, in which case it is too well named, for I have never known mules or horses, however sure-footed, to make their way either up or down the canyon, without leaving a trail more or less marked with blood. Occasionally one is killed outright by falling over some precipice like a boulder. But such instances are less common than the appearance of the place would lead one to expect, the more experienced when driven loose, picking their way with wonderful sagacity.

During the exciting times that followed the discovery of gold near Mono Lake it frequently became a matter of considerable pecuniary importance to force a way through the canyon with pack-trains early in the spring, while it was yet heavily choked with winter snow. Then, though the way was smooth, it was steep and slippery, and the footing of the animals giving way, they sometimes rolled over sidewise with their loads, or end over end, compelling the use of ropes in sliding them down the steepest slopes where it was impossible to walk.

A good bridle-path leads from Yosemite through the Big Tuolumne Meadows to the head of the canyon. Here the scenery shows a sudden and startling condensation. Mountains red, black, and grey rise close at hand on the right, white in the shadows with banks of enduring snow. On the left swells the huge red mass of Mt. Gibbs, while in front the eye wanders down the tremendous gorge, and out on the warm plain of Mono, where the lake is seen in its setting of grey reflecting the light like a burnished disc of metal, volcanic cones to the south of it, and the smooth mountain ranges of Nevada beyond fading in the purple distance.

Entering the mountain gateway the sombre rocks seem to come close about us, as if conscious of our presence. Happily the ouzel and old familiar robin are here to sing us welcome, and azure daisies beaming with sympathy, enabling us to feel something of Nature's love even here, beneath the gaze of her coldest rocks. The peculiar impressiveness of the huge rocks is enhanced by the quiet aspect of the wide Alpine meadows through which the trail meanders just before entering the narrow pass. The forests in which they lie, and the mountain-tops rising above them, seem hushed and tranquil. Yielding to their soothing influences, we saunter on among flowers and bees scarce conscious of any definite thought; then suddenly we find ourselves in the huge, dark jaws of the canyon, closeted with Nature in one of her wildest strongholds.

After the first bewildering impression begins to wear off, and we become reassured by the glad birds and flowers, a chain of small lakes is seen, extending from the very summit of the pass, linked together by a silvery stream, that seems to lead the way and invite us on. Those near the summit are set in bleak rough rock-bowls, scantily fringed with sedges. Winter storms drive snow through the canyon in blinding drifts, and avalanches shoot from the heights rushing and booming like waterfalls. Then are these sparkling tarns filled and buried, leaving no sign of their existence. In June and July they begin to blink and thaw out like sleepy eyes; sedges thrust up their short brown spikes about their shore, and daisies bloom in turn, and the most profoundly snow-buried of them all is at length warmed and dressed as if winter were only the dream of a night.

Red Lake is the lowest of the chain and also the largest. It seems rather dull and forbidding, at first sight, lying motionless in its deep, dark bed, seldom stirred during the day by any wind strong enough to make a wave. The canyon wall rises sheer from the water's edge on the south, but on the opposite side there is sufficient space and sunshine for a fine garden. Daisies star the sod about the margin of it, and the centre is lighted with tall lilies, castilleias, larkspurs and columbines, while leafy willows make a fine protecting hedge; the whole forming a joyful outburst of warm, rosy plant-life, keenly emphasised by the raw, flinty baldness of the onlooking cliffs.

After resting in the lake the happy stream sets forth again on its travels warbling and trilling like an ouzel, ever delightfully confiding, no matter how rough the way; leaping, gliding, hither, thither, foaming or clear, and displaying the beauty of its virgin wildness at every bound.

One of its most beautiful developments is the Diamond Cascade, situated a short distance below Red Lake. The crisp water is first dashed into coarse granular spray that sheds off the light in quick flashing lances, mixed farther down with loose dusty foam; then it is divided into a diamond pattern by tracing the diagonal cleavage joints that intersect the face of the precipice over which it pours. Viewed in front, it resembles a wide sheet of embroidery of definite pattern, with an outer covering of fine mist, the whole varying with the temperature and the volume of water. Scarce a flower may be seen along its snowy border. A few bent pines look on from a distance, and small fringes of cassiope and rock-ferns grow in fissures near the head, but these are so lowly and undemonstrative only the attentive observer will be likely to notice them.

A little below the Diamond Cascade, on the north wall of the canyon, there is a long, narrow fall about 2,000ft. in height that makes a fine, telling show of itself in contrast with the dull, red rocks over which it hangs. A ragged talus curves up against the cliff in front of it, overgrown with a tangle of snow-pressed willows, in which it disappears with many a surge, and swirl, and plashing leap, and finally wins its way, still grey with foam, to a confluence with the main canyon stream.

Below this point the climate is no longer arctic. Butterflies become more abundant, grasses with showy purple panicles wave above your shoulders, and the deep summery drone of the bumble-bee thickens the air. *Pinus Albicaulis,* the tree mountaineer that climbs highest and braves the coldest blasts, is found in dwarfed, wind-bent clumps throughout the upper half of the canyon, gradually becoming more erect, until it is joined by the two-leafed pine, which again is succeeded by the taller yellow and mountain pines. These, with the burly juniper and trembling aspen, rapidly grow larger as they descend into the richer sunshine, forming groves that block the view; or they stand more apart in picturesque groups here and there, making beautiful and obvious harmony with each other, and with the rocks. Blooming underbrush also becomes abundant — azalea, spiraea, and dogwood weaving rich fringes for the stream, and shaggy rugs for the stern unflinching rock-bosses, adding beauty to their strength, and fragrance to the winds and the breath of the waterfalls. Through this blessed wilderness the canyon stream roams free, without any restraining channel, stirring the bushes like a rustling breeze, throbbing and wavering in wide swirls and zigzags, now in the sunshine, now in the shade; dancing, falling, flashing from side to side beneath the lofty walls in weariless exuberance of energy.

A glorious milky way of cascades is thus developed whose individual beauties might well call forth volumes of description. Bower Cascade is among the smallest, yet it is perhaps the most beautiful of them all. It is situated in the lower region of the pass where the sunshine begins to mellow between the cold and warm climates. Here the glad stream, grown strong with tribute gathered from many a snowy fountain, sings richer strains, and becomes more human and lovable at every step. Now you may see the rose and homely yarrow by its side, and bits of meadow with clover, and bees. At the head of a low-browed rock luxuriant cornel and willow bushes arch over from side to side, embowering the stream with their leafy branches; and waving plumes, kept in motion by the current, make a graceful fringe in front.

From so fine a bower as this, after all its dashing among bare rocks on the heights, the stream leaps out into the light in a fluted curve, thick-sown with sparkling crystals, and falls into a pool among brown boulders, out of which it creeps grey with foam, and disappears beneath a roof of verdure like that from which it came. Hence to the foot of the canyon the metamorphic slates give place to granite, whose nobler sculpture calls forth corresponding expressions of beauty from the stream in passing over it — bright trills of rapids, booming notes of falls, and the solemn hushing tones of smooth gliding sheets, all chanting and blending in pure wild harmony. And when at length its impetuous alpine life is done, it slips through a meadow at the foot of the canyon, and rests in Moraine Lake. This lake, about a mile long, lying between massive moraines piled up centuries ago by the grand old canyon glacier, is the last of the beautiful beds of the stream. Tall silver firs wave soothingly about its shores, and the breath of flowers, borne by the winds from the mountains, drifts over it like incense. Henceforth the stream, now grown stately and tranquil glides through meadows full of gentians, and groves of rustling aspen, to its confluence with Rush Creek, with which it flows across the desert and falls into the Dead Sea.

At Moraine Lake the canyon terminates, although apparently continued by two lateral moraines of imposing dimensions and regularity of structure. They extend out into the plain about five miles, with a height, toward their upper ends, of nearly 300ft. Their cool, shady sides are evenly forested with silver-firs, while the sides facing the sun are planted with showy flowers, a square rod containing five to six profusely flowered eriogonums of several species, about the same number of bahias and linosyris, and a few poppies, phloxes, gilias and grasses, each species planted trimly apart with bare soil between as if cultivated artificially.

My first visit to Bloody Canyon was made in the summer of 1869, under circumstances well calculated to heighten the impressions that are the peculiar offspring of mountains. I came from the blooming tangles of Florida, and waded out into the plant-gold of the great Central Plain of California while its unrivalled flora was as yet untrodden. Never before had I beheld congregations of social flowers half so extensive, or half so glorious. Golden compositae covered all the ground from the Coast Range to the Sierra like a stratum of denser sunshine, in which I revelled for weeks, then gave myself up to be borne forward on the crest of the summer plant-wave that sweeps annually up the Sierra flank, and spends itself on its snowy summits. At the Big Tuolumne Meadows I remained more than a month, sketching, botanising, and climbing among the surrounding mountains ere the fame of Bloody Canyon had reached me.

The mountaineer with whom I camped was one of those remarkable men so frequently found in California, the bold angles of whose character have been brought into relief by the grinding effects of the gold-period, like the features of glacier landscapes. But at this late day my friend's activities had subsided, and his craving for rest had caused him to become a gentle shepherd, and literally to lie down with a lamb, on the smoothest meadows he could find. Recognising my Scotch Highland instincts, he threw out some hints concerning Bloody Canyon, and advised me to explore it. "I have never seen it myself," he said, "for I never was so unfortunate as to pass that way; but I have heard many a strange story about it, and I warrant you will find it wild enough."

Next day I made up a package of bread, tied my note-book to my belt, and strode away in the bracing air, every nerve and muscle tingling with eager indefinite hope, and ready to give glad welcome to all the wilderness might offer. The plushy lawns starred with blue gentians and daisies soothed my morning haste, and made me linger, they were all so fresh, so sweet, so peaceful.

Climbing higher, as the day passed away, I traced the paths of the ancient glaciers over many a shining pavement; and marked the lanes in the upper forests that told the power of the winter avalanches. Still higher, I noted the gradual dwarfing of the pines in compliance with climate, and on the summit discovered creeping mats of the arctic willow, low as the lowliest grasses; and patches of dwarf vaccinium, with its round pink bells sprinkled over the sod as if they had fallen from the sky like hail; while in every direction the landscape stretched sublimely away in fresh wildness, a manuscript written by the hand of Nature alone.

At length, entering the gate of the pass, the huge rocks began to close around me in all their mysterious impressiveness; and as I gazed awe-stricken down the shadowy gulf, a drove of grey, hairy creatures came suddenly into view, lumbering towards me with a kind of boneless, wallowing motion like bears. However, grim and startling as they appeared, they proved to be nothing more formidable than Mono Indians dressed in a loose, shapeless way in the skins of sage rabbits sewed together into square robes. Both the men and women begged persistently for whisky and tobacco, and seemed so accustomed to denials, that it was impossible to convince them that I had none to give. Excepting the names of these two luxuries, they spoke no English, but I afterwards learned that they were on their way to Yosemite Valley to feast awhile on fish and flour, and procure a load of acorns to carry back through the pass to their huts on the shore of Mono Lake.

A good countenance may now and then be discovered among the Monos, but these, the first specimens I had seen, were mostly ugly, or altogether hideous. The dirt on their faces was fairly stratified in the hollows, and seemed so ancient and undisturbed as almost to possess a geological significance. The older faces were, moreover, strangely blurred and divided into sections by furrows that looked like some of the cleavage joints of rocks, suggesting exposure in a castaway condition for ages. They seemed to have no right place in the landscape, and I was glad to see them fading down the pass out of sight.

Then came evening, and the sombre cliffs were inspired with the ineffable beauty of the alpen-glow. A solemn calm fell upon every feature of the scene. All the lower depths of the canyon were in gloaming shadow, and one by one the mighty rockfronts forming the walls grew dim and vanished in the thickening darkness. Soon the night-wind began to flow and pour in torrents among the jagged peaks, mingling its strange tones with those of the waterfalls sounding far below. And as I lay by my camp-fire in a little hollow near one of the upper lakes listening to the wild sounds, the great full moon looked down over the verge of the canyon wall, her face seemingly filled with intense concern, and apparently so near as to produce a startling effect, as if she had entered one's bedroom, forsaking all the world besides to concentrate her gaze on me alone.

The whole night was full of strange weird sounds, and I gladly welcomed the morning. Breakfast was soon done, and I set forth in the exhilarating freshness of the new day, rejoicing in the abundance of pure wildness so closely pressed about me. The stupendous rock-walls, like two separate mountain ranges, stood forward in the thin, bright light, hacked and scarred by centuries of storms, while down in the bottom of the canyon, grooved and polished bosses heaved and glistened like swelling sea-waves, telling a grand old story of the ancient glacier that once poured its crushing floods above them.

Here for the first time I met the Arctic daisies in all their perfection of pure spirituality — gentle mountaineers, face to face with the frosty sky, kept safe and warm by a thousand miracles. I leaped lightly from rock to rock, glorying in the eternal freshness and sufficiency of nature, and in the rugged tenderness with which she nurtures her mountain darlings in the very homes and fountains of storms.

Fresh beauty appeared at every step, delicate rock-ferns, and tufts of the fairest flowers. Now another lake came to view, now a waterfall. Never fell light in brighter spangles, never fell water in whiter foam. I seemed to float through the canyon enchanted, feeling nothing of its roughness, and was out in the glaring Mono levels ere I was aware.

Looking back from the shore of Moraine Lake, my morning ramble seemed all a dream. There curved Bloody Canyon, a mere glacier furrow 2,000 and 3,000ft. deep, with *moutonée* rocks advancing from the sides, and braided together in the middle like rounded, swelling muscles. Here the lilies were higher than my head, and the sunshine was warm enough for palms. Yet the snow around the Arctic willows on the summit was plainly visible, only a few miles away, and between lay narrow specimen belts of all the principal climates of the Globe.

About five miles below the foot of Moraine Lake, where the lateral moraines terminate in the plain, there was a field of wild rye, growing in magnificent waving bunches six to eight feet high, and bearing heads from six to twelve inches long. Indian women were gathering the grain in baskets, bending down large handfuls of the ears, beating them with sticks, and fanning out the rye in the wind. They formed striking and picturesque groups as one caught glimpses of them here and there in winding lanes and openings with splendid tufts arching overhead, while their incessant chat and laughter proclaimed their careless joy.

I found the so-called Mono Desert, like the rye-field, in a high state of natural cultivation with the wild rose and the delicate pink-flowered abronia; and innumerable erigerons, gilias, phloxes, poppies and bush-compositae, growing not only along stream-banks, but out in the hot sand and ashes in openings among the sage-brush, and even in the craters of the highest volcanoes, cheering the grey wilderness with their rosy bloom, and literally giving beauty for ashes.

Beyond the moraines the trail turns to the left toward Mono Lake, now in sight around the spurs of the mountains, and touches its western shore at a distance from the foot of the pass of about six miles. Skirting the lake, you make your way over low bluffs and moraine piles, and through many a tangle of snow-crinkled aspens and berry bushes, growing on the banks of fine, dashing streams that come from the snows of the summits.

Here are the favourite camping grounds of the Indians, littered with piles of pine-burrs from which the seeds have been beaten. Many of their fragile willow huts are broken and abandoned; others arch airily over family groups that are seen lying at ease, pictures of thoughtless contentment; their wild, animal eyes glowering at you as you pass, their black shocks of hair perchance bedecked with red castileias, and their bent, bulky stomachs filled with no white man knows what.

Some of these mountain streams pouring into the lake have deep and swift currents at the fording-places, and their channels are so roughly paved with boulders that crossing them at the time of high water is rather dangerous.

That Mono Lake should have no outlet, while so many perennial streams flow into it, seems strange at first sight, before the immense waste by evaporation in so dry an atmosphere is recognised. Most of its shores being low, any considerable rise of its waters greatly enlarges its area, followed of course, by a corresponding increase of evaporation, which tends towards constancy of level within comparatively narrow limits. Nevertheless, on the flanks of the mountains, drawn in well-marked lines, you may see several ancient beaches that mark the successive levels at which the lake stood toward the close of the glacial period, the highest more than 600ft. above the present level. Then, under a climate as marked by coolness and excessive moisture as the present by devouring drouth, the dimensions of the lake must have been vastly greater. Indeed, a study of the whole plateau region, named by Fremont 'the Great Basin', extending from the Sierra to the Wahsatch mountains, a distance of 400 miles, shows that it was covered by inland seas of fresh water that were only partially separated by the innumerable hills and mountain ranges of the region, which then existed as islands, forming an archipelago of unrivalled grandeur.

The lake water is as clear as the snow-streams that feed it, but intensely acrid and nauseating from the excessive quantities of salts accumulated by evaporation beneath a burning sun. Of course no fish can live in it, but large flocks of geese, ducks, and swans come from beyond the mountains at certain seasons, and gulls also in great numbers, to breed on a group of volcanic islands that rise near the centre of the lake, thus making the dead, bitter sea lively and cheerful while they stay. The eggs of the gulls used to be gathered for food by the Indians, who floated to the islands on rafts made of willows; but since the occurrence of a great storm on the lake a few years ago, that overtook them on their way back from the islands, they have not ventured from the shore. Their rafts were broken up and many were drowned. This disaster, which some still living have good cause to remember, together with certain superstitious fears concerning evil spirits supposed to dwell in the lake and rule its waves, make them content with the safer and far more important product of the shores, chief of which is the larvae of a small fly that breeds in the slimy froth in the shallows. When the worms are ripe, and the waves have collected them and driven them up the beach in rich oily windrows, then old and young make haste to the curious harvest, and gather the living grain in baskets and buckets of every description. After being washed and dried in the sun it is stored for winter. Raw or cooked, it is regarded as a fine luxury, and delicious dressing for other kinds of food — acorn-mush, clover-salad, grass-seed-pudding, etc. So important is this small worm to the neighbouring tribes, it forms a subject of dispute about as complicated and perennial as the Newfoundland cod. After waging worm-wars until everybody is weary and hungry, the belligerents mark off boundary lines, assigning stated sections of the shores to each tribe, where the harvest may be gathered in peace until fresh quarrels have time to grow. Tribes too feeble to establish rights must needs procure their worm supply from their more fortunate neighbours, giving nuts, acorns or ponies in exchange.

This 'diet of worms' is further enriched by a large, fat caterpillar, a species of silk-worm found on the yellow pines to the south of the lake; and as they also gather the seeds of this pine, they get a double crop from it — meat and bread from the same tree.

Forbidding as this grey, ashy wilderness is to the dweller in green fields, to the red man it is a paradise full of all the good things of life. A Yosemite Indian with whom I was acquainted while living in the valley, went over the mountains to Mono every year on a pleasure trip, and when I asked what could induce him to go to so poor a country when, as a hotel servant, he enjoyed all the white man's good things in abundance, he replied, that Mono had better things to eat than anything to be found in the hotel — plenty deer, plenty wild sheep, plenty antelope, plenty worm, plenty berry, plenty sagehen, plenty rabbit — drawing a picture of royal abundance that from his point of view surpassed everything else the world had to offer.

A sail on the lake develops many a fine picture; the natives along the curving shores seen against so grand a mountain background; water birds stirring the glassy surface into white dancing spangles; the islands, black, pink and grey, rising into a cloud of white wings of gulls; volcanoes dotting the hazy plain; and, grandest of all and overshadowing all, the mighty barrier wall of the Sierra, heaving into the sky from the water's edge, and stretching away to north and south with its marvellous wealth of peaks and crests and deep-cutting notches keenly defined, or fading away in the soft purple distance; cumulus clouds swelling over all in huge mountain bosses of pearl, building a mountain range of cloud upon a range of rock, the one as firmly sculptured, and as grand and showy and substantial as the other.

The magnificent cluster of volcanoes to the south of the lake may easily be visited from the foot of Bloody Canyon, the distance being only about six miles. The highest of the group rises about 2,700ft. above the lake. They are all post-glacial in age, having been erupted from what was once the bottom of the south end of the lake, through stratified glacial drift. During their numerous periods of activity they have scattered showers of ashes and cinders over all the adjacent plains and mountains within a radius of 20 and 30 miles.

Nowhere within the bounds of our wonder-filled land are the antagonistic forces of fire and ice brought more closely and contrastingly together. So striking are the volcanic phenomena, we seem to be among the very hearths and firesides of nature. Then turning to the mountains, while standing in drifting ashes, we behold huge moraines issuing from the cool jaws of the great canyons, marking the pathways of glaciers that crawled down the mountain sides laden with debris and pushed their frozen floods into the deep waters of the lake in thundering icebergs, as they are now descending into the inland waters of Alaska, not a single Arctic character being wanting, where now the traveller is blinded in a glare of tropical light.

Americans are little aware as yet of the grandeur of their own land, as is too often manifested by going on foreign excursions, while the wonders of our unrivalled plains and mountains are left unseen. We have Laplands and Labradors of our own, and streams from glacier-caves — rivers of mercy sacred as the Himalaya-born Ganges. We have our Shasta Vesuvius also, and bay, with its Golden Gate, beautiful as the Bay of Naples. And here among our inland plains are African Saharas, dead seas, and deserts, dotted with oases, where congregate the travellers, coming in long caravans — the trader with his goods and gold, and the Indian with his weapons — the Bedouin of the California desert.

from WEST OF THE ROCKY MOUNTAINS *1888*

The First Gentleman Backpacker

THOMAS DE QUINCY

There were already, even in those days of 1802, numerous inns, erected at reasonable distances from each other, for the accommodation of tourists: and no sort of disgrace attached in Wales, as too generally upon the great roads of England, to the pedestrian style of travelling. Indeed the majority of those whom I met as fellow-tourists in the quiet little cottage-parlours of the Welsh posting-houses were pedestrian travellers.

All the way from Shrewsbury through Llangollen, Llanrwst, Conway, Bangor, then turning to the left at right angles through Caernarvon, and so on to Dolgelly (the chief town of Merionethshire), Tan-y-Bwlch, Harlech, Barmouth, and through the sweet solitudes of Cardiganshire, or turning back sharply towards the English border through the gorgeous wood scenery of Montgomeryshire — everywhere at intermitting distances of 12 to 16 miles, I found the most comfortable inns.

No huge Babylonian centres of commerce towered into the clouds on these sweet sylvan routes: no hurricanes of haste, or fever-stricken armies of horses and flying chariots, tormented the echoes in these mountain recesses. And it has often struck me that a world-wearied man, who sought for the peace of monasteries separated from their gloomy captivity — peace and silence such as theirs combined with the large liberty of nature — could not do better than revolve amongst these modest inns in the five northern Welsh counties of Denbigh, Montgomery, Carnarvon, Merioneth and Cardigan. Sleeping, for instance, and breakfasting at Carnarvon; then, by an easy nine-mile walk, going forwards to dinner at Bangor, thence to Aber — nine miles; or to Llanberis; and so on for ever accomplishing 70 to 90 or 100 miles in a week. This, upon actual experiment, and for week after week, I found the most delightful of lives.

66

Life on this model was but too beautiful; and to myself especially, that am never thoroughly in health unless when having pedestrian exercise to the extent of 15 miles at the most, and 8 to 10 miles at the least. Living thus, a man earned his daily enjoyment. But what did it cost? About half a guinea a day: whilst my boyish allowance was not a third of this. The flagrant health, health boiling over in fiery rapture which ran along, side by side, with exercise on this scale, whilst all the while from morning to night I was inhaling mountain air, soon passed into a hateful scourge. Perquisites to servants and a bed would have absorbed the whole of my weekly guinea. My policy therefore was, if the autumnal air was warm enough, to save this expense of a bed and the chamber-maid by sleeping amongst ferns or furze upon a hillside; and perhaps with a cloak of sufficient weight as well as compass or an Arab's burnoose, this would have been no great hardship. But then in the daytime what an oppressive burden to carry! So perhaps it was as well that I had no cloak at all.

I did, however, for some weeks try the plan of carrying a canvas tent manufactured by myself, and not larger than an ordinary umbrella: but to pitch this securely I found difficult; and on windy nights it became a troublesome companion. As winter drew near, this bivouacking system became too dangerous to attempt. Still one may bivouac decently, barring rain and wind, up to the end of October. And I counted, on the whole, that in a fortnight I spent nine nights abroad. There are, as perhaps the reader knows by experience, no jaguars in Wales — nor pumas — nor anacondas — nor (generally speaking) any thugs. What I feared most, but perhaps only through ignorance of zoology, was lest, whilst my sleeping face was upturned to the stars, some one of the many Brahminical-looking cows on the Cambrian hills, one or other, might poach her foot into the centre of my face.

from CONFESSIONS OF AN ENGLISH OPIUM EATER *1822*

PART 2

Trails Through History

The writings in this section all have a particular association with the area they describe or the aspect of walking they depict — an association which is historical, in one sense or another.

In mood they vary widely. *Stravagers and Marauders* is a wry celebration of some stalwart defenders of ancient rights of way in Scotland; *The Kinder Scout Trespasses* does the same job in rather more trenchant style for England's open spaces. *Game Regions of the Upper Sacramento,* which really deserves a better title, is a vivid piece of writing that brings its period instantly to life.

The other contributions take us from one of England's oldest trading routes, the Ridgeway, to North Wales, to Scotland again, and across the Atlantic to celebrate the achievement of a remarkable lady — Grandma Gatewood of the Appalachian Trail.

Stravagers and Marauders

ROBERT AITKEN

I and my friends had no desire to see the proposed Club mixed up with any attempt to force rights-of-way. We did not desire the Club to become a stravaging or marauding Club, insisting on going everywhere at every season . . . *Professor Ramsay SMCJ* 4, p. 88

One of the endearing features of *The Scottish Mountaineering Club Journal* is the way it evokes the flavour of the mountain scene in Scotland — if not at the time, then thirty years on. Bygones become bygones, and the truth emerges — or something like it: the rowdy, reprobate and reckless of the last generation come out, blinking nervously, into the daylight of retrospective respectability, and Peaheid and Scrubbernut take up their niche in the hall of fame at last; the cause of history is served, the record put right.

There was a time, though, long before the dawn of the Duttonian* enlightenment, when such broad-mindedness was much less evident. In the days of Ramsay, the bourgeois academic, and of that land-owning reactionary, Munro, the activities and the achievements of a whole class of hillmen — a feature of the Scottish hills for half a century — went more or less unremarked. These were the advocates and exponents of Rights of Way and Access to Mountains, the deer-disturbers and signpost-erectors who walked outwith the pale of SMC constitutional precept: '. . . respect proprietary and sporting rights, and endeavour to obtain the co-operation of proprietors.' These bolshies of the Golden Age, the heyday of the deer forest, as well as of early mountaineering in Scotland, have rested largely in obscurity ever since. Perhaps it is time to rehabilitate some of them.

The task need not be a serious one, since there is no tradition of self-important solemnity in the Rights of Way movement; one of the prime movers was in fact noted for his sense of humour, and his contribution was almost clownish.

* Geoff Dutton — Editor of *SMCJ* 166

John Hutton Balfour is now remembered chiefly as professor of botany at Edinburgh University between 1845 and 1879, and for his work in the design and development of the Edinburgh botanic gardens, but in his time he was known as an entertaining and humorous lecturer, and held the incongruous post of Punster to the Cockburns' Bonaly Friday Club. He was particularly energetic in conducting field excursions with his students to all parts of Scotland — the kind of excursions on which the first SMC meets were modelled. His contribution to the Rights of Way movement came in August 1847, when he and seven of his students encountered the Duke of Athole in Glen Tilt. Sir Douglas Maclagan, a friend and contemporary of Balfour, commemorated the event in some of the most unforgettably excruciating doggerel of the time:

> The gerse was poo't, the boxes fill't,
> An' syne the hail clamjamphrie
> Would tak' the road by Glen o' Tilt,
> Awa' to whar' they cam' frae.
> The Duke at this put up his birse;
> He vowed, in English and in Erse,
>> That Saxon fit
>> Su'd never get
>> A'e single bit
>> Throughout his yett,
> Amang the Hielan' hills, man.

After a protracted argument with the Duke and his gillies about the disputed right of passage, the botanical party ended the deadlock and circumvented the opposition by scrambling over a wall. This, the so-called 'Battle of Glen Tilt', generated enormous publicity and led to a prolonged lawsuit in which the Edinburgh Association for the Protection of Public Rights of Roadway in Scotland, through various agents, established the public right on this ancient drove-road, and did much to clarify the law to their advantage: it was a vital precedent for what was to become the Scottish Rights of Way Society.

It has long been tacitly assumed that Balfour and his students were the innocent and inadvertent objects of the Duke's wrath. All the evidence, though circumstantial, suggests otherwise. There is the Professor's character; the fact that he had previously on the same excursion run the gauntlet of the Earl of Fife's keepers to ascend Ben Macdui by the forbidden Luibeg route; and the singular coincidence that less than six weeks before Balfour set out, the Edinburgh Association had held a meeting at which they explicitly stated their intention of taking up the cause of Glen Tilt, and indeed asked that pedestrians hindered in their passage should contact them. Not only was this meeting reported in the Edinburgh press, but there was also at least one close friend of Balfour's, Patrick Neill, on the committee of the Association. It is difficult to imagine that Balfour could have remained ignorant of these circumstances; it is easy to picture the impish anticipation with which he probably set off on his stravaging excursion.

Such anticipation would certainly have been justified, for it was a time of general feeling against landowning Dukes, and there could hardly have been a more appropriate subject than the sixth Duke of Athole (the change of spelling from Atholl was quite characteristic of the man). He was a litigious, irascible romantic who squandered vast sums in lawsuits to prohibit his neighbours from shooting his deer when they crossed to adjoining estates, in entertaining Queen Victoria on her Highland jaunts from Balmoral, and in equipping his Athole Highlanders with Lochaber axes and other antique arms. After Balfour, things went from bad to worse with the Duke: in August 1850 he was involved in a brawl with two Cambridge students walking through Glen Tilt, and in October of the same year at Perth Station he more or less assaulted the Provost, who had been active in raising local sentiment, not to say local money, for the case against the Duke. Even the *Times* was moved to suggest that 'it would be doing the public a service to bring this hot-headed foolish man to his senses,' while *Punch* was merciless in mock-Ossianic style on the black eye the Duke had collected in the fray with the undergraduates:

Lament; for the visual organ of Atholl is darkened. Raise
the sound of wail upon a thousand bagpipes! Closed is the eye
of him who would close Glen Tilt to the traveller. Ken ye not
the Chieff of Clan Atholl — the tourist-baffling Duke of the
impassable glen?

Probably nobody enjoyed all this more than J. H. Balfour. It
is sad, then, that he should so rarely get the credit for starting
it. Sir Henry Alexander, for instance, mentioned the 'Battle'
in the 1928 SMC Cairngorms Guide, but made the mistake of
ascribing it to Balfour's son, and the error persisted until
Adam Watson corrected it in the 1975 edition of the Guide.

Twenty years on, in 1867, it fell to one of Balfour's
colleagues to show how far the deer forest and its exclusive-
ness had spread. In August of that year John Stuart Blackie,
professor of Greek at Edinburgh, and passionate champion
of the Highland people, ventured to climb Buachaille Etive
Mòr against the wishes of the proprietor, who also,
interestingly enough, refused to provide him with a guide. It
is pleasant to record the sequel: "Arrived at Fort William, he
called upon the Fiscal, who, along with a hearty welcome and
some glasses of excellent port, gave him the information that
he had received instructions to have him prosecuted for
climbing Buachaill-more. Professor Tyndall was at Fort
William . . . . (visiting the Parallel Roads of Glen Roy) and
joined him in a hearty laugh at the baffled deer-stalkers,
whose attack expired in this letter."

The continued extension of the deer forests and the gradual
decline in use of the great drove roads combined in a threat to
the hill rights of way which became acute in the 1880s,
especially where the proprietor or shooting tenant was an
outsider. Such was the American, Walter Louis Winans, who
controlled over 200,000 acres of jealously guarded stalking
country in Affric and Kintail, paying nearly £10,000 in rents
for the privilege. "And for all this extravagance, he could not
be called a true sportsman," it is alleged; "He believed in
drives of deer and grouse, and in sumptuous hill pic-nics."

Such too was Duncan Macpherson, who purchased the
estate of Glen Doll with capital acquired in Australia. In 1885
he was the first proprietor visited by a notable stravaging

'deputation' which toured the Central Highlands on behalf of the revived Scottish Rights of Way Society. This expedition neatly combined the impudence of the Balfour tradition with a very Victorian logistical thoroughness: the party carried signposts previously prepared to mark disputed footpaths, which they erected in the appropriate place; obstructing gamekeepers were then intimidated by the 'taking of instruments' — an obscure and no doubt impressive legal process made much easier by the presence in the party of a notary public. The passage of the deputation led to a prolonged and ruinous lawsuit over Jock's Road in Glen Doll, in which the Society was at last successful in the House of Lords, and precipitated a decade of hectic activity in claiming and forcing rights of way, activity which abated only when the Local Government (Scotland) Act of 1894 made the maintenance of rights of way a local authority responsibility. One of the leading spirits in the deputation was Walter A. Smith, who was later to become an original member of the SMC and the sponsor of notable Edinburgh members such as William Douglas; he seems to have gone back over Jock's Road fairly often — it probably gave him as much satisfaction as a new route would to a different kind of mountaineer.

In fact, the SMC drew several of its early adherents from the ranks of the stravagers. Professor Veitch, J. Parker Smith, and Hely Almond, headmaster of Loretto and the original Salvationist, were members, and C. E. W. Macpherson, secretary of the Rights of Way Society. But the hard core of the Club was composed of Alpinists — often abroad in the critical months of stalking, and doing most of their Scottish climbing in winter and spring. And most were Glaswegian, with easy access by rail to hills noted more for their rocks and roughness than for their qualities as deer forest; almost without exception, the great right of way cases were fought in the eastern Highlands. It is not, then, surprising to find that the Cairngorm Club had its origins in a tradition altogether more radical than that of the SMC. The political background of the North-East was Liberal; the members, hillmen rather than mountaineers, were usually afoot on the Cairngorms during the stalking season; and the founders included Alexander Inkson McConnochie — a member of the Rights of Way Society — Alexander Copland, and Thomas Gillies. Under the unlikely pseudonyms of 'Dryas Octopetala' (the mountain avens) and 'Thomas Twayblade', these last two chronicled in the Aberdeen Journal of the 1880s their early expeditions across the High Cairngorms: expeditions notable not only for their adventurous bivouacs and cuisine on the tops, but also for their encounters with, escapes from, and diatribes against stalkers, ghillies, and lairds. Copland gave us the name Angel's Peak for Sgòr an Lochain Uaine of Cairntoul, to offset the Devil's Point, itself a euphemistic translation of the Gaelic; and he was first Chairman of the Cairngorm Club, which he regarded as ". . . . in some sense a reserve force in questions affecting rights-of-way to and on mountains." Gillies, his son-in-law, was an advocate who acted as local agent for the Rights of Way Society in the Glen Doll case, mustering ancient drovers and couthy shepherds to give evidence of historic use of Jock's Road.

In electing their first President, however, the Cairngorm Club demonstrated that their stravaging aspirations ran to more than mere footpaths; he was James Bryce MP, later Viscount Bryce, the originator of the campaign for Access of Mountains. Bryce is perhaps the least known of the great Scottish mountaineers of the late Victorian period; this may well be because most of his prodigious climbing experience was gained overseas, for he was the most travelled of mountaineers, and it is unlikely that many people have climbed more widely, even in these days. The Alps, Pyrenees, Norway, Etna, Caucasus, Andes, Rockies, Tatras, Hawaii, Ararat, Himalaya, Sinai, Iceland, Mashonaland, were all grist to his mill. He contributed a short chapter on 'Mountaineering in far-away countries' to Clinton Dent's Badminton Library volume on mountaineering, was a friend of Leslie Stephen and Freshfield, and was president of the Alpine Club between 1899 and 1901. Nevertheless, his ascents seem to have been almost incidental to other interests, such as history, law, education, and botany, and to his political career, first as a Liberal Member of Parliament from 1880 to

1906, and latterly as Ambassador to the United States from 1907 to 1913, a role in which he achieved singular success and popularity, including honorary membership of the American Alpine Club. He was never a member of the SMC, though he was almost an exact contemporary of Ramsay; indeed, they were both successful competitors for scholarships at Trinity College, Oxford, in 1857, when Ramsay described Bryce as "that awful Scotch fellow who outwrote everybody".

It was mainly during his period as Member for South Aberdeen, from 1885 to 1906, that Bryce waged his long campaign for free access to mountains for recreation, a concept of striking originality in Britain at that time. He did assist with the Parliamentary cause of Rights of Way, but his addresses to the Cairngorm Club, as well as his speeches in the House of Commons, show a very modern awareness of the need for areal, rather than simply linear access: ". . . . we are by no means content to be kept to a specified limited path in the centre of a mountain". As long as he was in the House, Bryce took every opportunity, and used every artifice of parliamentary procedure, to present and press his Bills; but while his often eloquent argument occasionally succeeded in carrying a resolution, detailed proposals were never given time. There was considerable support among Scottish MPs, but the opposition included many such as J. Parker Smith, who represented Partick, and who was, as mentioned earlier, a member of both the Rights of Way Society and the SMC. A piece by Smith in *Blackwood's Magazine* for August 1891 examines the access question, coming down heavily in favour of the 'amicable agreement' policy of the Club — not surprisingly, since Ramsay, Munro, Veitch, and Gilbert Thomson contributed 'evidence' for the article. Not surprisingly, too, Stott gave it a very favourable notice in the *SMC Journal* (1, p.328). John Stuart Blackie, by contrast, broke into verse as he took Bryce's side:

> Bless thee, brave Bryce! all Scotland votes with thee,
> All but the prideful and the pampered few,
> Who in their Scottish homes find nought to do
> But keep our grand broad-shouldered Grampians free

From tread of Scottish foot. . . .

The radical simplicity of Bryce's proposals for Access to
mountains has tended to obscure the breadth and the
farsightedness of his concern for the countryside. He watched
with dismay the extension of the railway network into the
Highlands, and its impact on the scenery of such areas as
Killiecrankie and Loch Earn, while he recognised another
potent threat in the destruction of the Falls of Foyers to
create Scotland's first hydro scheme. To counteract these
and similar future developments, he outlined a system of
controls that closely foreshadowed much of our present
planning legislation.

Bryce's experience of the United States also gave him an
almost uncanny foresight of the motorcar era — in the days
when Ford and his fellows were just tooling up for mass-
production. As ambassador, he urged the Americans to keep
cars out of the Yosemite National Park, in terms that were
entirely unequivocal: "Do not let the serpent into Eden at
all". It is intriguing to reflect that by 1912 Bryce was
thoroughly familiar with the national park concept, as
realised in the United States, Australia, and New Zealand,
but he seems never to have considered importing the idea, on
the grounds that private ownership of the land had rendered
it impossible in Britain. As it was, Bryce returned from
Washington only in time for the First World War, and died in
1922 at the age of 84. The parliamentary cause of Access of
Mountains, carried forward by Sir Charles Trevelyan and
others, merged imperceptibly at last into the national park
movement in England and Wales: but there was no such
momentum in Scotland. Perhaps Bryce had too many irons in
the fire; perhaps he was essentially too restrained and self-
effacing. Queen Victoria had said of him: "I like Mr. Bryce.
He knows so much and is so modest"; while Freshfield, a
much more astute and less amenable critic, saw in him
". . . a simplicity of character, an honesty, a breadth of
outlook. . . .". This most respectable of radicals remains a
prophet almost without honour in his own country; the
conservation of scenery he urged so strongly is now an

accepted objective, but the problems he sought to avoid still await solution.

Shortly after Bryce's death those problems were emphatically restated by Ernest Baker, leader of the notoriously dramatic climb of the Ben Nuis Chimney on Arran in 1901, in the introduction to his book, *The Highlands with Rope and Rucksack* of 1923. Re-published a year later in pamphlet form as *The Forbidden Land,* and dedicated to Bryce, it is an exhilaratingly comprehensive polemic against the Clearances, the deer forests, and every form of land-lordism and access restriction, with an apologia worthy of Haston thrown in for good measure: ". . . we were not imbued with any superstitious reverence for legal rights. Under stress of circumstances we committed some lawless things — even a burglary on one occasion. . . ." The review of Baker's book (*SMCJ* 16, p.320) is sympathetic on the whole, but coyly declines to join battle on the content of that lively first section — Baker was, after all, a member of the Club, even if his stravaging tendencies were rather too evident.

"Are you quite sure walkers aren't a protected species?"

No such complaint could be levelled against Arthur Russell or A. E. Robertson, whose credentials as SMC men were unimpeachable. Russell, whose death in 1967 closed seventy-one years of membership, served for fourteen years in various Club offices and was closely involved with Unna and the National Trust for Scotland in the acquisition of Glencoe and Dalness — these services concealing his sterling work as secretary of the Rights of Way Society for many years. Robertson was even more successful, plodding the Coffin Roads of the north and west with resurrectionist zeal, while doing all the Munros for light relief, and to establish his *bona fides* — achieving this so effectively that he became President of both the Club and the Society: and though the first to do so, he has not been the last — such schizophrenia seeming to be chronic, if not particularly malignant.

In fact, a relationship has always existed between the SMC and the stravaging faction, however little acknowledged it may have been; the Club may have done its best to ignore them, but they have patently not gone away, though the radical passions of last century have subsided. Perhaps now they can all, earnest or impish, be permitted to come forth from the shades of obscurity to which the scurrilous scribe Stott and his successors have condemned them. They're not so very wicked, after all.

from THE SCOTTISH MOUNTAINEERING CLUB JOURNAL *1975*

The Appalachian Trail

1 (previous page) Fording Baker Stream in Maine. *Photo: Kevin White*
2 (left) The trail in North Carolina.   3 (top) The ridge of
Charlie's Bunion in Great Smokey Mountains National Park in
North Carolina.   4 (above left) Commemorative plaque in Georgia.
5 (above right) A stop to brew up at Stover Creek, near Springer Mountain,
Georgia near the end of the Trail. *Photos: John Merrill*

6 (overleaf) In the Lakeland fells west of Derwent Water —
looking west towards Crag Hill from Barrow. *Photo: Derek Forss*

7 and 8 Ramblers enjoy free access to the moorlands of the High Peak following decades of protest: on the Bleaklow massif (Howden Moor) and at Kinder Downfall (below).
Photos: E. Hector Kyme and C. Douglas Milner

9 A ramblers' protest meeting on Kinder Scout in 1911.
Photo: Sheffield Telegraph

10 and 11 (below) Balfour and Bryce — pioneers of the
'free access' movement in Scotland. *Photos: SMC Collection*

Prof. John Hutton Balfour   James Bryce

12 (overleaf) A typical Scottish glen (Glen Nevis at Steall).
Many valleys like this had restricted access in the last century.
Photo: Ken Andrew

Grandma Gatewood — First Lady of the Trail

JAMES R. HARE

Grandma Gatewood had learned about the Appalachian Trail two or three years before from a magazine article. She remembered the description as being on the idyllic side: a smoothed footway with easy grades, a yard-wide garden path carefully blazed and manicured, with plenty of signs. She resolved to hike it all. She had always wanted to do something notable, and no woman had ever hiked the Appalachian Trail in one continuous journey. The length of the longest footpath in the world held an irresistible appeal for her. Her imagination was fired. It was a challenge worthy of the pioneer woman of the last century, some of whom she had known well. She herself had come of a pioneer family, born on the 25th October 1887, one of 15 children, on a farm in Ohio. Most of her life had been lived on farms, where she had hoed corn, raked hay, chopped tobacco, and raised four sons and seven daughters of her own.

For her hike she had fashioned a bag from denim. In it she carried any clothing not being worn; food such as bouillon cubes, chipped beef, raisins, peanuts, powdered milk, and salt; items of first aid like adhesive tape, Band-Aids, and Mercurochrome; hairpins, safety pins, needles, thread, buttons, and matches in a plastic matchcase.

Her basic outer costume consisted of hat, skirt, blouse and sneakers. She wore a single pair of socks, sometimes cotton, sometimes woollen. At night she would pull on a second pair of socks. She also had a scarf, a sweater, a jacket, and a light wool blanket.

Grandma had been a little cowed by the events in Maine; she knew it and she hated it.* She travelled to California to

* On a previous attempt to walk the Trail, Grandma Gatewood got badly lost and had to be rescued — *Editor's Note.*

visit with relatives, but as the months slipped by the pull of the trail became strong. One day in spring she boarded a plane bound for Atlanta, and a week later she signed the trail register on the summit of Mt. Oglethorpe in Georgia.

Her hiking gear had been increased by a flashlight, a Swiss army knife with nine miniature tools, a teaspoon, two plastic eight-ounce baby bottles for water, a rain hat and rain cape, and a plastic curtain. She had sewn a tail on the rain hat to shield her neck. The rain cape, made from two yards of plastic sheeting, protected herself and her denim bag when she walked in the rain. It was used as a ground cloth when she rested in some damp place or slept on the ground. The plastic curtain was used for shelter when it rained. A straw hat began the trip, but was lost when a stray wind blew it into Tallulah Gorge on the Georgia border. Other hats followed — a fisherman's cap, a man's felt hat, another hat with a green celluloid visor, and a knitted stocking cap. None lasted long before succumbing to some vagary of the trail, like being forgotten at a rest stop or falling into a mountain torrent. Grandma's pack seldom weighed as much as 20lb; 14lb to 17lb was more usual.

A chilling fog was shrouding the famed rhododendron thickets on Roan Mountain on the North Carolina-Tennessee line when she arrived there at the end of a June day. She heated rocks in a fire, laid them on the grass, and went to sleep on top of the rocks, wrapped in her blanket. The rocks gave off warmth for hours and the night was tolerable. During a cold snap on another mountain she pulled a wide board from the ruins of a tumbledown cabin and toasted it over the embers. This became her bed, and if the board rather quickly lost its heat the night had at least begun cosily.

Like many a hiker before her, she made the discovery that picnic tables in forest and park campsites could be used as beds if the ground was soaked, and they were no harder than the floors of the lean-tos. She did not depend on lean-tos much; she was a woman and alone, and sharing such primitive accommodation with chance strangers was not always satisfactory.

Tiny wood mice pulled at her hair as she slept, no doubt

regarding the strands as capital homemaking material. She thought of the mice as sources of amusement and company rather than as annoyances.

As she hiked through the southern hill country, Grandma soon learned that a stop at a home to inquire about the route or to fill her baby bottles at the hand pump in the yard was likely to make her the object of intense though well-mannered curiosity. She was often invited to stay for the night. While preferring the "company room" for slumber, she wasn't finicky; the hayloft would do nicely.

In Shenandoah National Park a black bear ambled onto the pathway. Its intentions seemed not unfriendly, although it was ambling her way. As the gap between them narrowed, Grandma let go with what she calls "my best holler".

" 'Dig', I hollered, and he dug."

The episode seemed to release a little extra adrenalin into Grandma's system. Up till then she had been doing from 12 to 16 miles daily, but by nightfall on this particular day she had logged 27 miles.

West Virginia and Maryland sped by under Grandma's sneakered feet. By now she had switched to men's sneakers, having decided that the soles of women's sneakers were too light and thin. The rocks of Pennsylvania, which on the narrow ridgetops stand on end like the fins of the dinosaurs, put her choice of footwear to a stern test. In its 200 miles of trail, Pennsylvania accounted for about one and a half pairs of the five pairs of sneakers she was to wear out on her journey. Usually a pair of sneakers were good for from 400 to 500 miles.

For almost three months she had managed without utensils other than jackknife, teaspoon, and baby bottles. At a spring in New Jersey she picked up an abandoned tin cup and liked it so well that she never hiked without it afterwards.

Where the trail precariously negotiated a cliff on Kittatinny Ridge, a blacksnake practically stood on its tail in a fighting attitude, but Grandma Gatewood knew all about blacksnakes from her years on the farm. She simply waited until the creature subsided and fled into a crevice.

In New York a rattlesnake made the mortal mistake of

shaking its tail at Grandma. And near the summer community of Oscawana Corners a German shepherd dog leapt a hedge and nipped the upper calf of her leg. As the skin was hardly broken, she painted the teeth marks with Merthiolate and hiked on, but more warily. When she ran into a patch of nettles she changed her mind about wearing a skirt on the trail. Dungarees became her usual garb after that.

In the Mohawk State Forest in Connecticut a bobcat circled around and "squeaked infernally" while Grandma was snacking from a can of sardines. "If you come too close I'll crack you," she warned. The bobcat kept its distance.

Coming down that choice little precipice in the Berkshires which Yankee humour has named Jug End, Grandma Gatewood slipped on the rain-wet slope. She grabbed at a tree limb; it broke and she slid hard against a rock. For some minutes she was unable to move and wondered if a shoulder was paralysed, but the numbness ebbed and she went on.

In Vermont the porcupine thrives. Its flesh is said to be as toothsome as pork or veal. On learning this fact, Grandma cornered a porcupine and gave it a crack with a pole. Mindful of the quills, she skinned it with caution, then spitted the carcass over a fire. The flesh smelled lovely as it roasted, but the first forkful was another matter. "My imagination got away on me," Grandma said. "All at once the porcupine meat filled my mouth. I just couldn't swallow."

She had been carrying a walking stick, flourishing it at hostile dogs and using it as a third leg to ford streams; in the White Mountains she found it of particular help in descending barren ledges where her legs weren't long enough to make the step down without extra support.

As Grandma hiked, word of her progress ran ahead. She had become news, and reporters from local papers popped up at the road crossings to get her story. Heretofore only the children of her children had known her as 'Grandma'. Now 'Grandma' was to become a fixed part of her name — and a part of the vocabulary of the Appalachian Trail.

The Maine Forest Service was on the alert as Grandma crossed the state line. If the service was astonished at seeing her again, after having issued a virtual writ of banishment, it

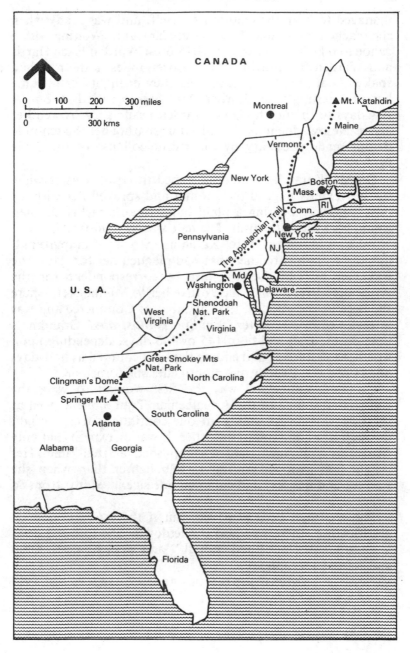

managed to keep the emotion to itself, and was ready when she reached the Kennebec River at Caratunk. Waiting with a canoe to take her over were Chief Forest Warden Isaac Harris and Warden Bradford Pease. A dozen miles in the rain had soaked Grandma to the skin, and they brought her in some haste to Sterling's Hotel, where Mrs. Sterling dried her out. A few days to the north Game Warden Francis Cyr rowed her across Nesowadnehunk Stream, thus sparing her the ten-mile detour made necessary by the recent collapse of the cable bridge.

On Mt. Katahdin Grandma signed the trail register while the low clouds hugged the summit and sprayed her with icy mist. She was wearing a plaid lumberman's jacket she had found back along the trail. The date was September 25.

When she returned to Katahdin Stream Campground, limping from a sore knee that had plagued her for days, she was met by Mrs Dean Chase, a correspondent for the Associated Press. Mrs Chase drove her to Millinocket, where she became the guest of the Chamber of Commerce and was interviewed by a reporter from *Sports Illustrated*. Grandma's time on the trail had been 145 or 146 days, depending upon whether the starting and ending days are counted as half-days or as full days. Exactly one month later she turned 68.

Grandma Gatewood was the first woman to walk the complete distance of the Appalachian Trail alone as well as the first woman to walk it in one continuous trip, straight through from one end to the other. It was an exploit that only five others, all men, had accomplished at that time. Her weight had dropped to 120lb, 30lb lighter than when she started, and her feet had enlarged one size in width, from 8c to 8D.

The goal had been achieved, but if there was a glow of gratification, there was also the letdown. She told the news media that she had "had enough" and went home to Ohio and started a scrapbook.

from HIKING THE APPALACHIAN TRAIL *1975*

The Kinder Scout Trespasses

HOWARD HILL

The great event which shook the rambling world in the early 1930s was the Kinder Scout mass trespass. The official ramblers' movement had tried everything they knew, yet they were further away from their goal of gaining access than was James Bryce 40 years back. He had won an affirmative vote for the right of access from a Parliament less representative of the ordinary people than were the post-war ones. What to do next? — that was the puzzling question in every rambler's mind.

It was a young unemployed motor mechanic from Manchester, Bernard Rothman, who along with a group of his friends, organised in the British Workers' Sports Federation, supplied the answer. On a fine morning, Sunday, 24th April 1932, a party of ramblers, estimated by Rothman between "600 to 800 — probably round about that mark", (the police put the number "at about 200", the *Daily Express* 500) set off from Hayfield, a village nestling in the Peak, to storm openly the fortress of Britain's most sacred grouse moor — the 2,000ft. high plateau of Kinder Scout. After a brief skirmish with stick-wielding gamekeepers, they achieved their objective. History had been made. They had, in full view of the police, walked on ground which up to 100 years before had been free land.

Little did Rothman and his friends realise what they had started. The rambling world was ablaze with excitement and controversy. There were those who were outraged with a Parliament which had in Ramsay Macdonald a Prime Minister who declared himself to be more committed to legal access than any of his predecessors, yet refused to give facilities for the discussion of Ellen Wilkinson's 1931 Bill. They saw in the Mass Trespass a new round of direct-action skirmishes, which would compel the small but influential landowning and grouse-shooting interests to give way. There

were others, such as Harold Wild of the Manchester and
District Ramblers' Federation and Stephen Morton, secretary
of the Sheffield Federation, who declared it had set the
campaign "back 20 years, at a time when we were beginning
to break the power of the owners and getting them to meet us
across the conference table". Whichever view was held, there
is no doubt all organised ramblers admired, as Tom
Stephenson said, the courage of Rothman and his friends.
They were particularly outraged by the prison sentences
which five of the mass trespassers received later at the Derby
Assizes.

The idea of a Mass Trespass arose out of a ramble which
started from a camp for young people at Rowarth, south of
Glossop, organised by the Lancashire District of the
Workers' Sports Federation, a body started on the initiative
of the Young Communist League in Manchester. A number
of these camps had taken place earlier, and this particular
ramble was going from Rowarth over Bleaklow. They were
stopped by gamekeepers, and this caused much annoyance.
During the ensuing discussion there emerged the idea that
"They might have stopped a few of us but they'll not stop the
lot of us". Bernard Rothman is unable to say which of the
incensed ramblers uttered the historic words "Mass Trespass".
He is certain these two words were the collective response,
arising out of the injustice to which they had been subjected.

Rothman and his friends felt so deeply aggrieved at the
denial of access by a handful of grouse shooters, and by the
failure of the official campaign by the National Council of
the Ramblers' Association to make any progress, that
nothing short of an open public demonstration upon Kinder
Scout would do. Whereupon they planned the biggest public
campaign possible.

On 18th April 1932, Rothman visited the offices of the
Manchester Evening News. Next day the plans were head-
lined: "Mass Trespass over Kinder Scout", embellished with
emotive phrases like "Assaults" and "Shock Troops". The
rest of the press immediately took it up. At the end of the
week leaflets were distributed which put the ramblers' case
succinctly: "It is a crime for workers to put their feet where

Lord Big Bug and Lady Little Flea do their annual shooting.''

But the Manchester Ramblers' Federation condemned the trespass, urging their members not to take part. This did not stop a few officials and many of their club members joining the Trespass, for it was not the first time some of them had walked over prohibited ground, or faced abusive game-keepers. Meanwhile the grouse moor owners were busy making their own preparations. A number of regular game-keepers, including the Duke of Devonshire's head keeper, were assisted by a few temporary keepers. In total, according to Rothman, there were around 18, although the *Daily Express* put the number at 60, as did the *Daily Herald*. They were all supplied with the usual gamekeepers' heavy sticks. Most important of all were the police. Sergeant Brailsford was one of the policemen there, and when interviewed after his retirement he said there were about 30 police, as well as a number of plain clothes officials. He said the presence of Superintendent Garrow, Deputy Chief Constable of Derby-shire, indicated how seriously the police regarded the Trespass. *The Sheffield Independent* of Monday 25th April claimed that Hayfield was alive with police, a number of whom were hidden in the local cinema.

Before the Mass Trespass even started, efforts were made by the police to prevent Rothman getting there. They were waiting at the Manchester and Hayfield railway stations with an injunction restraining him from attending the Hayfield meeting, which had been advertised to precede the actual Trespass. Unfortunately for the police, he and one other, knowing nothing of this, went early to Hayfield on their bicycles, and walked along the route which they had planned the Trespass should take; when he arrived at Hayfield to hold the advertised meeting a dense crowd had already assembled.

The police, under the command of the Deputy Chief Constable, ringed the recreation ground, and had already been in action stopping the playing of leap-frog. They had with them the Parish Clerk to read the regulations which had been newly posted, prohibiting the holding of meetings. This was quite unnecessary, for Rothman and his friends quickly realised that if they attempted to hold the meeting on the recreation ground it would be the start and finish of the Trespass. Accordingly word was passed round to leave the recreation ground and to move along William Clough up towards Kinder along a path which had been the object of a twenty-year struggle to force its re-opening at the end of the last century.

This initiative took the police quite by surprise, and before they realised what was happening, the ramblers were disappearing along the track, followed by perspiring bobbies, unaccustomed to moorland tramping. The first stop was near the Kinder Reservoir, but officials belonging to the Stockport Corporation Waterworks dashed along and banned it. As the Mass Trespassers' quarrel was not with them, they carried on until they reached an old disused quarry, a natural amphitheatre. There Rothman addressed the ramblers, insisting the Trespass was to be orderly, disciplined and non-violent. To ensure it was so, as Rothman explained later in his trial at Derby, he instructed them how they were to proceed once they left the footpath. One long blast meant advance in open order, the object being to walk round the keepers. This is in fact what happened to the overwhelming majority of the 800 ramblers, as was verified by Police Inspector Clews, the chief witness at the trials. "The fight," he said, "took place over a front of twenty yards," only a handful of ramblers being involved, while the others made for the top.

At the quarry meeting everybody was determined that the Trespass must go ahead, despite the presence of the police and gamekeepers. Rothman described the scene:

> Away we went singing along William Clough, so strong, it was impossible for the police to stop us — there were too many of us. It was a really dense crowd of young people, all picturesque in rambling gear, khaki jackets, khaki shirts, abbreviated shorts, colourful shorts, colourful jerseys — away we went in a jubilant mood, determined to carry out the assault on Kinder, also determined that no authority whatever would stop us.

The outwitted police were intent on stopping the Trespass, hoping to isolate Rothman and pick up any stragglers. But it was not to be — the ramblers guarded him, and at every stile the main body did not move off until everybody was through. It wasn't planned, explains Rothman, it just happened.

At Sandy Heys Moor — the predetermined point — a long blast on the whistle heralded the beginning of the Trespass. All the girls and youths left the path, crossed the stream and dashed up the steep side of Kinder. Some were met by game-keepers holding out their sticks which they used to belabour the advancing ramblers; other ramblers stood back aghast at the violence used by the keepers. Those attacked used their rucksacks as shields, seizing what sticks they could, breaking them, and then following the others on to the crest of the plateau. There they met contingents from Sheffield and Stockport who had carried out a trouble-free trespass across Kinder. "There we exchanged congratulations, held a short victory meeting and held a little council of war", for Rothman sensed this wasn't by any means the end. For, in addition to the police they had seen at Hayfield, the Sheffield reinforcements told how they had observed numerous police *en route*.

They decided to return as they came in a solid body, "full of determination, full of solidarity in maintaining our same tactics of waiting at every stile to prevent arrest", which they did. About one mile before reaching Hayfield they met the police who were stretched right across the road. The gamekeepers, accompanied by the police, moved amongst the ranks of the ramblers and picked out five who they claimed were responsible for the melée — the sixth had been arrested early after the scuffle, and was later charged with causing grievous bodily harm to Beevers, one of the temporary keepers. They were taken to the Hayfield Lock-up, but because of the efforts of the ramblers to release them — hammering on the door and threatening to break the Police Station down — they were transferred to New Mills and kept there overnight.

There are some surprising things about the trial. Although the judge adopted a pose of fairness, his treatment of the defendants is questionable, and political prejudice loomed large in the case. There was no evidence of violence from the ramblers, as all the newspapers reporting the Trespass agreed. What violence there was came from the keepers, who were provided with thick sticks for that purpose. In fact, the ramblers acted in a most exemplary way. The *Sheffield Telegraph,* reporting on the Trespass, declared that hooliganism was entirely absent, gates were closed, orange peel and paper buried. John Anderson got six months for assault, yet the police witness agreed he was trying to protect himself from being assaulted by the keeper, and the only injury Beevers sustained was a twisted ankle, resulting from falling over. Because the defendants were five minutes late in getting back into the court after the first day's lunch break, due to their difficulty in finding a café, the judge, in Rothman's words, "gave us a fearful lecture", and committed them to Leicester gaol for the night. It was in the semi-darkness of the cell that Bernard Rothman finished preparing his defence — and what a defence it was!

> After a hard week's work and life in smoky towns and cities we go out rambling for relaxation, a breath of fresh air, a little sunshine. We find, when we go out, that the finest rambling country is closed to us, because certain individuals wish to shoot for about ten days a year. For 25 years the Ramblers' Federation has carried on a campaign which has been futile. It was by united action on the part of the ramblers that the well-known path, Doctor's Gate, was opened.

He went on to reveal the failure of the prosecution to prove its case:

> We are not hooligans, we tried to avoid contact with the keepers by advancing in open formation. When the keepers raised their sticks we took them from them . . . The mass trespass of 24th April was a peaceful demonstration of protest.

from FREEDOM TO ROAM *1980*

From Nantlle to Llanberis —
A Walk from Past to Present

DEWI JONES

A Journey of Memories

Running along the westward boundaries of the Snowdonia
National Park there is a line of rarely trodden hills that are
very dear to me. They form a series of five 'humps' that
connect the Nantlle Valley, the Gwyrfai Valley and Llanberis.
I have lived, played and walked in these hills all my life and
they hold a very special place in my memories. In the villages
that nestle on the slopes lived a special brand of people, little
known to the brightly clad hordes that pour into Pen-y-Pass
car park every weekend. These were the *Tyddynwyr* (small-
holders) and the quarrymen, an almost vanished race. The
villages now, apart from the summer homes of a few far-
sighted English families provide abodes for commuters
working in shops, offices and factories at Caernarfon.
Happily these dormitory villages still speak the Welsh
language and some of the old ways still survive, but not to the
same extent as when I spent my happy childhood years here.

I began my walk from my present home village of
Penygroes, an important railway station in the days when the
valley's small quarries vomited slate. On the old high road to
Talysarn a Public Footpath sign points the way to Clogwyn
Melyn, my first top of the day. It is little more than three
fields at a height of 725ft., with a long drystone wall for a
spine. It provides the walker with good all-round views
provided he turns a blind eye to the striding rows of pylons.
Below, the canal-like river Llyfni flows placidly from Llyn
Nantlle, curving round the rise of the ancient fort of Caer
Engan. After passing beneath the bridge by the Old Mill it
bends sharply left and heads for the fine old St. Rhedyw
church before twisting out of sight on its way to the sea. On
the side of Clogwyn Melyn is a natural chair of rock, in the

93

past the scene of many a lovers' vow — and row! I have climbed up here on many a warm summer evening and found peace and solitude after a busy day at work.

Young curlews swooped off as I came by; the staring motionless sheep were unruffled by my presence — I had no dog with me. An old iron stile, then a carefully banked path running beside the wall to the 'kissing gate', or 'giat mochyn' (pigs gate) as they are called up here, squeaked to my touch, and then I passed one of the *tyddynod*. It stood silent and roofless, nettles and briar having taken over. More often than not the tyddynwyr worked daily in the quarries and kept sheep in his spare time to supplement the family income. Of course, there were tyddynwyr who lived entirely from the resources of their little farms. It was a hard life, but these mountain folk were practising self-sufficiency long before the hills echoed to the blastings of the slate quarries.

You go on past a sprawling slate tip to the hamlet of Cilgwyn. The first thing you notice on approaching these quarrying villages is the imposing chapels. Here in Cilgwyn it is obvious what an important part the chapel played in days gone by. It was the focal point of the community, for my forefathers possessed an undying faith.

From the little chapel the route up Mynydd y Cilgwyn goes past the telephone kiosk, rising gently over yellow grass and between grey rocks. There is a cairn, and a pause is rewarded by the best view of all, the Nantlle Ridges rising on the other side of the valley. Years ago sea-shells were found on this hill by students of geology.

Y Fron and Twll Braich

Y Fron is another village created by the great slate quarry boom of the last century. As I walked down the back of Mynydd y Cilgwyn the prominence of 'Cesarea' stood out above all else. This is the name of the village chapel that stands halfway along the long line of houses that is the village of Y Fron. This village, incidentally, is known by three names, Upper Llandwrog, Cesarea, and Y Fron. The first posh English name doesn't fit; Cesarea is Hebrew and the name of the chapel. Y Fron, or Bron y Foel, is its real name, and to me it will forever be Y Fron.

Here we used to come in the milk van helping deliveries, standing behind and clinging to the top while Gwyrfai, the milkman, bumped along the narrow winding roads. Here we came to the Eisteddfod at the big chapel — looking for girls rather than culture! On the flat green in front of 'Cwt Shave' our village played soccer against the team from Y Fron. This was all before we left Primary School. From here too came the party of singers known as 'Gennod y Fron'. They won all the Eisteddfodau prizes and performed in concerts throughout the county. I can almost hear them now; they were excellent, and I have never since heard their equals. I went by 'Cwt Shave' where in the past you could have your hair cut and a shave. It is now just a black empty zinc hut.

The broad quarry track mounts gradually out of the village, passing deserted cottages and a deep hole half full of water. This was Twll Braich, sign of man's exploitation of the wilderness in pursuit of wealth. Now there are signs of nature re-claiming her own. The sides of these old quarry and slate tips are slowly being re-covered in green growth, grass and moss. In time the scars left by the slate industry on the mountains will disappear, and nature — if left to develop — will prevail.

I went through a gate on to the open mountain, with a faint and very old track going my way. The signs of the slate industry are everywhere. Trial levels and rusted wire rope, derelict buildings and forgotten railway courses. Here stands the remains of Chwarel Moeltryfan (Moeltryfan Quarry), where my father spent most of his working life. The quarry of Gors y Bryniau is nearby, beyond Wales's answer to the Grand Canyon, a large yawning hole. Here my grandfather started work at the age of nine. My father was fourteen when he started working here, and his first weekly wage was five shillings. He had to pay two shillings (10p) for his measuring stick and two and six (12½p) for a trimming knife, fashioned by the quarry's carpenter and blacksmith respectively.

I paused. The slow steady dripping of water from some high hidden source was like a grim echoing count-down to the quarry blasting horn that will never again sound.

Passing by the edge of the water-filled working, I made for
the summit of the grassy hill. Here is a cluster of fortress-like
rocks which was our castle in childhood days — the first
mountain climb for a gang of eight-year-olds dressed in
corduroys and clogs, squinting through the swirling mists for
a glimpse of the giant Mynydd Mawr beyond a sea of
heather.

The Gwyrfai Valley

Below, where the slopes of the mountain ease, stands the
sturdy Hermon Chapel between the sentinel gravestones. Not
far is Nant Bach, the home of my forefathers. Here in this
low-roofed farmhouse lived my great-grandfather and his
brothers. They built Nant Bach and another cottage called
Bryn Llwyd. The latter had to be built, according to the law
of those days, between sunset and sunrise, and smoke had to
rise from the chimney at dawn in order to claim squatters'
rights. To overcome this difficulty they had built the chimney
first. Word soon reached the authorities of this illegal
procedure and a force of policemen was sent up to apprehend
the brothers. Warning of their approach reached the men and
there ensued a fierce battle. The brothers routed the 'lawmen'
and subsequently those who were involved had to leave the
district. According to tradition, one of the warriors was a
large woman wielding a long-handled spade.

The younger 'wanted' brothers moved over to the Ogwen
Valley and worked in the quarries there before emigrating to
America and freedom. A blind member of the family walked
every Wednesday, carrying food and clothes, over the hills to
the brothers at Bethesda. He was guided by a trusty dog and
they never failed in their mission. The remaining family
stayed in Nant Bach and gave land to build the Hermon
Chapel. The first thing to be buried in the Hermon cemetery
was my great grandfather's leg, which was blown off while he
was blasting for slate in the nearby quarry.

The grass of Moeltryfan gave way to the heather of Moel
Ysmytho. I gave a wide berth to a tangled array of decaying
automobiles down in the hollow. There they are, displayed
sideways and upside down, the Baby Austins, the Morris

1000's, and an old van eroded so badly that I failed to identify it.

The view from the top of Moel Ysmytho is wide and pleasant, including Yr Eifl, Caernarfon and Anglesey; but for my favourite viewpoint I moved north a little to some rocks we call Creigiau Llwynbedw. From here the whole wide Gwyrfai Valley can be seen, one of the finest prospects in Snowdonia.

There was a marked difference between my own Nantlle Valley, from which I had just come, and the one into which I was looking. Here the bright tents and caravans were abundant, whereas in Nantlle they are virtually unknown. I was looking down into the North Wales holiday jungle — pony trekking, bicycle hiring, ice cream vans and holiday homes. I had walked out of the peaceful past into the busy commercialised present. Down into the present I went, descending steep wooded slopes, where we once searched for a cave in which we were told lay the buried treasure of Sion Prys. We found the cave, but no treasure. Reaching a narrow lane at the bottom, I walked down it to join the busy trunk road that carries the tourists to Beddgelert and Snowdon and Caernarfon.

The road crosses the river Gwyrfai by an old stone bridge and enters the village of Waenfawr. The old Welsh Highland Railway passed this way in days gone by and recently there has been talk of rebuilding it. On the other side of the bridge I turned right at a public footpath sign, onto a path that enters the village near the inevitable large and mighty chapel. At the back of the chapel, and near a newly converted cottage, a path sneaks through the fields and emerges on to the old hill track which goes over to Llanberis. This path has recently been renovated by a job-creation scheme and it is a pleasure to find gates in working order and sturdy stiles.

It is an easy matter to gain the crest of Cefn Du from the old hill track. This was the last top of the day, a lofty heathery place full of old shafts. Looking down into the next valley you see an even greater upheaval taking place, for ahead is the site of the Dinorwic Hydro-Electric Scheme. This has brought new wealth into the area, and with the high influx of tourism in the Llanberis Pass it is the very opposite of my home valley, where the walk began. Down in the main street of Llanberis, where this ten-mile walk ends, the change from past to present is complete.

The lake is a nice place to sit by, but not as nice as it was before the new by-pass and car park came. Now there are rows of cars, ice cream and hot dog vans, all busy to the background music of the holidaymakers' car-cassettes.

Long may the Nantlle Valley retain its character unchanged!

from THE GREAT OUTDOORS *October 1979*

In the Steps of Deirdre

CAMERON McNEISH

Glen Etive my home,
It was there we raised our first house,
Lovely its wood in the smile of the early
   morning,
A cattlefold of the sun is Glen Etive

In the heart of Argyll, a county blessed with a super-abundance of loch, sea, and mountain, a long sinuous arm of water threads its way far into the mainland. To the north lie the pleasant hills and woods of Benderloch and Appin, areas rich in story of the royal Clan Stewart, while to the south, particularly to the south-west, stands a jumble of peak and crag culminating in the shapely top of Ben Starav; the Blackmount Forest.

Loch Etive is that thin arm of sea, its waters wearing their way inland for almost ten miles. It forms a glorious portrait; the mixture of sea loch and mountain, forest, moor and crag, the pulsating summer sea breaking in long curling billows on the rocky shoreline, and the crashing of the lively waterfalls as they escape the hemmed-in confines of the crags for the openness of the sea loch. Mix the tangy brine of the sea, the heady wine of western waters, and the freshness and pureness of a mountain breeze, and your nostrils will experience the superlative blend of Loch Etive.

But there is more to Glen Etive than beauty and freshness. No-one can savour the full flavour of a place without delving into the distant recesses of time and discovering something of the history of the men and women who have lived there. Glen Etive can whisk you back almost beyond the pure fact of history, back to that mysterious semi-mythological period which borders the frontier of fact and fancy; back to the great exploits of the Ancient Celts. Truth and legend have been blended with the passing of almost 2,000 years; whether mythology, folklore or truth we will never ascertain, but with a little help from maps and some knowledge gained from ancient manuscripts, one can trace the footsteps of these famous heroes and heroines along the corridors of time.

The Knights of the Red Branch

Glen Etive belongs to Deirdre of the Sorrows. Once beyond the Falls of Lora (Laoighre, an early Celtic hero) at Connel, one keeps company with the warriors of Fingal; the sound of the wind is the music of Ossian the bard, and the crashing of the waterfalls the battle roars of the Knights of the Red Branch, the order of knighthood from which the Kings of Ulster were chosen.

Across the flats of Benderloch once lay the home of the Fingalian chiefs, Beregonium, the Fort of the Rock. The rock still exists, although the fort has crumbled away through the continuous decaying action of the sea breezes. A solitary Standing Stone exists as a silent witness to times long past. On the shores of Camus Nathais, between Ardmucknish Bay and the Lynn of Lorne, the Stronghold of the Three Sons of Uisneach once stood; Dun Macuisneach, its thick walls facing south east over the waters of the Moyle (the ancient name given to the strait between Argyll and Northern Ireland) to Ulster, the birthplace of its occupants.

In the days of the first century, it was customary for the sons of the knights and kings of Ulster to be sent across the waters of the Moyle to Alba, as that part of Scotland was then known. There, in the mountains and glens, they were trained in the arts of hunting and combat. One of the most famous schools was that of Sgiathach, the warrior Queen of Skye. It was here, among the black hills and the mists, that some of Ulster's foremost warriors were trained. Cuchullin, 'the hound of the armourer', who was to gain notoriety by defending Ulster single-handed from the invading forces of the High King of Connacht; Fergus, son of Roigh, a poet and revolutionary general; and the Sons of Uisneach, of whom we shall hear more later.

Cathbad's Prophecy

The story of Deirdre (Daredra) is a bitter-sweet tale of love and treachery, a classic theme with underlying parallels in the Sanskrit Ramayana and Homer's Iliad. The story, along with other Tales of the Red Branch, can be read in the 15th Century Glen Massen Manuscript, which is kept in the Advocates' Library in Edinburgh. An older version appears in the Twelfth Century Book of Leinster. This can be seen in Trinity College, Dublin.

Deirdre was born near Emhain Macha, (pronounced Evan Maha), the fortress and shrine from which 39 Kings of Ulster ruled between 300BC and 330AD. Today, the old city of Armagh stands approximately in the same position. Her father, Phelim the Bard, was the king's harper, and he held a feast to celebrate Samhain, or Halloween. The High King, Concubar Macnessa, famed throughout all Erin and Alba as a great warrior and chief of the Red Branch, was in attendance as guest of honour.

In the course of the celebrating and festivities, the king became aware that his silver-haired prophet, Cathbad the Druid, was lost in thought, unseeing eyes gazing deep into the glowing embers of the open fire. The king grew apprehensive; what could he see? Cathbad the Druid, who had eaten the hazelnuts of knowledge, the interpreter of dreams and omens; one who could glimpse the unknown. And wasn't this the night of Samhain, when the supernatural powers of 'the other side' joined forces to appear to those mortals who did not perform the rituals to satisfy them?

Suddenly, as though waking from a dream, the prophet rose, and turning to the host Phelim, told him that his wife would bear him a daughter whose beauty would be unsurpassed, but for whose sake three great heroes of Ulster would perish.

"True, it is a daughter, and let her name be Deirdre. But out of her beauty will arise a sharp sword to split apart the Tree of Ulster."

"Better then that she should not live," cried Phelim.

"No," replied the High King, "Let her live, but keep her well apart from all men, until she is of age to become my queen."

As prophesied, a daughter was born to Elva, Phelim's wife, a daughter whose beauty, even at birth, was beyond doubt.

The baby was taken immediately from her mother, and a foster mother was found. The king, Concubar Macnessa, chose the nurse himself; a young intelligent woman called Lavercam, whose loyalty to the king was beyond question.

Under the guidance of Lavercam, and the instruction of Cathbad the Druid, Deirdre grew to womanhood on a lonely wooded island, far away from the coveting eyes of any other man. King Concubar visited the island from time to time, taking great delight and satisfaction from the increasing beauty and intelligence of the young Deirdre.

Naoise's Song

One day, the young girl found a calf lying dead in the snow. A raven hovered above it, inspecting the carcass for food.

"If there was a man whose hair was so black as that raven, whose skin was as white as that snow, and whose cheeks were as red as that blood, I would love him dearly forever."

"Enough of such talk," replied Lavercam, "You are betrothed to the High King of Ulster, and no other man will cast eyes on you until your wedding day."

This news greatly saddened Deirdre. Night after night she dreamt of her darkhaired hero, and during the days she grew listless and downhearted. Tears often filled her eyes when she thought of her future with the king that she did not love. One day, Lavercam could stand Deirdre's grief no longer. She greatly feared that the young woman would die of a broken heart, and her love for Deirdre was growing far greater than her fear of the king's wrath.

"Deirdre my dear, I know of such a man as you dream of. His name is Naoise (Neesha) and he is the eldest of the Three Sons of Uisneach (Wishna). He stands above all the sons of Erin, and he is the finest warrior of all the Knights of the Red Branch."

Not long after, Deirdre heard singing from the woods, a singing the like of which she had never heard before. It was the song of the Three Sons of Uisneach. The voice of Ainle the youngest was like the upper strings of the harp; the voice of Ardan was like the middle strings, and the voice of Naoise was like the deep strings, the bass notes which can draw the hearts of heroes.

As the three men drew closer, Deirdre immediately recognised Naoise as the lover of her dreams. Her beauty overwhelmed the brothers, and from that moment, Naoise gave up his soul for the love of the young woman of the woods.

Exile in Alba

Not long after, King Concubar Macnessa came to hear of the meeting between Deirdre and the Three Sons of Uisneach, and his anger grew so great that the very walls of Eamhain Macha shook with his wrath. For a long time, Deirdre and the three brothers ranged far and wide across Erin in an effort to escape the King of Ulster who was determined to kill them. They could not sleep at night for fear of being betrayed, and the threat of ambush lay at every corner. Eventually, they agreed to leave Erin, and flee to Alba, across the sea, where the three brothers had been brought up.

They sailed in galleys, taking with them 50 men and three times 50 women, all faithful servants of the house of Uisneach, and at last they reached the long sea loch of Etive. Here, on the shores of the Bay of Selma, they built a fortress, Dun MacUisneach, the fortress of the Sons of Uisneach.

Here they spent their winters, warming themselves within the fire-glazed walls of their stronghold. Often they would gaze from the windows across the water to the far shore of Erin, but their happiness was complete, consanguineous in their love of each other, and in the land around Etive.

During the summer months, the three brothers carried Deirdre beyond Ben Lora, to the head of Loch Etive, a mountainous land where the deer played and the eagle flew high above Ben Starav and the slabs of Trilleachan. Here they built a bower for her, a sun house beside a white cascading waterfall, where the beauty of the surroundings was only matched by the beauty of the young woman herself.

Return to Ulster

Soon, though, a serpent crawled into their earthbound paradise. King Concubar Macnessa had been warned of a prophesy by Cathbad the Druid, that a great war would break out in Ulster. Although the Knights of the Red Branch were strong in battle, all in Erin believed the King's forces to be incomplete without the Children of Uisneach. A royal pardon was issued on the condition that the three brothers would return to Ulster, and three messengers were sent to ask them home — Cuchullin, Connel and Fergus, three of the Red Branch's mightiest warriors.

The three Knights were well received by Naoise and his brothers, for their hearts, like the hearts of most gaels, were firmly rooted in their homeland, despite the joy and peace they had known on Etive side. They agreed to return to Ulster and fight with the Red Branch. At this decision, Deirdre was overwhelmed with dismay, and that night dreamt a dream. She saw three ravens arrive with a drop of honey in their beaks, but as they flew away, they carried three drops of blood in their beaks. She begged and beseeched the brothers not to leave Alba, but their loyalty as trained warriors was just too strong.

Galleys were prepared, and just as they were about to sail away, Deirdre decided she could not be left behind. As the ships sailed away from Loch Etive, Deirdre sang a song, the saddest song in all Gaeldom, the Lay or Lament of Deirdre:

> Beloved is that eastern land, Alba
>   with its lakes,
> Oh that I might not depart from it,
> Unless I were to go with Naoise,
> Oh that I might not leave the east,
> Unless it were to come along with me,
>   Beloved.

The brothers were given the house of the Red Branch to live in, a great honour but when Lavercam saw again her old charge she was greatly afraid. Deirdre's beauty had increased during her years in exile, but Lavercam told the king otherwise. Before long, however, word reached the king's ears of the great beauty of this woman to whom he was once betrothed, and he was inflamed with a renewed passion for the Beauty of the World. The House of the Red Branch was surrounded by the king's men, and set on fire. Ardan and Ainle climbed out through a window, and a terrific battle ensured. Naoise joined the throng, holding Deirdre aloft in one arm, and cleaving with his great sword with the other. The battle raged, but the sheer odds were too much for even the mighty Sons of Uisneach. They were captured, bound together, and taken before Macnessa.

The king overcome with a hatred born of desire, ordered the brothers to be slain. Their heads were struck off as one by a mighty blow, standing together in death as they had stood in life. Deirdre, frantic with sorrow, begged Cuchullin to find the head of Naoise, and as the brothers were buried standing upright, as was the custom with Ulstermen, she kissed the severed head and placed it on the shoulders of her dead lover. Frantic with grief, she leaped into the grave and clasped the body of Naoise in her arms, and so died.

Such is the story of Deirdre, a tale long remembered by Celts. The Song of Deirdre will be sung forever.

The Land of Deirdre

Today, the footsteps of Deirdre and the Sons of Uisneach can still be traced around Glen Etive. The promontory near where Dun Macuisneach stood is called Fionn Aird, after the Fingalians of Celtic mythology. The great rock, where many believe the stronghold was situated, can be seen on the shores of the Bay of Selma, or as it is known nowadays, Ardmucknish Bay. This is near the village of Ledaig, a few miles north of Connel Bridge and the Falls of Lora. A solitary standing stone marks the spot where mysterious Druidic rites were performed. Near Taynuilt, on the southern shore of Loch Etive, is a wood called Coile Naoise, and Deirdre's Sunny Bower, Grianan Deirdre, although not placed on modern maps, was probably on the slopes of An Grianan (1,795ft.) west of Kinlochetive in upper Glen Etive.

With a little imagination one can trace the spot, a green meadow, at the foot of a long white waterfall. Glen Etive is still the land of Deirdre, the deer wander across the hillside like a slow moving cloud, and her eagles still soar high above Trilleachan.

Above all, her song survives, the heart-rending sorrow that was later adopted by other emigrants leaving the shores of Scotland for the last time; the powerful expression of a once common experience. The emigrants of the Highland Clearances knew the story of Deirdre, and more than likely sang the song themselves as they were transported abroad to a new life and new ways.

from THE GREAT OUTDOORS *October 1979*

A Very Special Place

ROGER A. REDFERN

Of all the remote and beautiful spots in the Hebrides known to me one is, above all others, my favourite — a sort of mecca of which I could never grow tired. It lies in the south-west of Rhum, far from any well trodden track and facing out across the Atlantic where the sky is ever changing.

The place is called Papadil. It is a secret sort of place, hemmed in by the mountains against the sea and possessing a ghost better known by far than the place itself. Whether one goes to Papadil by way of the west or east coasts the way is steep and rugged. I much prefer a circuitous route — out by the west coast and back by the east.

Anyone getting permission from the Nature Conservancy Council to explore the southern half of Rhum will probably start from Kinloch, now the only inhabited place on the island, at the head of Loch Scresort. The rough track follows the Kinloch Glen and near the centre of the island swings south-westwards to the wild and rugged western shore at Harris. Glen Harris once contained a large population but in 1827-28 all Rhum's inhabitants were assisted to emigrate to Canada because living conditions had fallen to such a low standard. The old 'lazy beds' and foundations of hovels can still be seen on the floor of the glen.

Out at the edge of the sea, upon a broad and grassy terrace maintained like a bowling green by the red deer, Highland cattle and westerly gales, stands the former shooting lodge (inhabited by a shepherd up to 1957) and the Bullough family's mausoleum*.

From Harris the steep, tussocky slopes are tackled south-wards, keeping high above the sea and not far below the rocky upper part of Ruinsival (1,700ft.). By careful observation in clear weather a few cairns of stones can be followed around the flanks of the mountain. All the vistas to

* The Bulloughs bought Rhum in 1887 and it remained in their possession until presented by Monica Lily, Lady Bullough to the Nature Conservancy in 1957.

the right are filled by the Atlantic. In perfect conditions it is a sheet of azure, when showers race in the sea gleams like a golden cauldron, punctuated by dark islands of cloud shadows.

Contouring at about 800ft. across the southern slope of Ruinsival the scenery quickly becomes grander and soon a steep gully must be crossed. It contains a torrent which falls to the rocky shore at Inbhir Ghil, guarded by pinnacles and stacks and great, tumbled boulders. By taking a diagonally descending line beyond the gully a shoulder is crossed, and Papadil lies in full view below. In spring this sunny mountainside is dotted with primroses and early violets; looking up across the south-western slope of Sgurr nan Gillean one is as likely as not to see a group of red deer crossing the screes.

Loch Papadil is a roughly circular body of fresh water which is separated from the sea by a bank of grass-covered beach and boulders. Where the water drains out of the loch are the sheep-pens long used by shepherds prior to the removal of all sheep from Rhum in 1957. Rising from the steep boulder beach is Papadil Pinnacle. It is about 50ft. high and has twin tops. The first recorded ascent was by yachtsmen in 1937 but it has often been climbed since then. From its sharp summit there is a pretty view of Loch Papadil and the huge sweep of Sgurr nan Gillean's south-western flank.

Until the Nature Conservancy Council began their comprehensive tree planting programme on the island the only mixed woodland was at Kinloch and here beside Loch Papadil. This little wood was planted about the turn of the century and helps to make this such a charming corner of Rhum. It is here, also, that mystery lurks.

The Bulloughs built several lodges near the coast of their island, one at Kilmory, another at Harris and a third here at Papadil. It is by far the most inaccessible house on Rhum and made all the more so by the boulder beach which prevents a landing by boat in all but the calmest weather. Papadil lodge was one of the Bulloughs' favourite corners of their island. The single-storey building was well furnished and parties often stayed overnight in the stalking season to save the long walk or ride on ponies back to Kinloch.

The lodge was not the first habitation at Papadil for there still remain the ruins of a couple of old cottages. They are typical Hebridean structures, with rounded gables to turn the severest gales and formerly had roofs thatched with rushes or heather. It is likely that these remote dwellings were inhabited up to the 1827-28 clearances.

Papadil possesses a strange charm and there is little wonder that it has a powerful spirit. Many are the stories of people staying overnight in the lodge and feeling a supernatural pressure upon their chests. Some have fled from this magic hollow by the sea in the middle of the night, others who know the island intimately vouch they would never spend a night there. Nevertheless Papadil lodge has suffered greatly from thoughtlessness in recent years.

In glorious weather in the spring of 1971 I remember descending from Inbhir Ghil, across banks of primroses and violets, to Papadil. The lodge was still almost intact and contained brass bedsteads, wicker day-beds and a brass candelabra. Subsequent visits have revealed increasing damage to the building and its contents. During the spring of 1974 the Nature Conservancy Council removed the slate roof and had the roof timbers burned in an effort to stop deer poachers using the lodge as a base. The poachers come by water in favourable conditions and carry off red deer to the mainland.

George MacNaughton, acting Head Warden on Rhum and now the island's only native resident, believes that the restoration of the shepherd's cottage in neighbouring Glen Dibidil by the Mountain Bothies Association has helped to increase damage at Papadil. Parties getting permission to stay at Dibidil overnight have relatively easy access around the coast to Papadil.

When Lady Bullough handed over the island in 1957 one of her stipulations was that Papadil lodge be burned to the ground, but for some reason, this stipulation was never complied with. Only now, 17 years later, is the lodge being destroyed.

The ruin stands forlorn, almost totally engulfed by

rhododendrons and great trees, many of them blown down and rotting in the swamp caused by a change in the course of the stream coming down off Sgurr nan Gillean. On still days in summer the loch's margins are thick with dancing midges and then Papadil is not a pleasant place to be.

A path climbs eastwards to 500ft. by Loch Dubh an Sgoir and so takes one round in 2½ miles to the mouth of Glen Dibidil. At the head of this wild valley rears Askival (2,664ft.) Rhum's highest peak and "the most beautiful mountain in Scotland," to quote Sir Hugh Munro. A winding path high above the sea continues around the island's eastern coast for 5½ miles back to Kinloch. The complete circuit here described measures almost 19 miles of rough track, path and mountainside.

from THE GREAT OUTDOORS *August 1978*

The Ridgeway Path — A Walk Through History

HUGH WESTACOTT

During the dark days of the war I was given for my tenth birthday a copy of Rudyard Kipling's *Puck of Pook's Hill,* a book which has had a considerable influence on me. I have read it so many times that I can repeat whole passages by heart and I have only to turn its pages to feel a tingling sensation of pleasure. Twenty years ago it was fashionable for critics to dismiss Kipling's books as jingoistic and even containing fascist undertones. It is true that some of his later works contain references to the 'White Man's Burden' and similar sentiments that are not now generally acceptable.

Kipling had a profound and original feeling for the spirit of British history and in *Puck of Pook's Hill* he tells the story of two children who, by acting part of Shakespeare's *Midsummer Night's Dream* in a fairy ring on Midsummer

Eve, invoke the spirit of the hills and meet Puck, the archetypal British fairy or, as he not unnaturally prefers to be called, one of the 'Old Things' or 'People of the Hills'. Puck brings before Una and Dan characters which in some way epitomise the various strands which run through British history. He tells them of the myths and legends before the age of recorded history and introduces them to a British Roman centurion who fought the Picts and the Saxons on the Great Wall when the Empire was crumbling and to Sir Richard Dalyngridge, a Norman knight who came to conquer England with William and ended up by allowing England to conquer him.

Kipling was fascinated by the concept of law as the basis of civilisation and a well-ordered society and believed that the genius of the British is our ability to uphold and respect the law and yet to adapt it as circumstances required. He believed that our stable society is based on our ability to absorb new ideas and to digest the few invaders who have landed on our shores, and ultimately to make them all British.

In these days when it is so fashionable to denigrate ourselves, let us remember what an extraordinary people we are. We live in a tiny offshore island which for most of our history was to all intents the furthest limit of the civilised world. Yet we have given the world the richest literature and the most widely spoken language that has ever been known; at one time within living memory we ruled one third of the world and on the whole governed benignly; we invented parliamentary democracy, which has been widely copied; and the industrial revolution which is the foundation of modern prosperity started in Britain.

It is evident, too, that what has become known as the 'matter of Britain' occupied a leading place in European myth and legend long before the Romans settled here. Although I cannot subscribe to the theories of the British Israelites that we are one of the ten lost tribes and do not believe that the great monuments of prehistoric Britain such as Stonehenge, Avebury and Silbury Hill have anything to do with alien beings from another world, I do believe that the seeds of the peculiar British genius may lie in our prehistoric past. The art of writing was unknown in Britain until the Romans came and as a result we have no real knowledge of the beliefs of these early people. Archaeologists can tell us *how* they built their impressive monuments but can offer very little explanation of *why* they were built.

An Ancient Way

There can be little doubt that the Great Ridgeway, with its splendid hill-forts and close proximity to Avebury and Silbury Hill, and its network of old tracks which link it to other important centres such as Stonehenge, was of great importance to early man, so instead of treating the Ridgeway Path as just another lovely long distance route, let us gain some understanding of its place in our history. It is one of the most popular of the long distance routes and most people know that it runs for 89 miles from near Avebury in Wiltshire to Ivinghoe Beacon in Buckinghamshire. The first 40 miles to the Thames follows for almost the whole of its length the ancient Ridgeway, but the section east of the river is a modern creation, although at times it follows the route of the Icknield Way, another ancient highway.

There is strong archeological evidence that the original Ridgeway ran along the chalk escarpment from Axmouth in Devon to the Wash. We now have to ask ourselves *why* this particular route came into existence. The reasons seem fairly obvious when we consider what the landscape was like in pre-historic times. The modern walker on the Ridgeway will journey through a landscape made almost entirely by man. He will see well tended farms and neat fields, small areas of woodland and coppice, and a complicated network of drainage channels which allow the surface water to run off and eventually reach the sea.

But 10,000 years ago, when our story begins, things were very different. The country was covered with virgin forest; the rivers were not channelled and frequently flooded, leaving large areas of swamp; and the tiny human population eked out a precarious existence by hunting. Because the soil on chalk is relatively poor (it is only in the last 30 years that modern fertilisers have made it worth while to plough the downs), the forest was thinner on the chalk uplands, which made it easier for early man to follow the chalk ridges in pursuit of game. No doubt when he reached an area where game was plentiful a settlement would be established and the men of the tribe would descend into the forest to hunt. Indeed, remains of a primitive settlement have been found in the chalk hills of Surrey. When the food supply was exhausted it was necessary for the tribe to move on and it was natural to follow the chalk where the going was somewhat easier.

It is fairly certain that at this time Britain was part of Europe and it may well be that these early hunters entered Britain by means of the land bridge. About the year 6000BC the sea broke through the narrow isthmus which connected England to the continent and we became an island, thus cutting off our early ancestors from outside influences.

Windmill Hill

In about 3000BC the first farmers arrived in Britain. It is interesting to speculate on why they came. Anyone living in the neighbourhood of Calais can, on a fine day, see England and it is also possible that fishermen were blown out to sea, made a landfall, liked what they found and decided to settle. Yet a third theory suggests that these early farmers had no knowledge of crop rotation and when the soil became exhausted they were forced to move on. In the course of time they reached the sea and crossed it in search of new and fertile land. We know something of these early farmers because they left behind them significant artefacts, and the fact that they were able to cross the sea and tilled the land indicates that, culturally, they were far superior to the nomadic hunters.

A little to the west of the Ridgeway, and just north of Avebury, lies the causewayed camp of Windmill Hill which has given its name to the culture of those early farmers. It consists of three concentric rings of earthworks and has been dated reliably to about 2750BC. Contrary to popular opinion, it is not a fort but an enclosure for sheltering cattle; the community lived outside in thatched huts. The Windmill Hill people buried their important dead in massive long barrows of which the two most famous examples are West Kennett, just south of the Ridgeway, and Wayland's Smithy, which is on the Ridgeway itself. These barrows are massive structures which must have made enormous demands on the labour force available (hence the supposition that they had some regal or religious significance), and consist of chambered tombs constructed from stones covered with earth.

One of the most important requirements of the Windmill Hill people was flint for making tools. At Grimes Graves near Brandon in Norfolk there are extensive prehistoric flint mines in which have been found antler picks and the shrine to a goddess, and the Ridgeway was almost certainly used as a trading route to bring these goods to the Windmill Hill people.

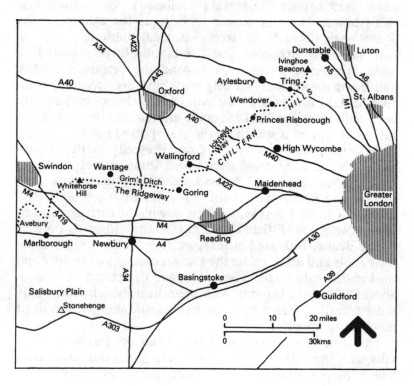

The Beaker Folk

Metal tools were introduced into Britain about the year 2400 BC by the Beaker people who derive their name from their characteristic pottery. They were a remarkable people, achieving a very high level of social organisation. It was they who built Avebury, the largest stone circle in Britain, which consists of a huge bank and ditch enclosing a stone circle 1,400ft. in diameter and covering 28 acres. Nearby is Silbury Hill, another remarkable enterprise of the Beaker people. It is an artificial mound 130ft. high, covering 5½ acres and surrounded by a ditch 125ft. wide and 30ft. deep. Although Silbury Hill has been excavated recently, nobody has yet put forward a convincing explanation of what it is. Modern man can only marvel at such enterprises and although we do not know for certain what purpose they served, they must surely have had some important religious or ceremonial significance. There is reason to believe, for example, that Stonehenge was used for astronomical calculations.

It has been estimated that the labour force required to build these monuments was beyond the resources of the native population and that help must have been received from continental Europe. The first part of Stonehenge had already been built when the Beaker people arrived and they set about extending it, and it was they who transported the bluestones, each weighing some 40 tons, from Prescelly in Pembrokeshire. This in itself must have posed some interesting logistical problems and it is assumed that the stones were transported as far as possible on rafts by water and then towed on sledges across the firm downland turf; the sarsen stones came from Fifield Down just off the Ridgeway Path.

The Beaker folk used bronze, a difficult alloy to make, for their tools and after a time the known deposits of copper and tin became exhausted. The next wave of settlers arrived in about 700BC and brought with them iron, which is not only more plentiful, but is much easier to work and gives tools of much better quality.

The iron age settlers, or Celts, lived on farms in small villages. They kept cattle, sheep and pigs and grew corn which they stored in underground granaries. Sheep need more open pasture than arable farming and in the centuries after the arrival of the Celts there was much clearance of the forest and scrub by burning, felling and the rooting of pigs. The clearance of so many obstacles facilitated communications and it is known that artefacts were traded all over England.

It was around 500BC that most of the Celtic hill forts were built, including Barbury Castle, Liddington Castle, Uffingston Castle and Letcombe Castle, all of which lie on or near the Ridgeway. They are very impressive and appear to be constructed to defend the upper Thames valley. As they lie above the spring-line it is assumed that they either relied upon dew ponds for water or, at the time of their construction, the water table was higher.

After the Romans

As everyone knows, the Romans invaded in AD43 and within five years had occupied and colonised much of southern England. It is doubtful whether they used the Ridgeway to any great extent as they preferred to build their own superb road system which connected their settlements and facilitated trade and the swift movement of troops. The Ridgeway forts fell into disuse during the Roman period but were reoccupied when the Romans withdrew and the Saxons started to penetrate southern England. We know from the *Anglo-Saxon Chronicle* that the Britons were defeated by the Saxons near Barbury Castle in AD556.

In the centuries following the Dark Ages, the Ridgeway remained a well used highway, and from mediaeval times onward was used by drovers bringing sheep and cattle from Wales to London. This trade increased as the population of London grew, and was given a new impetus with the coming of the turnpikes in the eighteenth century, as the old highway provided an easy way of avoiding the tolls levied for the use of turnpikes. The coming of the railways destroyed the droving trade almost overnight and the Ridgeway reverted to a little used track until it was rediscovered by modern walkers and became a recreational route.

And so, dear reader, when you walk the Ridgeway, start at

Ivinghoe Beacon and make your journey a pilgrimage through ten thousand years of history, with the ancient stone circle of Avebury as your goal. Take time to savour the atmosphere of this route so redolent of the past and muse upon the ancient things along the way. And on reaching Hackpen Hill, stop before descending to the Ridgeway café and that well-deserved cup of tea, take off your pack, lie in the long grass, hug the dear earth to you and if the mood is right and the 'Old Things' are kind you may just hear above the murmur of insects and the wind, the whistling flight of an arrow from the bow of a hunter; the fluting of a bronze trumpet from the funeral procession at Wayland's Smithy; the measured tramp of a Roman Legion marching from Aquae Sulis to Londinium; the despairing sounds of battle from Beran Byrg; or the incessant lowing of cattle as the drovers pass. And remember that these old, unhappy, far-off things are more than whispers from the past; that they have helped shape each one of us into what we are; and rejoice and be glad that we have such a glorious heritage.

from THE GREAT OUTDOORS *September 1979*

Game Regions of the Upper Sacramento

JOAQUIN MILLER

Were I asked to put a finger on the one most favoured spot to be found on the map of the world for rod and gun and restful camp, I would indicate the tributary waters of the Sacramento, with Mt. Shasta for a tent. And not because the first and best years of my life lay there, nor because I owe all I hope to be to this mighty, throbbing heart of roaring, white waters; but solely because there is gathered in and about this pre-eminent place more of the great things of earth than enter into the delights of a strong, healthful man in love with nature than can be found in any other one part of the world.

Back of all this lies the comfortable fact that this focus and centre of the sportsman's Eden is now quite as accessible as a city park. The Englishman in his journey around the world may arrive in San Francisco this evening, go to bed and be awakened next morning by the roaring waters from the melting snows of Mt. Shasta, with the mountain lion and the grizzly bear on the overhanging crags for a background to the view as he looks from the window of his palace car. Thirty-five years ago it cost half a year, a small fortune, much patience, peril, often life itself to reach this paradise of the 'mighty hunter'. But now at last, and within this year, time, cost, peril — all have been swept away together, while the mountains in all their black-white majesty remain, and ever must remain, thank God, as unchanged as the ocean. And the huge wild beasts are there in their fastnesses as of old. The trout in the sparkling waters are still eddying about under the overhanging rocks and beneath the gnarled and mossy roots that reach from giant trees, 'bald with antiquity'.

Go with me to this heart of the world's heart for an hour, for who should know the haunts and the habits of all things here so entirely? In the first place few equipments are needed. You want your favourite gun, of course, good substantial boots, and that's about all. The best of hotel comforts, all the detail of fishing appurtenances, tents if you tire of the hotels and wish to penetrate farther than the farthest, all these things are on the ground and to be had at fair cost. But there is one sort of outfit you must surely have before starting, and that is a kind of mental equipment. You must catch the colours. Do this and you will come away content. Your catch of trout, your deathshot at the black, brown, or grizzly bear — all this will to the end of life be mere detail in comparison of results. This intensity and emphasis of colour is due to the sapphire and purple of the skies and the mighty mountain of snow. The vast and high-held world of whiteness above you, only a little below the sapphire of heaven, as it seems when you look up through the black immensity of trees overhead; this Mt. Shasta heaven and earth coming so close together — these two things make a new or at least a magnified and an intensified world of colour. And this element enters into all things there, even down to the fiery red blossom that bursts through the snow at your feet. I implore you go prepared to see and comprehend, so far as possible, the indescribable calm of this colossal Shasta world. The soul grows there.

Make your first, if not your final, stopping place at Lower Soda Springs. This spring is of itself, to say nothing of its fabulously invigorating waters, a curious study. Besides that, it is the first spot ever occupied by the white man in all its region. And such men as Hastings, Lane, Frémont, made few mistakes in selecting camps. Here too some battles were fought in the old days. When 'Mountain Joe' and myself owned the place the house was sacked and burned. The Indians retreated across the Sacramento river with their plunder and climbed to near the summit of the almost inaccessible crags that pierce the clouds over against Mt. Shasta. And here on these gray and glorious heights we fought and vanquished them on the 15th day of June, 1855. The deep cleft in the left side of my face is the work of an Indian arrow received in that deadly little engagement.

Do not pitch camp closer to Mt. Shasta than Soda Springs. It is a mistake to ram your head right up against a mountain, as if you were afraid you could not see it at a respectful distance. There is an impertinence in that sort of doing, and it has its punishments, such as snow-blindness, rheumatism, and so on. Mountains are like pictures; made neither to smell nor to eat. And yet in the Vatican at Rome and in the Sierras of California you see herds of people who push themselves as far to the front as the bar of iron or the bank of snow will allow. The best in nature, like the best in art, is sacred. Look upon it respectfully, reverently, or not at all. Even the wild beasts know that much.

The haunt of the bear changes somewhat with the season, although he is perhaps less of a nomad than any other inhabitant of these altitudes. The grizzly has been known to remain within an area of a few miles of dense wood and trackless rocks for a generation. And that is the meaning of the little mounds of stones which you find on the old Indian trails that track from one tributary to another on the head waters of the Sacramento River. It was the custom for each Indian as he passed the place where one of his people had been killed or maimed by one of these monsters, to pitch a stone or pebble onto the spot. And thus from year to year the mound of stones was formed. No doubt some sentiment of pity or respect lay at the bottom of the custom; but back of that lay the solid and practical fact of a warning to all unwary passers-by, that the grizzly bear had been there and probably at that moment was not many miles away.

I beg here to digress enough to state that the Indians, until taught better by the white man, would not harm a grizzly bear, even in self-defence. For they held that the grizzly bear was the father of the Indian. The mother of the Indian they asserted to have been the daughter of the Creator, who dwelt in Mt. Shasta. They held that the mountain was, of old, hollow like a tent; that they could see the smoke coming out from the top of the great wigwam. And their story is to the effect that once when the wind was blowing fearfully from the ocean — which may be seen from the summit of the mountain on any day of exceptional clearness — the Great Spirit sent his daughter up to beseech the wind to be still; that he warned her not to put her head out for fear the wind would get into her hair, which was long as the rainbow, and blow her away. Being a woman, however, she put her head out, and so was blown out and down to the very bottom of the snow where the chief of the grizzly bears was camped with his family.

The Indians further insist that the grizzly bear at that time talked, walked erect, and even went hunting with bow and arrows and spear, and the story goes on to say that, in violation of all the laws of hospitality, the daughter of the Great Spirit was made captive and compelled to be the wife of the chief's son, and so became the mother of all good Indians. Finally, when the Great Spirit found out what had happened to his daughter, he came out and down the mountain in a great fury; and calling all the bears together he broke their hands and feet with a club and made them get down on their all-fours like other beasts. He made them shut their mouths so that they could talk no more forever, and then, going back and down into the hollow of Mt. Shasta, he put out the fire in his wigwam and was seen no more. They point to the three great black spots on the south side of the mountain and say these are his footprints and explain that he descended the whole vast cone in three long strides, showing how very angry he was. And as evidence of the truthfulness of what they say about their origin, they point to the fact that the grizzly bear is even yet permitted to use his fists and stand up and fight like a man when hard pressed.

All the Indians believe to this day that the grizzly bear can talk, if you will only sit still when he comes up and hear what he has to say. But this may not be advisable. However, I know one wrinkled and leathery-looking old woman, a century old perhaps, who used almost daily to go out to a heap of rocks on the edge of a thicket and talk, as she said, with a grizzly bear. She was greatly respected.

Late Autumn or the very early Spring is the best time for hunting this king of the Sierra: the only safe time, indeed. For when the she-bear has young it is simply folly to be found in her vicinity. At other times this brute is not more to be dreaded than any other wild beast equally strong and reckless of danger.

All that wide and savage watershed of the Sacramento tributaries to the south and west of Mt. Shasta affords good bear hunting at almost any season of the year — if you care to take the risks. Quite often, when and where you think you are alone, just when you begin to be certain that there is not a single grizzly bear in the mountains, when you begin to breathe the musky perfumes of Mother Nature as she shakes out the twilight stars in her hair, and you start homeward, there stands your long-lost bear in your path! And your hair stands up! And your bear stands up! And you wish you had not lost him! And you wish you had not found him! And you start home! And you go the other way, glad, glad to the heart if he does not come tearing on after you.

More than 30 years ago in company with a cultured young man, Volney Abby by name, I went hunting for bear up Castle Creek, about a mile from the banks of the Sacramento. Pretty little dimples of prairie lay here and there, breaking the sombre monotony of pine and cedar, and, as we leisurely walked on, the waters sang among the mossy boulders in the bed of the creek with a singularly restful melody. My companion took out his Homer and as we sat on a mossy log he read aloud of the wanderings of Ulysses till twilight made him close the page. Our path, an old Indian trail, lay close by the singing waters that foamed down their steep way of rocks. To our right and up and away from the stream stretched a little crescent of wild clover. As my companion closed the book I caught sight of a pine tree dripping with rosin. The Indians peel off and eat the inner portion of pine bark at certain seasons of the year, and all through the Sierra you can to this day see evidences of this meagre means of subsistence. An Indian had been resting and feasting in this same sweet little clearing by the singing waters only a year or two before. I struck a match, touched it to the scarred and dripping white face of the pine — and such a light!

A grizzly! A grizzly! God help us! He came bounding down upon us like an avalanche, fat, huge, bow-legged, low to the ground, but terrible! He halted, just a second, to look at the fire perhaps, when my companion, bolder than I and more prompt to act, blazed away. The bear rolled over, being badly hit. But he kept rolling and tumbling straight in our direction, and not a tree or stump or stone at hand; only the old mossy log on which we had been sitting. I wanted to run. "We must fight!" yelled my friend. I jerked up my gun and he got at his knife, as the monster with his big red mouth wide open tumbled over the log full upon us, breaking my gun in two at the breech and taking the most of my companion's red shirt in his teeth as he passed. But he passed, thank heaven, passed right on. He did not pause one second. He did not even seem to see us. I think the fire may have blinded him and so saved our lives.

The next animal in rank, both in size and importance to the sportsman of this region, is the mountain elk. And he also is much larger than his brother in the valleys — like the grizzly bear, which often attains to the weight of 2,000lb. He is also full of battle when pushed to the wall, his nature thus taking to itself something of the unconquerable splendour of his lofty environments. The haunt of this noble and high-headed creature is (or was, until driven farther up the savage spurs of Mt. Shasta by the invasion of our armies and the shock of battle), not far from the Modoc lava beds, or rather between these rocky fastnesses and the snow-belt on the eastern and south-eastern base of the great snow peak. This large elk, certainly the largest in the world, seems to have been born of the thermal springs that burst from the savage and sublime mountain along the lower edges of everlasting snow. To find him at home the hunter will have to change his base from Soda Springs, on the banks of the Sacramento, and move around the mountain about 25 miles to the eastward. He is a gregarious animal, more so than any other creature on the continent, save perhaps the buffalo, and so you may have to search long before finding him. True, if there have been invasions, as is not unlikely in the progress of civilisation, you may find his large family broken up and scattered about through the dense wood and dimpled little valleys that prevail here. But in his undisturbed state, as I knew him, he is a great lover of his kind, and is to be found only in herds numbering from 50 to 500.

In the Winter of 1856-7 I set out from the sweet little Now-ow-wa Valley (since named 'Squaw Valley' by the coarse and common hunters who kill game as a source of livelihood) with two fine young Indian hunters from the McCloud River, in quest of a band of elk. The winter had thus far been terribly severe and the large tribe of Indians encamped on the banks of the McCloud, some ten miles distant, were starving. The snow had been falling soft and continuously for a long time. It lay from five to ten feet deep and was so wet and soft that the Indians even on their snow-shoes had been unable to move; hence their destitution. But now clear, cold winter was suddenly upon us, and this was their opportunity. The snow was as hard as a floor. The sky was sapphire. The air keen and crisp and full of spice and energy. The perfume of the frosted fir and spruce and pine and tamarack filled us with such an intoxicating delight as I never shall know again. We struck straight up the mountain, right against the gleaming world of snow. We must have made 40 miles that day and encamped under one of 'God's tents' — this is the name given them by the Indians. They are formed entirely of the snow, with a huge and bushy fir-tree whose broad and low boughs reach out and over and down till pinned to the solid snow-bank. And thus is formed a perfect and most shapely tent of solid snow with dry quills for bed, and little dry, resinous and most fragrant cones for fire. And, oh! the perfume that fills this tent of snow, when the gentle flame starts and the indolent smoke lazily reaches up and loses itself in the lofty arches overhead!

The next day we came upon one of the warm springs, a bad, boggy hole in the side of the mountain containing perhaps two acres. The elk had been there only a few days before. Everything had been eaten to the earth, the vine maple, the birch, the alder, all things. There were stumps of willows here and there as large as my arm. The elk were evidently as hungry as the Indians and were eating solid wood. We found where they had broken this corral of snow. It looked as if some huge saw-log had been drawn up the mountain by lumbermen; only this one deep track, and that leading sharp and steep up the world of solid snow. The Indians tightened their belts, tied their moccasins, loosened their arms, and with blazing eyes bounded forward. I followed as fast as I could. The banks of snow on either side of this trench stood higher than my head. Now and then I could see where the big bull leader of the herd had rolled aside in the snow to fall into the rear while another took his place. On the crest of a canyon I came upon my Indians crouching down under the snow-bank in a blaze of suppressed excitement. Peering over them I saw a herd of many hundred elk, all lying down and ruminating under the dense trees on little hillocks that rose among the steaming warm springs.

The Indians conceded me the first shot, and I made my mark the shaggy tuft of hair that lay between a pair of most majestic horns. Over the knoll of snow and down into the corral the Indians leaped, bows and bunches of arrows in hand, leaving their guns behind them; and before the poor cattle were yet fully on their feet their eager captors were sinking arrows up to the feathers in their sides.

And what a slaughter! Some of the bulls sullenly shook their stately horns, and struck out with their sharp and deadly hoofs, trying to fight. The Indians, however, lost no time in hesitation. They drove the elk into the crusted deep snow on every side, broke all discipline of the kingly camp, and darting around on the snow where the poor beasts wallowed helplessly, soon had the band in their power. A tribe was starving. There was no time for pity or sentiment; and they were equal to their bloody work. And the wolves! the wild-cats! the California lions that night! If you want a wild and a terrible sight, if you want to see savagery, to hear the howl of fiends, go high up Mt. Shasta and put the scent of blood in the air on a mid-winter night!

For nearly half a century these cool and flashing head-waters of the great California river have been counted the best fishing grounds, even in a country celebrated as the very elysium of Izaac Walton's disciples. In them is to be found a new fish not known elsewhere in the world; as full of fight as it is possible for a fish to be with a hook in its mouth; proud too, disdaining small things, despising worms and warm pools and all shallow waters. This fish is of the trout family, and, as his great size and strength suggest, he is the king of all trout. He is to be found, so far as I can learn, only in the McCloud river, and that too only far up in the fresh snow-water, even laying his head and glittering sides against the icy banks of snow. His beautiful and varied colours have given him among the fishermen of this region the name of 'Dolly Varden'. But science knows him not and I think he has no other name save that of his Indian appelative 'Wi-la-da-it' or 'Fighting Fish'. I sent a skin of one of these fishes some years ago to Hon. R. B. Roosevelt, famous as an authority on such matters; but, as said before, this fish is, or was at that time, new to the learned. Only last season one of these bright beauties, after he had fought for half an hour and was apparently dead, pulled a man into the river and nearly cost him his life. He was saved from drowning by his companion, who plunged down the steep bank into the deep water where he had fallen and contrived to get him to the shore before he was carried over the falls only a short distance below — a rare instance of getting advantage from fishing in company with another, which, I must say, savours of profanity in a temple. Of course there are fishermen and fishermen; but the man who, to my mind, has any right to fish, fishes alone. The light, the peeps through the trees, the fragrance, above all the perfume of the cool and perfect temple of nature — all these are lost with a crowd, are made less sacred with the sound of voices.

To take the ordinary trout — and you will always have great respect for this spirited fish, till you have encountered the Wi-la-da-it — you have only to visit these head-waters made from the melting snows of Mt. Shasta, and then cast in your line. Under the shadows of the huge sugar pines, beneath the gnarled roots of ancient trees at the base of the steep red hills, you will find them eddying about by the basketful in almost any one of the thousand white streams that come tumbling headlong down from out the awful canyons — as if afraid of the grizzlies there. But go on up and up and up, find new grounds and take your trout skilfully and sparingly like a gentleman. There is a great difference in dollars. How much bigger and how much better is a dollar quietly made by the pen or the plough than a dollar obtained by selling beer and washing glasses for a garrulous mob! And so it is with your catch of trout. When the day's hard tramp is done let each crisp little trout taste of the perfumed woods, of the flashing white waters, the mossy brown rocks under foot, the emerald world of woods overhead, the gleaming snow beyond, and over all and still beyond, the fervid sapphire skies of California; and, although you may have disdained to take but the one trout, it will be enough — and the miraculous draught of Galilee was no more.

from WEST OF THE ROCKY MOUNTAINS *1888*

PART 3

Classic Trails

This section deals with walks that are in some way famous, notorious, or classic examples of their type.

From England we have the Lyke Wake Walk, 42 miles over the North Yorkshire Moors, a walk attempted by thousands of people every year; the Cumbria Way, through the inspiring scenery of the Lakes; and the Wolds Way, a path in Yorkshire established only after many battles over the right of foot passage.

Scotland is represented by the Lairig Ghru, one of *the* great walks, from Speyside to Deeside through the Cairngorm mountains; Ben Alder, whose difficulties of access and uncertainties of weather can frustrate the intending climber, as Philip Gribbon found out; and Skye, most magnetic of islands.

Other articles come from widely differing areas of North America. The celebrated Appalachian Trail is here described by Eric Ryback, while John Hay takes us round Cape Cod and Les Scharnberg leads us to the deserts of the Great Divide.

Along the Cumbria Way

BRIAN ATKIN

The idea was born on a winter's day in Derbyshire. My wife and I had come North for a rambling reunion with some old friends. The deep snow was thawing and rain carried on the wind from an ominous sky did not augur well for the next two days. But the moors were sheer magic after many months' absence. The white treeless expanse of the tops marched into the grey hazy distance, broken only where stone walls and rock outcrops penetrated the covering. The old feeling of excitement returned. I resolved that I would never again stay away from the northern hills for so long. We dropped down to the valley bottom and were drawn like a magnet into an outdoor equipment shop. In a prominent position on the book-rack was a guide to the Cumbria Way. I picked it up and knew immediately that this had to be the long distance walk which my eldest son and I were scheduling for the first week in May. In retrospect the snow of that day was an unrecognised omen for the future.

Day One — Ulverston to Coniston

The morning was bright and sunny yet a cold northerly wind soon pierced our clothing. This weather was a very pleasant change from yesterday's dull, wet motorway journey. The hills around Ulverston have a distinct Lake District look to them, a sort of miniature ruggedness, but we were still half a day's walk away from the mountains. The initial stages of the Cumbria Way are through hilly country along paths and tracks between farms, thus avoiding metalled roads. It is the type of country where way-finding can be a problem. With little evidence of previous walkers, it was necessary to make frequent references to the guidebook.

A long mountainous horizon stood in front of us. The nearest and most prominent peaks were the Coniston group, dominated by the Old Man. Beyond them the Scafell range looked alien and dramatic, highlighted by the long white streaks of snow-filled gullies. What had first been a suspicion was eventually confirmed. Snow showers were developing on the high fells, draping each peak in a gossamer of white. The countryside became increasingly rough, meadows giving way to bracken-covered grazing and greater numbers of sheep. The first flurries of snow came our way. The boundary of the National Park was crossed at Gawthwaite and we took lunch under the limited shelter of a field wall near Tottlebank.

Beacon Tarn was special, reviving many memories. Although only 500ft. above sea level it had every appearance of a remote mountain lake. Substantial waves created by the bitterly cold wind were beating on the rocky shore. Banks of dead bracken rising above the clear water were topped by a shrouded outline of the Old Man. We had arrived back in the Lakes.

The ground dropped to a marshy depression, the site of a former tarn, and then we skirted round the edge of an extensive Moss. The descent continued along the side of a beck to where it was joined by a bigger volume of water coming down from the lofty mass of the Old Man. The much enlarged beck was in spate, the stepping stones covered and treacherously slippery. The single and rather loose wire strand serving as a hand-hold was some comfort, but would have been little use in the event of a lost foothold. A heavy snow shower passed over and ice-blue Coniston Water came into view with the returning sun. The lake shore was sheltered, but nearby trees looked bare and wintry. On closer inspection it was apparent that new life was just about to burst. Things were more advanced on the opposite sunnier shore, where multitudinous buds gave the bank of trees a gentle green, almost fluffy, sheen.

It was very quiet here, especially as we were away from the wind. As might be expected, the Way now showed signs of considerable use. But two sailing dinghies sliding along near the far shore, and chaffinches ever eager for our biscuit crumbs were the only company. On the last leg of the day's walk more snow was visible on the Old Man as we worked our way round to its eastern side, and then the steep fells

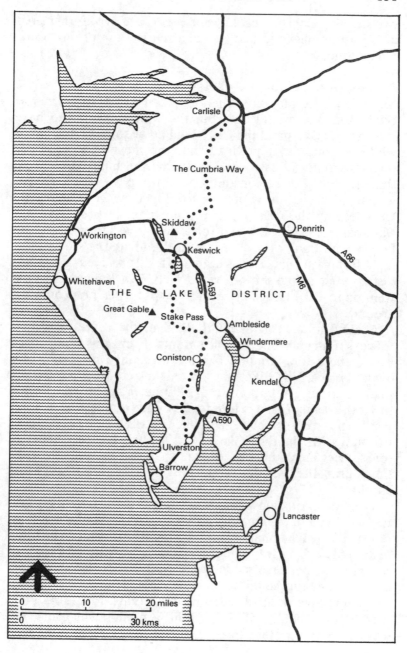

overhanging Coniston caught our eye. We arrived rather tired at Coniston village just as the children were returning home from school.

Day Two — Coniston to Rosthwaite

May Day, the old day when the arrival of summer was celebrated. It was still cold but the wind appeared to have moderated. Overnight the Old Man had acquired a dusting of white. A long day lay ahead, but the morning's walk was through relatively easy country below the high fells. These same fells provided a constant backdrop to the meadows and woodland along our route. A fox loped away through the trees leaving the nearby sheep quite undisturbed. The Old Man had passed behind and for a time it was the turn of the huge rough flank of Wetherlam to dominate the scene. At a high farmyard, gable ends and daffodils framed a sombre distant view of the snow-covered Helvellyn Range. Then we went on to Tarn Hows, an attractive spot when no people are around.

Around midday at Skelwith Bridge, the route turned in towards Langdale and the mountains. From this point there was to be a long gradual climb and change of scene. The distant view of the Pikes and Pavey Ark across Elterwater is justly famous. A background of blue crags streaked with snow was set against a gentle foreground of quiet water, long reeds and trees in bud. We had a drink at the familiar Britannia Inn in the village of Elterwater. The sheltered forecourt gained full benefit from the warm sun; the only time during the walk that it was possible to sit out-of-doors in comfort.

The first major snow squall of the day came over the tops. For a time all the mountains were blotted out, and when they returned Bowfell remained under a mantle of white. The head of Langdale is a great wilderness shaped by the Ice Ages. It contains neither man-made stone walls, nor even trees and bushes. Only rugged boulders and glacial debris stand in that vast amphitheatre surrounded by mountains. I had forgotten the awesome majesty of the place. It is a blind valley and our way out was over Stake Pass, an increasingly steep climb over the bare slope until the lip of the valley is reached. On the way up I realised I had also forgotten the size of the Lakeland hills — or perhaps it was the passing years?

After negotiating a tussocky tundra at the top we gained our first but brief view into Langstrath which was being obscured by another heavy snow shower coming along the valley. As we descended, dense clouds of large snowflakes came up to meet us from below. We and the snowfall stopped on reaching the valley bottom. Not far from the beck a few old gnarled trees were struggling to survive in that magnificent desolation. Just then the hectic cities of my working life seemed very far away.

Perhaps we were tired, but it seemed a long walk down the valley to the first field walls. At the junction of Langstrath and Greenup Gill there was another heavy snow shower which left everything, including ourselves, a dazzling white, for immediately afterwards a brilliant evening sun came out from behind the clouds. Our lodgings for the next two nights were with Mrs. Bland at Nook Farm, and we arrived in Rosthwaite as the fires were being stoked for the evening. Woodsmoke drifted over the rooftops of the hamlet. As the sun set, the snow began to fall again, and so May Day ended.

Day Three — Great Gable

The Cumbria Way is essentially a low level route. The only climb which is unavoidable is Stake Pass. You spend a lot of time each day gazing at the multitudinous procession of peaks, and in the planning stage we resolved to climb at least one. This was the reason for the two-night stay in Borrowdale. Our objective was the queen of them all, Great Gable.

We awoke to a white world. A morning sun encouraged birdsong, the bleat of the lambs, and the snowline to retreat up the hill.

The first stage of the walk was along the valley-bottom path passing both the Youth Hostel and the CHA guesthouse. We used the old road on the climb up to Honister Pass. Although some parts survive intact, in others it has been reduced by erosion to little more than a trench. For the walker it makes a very acceptable alternative to the modern highway. Above the treeline we were caught in a cutting wind and were obliged to wear our anoraks. From the Honister Quarry workshop the route continued up the line of the old cable railway. On this stretch we overtook the retreating snowline. At the scant remains of the winding house the path turns southwards towards Grey Knotts and Brandreth. The rewards of the climb become apparent; first there are extensive views westwards to the lovely Buttermere Valley and its lakes, and then into lonely Ennerdale with Pillar towering above.

This was the only time that week that we met other walkers. I think of the lone old man hobbling slowly but gamely along over the flank of Brandreth with the help of a stick and wonder whether his goal was Great Gable and if he ever achieved it. The snow grew deeper as the climb continued until only the exposed upper surfaces of the stones and boulders showed through. This is a secret route to Great Gable. The mountain remains hidden until Brandreth is breasted. Suddenly there it stood, a great forbidding dome of crags and snow set against a wild sky, a daunting view for someone who had become a little too acclimatised to the Sweet South. We made careful progress along the footsteps of our predecessors to avoid dropping into deep snow-covered holes. At the summit of Green Gable the last obstacles were in full view, the dizzy spaces of the appropriately named Windy Gap and the long scramble over the rocky buttress of Gable Crag to the summit.

On arrival at Great Gable summit the sun came out, and, blessed relief, the wind died away for a short time. The superlative views ranging from the dark depths of Wasdale immediately beneath, to the rugged white Scafell range to the south defy description. To many walkers this spot is the ultimate goal, and it is fitting that it was given to the nation as a war memorial 60 years ago.

The sun went in and the bitterly cold wind returned. Our time to leave this jumbled desert of rocks surrounded by massive space had come. We followed the tourist path which starts as a gentle slope and then becomes an unpleasant but reasonably safe scree on the steeper reaches in the vicinity of

Tom Blue rocks. We passed through the snowline well before Styhead Tarn, a cold aloof water in spite of the many thousands who visit it each year. Very little vegetation grows in and around its clear waters.

Borrowdale was now in view ahead. Before descending further I took one final look back at the rugged Scafell range and its wild sky before it disappeared below the immediate skyline. Three walkers who had just climbed past us were, for a moment, silhouetted against the snow of the higher mountains. Then they were gone, leaving the whole scene to us. The first trees above Stockley Bridge were a welcome sight after the desolation. From Seathwaite we progressed to Seatoller and back to our temporary home among the cluster of houses and cottages in Rosthwaite.

Day Four — Borrowdale to Keswick
This was to be a rest day, a gentle walk down the valley to Keswick. Accompanied by a fitful sun and the cry of lambs we made our way through meadowland to the narrow neck which divides the upper and lower valleys. The busy river has cut through rocks which show evidence of former mining operations much healed by time. Hereabouts the scenery of the Lake District undergoes a marked change. The rugged volcanic rocks which had been with us for the previous two days were replaced by the smooth slopes of softer slate.

The valley opened out again and we soon reached Derwentwater. This is my favourite lake. Although surrounded by mountains, they stand back so that the scene can be enjoyed in full. Its still waters in turn presented reflections of Walla Crag, Blencathra and the dominant mass of Skiddaw to the north.

The Cumbria Way follows the shoreline for a considerable distance. There are two paths. The one which we took passes over alternating rocky beaches and tree-covered headlands. The second path, which cuts a number of corners, is some distance back from the shore. Following the usual daily pattern, the summits of the mountains became gradually hidden in snow. These distant phenomena seemed to have little relevance to us enjoying the sun surrounded by daffodils, green grass and bursting buds. But by the time we reached Portinscale the sky had become very overcast and our midday walk over the meadows to Keswick was accomplished in a heavy storm of hail and sleet.

Day Five — Keswick to Potts Gill

The noise of the inhabitants of Keswick bustling in preparation for the tourist season was left behind before we had climbed up and behind Latrigg, to the point where the tracks divide. One goes straight up the steep bare flank of Jenkin Hill to the summit of Skiddaw, and ours contoured round the great curvaceous slope, which, dare I say it, had the appearance of a massive South Down. The pervading peace and emptiness made a pause appropriate. We looked back for the last time at the vast panorama of mountains through which we had come. Snow still covered the tops of the higher peaks, and Great Gable stood out massive and aloof from the rest.

The scene changed abruptly when we turned into the precipitous Glenderaterra Valley and met our old companion, the north wind. The track dwindled to a stony path hugging the outcrops half way up the western wall of this gap which divides Skiddaw and Blencathra. Where the contours ease below Lonscale Fell, we passed what appeared to be remnants of former cottages and found ourselves in Skiddaw Forest. The only trees in evidence were the rather scrawny coppice close to the weatherbeaten lodge which goes under the name of Skiddaw House.

The forest is a great bowl of heather and bracken-covered hills. Both Skiddaw and Blencathra are part of the rim, but on this northern side they do not display the grand mountain faces which can be seen from the south. It is as if they now want to merge into the moorland scenery of Northern Lakeland. The rim of the moorland bowl is broken in three places, the Glenderaterra Beck by which we had arrived, the Dash Beck which provides the Cumbria Way bad weather escape route, and the River Caldew which we followed. This whole area is unknown to most Lakeland visitors. It was a pleasure to walk along and not see rubbish and the ubiquitous can rings. For some miles we stepped briskly down a gentle valley beside the sparkling River Caldew.

Just as meadowland becomes visible at the entrance to the valley, the Way turns up into the side valley of Grainsgill Beck. We had been warned, but it was still a shock. The mess, noise and activity of the Carrock Wolfram Mine needs no more description. Electric light bulbs are essential to our society, but one was left with the hope that the mine operators will be obliged to do some tidying up before they finally depart. There was no obvious path up the fell to the shooting box which serves as a marker. It was a long hard slog, but we could not get up fast enough.

Apart from the wind, peace was reigning again on the wide tops. First on a track and then across open moor, our way led over tough grass, peat and shining lumps of quartz. The top of High Pike was all space. This is the very last mountain of the Lake District but it is so different from the rest that it did not seem like the Lakes at all. The highest point is almost flat, marked by a cairn and stone seat. It seemed that we were suspended far above the farmland of the Eden Valley and the coastal plain. The hazy hills of Scotland could just be seen across the Solway Firth and eastwards lay the long snow-covered ramparts of the Pennines. Parts of this great panorama were hidden by marauding showers of hail and snow. We went down a gentle slope past several old mines to arrive at a cluster of stone farm buildings sheltering beside a beck at the foot of the fell. It was here, at Potts Gill, that we spent the night, looked after by Heather and Robin Highton and their dogs, in a seventeenth century farmhouse, full of unexpected nooks and angles, low ceilings, and with a magnificent front door whose ancient timbers were fastened together by rows of wooden pegs.

Day Six — Potts Gill to Carlisle

There was a problem: we were planning to walk to Carlisle and travel home that day. Potts Gill is 16 miles from Carlisle, our car was in Lancaster and the train service between Carlisle and Lancaster is rather limited. Heather kindly provided us with a very early breakfast so that we might catch a train at 1 p.m. and we were on our way before 7.30 a.m. Something else had been active early; snow had been falling heavily since the first glimmerings of dawn. Our muffled footsteps traced across the yard and out onto the track, and Potts Gill was soon lost to sight by a fold in the ground. Caldbeck seemed to be asleep. Its well known early rising inhabitant* in his 'coat so grey' has been in the graveyard these many years.

The snow turned to slush as we hurried along muddy paths through woodlands. After Sebergham, way-finding was easier as the Way lies mainly on the river bank and the firm turf helped us maintain our pace. The snow had thawed and the sun appeared, but the now distant white hills were still partly obscured by cloud.

This is lowland farming country. In sharp contrast to the previous days, mature lambs stood in rich green pastures. Local buildings are of red sandstone, ranging from the simple fortress-like church at Churchtown to the impressive array of buildings at Rose Cottage. The character of the country changes at Buckabank with its factories, mills and commuter houses. We floundered for some time trying to find our way in a semi-industrial area, but eventually got back on track.

The last stage of the walk was again beside the Caldew, which had become a sad old river. The youthful moorland stream of yesterday was but a memory. Its broad, slow and polluted reaches led to the factories, gasholder and railway station of Carlisle. The destination was of no account: the journey was all. We arrived at the station 25 minutes before the train was due, and it arrived 15 minutes late. The walk was over.

from THE GREAT OUTDOORS *March 1980*

---

* John Peel — the subject of a celebrated English folk song.

Lairig Ghru

ALASDAIR BORTHWICK

Scotland has two great passes which, relatively small though they are, exercise as vivid a local appeal as the giants of Europe, and northern India. They are the Corrieyairack, where Wade's old military road climbs over the Monadhliaths from the Great Glen to Speyside; and the Lairig Ghru, chief pass of the Cairngorms. Both are long, and both fulfil the prime function of a pass, which is that it should link, across some desolate region, two centres of civilisation. They have become the pilgrim routes of those who like to take their pleasures strenuously. By far the finer of the two is the Lairig Ghru.

At 8 p.m. my brother dropped me at Coylum Bridge, a few miles from Aviemore, and promised to pick me up on the far side of the Cairngorms on the following afternoon. I said goodbye, and turned along a little track to the Rothiemurchus Forest, where a signpost points a single arm labelled 'Braemar' as if it heralded a motor road instead of a scratch on the bare bones of the earth without so much as a house to grace it for more than 20 miles.

No road goes over the Lairig Ghru. The mountains which we now know as the Cairngorms were once a high, level plateau covered with ice which, forming glaciers, gradually carved out beds for itself in the rock as rivers do today; and when, in the fullness of time, the glaciers melted, the plateau had been cut up into a group of separate mountains. The Cairngorms cover a large area. Most of the glaciers could only carve glens which ran back a few miles into the mountains before disappearing; but in the centre of the range they cut a way clear through, a deep V running for more than 20 miles through the heart of the old plateau.

Near one end today is Braemar, and near the other is Aviemore; but, as the summit of the pass is 2,700ft. above the sea and blocked with snow throughout the winter, not even the indefatigable General Wade ever had the temerity to drive a road through it. It has been left for the pleasure of stalkers, hikers and climbers.

I knew I should have enough daylight to see me to the top of the pass, for it was a fine night in July and in these latitudes the sun at that time of the year never sinks very far below the horizon. The going was pleasant, for the Rothiemurchus is a beautiful place, and is a real forest. It actually has trees in it. It is not, for example, like Lord MacDonald's deer forest in Skye, which, so far as I have seen, has no trees at all; nor is it like any other of the skimpy woods or wastes of peat which are called deer forests simply because deer happen to be shot in them. The Rothiemurchus is a forest, dense and green, where thousands upon thousands of firs cling to the foothills of the Cairngorms so profusely and without plan that anyone straying from the Lairig path might easily lose himself amongst them.

My way climbed gradually upwards through the trees, which opened out every now and then into a clearing with sometimes a deer or two standing there watching me; and the farther I climbed the more did the path twist and squirm as it avoided hummocks where heather had grown over ancient roots and fallen trunks.

And then the trees thinned out, and I emerged on to a species of natural midden right in the mouth of the Lairig. The old glaciers had picked up all sorts of odds and ends on their way down to the plains — boulders, and mud, and rocks of all sizes and in vast quantities — because glaciers flow like rivers and when they reach low levels they melt, dumping all the solids they have collected on their way. These rubbish dumps, or moraines, are common all over the Highlands, and there is a particularly fine example where the Lairig Ghru begins and the Rothiemurchus stops. The mouth of the pass is silted up with a great conglomeration of mud and rock overgrown with heather. Into this soft stuff a burn has cut its way, so that when I came out on to the open hillside I found myself on the lip of a cutting, steep and deep out of all proportion to the tiny burn which flowed at the bottom on the bare rock of the mountains. So enormous was this accumulation of silt that I had to walk nearly two miles uphill before the bed of the burn rose to meet me and I too was travelling on rock.

It was now past 10 p.m., and I was keeping my eyes open for a convenient place to sleep, with a fairly clear suspicion that no such place existed. The wind had risen, which was awkward. Once an enthusiastic half-gale finds its way into the funnel of the Lairig, the tentless traveller feels like a customer's change coming down one of those suction tubes used in department stores, for the wind is concentrated and, once committed to the journey, has no option but to sweep over the summit and down the other side.

It seemed I had the choice of two evils. I could choose a sheltered bed among the masses of rock which had fallen from the cliffs on either side of the pass, thereby assuring myself of a windless but abominably uncomfortable night, for no grass or heather grows among the rocks there, and rock makes a hard bed. Or I could choose a good, soft, heathery place and be blown off the face of the earth. So I had to resort to guile.

I have found that in a confined funnel such as the Lairig, the wind behaves like a car on a race-track or water in a river: when it comes to a bend, it tends to swing to the outside of it. This is a useful thing to know when one is carrying no tent and has to rely upon what the ground provides. The method is not entirely efficient; but the chances are that an island of comparatively still air will be found on the left-hand bank of a left-hand bend, or the right-hand bank of a right-hand one, though the place may appear to be no more sheltered than any other part of the landscape.

So when I reached a point only a hundred feet or so below the crest of the pass and found that the track bore slightly to the left, I crossed to the left bank and dumped my rucksack. It did not appear to be at all a bad spot, though an annoying little current of air branched off the main stream and came sighing past from the direction of Aviemore. But that, I thought, could be baulked if I built a little dyke of stones at my head and lay with my feet to Braemar.

Stones were plentiful. The wall of the pass was steep, so

that by climbing up a short distance and heaving down every-thing manageable within reach, a very fair collection had soon rolled down and come to rest beside the patch of grass where I intended sleeping. Then I built my dyke. I built it lovingly and with care. It was four feet long, three feet high, two feet thick, and the only dyke I ever built that stayed up for more than five minutes. I still like to think of that dyke. It was a masterpiece. I wasted an hour and all the knuckles of my left hand in making it, and my grunting would have been fearful if there had been anyone about to hear it other than two ptarmigan which watched operations from a nearby boulder, drawn, apparently, by the same form of hypnotism exercised in cities by pneumatic drills or men digging holes by any means whatsoever.

At last it was done. Ten minutes before midnight the two ptarmigan and I stood back in the half-light and admired my handiwork. And immediately the annoying little current of air branched off the main stream and came sighing past from the direction, not of Aviemore, but of Braemar. At this stage of the proceedings I had much wicked pride removed from my system, and eventually crawled into my sleeping-bag in a very bad temper indeed, for a boulder prevented my lying on the other side of the wall. The wind blew the wrong way all night.

I should like to digress here long enough to point out that, if the weather is at all reasonable, sleeping without a tent is ten times better fun than sleeping with one, provided only that you should not spend more than one night in the open. There is nothing extraordinary about it. The one is as comfortable as the other if the proper spot is picked. All that is needed is a lightweight sleeping-bag — preferably eider-down, which is light and warm — and two lightweight groundsheets loosely stitched together down one side. You simply get into the bag and roll yourself in the groundsheets. Rain may mean damp feet; but if only one night is spent in the open the bag can be dried at the end of the journey, and conditions are seldom bad enough to interfere with sleep. This is obviously not wild weather equipment, but it serves the pinch and has the merit of weighing less than 3lb.

And it is good to lie with your head projecting from one end of the cocoon — wear a balaclava helmet, by the way — with nothing between you and the stars, and all sorts of things going on around you which normally would never be noticed. Three deer went past me that night, walking very quietly, less than 20 yards away. That was after midnight, but it was still quite light. One of them disturbed a pebble, and I looked round, and there they were. They looked at me, but did not seem frightened. They moved slowly uphill until I lost sight of them.

There were other things, too. Even at that height, 2,700ft., there is plenty of life. Something set a stone rolling only half a dozen yards away, and to this day I do not know what did it. It was probably a ptarmigan, rooting about among the rocks, though what it was doing out and about at that time of night I do not know. I thought, too, that I heard a fox bark.

The wind roared by on the far side of the pass; the cliffs above were black against the sky; a little burn trickled past almost under my elbow. It was a grand night. I wrapped my scarf firmly round my seat (where, I find, it does most good: camp nights are cold), and slept.

At 9.30 a.m. on the following morning I met the first of the pilgrims. I was over the summit by that time and a good half-hour down the other side, just beyond the Pools of Dee, which are three or four brackish puddles near the top of the pass. I had been walking on rock and loose screes almost since I started, up and down through a landscape of boulders. The hikers, who were the first human beings I had seen for 13 hours, were two lads from Edinburgh, and they had been walking since 3 a.m. They had to reach home by evening, so they must have had a fairly crowded weekend: when I saw them they had covered about 11 miles from the road-end at the Linn o' Dee, and were roughly halfway to Aviemore.

After them came a steady stream. First were two lads on the far side of the burn, then three who had been on the way since 6 a.m., then two from Corrour Bothy, a tiny hut dumped in the Lairig itself and the only shelter within miles. By this time the Lairig had widened from a notch in the skyline into a valley, and the trickle of water which seeped through the screes below the Pools of Dee was a young river. Beyond the river were the endless slabs and overhanging crags of the Devil's Point, a monstrous black mass of rock which fell over a thousand feet sheer to the level carse on the floor of the glen. Below it, looking absurdly lonely, was Corrour Bothy. I saw people moving about outside it, so I left the track where a cairn marks the ford, waded the river, and joined them.

The bothy is no more than a small shed with an earth floor, and a leaky roof; but there were six people living in it, and two of them — Edinburgh lads again — had been there for a week, using it as their base for climbing and walking. I do not know how they manhandled all their food up to it, but they seemed quite happy. The situation was worth the effort, for the bothy was surrounded by 4,000ft. tops — Ben Macdui just across the way, and Braeriach and Cairn Toul behind — with not a living soul in miles and miles. They said it was the most peaceful holiday they had ever spent.

We fell to talking, sitting on biscuit tins in the middle of the floor; and one of the lads said: "Do you know So-and-so?" and I said, "Yes. Do you know Whatsisname?" And, as usually happens in these places, we found we had met most of each other's acquaintances and were not at all sure that we had not met each other too, years before. So we talked a little more; and a middle-aged man from Aberdeen sat in a corner puffing his pipe, listening but saying nothing.

After a while I said: "Any more word of the Great Grey Man?" to which the Edinburgh fellow said no, he had not heard anything lately, and did I think there was anything in that story? And I said I did not know, but it was a queer business just the same, and I should like to see the Great Grey Man myself.

Then the Aberdonian took his pipe out of his mouth long enough to ask who the Great Grey Man was. And we told him.

The Great Grey Man of Ben Macdui, or Ferlas Mor as he is called in the Gaelic, is Scotland's Abominable Snowman and the only mountain ghost I have heard of in this part of the world. He ranks high in the supernatural Debrett, for he has been seen by responsible people who have reputations to lose, most of them expert mountaineers accustomed to hills at night and not given to imagining things.

He first reached print about 20 years ago, when Dr Norman Collie, a mountaineer of international repute who not only made first ascents of most of Scotland's major cliffs (a route in the Cuillin is named after him), but climbed extensively in the Alps and was with Mummery on Nanga Parbat in the Himalayas, admitted that strange things had happened to him on Ben Macdui. He had been alone on the summit at midnight; and so peculiar were the things he saw there that he did not stop running until he was half-way down to the Rothiemurchus.

He related this experience at a dinner of the Cairngorm Club; and immediately others, equally reputable, came forward and admitted that they, too, had seen queer things on Macdui. According to their descriptions the Great Grey Man is a tremendous shadowy creature, and his height is variously reported to be anything from 10 to 40 feet. He appears generally at night; and one's natural reaction is to run as fast as possible in the opposite direction.

There are two interesting points about the circumstances under which he has appeared. First, several men claim that they saw him before they knew of his existence: only when Dr Collie gave the lead did they admit that they had seen something too, so they did not hear the tale and then imagine themselves into meeting Ferlas Mor. And second, there is no known mountain phenomenon which could account for him. If the sun is shining, it frequently happens that a climber's shadow is cast on a screen of mist some distance away, so that he can march along a ridge with a huge shadow stalking along in space beside him. But this is a common trick of mist and sun which would scare no one. I have seen it half a dozen times. It is interesting, but not in the least eerie. Anyone who makes a habit of climbing knows what causes it; and, instead of running away, whoops with delight, rakes his rucksack for a camera, and tries to photograph it. It is known as the Brocken Spectre, after the peak in the Hartz Mountains where it commonly occurs. But Brocken Spectres cannot live without sunlight: the moon is not sufficiently bright. And the Great Grey Man walks at night.

I know two men who claim to have heard Ferlas Mor. The first was alone, heading over Macdui for Corrour on a night when the snow had a hard, crisp crust through which his boots broke at every step. He reached the summit, and it was while he was descending the slopes which fall towards the Lairig that he heard footsteps behind him, footsteps not in the rhythm of his own, but occurring only once for every three steps he took. He described the following strange experience.

> I felt a queer, crinkly feeling on the back of my neck, but I said to myself, 'This is silly. There must be a reason for it.' So I stopped, and the footsteps stopped, and I sat down and tried to reason it out. I could see nothing. There was a moon about somewhere, but the mist was fairly thick. The only thing I could make of it was that when my boots broke through the snow-crust they made some sort of echo. But then every step should have echoed, and not just this regular one-in-three. I was scared stiff. I got up, and walked on, trying hard not to look behind me. I got down all right — the footsteps stopped a thousand feet above the Lairig — and I didn't run. But, man, if anything had as much as said 'Boo!' behind me, I'd have been down to Corrour like a streak of lightning!

The second man's experience was roughly similar. He was on Macdui, and alone. He heard footsteps. He was climbing in daylight, in summer; but so dense was the mist that he was working by compass, and visibility was almost as poor as it would have been at night. The footsteps he heard were made by something or someone trudging up the fine screes which decorate the upper parts of the mountain, a thing not extraordinary in itself, though the steps were only a few yards behind him, but exceedingly odd when the mist suddenly cleared and he could see no living thing on the mountain, at that point devoid of cover of any kind.

"Did the steps follow yours exactly?" I asked him.

"No," he said. "That was the funny thing. They didn't. They were regular all right; but the queer thing was that they seemed to come once for every two and a half steps I took."

He thought it queerer still when I told him the other man's story. You see, he was long-legged and six feet tall, and the first man was only five-feet-seven!

Once I was out with a search-party on Macdui; and on the way down after an unsuccessful day I asked some of the gamekeepers and stalkers who were with us what they thought of it all. They worked on Macdui, so they should know. Had they seen Ferlas Mor? Did he exist, or was it just a silly story?

They looked at me for a few seconds, and then one said: "We do not talk about that."

When we had finished this harangue, the Edinburgh lad and I, the Aberdonian scratched his head and said: "Well, I'm glad I didn't know about that last night" and then told us, quite casually, of the energetic time he had been having. He had walked 14 miles from Braemar to the bothy on the previous night, and had then been smitten by an urge to see the sunrise from the top of Ben Macdui, which is over 4,000ft. high, the second highest mountain in Britain, and a good three miles farther on.

He had reached the summit and so nearly frozen on the way that at one stage he thought his fingers were frost-bitten. Feeling rather sorry for himself he had stamped round in circles, waiting for a dawn which arrived, swathed in mist and completely invisible, at 4.15 a.m. In disgust he had returned to the bothy and slept for two hours, a period which he apprently deemed sufficient, for he left with me for the Linn o' Dee. There I waited for my brother, glad to stretch my weary bones on a heather bank, and let the world go by; but he, still restless, plodded onwards another six miles to Braemar. All told, he must have walked at least 35 miles with a mountain thrown in, which is more than enough for a young man, much less one in middle life. He finished fresh, too.

We met a dozen people with rucksacks before we reached the Linn. That was after we had signed the visitors' book at the bothy. It was the sixth visitors' book which had lain there; and, like the other five, contained some famous names, even if the roof did leak and there was scarcely room to turn round. On the fly-leaf some wag announced that the tele-graphic address was, 'Comfort, Cairngorms'.

The Lairig grew wider as mile succeeded mile, growing softer and more like the tourist's conception of the Highlands as the notch in the skyline fell behind, and in the end merging into Glen Derry, where the slopes are gentle and there are trees and the cottage of Luibeg stands by the river on the level strath. Outside the cottage, lying on the grass, were a neatly trimmed tree-trunk and several rounded stones taken from the river. Ian Grant of Luibeg is a great man at the Games with the caber, and he putts the weight like Ossian himself: here, evidently, he practised with no audience but the deer.

The track which had started high in the mountains as a few scratches on the rock had by now become a road of sorts, dusty and rutted, but still a road. The trickle from the Pools of Dee was a river, full-grown. Arguing with violence about diet and unemployment, two subjects about which I know practically nothing, the Aberdonian and I turned a bend and heard the cries of an ice-cream vendor and the voice of the internal combustion engine. We were at a beauty spot, a province of picnic-land. The fringes of civilisation were upon us.

from ALWAYS A LITTLE FURTHER *1939*

On the Appalachian Trail

ERIC RYBACK

When I had started at Mt. Katahdin the weather had been cold and rainy. Now it was becoming spring and the walking conditions were better. I was no longer so concerned with the terrain. In the beginning I had made every footstep with caution. I would need three or four rest stops to climb a mountain. Now I could climb all the way up and down a mountain without stopping. I was not fully conditioned yet, and still had a few problems, but I no longer thought about my problems every minute. This was one reason why I began to get lonely. I had more time to think of other things now, especially at night. It no longer took all of my thoughts and energy just to survive and keep walking.

For the first few days I had spent a lot of time studying my maps and trying to figure out the terrain ahead. Now I had travelled some 220 miles over some of the roughest terrain at the worst time of the year, with rain and blackflies continually plaguing me, so I knew what to expect. I was growing stronger; originally it took me 18 hours a day just for the hiking. Now I made my miles in much less time.

Because I had a lot of time to think, I began to suffer from loneliness. Night was the worst time. I wasn't completely exhausted now and would sit listening to the quiet. I could hear the animals moving through the forest, and the frogs, and the general animal activity. I would see the stars, and then I would think about my family at home. I would wonder what they were doing. If I thought about home too long, it would make me very lonely, so I would try to think about something else, or amuse myself about how it would feel to reach certain points down the trail. Such thoughts would make me want to get going again, but I did no night walking in Maine.

Sometimes I would clean my pots and pans, scrubbing them with sand over and over, just to keep busy. Small details of living, which were performed mechanically at home, became of great importance. I thought about how I could improve on my equipment and of better ways to store items in my pack. I spent hours waxing and greasing my boots. I realised how valuable they were, now that I had almost ruined them.

The boots were now like a part of me. My feet had moulded the boots. When I put my boots on they gave me a sense of power. I began to feel that my legs were pistons, and the boots made them stronger.

I was feeling good. Since leaving Caratunk, the weather had been great. However, the increasing loneliness had almost destroyed my peace of mind in the last few days. I had been on the trail for two weeks, and had not met anyone since

I left Chris and Mary Joe. With only 11 miles left to go in Maine, I felt sure I would spend the night in New Hampshire.

It wasn't to be so easy, getting to New Hampshire, for now I learned why Maine had tested and hardened me. I stood facing Old Speck! It was 4,180ft., and looked like it went straight up to the clouds, a sheer granite wall that extended almost as far as I could see. This peak was the first mountain of the Mahoosuc Range.

I rested at the base of the mountain, playing with the squirrels, before I shouldered my pack and set off. The first 300ft. consisted of large boulders set down in a heavy growth of pine trees. Working my way in between the rocks, grasping tree branches, I slowly worked my way up, carefully placing each foot, making certain not to take long steps. This was to conserve my energy. I continued, step after step, and never looked back and never stopped to rest, thinking that if I did stop I would never get going again. I started to sweat and was soaking wet as I climbed higher. Pausing briefly to catch my breath every few steps, I would scan the area above me. It was very steep. I found a place called the Halfway House. It was used as a shelter in severe weather by any hiker unlucky enough to be up here in a storm. I wondered if I should rest or continue, but experience told me to go on. I had found that once I rested, it took twice as much energy to continue. Slackening my pace a little to help my breathing, I continued upward. My body became dehydrated again, but I was saving the water I carried as my reward when I reached the top. My breathing became laboured and my throat burned. I felt a breeze stirring and knew I must be within a few hundred feet of the top. Finally I reached the crest, utterly exhausted, I lay down without even bothering to take off my pack.

After catching my breath I took my canteen and gulped the water down, letting it run all over my face and down my neck. I could see why the Mahoosuc Range was considered one of the roughest sections of the Appalachian Trail.

After resting and drinking most of my water, I set out to conquer more mountains. I finally made my way to the border of New Hampshire. Someone had been there before me and ruined the sign I wanted for a picture. Mr Bear had raked the sign and splintered the wood into small fragments.

I picked up the splinters and tried to fit them together but the sign just wouldn't stay together. This seemed very important at the time and I was struck with the thought of how small incidents become of major importance in the wilderness.

Wanting to complete the Mahoosuc Range, I continued hiking even though dusk was approaching. There was supposed to be a lean-to at Rattle River, yet when darkness set in I hadn't found either the river or the shelter. Using my flashlight, I went on. I needed to find a stream or spring in order to prepare my dinner properly. I had neglected to refill my canteen at any of the numerous streams I had crossed. After a half-hour of night travelling, I came to the lean-to. Luckily, it was located right on the trail. The night was completely black. After building a fire and cooking some *chicken-à-la-king,* which I stuffed down to maintain my strength, I stacked heaps of wood on the fire. I felt elated because of the day's accomplishment. The night was beautiful. It was calm and peaceful and I was content.

from HIKING THE APPALACHIAN TRAIL *1975*

Hiking the Great Divide

LES SCHARNBERG

Thére were a lot of sceptics among those who heard of my plans to hike the Continental Divide through New Mexico. The only account I had read of such a hike was in the book *The Ultimate Journey* by Eric Ryback. It was full of phrases such as: ". . . . This ungodly country" and, ". . . tired of the dreary landscape". A final comment by Ryback, which seems ironic in light of the wonderful photography of the area by David Muench: "There is nothing to photograph, nothing to see".

My wife, Blue, and I began the trip on a windy day in March at the United States-Mexico border, not too far from the old Culberson's Ranch. Our topo indicated the R.I. Brass Ranch not far from the border, but as the survey was made in 1917, it was understandable that the only remains of the ranch were the stock tank and a windmill. The going was slow but we were treated to the wonderful sight of 20 antelope only a mile and a half from the border. Most of our travel would be by compass as the route is largely cross-country in New Mexico. We walked westward up the San Luis Pass where we made camp on 23rd March. The next day we hiked down into the Animas Valley and turned north. We seemed to be but specks in the vastness of blue sky and yellow grass.

The land offered little protection against the wind; the cold was incredible. The entry in my journal for that day says, "The wind howls at us . . . it wants to lift our little tent and toss us out, like an old woman shakes her rug to rid it of the dust. Mid-morning the thermometer reads 32°F."

Two days north of San Luis Pass we headed east for Animas Mountain. On the morning of 27th March everything was covered with a few inches of snow. The cholla cactus, with its yellow fruit on spindly arms, was to be the only thing vaguely resembling sunlight during most of the next three days. We wound our way through heavy snowfall along Double Adobes Creek for the next two days, then turned north along the Divide.

Flash floods are always a potential danger in this kind of terrain, and we were conscious of the fact when we made camp in a small wash named Bennett Creek. About 1.30 a.m. I awoke with horror to see the sand up the wash shimmering with 'water'. Grabbing socks and shoes, pots and pans, sleeping bags and stuff bags, packs and hats, we ran up the bank depositing one load after another. Safely on the banks of the wash, we could not *hear* any water. I went to check and, to my chagrin, found our 'flash flood' was only the advancing reflection of moonlight on the silica of the sandy wash.

In the Playas Valley came the decision that both of us knew was coming. Blue was four months pregnant when we began the hike and she decided that it was too rough for her to continue. From 1st April on, she would join me occasionally by means of our four-wheel-drive. Now I was alone.

Loneliness does not last long in this magic land. The meadowlark begins singing and the earth reveals beauties beyond counting. This is the land which gave the Navajo the lovely words to a prayer, "In beauty may I walk . . . In beauty may my walk begin, in beauty may my walk be finished". As I walked, the wildflowers were beginning to bloom and the land hinted a fragrance of honey in its yellow carpets.

On 5th April, I passed through the oldest mining spot in North America. Mined for turquoise by Indians in pre-historic times, Old Hachita is now the dying remains of its former self. A decaying cabin, a crumbling mine, and rusting relics scattered here and there are the only markers. There is no monument, no park.

Most of the land on the Divide in New Mexico is private property. In asking permission to camp, I always promised three things: no campfires, no firearms, and no camping near stock watering spots. This policy persuaded the cautious ranchers to grant permission.

During the hike, I crossed several big ranches — among them the Diamond A and the Gray Cattle Company. The McDonalds and McCauleys, the Woods and Towners, and

many other ranch families were models of the famed south-
western hospitality. It seems to me that in New Mexico, the
people and the land have become one — more than any other
place I've been. For better or worse, the story of the
Continental Divide, and its people, are inextricably
intertwined. There were the Fosters in Piños Altos, whose
museum is replete with the names of people like Mangas
Colorado, Cochise, and Judge Roy Bean. The Boltons of Pie
Town and the Howells of Winston were generous in offering
assistance and recounting the local history.

Crossing the old Butterfield Stage route near Soldier's
Farewell Hill, I went north up Burro Cienega Canyonland on
to Piños Altos. To this point, I had travelled over 180 miles,
walking mostly along small ranch roads close to the Divide or
cross-country. Above Piños Altos, on Black Mountain, I
reached the southern terminus of what the Forest Service calls
'The Continental Divide Trail'. I continued past the 'Twin
Sisters' and headed down the lovely canyon made by Allie
Creek. On 14th April, I hiked into Thunderbird Campground
near the Mimbres River for supplies.

As I headed for the big peaks of the lovely Black Range, I
crossed and recrossed the twisting Mimbres River a hundred
times or more. I spent five days in the Black Range on snow-
shoes — five marvellous days following a wild turkey's tracks
and waking on the 19th to his calls. For 30 minutes that
morning I was treated to a beautiful, magical dance. With a
display of his tail fan, his wing tips spreading downward, the
male turkey strutted back and forth around the female, his
small feet shuffling and stamping to an inner music.

After picking up supplies at the Beaverhead Ranger
Station, I headed north-west out of the Gila National Forest
skirting the Plains of San Augustin. I camped at Dutchman
Springs on 28th April, then went over John Kerr Peak and
turned toward Mangas Mountain. Most of this travel was
cross-country.

On a long backpack trip, a feeling of belonging, a spiritual
kinship, begins to develop. The closer I came to the Ramah-
Navajo Reservation, the richer this feeling became. I truly
believe there come moments when there is dialogue with

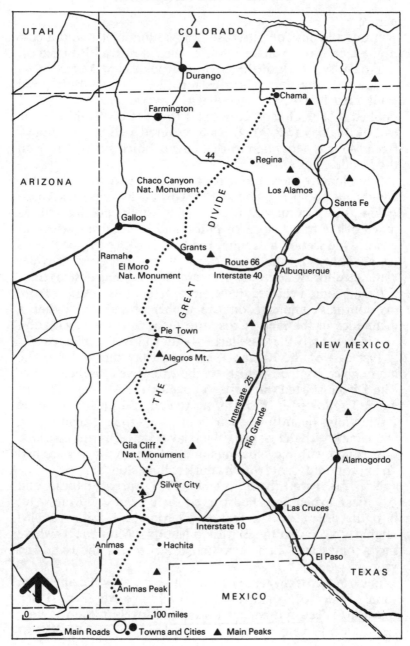

UTAH

COLORADO

Durango

Chama

Farmington

44

Regina

Chaco Canyon
Nat. Monument

ARIZONA

DIVIDE

Los Alamos

Santa Fe

Gallop

Grants

Ramah
El Moro
Nat. Monument

Route 66
Interstate 40

Albuquerque

GREAT

NEW MEXICO

Pie Town

Alegros Mt.

Interstate 25

THE

Rio Grande

Gila Cliff
Nat. Monument

Alamogordo

Silver City

Las Cruces

Interstate 10

Animas

Hachita

El Paso

TEXAS

Animas Peak

MEXICO

0   100 miles

Main Roads   Towns and Cities   ▲ Main Peaks

nature.

Along the base of Little Alegro Mountain, I found a cow trail which was, without a doubt, the finest trail I'd been on in the entire length of the Divide through New Mexico. (No criticism of the Forest Service intended; but the only good trails they had were covered with several feet of snow.) I dubbed it 'The Great Continental Divide Cow Trail'. By the end of this day (2nd May) I had covered well over 30 miles, from Mangas Mountain to Pie Town, which sits squarely on the Divide.

Occasionally there was a road which ran very close to the Divide. State 36-117 above Pie Town was one such road. Hiking this section was a distressing experience for me, as much of the forest cover of piñon and juniper was being cut down. One section at a time, the land is being stripped of its trees. There, in the mountains along the Great Divide, watershed for two oceans, the watershed is being destroyed.

On 6th June I entered the Ramah Reservation. A note from my journal comments on the timber situation: "What a difference in the land! Cross the fence into the reservation and immediately there are large stands of lovely ponderosa."

Just east of the Ramah Reservation lay the *Malpais,* the name given by the Spanish to the extensive lava beds here. The Divide skirted the western edge of the Malpais. On 7th June, I followed it, discovering the rugged lava flow to be fascinating. Beautiful aspen contrasted their fragility and white bark with the jagged, black lava. Barrel cactus splashed the ground with red blossoms and the afternoon sky seemed an appropriate escort with its dark rolling clouds.

Not far from there, members of early Spanish and American expeditions had carved their names and messages into the great rock known as El Morro. I followed NM Highway 53 to visit the El Morro National Monument, where the Acomas and Zuni once had travelled for thousands of years.

Back on the trail, just north of the Ice Caves, I came upon some of the most beautiful meadows I have ever seen. Aspen trees three feet in diameter dotted the lovely meadows near Oso Ridge. I spent several days there lounging in the tall grass and drinking.

Shortly after I left the meadows, I crossed US Highway 66. From this point, the land was strewn with mesas. In the flat lands one could see the red cliffs looming on the horizon for many miles; then, suddenly, one would be on the ledge of a large cliff. From Hosta Butte, I hiked eastward for a full day. Then the Divide swung north toward Hospah, a small Navajo centre, and northeast to the huge Chaco Mesa, which I reached on 20th June. Not far from the mesa, which is famous for its many ancient Indian dwelling sites, I detoured to meet Blue and to see Chaco Canyon National Monument.

Back on the trail, I went up a canyon east of the Divide and made camp near a small juniper. As usual in rainy weather, the tent was up first. I had finished with the flysheet and had two rocks for anchors on it. My pack was in the way, so I moved it to the side of the tent, a few inches from the side stakes I had set earlier. In spine tingling rasps, a small rattler let me know it had had enough! It coiled back to strike; but I had already let go of the pack and backed away. It started to crawl toward the tent and I killed it with one of the rocks.

For days that incident was to haunt me. The snake had been there all the time. I had been on that side of the tent much of the time. He could have struck me many times but he never made an attempt. Yet, when *he* let me know he was there, my first response was to kill him. There was certainly something very unequal in our attitudes.

At Star Lake, an area once used as a trading post, I spoke with a minister who was a climber. He was a bit surprised that I had climbed Chaco Mesa without ropes.

In this area the land was virtually without trees. The sun was hot and the wind dry. Waterholes were many miles apart. Again, most of my travel was by compass.

After three days, I was winding along small ridges and hills toward NM Highway 44. There were cyanide traps set out to kill coyotes in this area, but animals from crows to porcupines were lying dead near them. Across the highway I entered the Jicarilla Apache Reservation.

The forests on the reservation were so thick that hiking was often difficult. After following a ridge named 'The

Badlands', I crossed into a lovely valley, then climbed up the steep little ranch road west of Regina. It was 23rd June and Blue was waiting for me. It was time to take a break. I wanted to go to California for a few weeks to attend a month of seminars at Goddard College.

On 4th August I took up the trail again, following NM Highway 96 north for a few miles before turning toward the ridge. I was hiking while Blue drove along nearby roads or Jeep tracks, joining me at trail heads or where the trails crossed the roads. We camped on the Divide above Laguna Gurule. There had been many signs of elk and we saw our first one here. Lovely scarlet gilia were in bloom and most of the high country was covered with wildflowers.

Rains fell in the night and the caliche (red clay soil) was incredibly sticky on the boots and slippery to walk on. Blue found the terrain practically impossible to drive on. Near the Collins Ranch we noticed our first clear petroglyphs. During the rains, I tried pushing for Boulder Lake and twisted my ankle very badly. To rest the ankle, we stayed at the beautiful Stone Lake Lodge on 9th August.

At noon on 11th August, I hiked into Chama, the southern terminus of the Denver, Rio Grande and Western, one of the few narrow gauge railroad lines operating in the United States to still use the narrow gauge railroad tracks. Blue left me just before sundown. The baby's birth was close now and she would no longer be joining me along the trail.

Twelfth August was clear with no sign of rain. I got an early start up Highway 17. Several miles later, at Lobo Lodge, I turned north and followed the small valley of the Rio Chama. This was my last day in New Mexico. A female mule deer and a marmot bid me farewell as I crossed the line into Colorado shortly after 2.30 p.m.

I hiked nearly 800 miles of the Divide in this lovely state, covering every kind of terrain from Sonoran-Chihuahuan Desert to sub-Alpine, and I have not once seen another backpacker on the trail! What more could you want?

from BACKPACKER 34 *1979*

Five Times Lucky at Ben Alder

PHILIP GRIBBON

"Of all the remote unget-at-able mountains in Scotland,
Ben Alder ranks among the first." *W. H. Murray*

This gem, give or take a few inexactitudes, comes from W. H.
Murray's classic work, *Undiscovered Scotland*. I have begun,
with hindsight, to appreciate his title from a fresh viewpoint.

Ben Alder lies somewhere amidst the ranges that roll
through the hinterlands of the Central Highlands. Ben Alder
is "troublesome to reach". Choose a loch at any point of the
compass: Rannoch, Laggan, Ericht or Treig. Ah yes, it's
going to be a fair hike-in, but with some time, energy,
ambition, and luck it should be no problem to knock off this
lump, a big Munro, "so shapelessly graceful", ash-pale
under an Empty Quarter of the skies. Just the same as any
other Munro. Put it in your mind, and climb it. Nae bother!

Nonetheless Ben Alder threw an indefinable aura around
its flanks. There are tall tales about the mountain. People
who swam into the frigid winter waters, or strode on frost-
bitten feet under the moonlight. Ben Alder, a mystery
mountain, a wide land with a jinx.

In the beginning, it was a perfect weekend with the summer
sun spitting out of the sky, the gorse burnishing the slopes,
the trees splashed green with late spring fever, and the hills
a-beckoning. What could be more desirable than a voyage up
the entrenched Loch Ericht to the eastern spurs of Ben Alder,
camping by the canoe, and even climbing the hill, if the spirit
moved us. However it didn't matter how serious, or otherwise, were our intentions, because we got no further than a
wee glen in the Angus foothills, and that, my friend, is
nowhere near Ben Alder. We came over the Dundee hillroad
and had a brief glance over the Carse of Gowrie at the
Grampian hills spread out sharply across the blue horizon,
Ben-y-gloe, Vrackie, Schiehallion, and all that lot, with
somewhere Ben Alder, unseen but not unseeing, unknown
but not unknowing, its topmost tantalising tip thrust up

derisively on a western back-cloth. It was a revealing moment, but fraught with inanimate disintegration, because at the sight of our promised land the timing chain jumped joyfully off its sprocket, snarled a nest of links round the driveshaft, and in sheared delight demolished the car engine, once and for all.

Let's try again. Take him stealthily from the back, with gay abandon. We crammed into a tent on the first winter snows beside the concrete bridge near the outlet from Loch Laggan. That's miles away to the north of Ben Alder. Sure, I know that. Now. We were to travel light, to storm over the intervening hills with minimum gear. Some friends agreed to carry our food in to the bothy; some friends could have found less devious means of getting some extra grub. We made such reasonable progress towards the bealach that the dynamic hillbashers decided to take in a Munro. Soon over the bealach we were floundering in a desert of powder snow with all the lee slopes transformed to fluffed meringue pies. The woman was sinking up to her oxters; I was delving even deeper. We hit the stalker's road with relief, and saw the last roseate tinges on the dusken clouds at the same time as we saw the bothy. She thought we had made it, but I knew it was the wrong bothy. Somewhere beyond the sinuous spines of the ridges, further even than the ashen headwalls of the corries, some friends would be sitting comfortably in the other bothy, now lost for the night in a distant valley. Ben Alder had blocked us from our food. Still, Culra Bothy accepted us thankfully: we had half a tart and some coffee and there was a wee rodent-ravished clump of solidified sugar on the shelf. We had been on the beds for hours when the straggling crawlers walked through the door: the hill had bashed them. On the morrow I got Geal Charn and Creag Pitridh on the scorecard; perhaps, it was the inspirational brilliance of the successive waves of white hills a-sparkle in a sun-shimmering plaster of snow, with ne'er an icy twist of chill breath to cut the still air, or perhaps, I was hunger-struck, daft, and deranged; it could have been the sun. . . .

All right, let's make a full frontal approach, and to hell with the ghosts. This time Benalder Cottage would be the right bothy, the spirits would ensure we got up at the strike of dawn.

However, we arrived too late to walk in from the hydro-dam at the southern end of Loch Ericht. We had to use our tents. They were fully aerated, wind-billowed fridges, wistfully sucking in the snow; encouraging shivering submersion in the bags and discouraging disgorgement to face the winter shroud slipped across the pale hill shoulders. Bothy-bound, with the Colonel in his canoe weaving an erratic pewter-boned wake across the loch, and with the wandering walkers trudging disconsolately around the shoreline indentations, we approached the mists on Ben Alder. A curtain of drifting snow, first to mottle, then to scour, came soft-fingering through the desolation, plastering the pines, huddling the deer, burying our footsteps with silent whispers. We found the cottage in the dusk, our firewood in the dark. Our shadows hung flickering on the walls; we basked in the warmth, our thoughts roaming far and wide, no thought for the coming unknown.

Cur. .rumble! Its sound was shattering and overwhelming in the deep intangible darkness of a claustrophobically confined space. It was inexplicable, indefinable, all-pervading, nebulous and unnerving. The vibrations ran to their decay out of the floorboards, each to match the awesome tremors of our unmitigated shock. Gone the quiet patterns of half-somnambulance, the unconscious beat of tired bodies, to be overtaken by stifled gasps, throbbing hearts, listening, waiting, wondering. Everyone suspended in disbelief, burrowing deeper to limbo within their bags, incommunicado. The tense minutes flew; the slightest creak in the rafters, a dying quiver in the fire embers, and the primitive alert signals flashed up out of our subconscious. Cluny MacPherson perched in his cage, McCook at the front door, I fitfully dozed into a lifeless dawn, awakening to a mouthful of her long silken locks, and the blown snowflakes splattering on the window panes. We never broached our reason for staying at Benalder Cottage: we knew that the highland plateau was blizzarded whiteout.

We gathered some deadwood under the swaying branches

of the larch trees. We were buffeted by the squalls marching down Uisge Alder. We toiled back to the cars. Oh yes, what about the poltergeist! Damn't, but hadn't the Colonel with his last indolent sleepy stretch mischievously tipped with his toes one of the unstable fireside boulder seats into a rocking, rattling spasm of damped oscillations that had shattered our slumbers? He was quite unrepentant. . . .

My lack of success was becoming noticeable. We tried the same approach in early summer, but we couldn't even get through the locked gate beside Loch Rannoch. She appreciated her afternoon tea, with the rain lashing solidly across the Moor, and a shadowy electronic snowstorm bringing a glorious day on the turf at Hampden Park. We came ashore on an island paradise in the heart of the wilderness, the sunset a-glimmering through the night over the ringing hills, the air scented with bluebell, birch and burning bracken. We steamed beside the fire, while herons slowly wheeled over the waters. Ben Alder was lost in the quiet reflections dancing off the dappled surface of the loch.

The mountain of the rocks and the waters was acting with a coy and hesitant reticence. The game had gone on too long. Who wins?

The gates were open, Ben Alder was beckoning in the sunshine. We were sharing our fortune. We walked awash through the crunching sands, following the Culra river to the bothy. We were alone, with the mountain waiting.

Rain Belts, ploughing in quick succession down the glen, raced each other on their way. Each northern ridge presented its undoubted charms for our choice and glistened silver-gilt in the late summer sun. The swollen streams, free in their turmoil, rushed from the Bealach Dubh, tumbling below the purple sheen of the ling fields, and the unchastened deer browsed among the blaeberries. We ambled, under the curses of the blackbirds, over the rocky outcrops up the Long Leachas ridge to the bleak undulations of the high plateau; we skirted the lips of Garracoires; we reached the summit of Ben Alder in the mist. Done! She had enjoyed our wee dander. . . .

I had enjoyed the knowledge of the days of failure. I had

had to anticipate the inevitable moment of a so-called success. The Ben Alder saga appears to be complete. I harbour still a few regrets. . . .

from THE SCOTTISH MOUNTAINEERING CLUB
JOURNAL *1976*

Mountain Dawn

SETON GORDON

The beauty of sunrise is appreciated the more when it is seen at the end of a long walk, arduous and sometimes wearisome, across moors and hill slopes during the shadowy hours of a Hedridean summer night. That night, sunset behind the hills of Harris had been at 10.20 p.m., visibility had been good and it seemed that a clear sunrise might follow. Half an hour before midnight, Morag, the Cairn terrier, and I, left our home in the north of Skye. Had Morag known that our destination was the small cairn on Meall na Suireanach above the Quirang, at 1,779ft. above sea level, she might have shown less enthusiasm for a night walk. Of the thousands of visitors who have climbed to the Quirang, few have stood on the hilltop close to and almost immediately above it, for the rocky face is inaccessible and a long detour is necessary in order to reach the cairn. The night was warm after a day of sunshine when a shade temperature of 75°F (the highest reading for two years) was recorded. Across the Minch came the friendly flashes, in threes, from the lighthouse on Glas Eilean on the island of Scalpay near the Harris coast. The scent of a myriad early July flowers lay above the sun-warmed moor: large white moths drifted past, seeking nectar from these flowers. The crofters of Skye believe in burning the midnight oil although, now that electricity is supplied them, oil is almost a thing of the past. Half an hour after midnight I could see in the distance a number of houses still brightly lighted. The Hebrides lie so far west that even by Greenwich Time the clock is half an hour ahead of the sun. During Summer Time, the clock is an hour and a half ahead of the Small sun — the Islesman calls it an hour and a half 'fast'.

At 1 a.m. therefore, twilight was still deepening. We were then approaching the shore of dark Loch Sneosdal from which the crags of Creag Sneosdal rise almost 1,000ft. On this precipice there is a geological 'fault' which appears like a great wall, at least 20ft. high, built almost vertically up the cliff. Its local name is Garadh na Feinne, the Fingalians' Wall. When an old lady of the district was asked what reason those half-mythical Celtic warriors, the Fingalians, had for building that great wall she replied, "Maybe they had nothing better tc do". It is said that these heroes were so tall that they were able, as they sat at the top of the precipice, to cool their feet in the waters of Loch Sneosdal. There is a strange atmosphere in the neighbourhood of this loch. Here, it is said, the dreaded *each uisge* or water horse has his home and there is a pass here known as Bealach na Beiste, Pass of the Beast or Monster. Had we been at home Morag would have been sound asleep at this hour, but as she sat beside me on the shore of the loch she would not rest, but started often to her feet, ears cocked, as she gazed intently through the dusk. The moon, past the full, was obscured by clouds that drifted past slowly from the south. As, large and egg-shaped, the moon showed herself for a moment, her pale light mingled with the afterglow on the far northern horizon, whence came a single stab of white light from the lighthouse on Tiumpan Head close to Stornoway and at least 40 miles distant. Later the clouds dissolved and I found that the dazzle from the low, unclouded moon made walking more difficult. The moon, a few of the brighter planets and stars, and the afterglow creeping imperceptibly northward produced a soft twilight through which the hills of the Outer Hebrides could be seen rising faintly on the horizon. Dawn was breaking as I reached the watershed and came in sight of the island of South Rona and the powerful flashes from its lighthouse. There was no hint of chill in the midsummer dawn. Faint currents of wind, fragrant with the perfume of hill flowers and plants drifted across from the south. At 3.45 a.m. a meadow pipit rose into the air and flew waywardly higher and higher in the direction of the waning moon until lost to view. The dawn, as I could see was strengthening behind the hill top, but there was no hint of sunrise from the south slopes. It was therefore a surprise when I reached the small cairn to find that I was only just in time for sunrise. On the far north-east horizon rose the hills of the Reay Forest. One of them, Farraval, 80 miles distant, a hill usually of no great distinction, was now dark and imposing against a red, glowing sky, the time being just 4.16 a.m. As I sat and watched this scene of changing beauty, I noticed that Morag, now beyond the influence of the haunted loch, had curled herself in a tight ball and was fast asleep. A golden plover arrived and stood only a few feet from me, uttering his mournful flute-like whistle. The far north-east horizon brightened and at 4.26 a.m. the sun's orb, enormous and with tenuous clouds streaked across his red disc, climbed very slowly above the horizon and seemed to fill the strath of the far distant Dionard River, 80 miles away. The sun had travelled far since, six hours before, he had dipped behind the summit ridge of Clisham in Harris, and his coming signalled a new day of warmth and sunshine. When next I noted the hour of the fairy scene the time was 4.39 a.m. and the sun was poised above the long hill of Foinne Bheinn, distant from Farraval, as the eagle flies, some five miles, and now threw a golden pathway on the sleeping, almost windless, ocean. Farraval, the sun's glow no longer behind it, now lost its glory and was almost invisible in the haze of distance. The pillar of reflected sunfire on the sea became more glowing, and gained in distinction when the sun for a few seconds was hidden by a distant cloud. By 5 a.m. the hills of the Reay Forest had become dim in haze but the sea near Rudha Reidh, a promontory of Wester Ross, was afire in the sun's rays and a dark red glow burned on the cliffs of Beinn Eadarra of Skye. Before sunrise Trodday and the Shiant Isles had been dark and very clear: now, although the sun shone on them, they were less distinct and the magic of the sunrise hour had faded from the scene.

It is a peculiarity of the common ling or heather that it

flowers earlier on hill tops than at lower levels, and well-formed pink buds were showing on the hilltop where I had seen sunrise that early morning in July while 1,500ft. below, on the low moors, not a bud showed.

Larks were joyously soaring and cheerful families of wheatears were passed during the descent that morning: it was 7 a.m. when I again approached Loch Sneosdal and rested awhile on its shore. The loch was no longer gloomy and mysterious and the morning sun shone brightly on the water and on the high rocks, which are in sun only in the early morning. Small trout were rising to a hatch of fly, or were sunning themselves in the shallows. A sandpiper flew out over the loch, the waters of which, near the far shore, were still opaque from a cloudburst towards the end of June. Before that cloudburst the Isle of Skye had been for many days an isle of sunshine. The rain, that evening of 23rd June, gradually became of tropical violence. Hill torrents appeared where none had been known before. Darkness descended before sunset and in three hours the rain gauge recorded a fall of two and a half inches. Early next morning the sun was shining on hill and sea. The grassy face of Creag Sneosdal was changed in a remarkable manner. Here two great scars showed where thousands of tons of rocks, earth and grass had slipped like an avalanche down the hill face. They will remain for many years, perhaps for centuries, to commemorate that tremendous rainfall on 23rd June 1955.

A heat wave in early June is marred by neither of those two Highland pests, the midge and the cleg. A hot spell in early July encourages them both. The cleg or gadfly gives the walker, or the worker in the field, no peace, and its bite is more formidable than that of the midge. Fortunately it is not wily like the mosquito, and should a first attempt to slay it fail, it returns at once, and is usually liquidated at the second attempt. The name cleg is an unusual one; I used to think it was Scottish until I heard it was used in Norway. It may, like so many Scottish place-names, be a relic of the Norse occupation of the Hebrides.

The small cairn from which I had seen sunrise is named Carn Mhic an t-Sagairt (Cairn of the Priest's Son). On my way across the common grazing at the foot of the hill I passed near Buaile an t-Sagairt (Sheepfold of the Priest), and Clach an t-Sagairt (Stone of the Priest). It would seem that, like the cairn on the hilltop, these names commemorate a priest of olden times. Saint Maolrubha was known as the Red Priest of Applecross and he was often in Skye; the names may commemorate him, or one of his followers.

Earlier in this essay I have mentioned the sunrise burning dull red on the high rocks of Beinn Eadarra. It was some months later in the year when a friend and I, this time accompanied by Dileas the collie and Morag, climbed the hill, which is just 2,000ft. October gave summer warmth that year. Although the heather was over, hill violets were flowering out of season. The grass was green beside a clear stream where stand the foundations of summer shielings more than 100 years old. The people of the glen lived in these shielings during the summer months, taking with them their stock in order that the grass on their small fields might recover from the close grazing of the winter months. These small ruins tell of a way of life that will return no more. High above these shielings, on stony ground almost 2,000ft. above sea level, were a number of large wheatears, pursuing insects with quick, fluttering flights, or playfully chasing one another. These were almost certainly Greenland wheatears, held up by the south wind after a hard oversea migration, and finding a plentiful supply of food and unexpected warmth. Near the hilltop, where black-faced sheep had cropped the grass close as a lawn, rosettes of cyphel were green. The cyphel *(Arenaria)* has very small green-tinted flowers without petals. Even on this October day flowers were on the green cushions, close to the ground to withstand the gales at this height. A raven, sailing high over its mountain territory, turned joyfully on its back, then closed its dark wings and dropped like a stone behind the east-facing precipice. A few minutes later excited croakings were heard and we saw a thrilling sight for bird-lovers. Close overhead a golden eagle appeared, the raven, seeming no larger than a blackbird by comparison, in hot pursuit. Both birds were heading into the strong breeze and the eagle was driving himself forward by powerful thrusts of his strong, broad wings. In less than half a minute raven and eagle disappeared from sight behind the line of cliffs; shortly afterwards the raven returned, to sail backwards and forwards above its territory as before.

Five minutes' walk from the summit cairn is a pass which leads east through the cliffs which form the eastern face of Beinn Eadarra. Its name is Bealach a' Mhorgainn and it is famed as the haunt of Colann gun Cheann, the Headless Spectre, in whose memory a bagpipe tune was composed. The history of the Headless Spectre began centuries ago when he terrorised the district of Morar. MacLeod of Raasay was on a visit to MacDonald of Morar and offered to rid the district of the pest. On the Straight Mile, between Morar and Arisaig, he met the spectre at midnight and, after a hard struggle, got the better of him. Tucking the spectre under his arm, he told him that he would carry him to the laird's house in order to inspect him by candlelight. The ghost, well aware that this would be fatal to him, a spectre, begged his captor to release him, promising that he would obey any order he might be given. MacLeod agreed, and the spectre swore he would leave the district for ever and would flit across the sea to Beinn Eadarra in Skye and would make his home there. He now lives on this bleak pass, 70 miles from his former home.

Besides Bealach a' Mhorgainn there are two other hill passes within a couple of miles of the summit of Beinn Eadarra. One of them is Bealach Uig, the other is Bealach nan Coiseachan, Pass of the Walkers. Before roads were constructed in Skye, people made frequent use of these passes in their daily life. Bealach Uig has a small moss-grown cairn to mark it at the watershed, where it drops down a steep grassy slope eastward. In mist, or driving snow, the cairn would have been a guide to those who crossed here. On some of the Skye passes are small cairns to the memory of those who lost their lives while crossing them. These passes were also used in olden days by the men who went from the west of Skye to the herring fishing on the east coast of Scotland. There was no thumbing of a lift in those days, nor were there sympathetic motorists to supply free transport.

from HIGHLAND DAYS *1963*

Cape Cod – An Unimagined Frontier

JOHN HAY

One afternoon in the middle of June I set off from Race Point at Provincetown, carrying a pack and sleeping bag, with Nauset Light Beach in Eastham, 25 miles away, as my destination, and my purpose simply to be on the beach, to see it and feel it for whatever it turned out to be, since most of my previous visits had been of the sporadic hop, skip, and jump kind to which our automotivated lives seem to lead us.

The summer turmoil was not yet in full voice but the barkers were there on behalf of beach-buggy tours over the dunes, and a sight-seeing plane flew by; cars drew up and droned away, and families staggered up from the beach with their load of towels, shoes, bags, or portable radios. The beach did not contain quite the great wealth of paper, cans, bottles, and general garbage that it would later on, in July and August, but one of the first things to catch my eye as I lunged down on to the sands were an electric-light bulb floating in the water, a can of shaving soap, the remains of a rubber doll, and a great scattering of sliced onions — probably thrown off a fishing boat.

The air was dancing with heat. The sun seemed to have the power to glare through all things. With the exception of a camper's tent on the upper part of the beach, and a few isolated gray shacks perched on dune tops behind it, there was nothing ahead but the wide belt of sand curving around one unseen corner after another with the flat easing and stretching sea beside me. Two boys waved to me from where they were perched high up on a dune, and I waved back.

Then I heard an insistent, protesting bird note behind me, and a piping plover flew past. It was very pale, and sand coloured, being a wild personification of the place it lived in. It suddenly volplaned down the slope of the beach ahead of me, fluttering, half disappearing in holes made by human feet, side-winged, edged away, still fluttering, in the direction of the shore line, and when it reached the water, satisfied, evidently, that it had led me far enough, it flew back. These birds nest on the beach above the high-tide line, and like a number of other species, try to lead intruders away when they come too close to their eggs and young.

With high, grating cries, terns flew over the beach and low over the water, occasionally plummeting in after fish. Among the larger species, principally common terns, there were some least terns — a tiny, dainty version of the 'sea swallow', chasing each other back and forth. They have the graceful, sharply defined bodies and deep wingbeat of the other terns, but in their littleness and excitability they seem to show a kind of baby anger.

Also there were tree swallows gathering and perching on the hot, glittering sand, and on smooth gray driftwood just below the dunes. It was a band of them, adults, and young hatched during the early spring, chittering and shining with their brilliant blue-green backs and white bellies.

It seemed to me that out of these birds — my unwilling or indifferent companions — came a protest, the protest of a desert in its beauty, an ancient sea land claiming its rarity, with these rare inhabitants, each with its definition and assertion, each having the colour and precision of life and place, out of an unknown depth of devising.

Behind the beach at Provincetown and Truro are eight square miles of dune, making a great series of dips and pockets, innumerable smooth scourings, hollows within wide hollows. Standing below their rims are hills, mounds, and cones, chiselled by the wind, sometimes flattened on the top like mesas. These dunes give an effect of motion, rolling, dipping, roving, dropping down and curving up like sea surfaces offshore. When I climbed the bank to see them I heard the clear, accomplished notes of a song sparrow. There were banks of rugosa roses in bloom, with white or pink flowers sending off a lovely scent, and the dunes were patched with the new green of beach grass, bay-berry, and beach plum, many of the shrubs looking clipped and rounded, held down by wind and salt spray. The purple and pink flowers of the beach pea, with purselike petals, were in bloom too, contrasting with dusty miller with leaf surfaces like felt, a soft, clear grayish-green. Down at the bottom of the hollows the light and wind catching heads of bunch grass, pinkish and brown, waved continually; and the open sandy slopes were swept as by a free hand with curving lines and striations.

A mile or so at sea, over the serene flatness of the waters, a fishing boat moved very slowly by. I started down the beach again, following another swallow that was twisting and dipping in leafy flight along the upper edge of the beach. On the tide line slippery green sea lettuce began to glimmer as if it had an inner fire, reflecting the evening sun. I stopped somewhere a mile or two north of Highland Light in Truro, built a small fire of driftwood to heat up a can of food, and watched a bar appearing above the water as the tide ebbed. Low white waves conflicted and ran across a dome of sand, occasionally bursting up like hidden geysers.

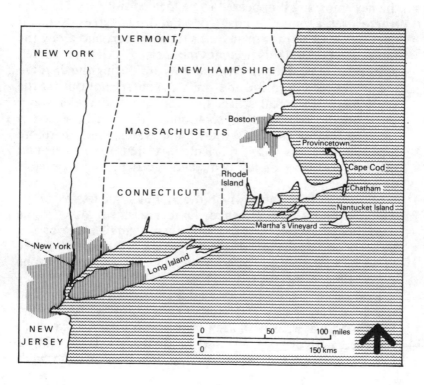

The terns were still crying and diving as the sun's metal light, slanting along the shore, began to turn a soft yellow, to spread and bloom. They hurried back and forth, as if to make use of the time left them, and fell sharply like stones into the shimmering road of light that led across the water.

Where I live on the lower Cape, that part of it which lies between the Cape Cod canal and Orleans, the land heads out directly to the sea, toward the east from the continental west. Cape Cod Bay lies to the north and Nantucket Sound to the south. The arm of the upper Cape turns in the Orleans area and heads up on a north-south axis, the head of it, or hand if you like, curving around so that the sandy barrens in the Provincetown area are oriented in an east to west direction again. I am used to looking toward Kansas to see the setting sun, and from the curving shore line at Truro I had the illusion that it was setting in the north and that when it rose the next morning it appeared to be located not very far from where it set, a matter of ninety or a hundred degrees. In fact it does set closer to the north at this time of year, and along the flat ocean horizon this becomes more clear to the eye, as well as its relative position at dawn and its arc during the day. On the open beach in spring and summer you are not only at the sun's mercy in a real sense, but you are also under wider skies. In the comparative isolation of the beach, which is convex, slanting steeply toward the water, and therefore hides its distances, I felt reoriented, turned out and around through no effort of my own, and faced in many possible directions.

Shortly before sundown a beach buggy, curtains at its windows and a dory attached, lumbered slowly down some preordained ruts in the sand, and then a smaller one passed by at the top of the low dunes behind me. Fishing poles were slung along the outside of both machines. It was getting to be a good time to cast for striped bass.

I sat on the sands and listened to the sonorous heave and splash of low waves. The sun, like a colossal red balloon filled with water, was sinking in to the horizon. It swelled, flattened and disappeared with a final rapidity, leaving a foaming, fiery band behind it. I suddenly heard the wild, trembling cry of a loon behind me, and then saw it fly over, heading north. The wind grew cool, after a hot day when the light shone on metallic, glittering slow waters, and sharp, pointed beach grasses clicked together, while I watched the darkness falling around me.

A small seaplane flew by at low altitude, parallel to the shore. A sliver of a moon appeared and then a star; and then single lights began to shine on the horizon, while from the direction of Highland Light an arm of light shot up and swung around. A fishing boat passed slowly by with a light at its masthead and two (port and starboard) at its stern. A few night-flying moths fluttered near me. The sky began to be massive with its stars. I thought of night's legitimacies now appearing, the natural claim of all these single lights on darkness, and then, making my bed in a hollow just above the beach, I lowered down into infinity, waking up at about one o'clock in the morning to the sound of shouting, a strange direct interruption to the night. It was the loud implacable voice of the human animal, something very wild in itself, filling the emptiness.

"For Chrissake bring her higher up! I can't have her dig in that way." The tide had come in and someone was having trouble manoeuvering his beach buggy along the thin strip of sand now available.

The light of dawn opened my eyes again before the sun showed red on the horizon, and I first saw the tiny drops of dew on tips and stems of beach grass that surrounded me. A sparrow sang, and then, somewhere behind the dunes, a prairie warbler with sweet notes on an ascending scale.

When I started walking again I caught sight of a young fox. Its fur was still soft and woolly and its gait had a cub's limpness where it moved along the upper edge of the beach. I wished the young one well, though I suspected it might have an uncomfortable life. In spite of an excessive population of rabbits, and their role in keeping it down, foxes have not been too highly regarded on the Cape. In recent years they seem to have been a skinny and somewhat dilapidated bunch for the most part, suffering from parasitic skin diseases, and ticks in season. I once saw a fox out on an asphalt road sliding along on his chin and side, shoving and dragging himself in such a frantic way that I began to feel very itchy myself. I have heard them referred to in scornful way as 'spoilers', fond of scavaging and rolling in dead meat. In other words, they are smelly, diseased and, to add another epithet 'tricky', not to be trusted.

Yet this cub exploring an early morning on the sands had a future, however limited, and I remembered the lively trot of foxes when they are in good health, and their intelligence and curiosity, and simply their right to whatever special joys they might inherit.

I carried a pair of field glasses with me, along with the somewhat thoughtlessly assembled equipment I wore on my back, which seemed increasingly heavy as time went on. When not too conscious of my burden I would use the glasses to bring an inland or offshore bird closer to me. I noticed five eider ducks across the troughs of the waves, a remnant of the thousands that winter off the Cape along with such other sea birds as brant, Canada geese, scoters, mergansers, old squaws, and various members of the auk family. I passed a dead gannet lying on the sand. It had been badly oiled, reminding me of the hazards of jettisoned tanker or freighter oil to all these water birds which land on the sea to rest or feed.

There were a number of kingbirds on the dune rims, and they kept dropping down over the beach in their special way, to hover with fast wingbeat and flutter after flying insects. I heard the grating call of redwings, indicating marshy areas inland of the beach, but the cliffs above began to increase until they were 100 to 150ft. high or more, and the sun was so fierce that I had little interest in trying to scale them to see what was on the other side.

I plodded on, noticing very little after a while, my attention blunted, reduced to seeing that one foot got in front of the other. The more level upper parts of the beach provided fairly good walking, but the sand was soft, and to relieve my aching muscles, I would then angle down to the water's edge where it was firmer, and there I was obliged to walk with one leg below the other because of the inclination of the beach. So I would return to the upper beach again and push ahead. I walked on, very hot and slow, seeing no one for miles until I came up to a group of bathers below a road and parking lot giving access to the beach, of the kind that are scattered along its reaches; and there I refilled my canteen at a cottage and went on.

I found that if I rested too long during this hike I had little desire to go on again, so I confined myself to an army 'break' of ten minutes every hour. Renewed walking unlimbered me a little and the wind off the water cooled my sweating skin. I listened to the sound of the waves. In addition to their rhythmic plunge and splash, their breathing, they clashed occasionally with a sound like the breaking of heavy glass, the falling of timber, or a load of bricks.

I passed what was left of two shipwrecks during the day, a reminder of the dangers that still face ships along this coast with its fogs, its shifting winds, its storms, the hidden, treacherous offshore bars. The sands often reveal the timbers of old ships. One day their ribs, sodden and dark, barnacle encrusted, may reach up out of oblivion, and not long after that the water buries them under tons of sand. From them a local history calls out for recognition. Thousands of ships over three centuries wrecked on shoals, engulfed by violent seas, men with the dark of doom in them, to drown or to survive, and only a few timbers left to declare the ultimate dangers and their terror.

I was not in Death Valley, or on a raft at sea. My walk was not unusually long, and I could leave the beach if I had to, but the enormity of the area filled me more and more. It had so much in it that was without recourse. Its emptiness, the great tidal range beyond it and through it, the raw heartbeat of the waves, the implacable sun, established the kind of isolation and helplessness in me which the commerce and community of our lives tries so hard to disguise. Even the birds, I began to think, were more secure than I. They had their strong bright threads of cognisance to the areas they came to, the water, the sands, the marsh. They were fixed in entity and grace, eating what was theirs by evolution to be eaten, using land and air in the ways that had come to them, knowing this place and all places like it in terms of its bounds and boundlessness, meeting its naked eye in the ways they had been sent to do.

I started off in the morning admiring the brilliance of the sun, the small shadows from the dunes and across the beach, through driftwood, isolated beach plants and tidal wrack, with the wide flooding of light ahead and the variation in reflected light across the sea. I felt the sea moving quietly beside me. The waves heaved and sighed and spray was tossed lightly above the sand. Everything was continuous, untroubled, and deliberate; but as the day wore on the sun became my enemy, and I had very little rage or resource in me to fight it with. I was not fitted to environmental stability, like a bird, or fox or fish. I found myself in an area of whose reaches I had never been wholly aware, and in me there was no mastery. The sun was not only hostile. It was an ultimate, an impossibility; and the waters beside me began to deepen from their pleasant daytime sparkle and freshness into an incalculable realm which I had hardly entered. I was touching on an unimagined frontier.

I spent my second night on the beach a few miles from Nauset Light where I left it the following morning. It was in the South Wellfleet area, and as I started to sleep on the sand a little above the high-tide line, I remembered that this was about the same place where a fishing boat had been wrecked two years before and two men drowned. I had seen the boat, with its cargo of fish, and some of the men's clothing strewn along the shore and I had heard a little about the depths of their ordeal. The story haunted me; and then I began to feel that I might be caught by the tide while I was asleep. There was only about 12ft. between the bottom of a steep cliff and the high tide line. I would soon be lying on a narrow shelf at the sea's edge. So as the vague thought of being engulfed began to invade me, I took up my pack and sleeping bag again, retraced my steps down the beach, and found a way to the top of the cliff, where I spent the night in another hollow.

The light of dawn, lifting quietly out of the sea, flooding into the range of low-lying land, woke me up again, and it signalled to the birds, who started singing in all the thickets

and heath around me with a sweet, high, shrill intensity, a
kind of automatic worship; and after a while they quieted
down again.

Little dirt roads dropped back from headlands through
green slopes covered with bearberry and patches of yellow-
flowered Hudsonia, or 'poverty grass', and there were
hollows dipping back inland and woods of stunted pitch pine.
From the top of the cliff I watched the sun starting to send
light running across the blue table of the sea, making it glitter
and move. The intensity of light and heat began to grow
steadily as I walked down the beach again for the last stretch
toward Nauset.

The beach is not so very far from where I live, or for that
matter where anyone lives on the Cape. It is a few miles down
the road, beyond the trees; and yet when I came back from
my walk I felt as if I had been at enormous remove from my
surroundings, caught out where I might have feared to be.
The long line of sand and surf, the intensity of the sun, the
cover of stars had come close enough to put me in council
with that which had no answers. I was in awe of nature; and I
understood that the sun and sea could be our implacable
enemies. It was in this context that I saw our human world as
subject to a stature that it never made.

from THE GREAT BEACH *1980*

Two Dry Feet

DIANNE BULLARD

Memories of thick sea roke seen dimly in fading torchlight as
one drags one's feet onwards, so shattered that even upon
reaching the short stretch of road it is impossible to see where
the next road marker is, before heading resolutely yet further
into the moor. You think almost lovingly of the deep,
squelching, slippery, smelly bog which adds an almost
tangible aroma to your breeches after deep immersion, an
aroma that lingers.

There was a time hundreds of years ago when you did not have appalling blisters, when you could feel that you had nearly completed half the walk and yet still felt quite fresh and could look wonderingly at the three 'golf balls' on the distant horizon — but that was centuries ago, yet all part of the ambience of the walk.

What is it that drives people on despite the personal knowledge of diabolical Crossings of over 22 hours, of getting incredibly lost on Fylingdales Moor and then being assured by a local that you had just come down off 'Paradise Valley' — the stupidest name for the moor when you are so tired that you cannot see straight, and have a touch of the 'Frank Smythes', thinking there was a whole group of people walking behind you who you had to wait for! Impossible to give the answer; you either hate the place or it captures some part of your heart and imagination so that even if you haven't been near it for years the pull is still there. It's as if the fact of having made the Crossing a number of times and thus turned oneself into a witch renders the pull of the moor over-powering and you become unable to resist the call of the Dirge . . . only something went wrong this time and a Double Lyke Wake Walk was the only means of appeasing the gods of Urra Moor.

If you have had any kind of walk that went completely right from start to finish, there must be something about your lucky stars that is not in my experience at all — things seem to go wrong from the minor to the disastrous! This walk was no exception and proved far tougher than expected. The idea was to utilise the whole of the Summer Bank Holiday by travelling up to Yorkshire, having a night's sleep, and then setting off fresh the next morning, taking up to the permitted 48 hours for the Double Crossing (84 miles), and then sleeping it off before returning home. The gods of Urra Moor decreed otherwise.

After a hard week with my Guides at camp and a particularly busy last day to boot, I arrived at Coventry Station to be greeted by Mike Robertson with the news that as he only had two days free, we would have to start walking immediately upon arrival and would only have time for a transport meal. Thus there was no sleep, and we found Derek Dodd and Colin Bryan so well ensconced in their tents that we had a job waking them at 2 a.m. and they were both irrevocably determined not to move until a sensible time in the morning. Enviously, we left them to their slumbers.

It was damp but clear as we set off from the Beacon, trying not to go too fast — we kept telling ourselves "don't forget we're coming back as well". Eyes quickly acquired 'night vision' as we made our way along the path, with nothing to distract our attention except an occasional gleam of light from one of the offshore lighthouses. The miles seemed to revolve under our feet, and suddenly we were faced with a most incredible sight — the Warning Station at Fylingdales in all its night glory. So many lights after so much darkness was almost unbelievable, something out of a fairy tale, so that we found we were unable to stop looking at this sight and Lorelei-like it lured us on until we found ourselves going towards York Cross. The drudgery of having to retrace our footsteps in pitch darkness was very trying, particularly as we had lost our night vision and were condemned to stumbling over rocks, bracken, heather, and into streams.

Nevertheless it was light by the time we reached Eller Beck. Normally this is a good stopping place, with a quarter of the route completed, but we stopped only briefly as our resting place would be the stepping stones by Wheeldale Lodge. Spurred on over Simon Howe by the thought of a rest, we reached the river and settled down for a brew-up. I think we dozed off but it can't have been for long as the midges were so bad it was a relief to get going again.

It was now mid-morning and we began to meet people — at first the lone walker, then a couple, more couples and then numerous groups until the place seemed to be swarming with walkers. I remember one lengthy and interesting discussion about war and its consequences, so that the time passed quickly to Hamer (having passed the Blue Man i'the Moss ludicrously daubed with blue paint — utterly out of keeping with the surroundings). Our thoughts turned to Fryup Lane, our next stop. The next stretch of the walk was incredible as this section is *always* a trap for walkers, who cannot hope to escape from getting wet feet from the bogs. This time it was so dry it didn't seem true; you could just walk through the bogs dryshod!

When we reached the road the temptation to get going was too strong and we walked briskly past Fryup Lane and around the three miles of road to Margery Bradley, where we stopped to consider our progress. It was pleasant just sitting and looking across the moors, but we were going well and didn't want to have a brew-up until we were nearer Hasty Bank, so we didn't take advantage of the river running down to Esklets — a mistake we were to regret bitterly later.

The weather was ideal for walking, fine and crisp but with the sun occasionally coming through the clouds. At the end of the railway we tried to find water but the streams were dried up and the trickle remaining was so thick with brilliant green slime that we carried on. No matter how well you seem to be going, the railway section always takes its toll and makes you tired. This certainly was the case with us as we continued across Urra Moor and down, down into the valley

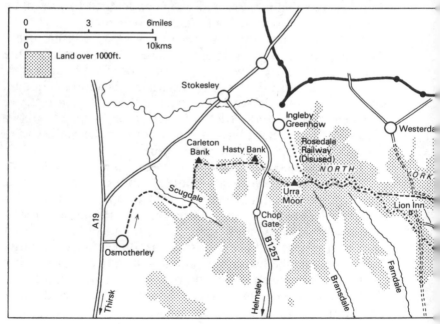

at Hasty Bank. Going up the other side seemed to suit Mike but I was going my usual snail's pace uphill. We were getting rather bothered by thirst as there was little left in our water bottles — we had not replenished them since Wheeldale.

Near the top of the Wainstones there should be a spring but it was dried up and some local people climbing there said that all the streams were dry except for the main rivers. This meant that the next water supply would not be met until we had passed Huthwaite Green, many miles ahead. We sat down to think — and awoke to find we had slept for half an hour.

Our problem was that we were getting dehydrated and in need of a good brew-up, starting with thick soup and following with numerous cups of tea. Mike's food needs and mine are totally opposed. He is like a horse that needs regular fodder, while I am more like a camel that fills up at the start and then keeps going. Mike's major problem, though, was one of time: he had to be back at work on Monday morning, so the time available to finish the walk was critical. Add to

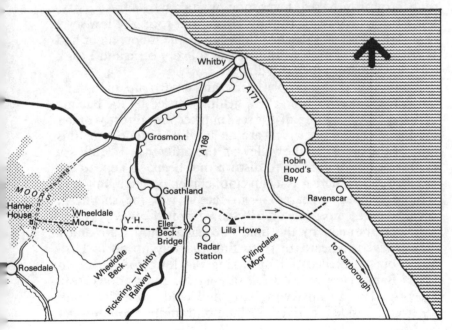

this the fact that we had slowed up over the last section, and the decision had to be made; Mike reluctantly headed for the valley and the route back towards the sea whilst I plodded on to Carlton Bank.

I hoped to reach the trig point above Osmotherley by 8 o'clock and as the evening was fine I quite enjoyed this part of the walk, particularly as the shop at Huthwaite Green was still open and I was able to buy some cans of lemonade, then fill up the water bottle in the river further on. It seemed much longer going round Coalmire before the final pull up to the trig point, but I got there at a quarter to eight.

The Return

Ahead lay the challenge — how would the return crossing go? The sheer mileage involved is obviously the main consideration, but the effects of fatigue, both physical and mental, would play their part. However, this was all interesting and probably the main reason for attempting a Double.

With these and other questions revolving around my head I set off towards the sea. I was soon overtaken by a fresh party, but I turned off at Huthwaite Green and took the low-level route. By the time I reached the edge of the moor, night had fallen and the moon was full. It was all very eerie and I took care not to disturb the farm dogs.

I didn't find the proper track and ended up ploughing through shoulder-high bracken, getting startled by the baa-ing of sheep and neighing of horses, but keeping directly under the telephone wires, which are an infallible guide over this part of the moor. In the valley on the other side I could see the farms but didn't like to disturb the sheep, so kept to the bracken. Soon there was a clip clop, clip clop, and a knight in shining armour appeared — in fact it was the shepherd, needless to say most welcome in showing me the way.

It was midnight by the time I reached Chop Gate and I didn't have the heart to try to find the way up on to Urra Moor but chickened out by taking the long road back to Hasty Bank. Here at last I felt safe again, and stopped for a brew-up. I woke up feeling stiff and cold, with the drink lukewarm beside me. Even pushing on rapidly I couldn't get

warm and the effort was rather pointless; I knew I had had it.
I gave up. I got out the bivvy sack and sleeping bag and my
last memories were of lights coming down Hasty Bank fast
and the mist descending even faster.

Some people going past at 6 a.m. woke me and I set off at
once, though not at all optimistic that I would have enough
time left. The early morning mist had cleared by the time I
caught the two walkers up, near the railway line. They said
that when they saw the bivvy sack they wondered if I was
alive, but then an eye opened as they walked past! It was very
interesting talking to them as it was their first Crossing and
the unknown loomed ahead of them. They seemed to be
making heavy weather towards Hamer, so I pushed on ahead.
I reached Hamer just as a kettle was boiling, and was given
tea by one of the support parties waiting there, a much
appreciated gesture.

The final 17 miles were a positive delight. It is difficult to
find superlatives, but never have I seen the moor in such good
condition, with mile upon mile of heather, all shades from
white to mauve to deep purple, as far as the eye could see; in
fact as far as the sea those many miles ahead. There was no-
one about and the stillness was profound. Even at the
stepping stones the riverside was empty, and the next lot of
people were at Eller Beck, where there were numerous cars
and an ice-cream van.

This made a delightful short break before heading on to
Fylingdales and through the heather to Lilla Cross. Here
there were a few people out to enjoy the moors and with no
intention of doing the Lyke Wake Walk, ever. There were no
problems of navigation now as the track is a major highway
despite the fact that one of the cairns pointing South had
been marked with orange markers whilst I wanted to continue
West; obviously there was a party wishing to take a different
route.

I stopped again in a sheltered spot at the top of the steep
rise from Jugger Beck, and then the Beacon was my final
aim. Going across Stony Marl Moor there was a dark spot in
the distance and another spot that kept moving about in a
different rhythm. This kept me puzzled for a long time until I

got nearer and saw it was a man with a dog. Then I reached the trig point and the Walk was over.

All that remained was to walk along the lane and into Ravenscar. It was more pleasant to use the verge as the road was unpleasantly hard on my feet, and I reached the café in about ten minutes. I signed off — Double Lyke Wake, 38¾ hours. Contented, I ordered a meal and in came Mike.

from THE LONG DISTANCE WALKERS' ASSOCIATION
NEWSLETTER *August 1975*

PART 4

Epic Trails

Man's appetite for challenge, for stretching himself to the limit both physically and mentally, seems to be undiminished in this technological age. Walkers still find new expeditions and push the horizons further; and probably will always go on doing so.

This selection of articles range in ambition from the editor's own 72-mile trek round the Lake District, to Sebastian Snow's attempt to become the first person to walk from Tierra del Fuego to Alaska.

The walks all include some element of competition, whether directed inwardly or against other people, and in mood they range from the mocking hilarity of Dick Sale's *Wet Welsh Three-Thousanders* to Michael Tobias's description of his untrammelled plunge into the Sinai Desert.

Reality Recrudescent

HAMISH BROWN

In the 1974 edition of *The Scottish Mountaineering Club Journal* I made a light-hearted appeal for a cleaner approach to the hills, little foreseeing that petrol prices would double, and strikes reduce the car-owner to a garage-groveller. We may, 'perforce, he'e to use Shanks' pony a bit mair'.

Nor did I then realise that I was already committed to this attempt on the 279 Munros, Ancient and Modern, in a single, car-less venture. It succeeded no doubt in desperation of the thought of what car-using weekend supporters might do if I weakened. The piston was held to my head.

So the mouse scuttled on among the mountains, the route on the map looking just like those labyrinthine tracks when the snow melts and the winter tunnels are laid bare on the hillsides.

'The sea is so large and my ship is so small' has its counterpart among the mountains. What a marvellously wholesome yet piquant landscape we have — a veritable geological curry: richly varied ingredients and spiced with the unexpected. In so many larger lands you can travel hundreds of miles, days on end, with very little scenic variation; here, in a step so to speak, you can swap Cairngorms for Cuillins, Schiehallion for Sheneval, Heasgarnaich for Hope (etcetera). They all have their fine points. Even the Monaidh Liath! Munro's Tables ensured more than he envisaged. If for no other reason than the satisfied feelings of a good meal, they are worth devouring: you will have relished a large portion both of meat and of the cream of the country.

Having had pupils from my old school up every Munro, ditto dog, ditto various other combinations, a new excuse was needed. (One does not just give up walking; the alternative). The incentive came. A year as an office-bound bureaucrat was driving me, in the words of a mountaineering Chancellor, bonkers.

O some grow old and dream no more
And some do dream by day, lad;
And some put feet upon their dream
And have a song to sing, lad.

That was pretty well the progression of it. The 'logistics' were quite complex but a grand antidote to boredom.

The data then; a sort of glorified Cousins *réchauffé*.

It always puzzled me why Sandy Cousins should have travelled north-south, ending in a city, albeit the fine one that is his home. My natural inclination was, and is, to head west and north, 'where all dreams lie'. Ben Hope *had* to be the finish. Given that, the route was a mere joining up of 279 dots to cover the ground as easily as possible. (It was 277 at the start but the new two were on a natural round anyway. Quick reference also set the mind at ease over Kitchy, the dog. "Done 'em", he smirked in self-indulgence and sank back into merited retirement.)

Planning such a route is another game for climbers to play on wet days. There is hardly a map of Scotland at home now which has not been covered with the doodles of tentative routes. The evolution of their convolutions went on for months. If wealthy, I'd offer a prize for improvements. Being lazy, it had to be as short as possible. Never have I worked so hard to be so lazy.

Setting up this trip proved every bit as complex as any to the Andes or Africa. Eating, sleeping and progression is the common element of any expedition, whether in a vertical or horizontal dimension. Some fools combine both.

This proved not far off the longest UK walk: 1,639 miles. Fred Wescott in 1966 walked from John o' Groats to Land's End *and back,* 1,760 miles, but presumably he was avoiding the vertical whereas over the 279 Munros and other worthy summits ('Tops' I never really recorded), 289 in all, I ran up 449,000ft. of ascent.

'Ran up' is perhaps the wrong term. It was invariably taken very slowly and steadily — so much so that on odd occasions I read a book on the way along or up. (Twice walking into gates thereby). It took a few days in the Cuillins immediately after the end (the joys of *rock* vertically) to regain the old speed. Quite a bit of blubber was lost and I've never felt so fit yet could not manage vast meals. Over-eating is a result of stress, of civilisation so called.

John Hinde was an enthusiast for long treks when at RAF Kinloss (now he just makes the poor *Captain Scott* trainees suffer) and Sandy Cousins' trip was also well known. Various others I found had not succeeded, and above all, in 1967 the Ripley brothers' attempt on the Munros had not come off. Various reports tell of diet troubles and so on. Presumably they did not know the ground so well either, as when they gave in — at 230 — they were heading for a greater mileage, footage and time.

So plans were made to ensure steady progress, with at least one day in seven off, food was carefully organised to give a balance of fresh, tinned and dehydrated, and I had the advantage of at least three previous ascents of all the Munros.

It took 22 maps (one inch) and eventually I had two notebooks with day stints outlined, plus probable days-off spots, often coinciding with hotel, hostel or such where clothes could be washed and a bit of hot water enjoyed. Telephones were marked too.

One of these notebooks was kept by my brother and his wife, David and Marina, in Dollar and planned telephone messages kept track of my progress. Failure to check in on the next schedule would start emergency procedures.

Dollar also provided a weekly box of fresh food, film, mail, etc. which was brought out by a succession of 'week-enders' who called via Dollar and marvellously kept such cryptic meetings as '9 a.m. by Loch Quoich dam on Saturday'. 'Friday night at Corrour Bothy'. This element of always having a schedule to keep was both useful, forcing on the issue when the flesh was weak, and infuriating, a shackle to the spirit when it fain would linger. (Far more often the latter). Time and time again the beautiful spots pleaded for longer acquaintance. I had two mottos by the end. 'Push' and 'Tomorrow might be worse'. In many ways I was a slave to the very things I resented: telephones and motor cars.

The second motto was often true: July gave 9 days of

increasingly foul weather, until on Conival's Pinnacle Ridge I
had the unique experience of being lifted by the wind off *all*
the holds while climbing up a chimney. Seldom have I been
high in such appalling conditions. My companion turned
back, muttering something about one being enough for a
sacrifice. The other extreme was April's 23 dry days: 55
Munro summits before one obscured. (Expensive in film — I
took a thousand slides before losing the wee Rollei on Beinn
Alligin).

Basic weight lies in rucksack, tent, stove and sleeping bag
— the rest is largely determined by personal choice. Having a
rheumatic shoulder and an arthritic hip I have to pare down
drastically. My burden was never ever as much as 30lb. and
usually only about 24. The Tiso sack I've used happily for ten
years all over the globe. It's comfy and can be slept on or in.
David Challis of Tulloch Mountaincraft provided a superb
3½lb. nylon tent which really seems to have cracked
problems of condensation, etc. I was never damp and with
camps over 3,000ft. and some real storms, it could hardly be
bettered. For cooking I used a Camping Gaz 120, as I had one
and they were clean, easy and no danger of contaminating
spills. Refills were easily stored or carried. I also used a Meta
Stove periodically but for long use it is a fiddle and the new
stands are uselessly weak. In Knoydart I ran out of Gaz and
had two days cooking on messy firelighters — all the shop
could provide, though it had a good selection of wines!
Black's Nordic sleeping bag at 4lb. was my heaviest item but
satisfactory. In addition, I used a two-pint billy and a spoon,
and had a squashy gallon container which meant I could stay
in the tent (and forget rain and midges for the night) and one
plastic jar for honey. All other things were carried in double
poly bags. Finance and availability as much as desire dictated
gear really.

A party at home in early February had all the 'week-enders'
and others busy breaking down things into two/three day
one-man size pokes, and then my mother and I spent days
parcelling them up. Depot labels would be scattered round
the house, then a box of sugar pokes be lugged round, then
meats, then candles, maps — all the possible items for each

varying parcel. I never want to tie another parcel in my life! There were 42 of them. Three tours by car delivered them and checked odd route points, telephones, etc. What a variety of people I met, what welcomes to the stranger at the door holding a parcel (try it in Ulster). Some professions I recall: banker (Jim Donaldson), sailing school director (Clive Freshwater), YH wardens (several), foresters, farmers, campsite manager, shopkeeper, roadman, outdoor centre folk (Dave Challis, Tony Montgomery), hoteliers, toymaker (Charlie Rose), gamekeepers, teachers, doctor (Catherine MacInnes), railwayman, shepherds. . . .

Barclay Fraser and Robert Elton were other SMC helpers. Barclay sped me over the Lui hills and Robert went dashing off to Crete after dining at Strathyre. Ann Winning of the LSCC came twice and stalwarts from our local Braes o' Fife MC helped the rest: Ian and Mary McLeod (who landed a rescue in the Cairngorms), Ian Mitchell (who had money stolen from his car at Glen Dessarry!), George Luke (Nevis), Bob Binnie and Lorna Marsh (bikini days on Ben More, Mull, a deluge in Dalwhinnie and midges at Loch Quoich). There was also John Lawton from Australia and Charles Knowles, who with Donald Mill and myself spent March in the Polish Tatras, a trip which at least meant some fitness at the start. Charles came and sat for two days in the CIC while the snow fell: the only days stormed off, though to be fair, two of my 12 'compulsory rest days' would have been as well.

Ten Munros in a day on the Mamores was the most ever and 15½ hours from Glen Affric YH to Strathfarrar over the Lapaichs the longest. Sixty-two nights were spent under canvas and ten in huts while ten bothies and ten hostels were used. Seven hotels doubled the nights I've ever had in such doubtful comfort! The daily average worked out at about 4,000ft. and 14½ miles (Sandy Cousins' 3,500ft. and 15 miles) and the average for a Munro is 1,500ft. and 4 miles. I had 213 clear summits — unusually high due to April's run. I was alone on all but 12 hill days, met or saw people on 44 peaks (inevitable at weekends until well into June). May alone gave 105 summits. The 112 days (exactly the estimate) ran from 4th April to 24th July.

The route can be hinted at generally by the following summary: Mull, Cruachan, Glencoe, Achalladair, Lyon, Lochay, Lui, Cobbler, Strathyre, Chonzie, Lyon, Ghlo, Keen, Braemar, Avon to Feshie, A9, Alder, Mamores, Nevis, Treig, Bealach Dubh, Monaidh Liath, Mheagaidh, Lochy, Gulvain, Knoydart, Quoich, Glenelg, Cuillins, Shiel, Affric, Loch Monar, Torridon, Sheneval, Fannichs, Wyvis, Deargs, Loch Shin, Klibreck, Hope.

A day-to-day account would fill a book — something I hope is happening by the time this sneaks out in the new monsoon season. So that can keep. In it too I hope to give a bit of the history of the infectious foot disease of Munro-itis; so this is very much a statistical account. A. E. Robertson was once asked why he should want to climb every hill, "no one has ever kissed every lamp-post in Princes Street". A. E. confessed that he had never looked at it in that profane light and that for many years he had very much wanted to kiss every summit in the historic Tables. It is an old SMC custom anyway: of the first two dozen at least 15 were SMC members and does not this ultramontane journal still keep these salvationist statistics? But back to the scoring.

Loch/Ben Lomond saw a canoe used: Inveruglas to Rowchoish to Inverarnon (where the renewed hotel welcomes hillmen again). A cycle helped for the A9, Oban, Skye and northern sections. Legally it's an 'aid to pedestrianism' though I doubt the definition having had contrary winds every time and being ditched three times by juggernauts on the A9. The rule of being entirely self-propelled was kept throughout.

On remoter summits I left a questionnaire when I remembered, and asked the question: "Are you using a car or public transport?" Over 20 of these have come back showing all but one using cars as transport, the one odd answer being, "No, a ship". This was the *Captain Scott* again.

This I'm sure accounts much for the popularity of Munro-bagging. The remoter the Munro the fewer summits the person was likely to have left to do — i.e. the really remote areas are penetrated only of necessity or by those who love

20 Near the River Mole at Dorking — at the point where
the North Downs Way and the Pilgrim's Way converge,
below Box Hill. *Photo: Derek Forss*

loneliness for itself; the majority like the thrall of car it seems! Most forms were found the following weekend showing it is very much a weekend sport — until mid-June. Only then did I start to meet people mid-week at all. The further north and west, the usage drops steadily, with exceptions (e.g. the western Fannichs, because of the Smiddy). Ages ranged from 18 to 62 with peaks at 23 and 30 and 42. Annual days on the hills came in two ranges: 'once a month' weekenders and 'every' weekenders.

April's fine spell was enervating but allowed a good push to clear out below a line joining L. Leven, L. Lyon and L. Tay. Once across the A9 the country is very easy (even Braemar is c.1,000ft.). Lochaber and back was fun, entirely using bothies, lots of snow and friends for parts of it. Laggan was endlessly wet but crossing the Great Glen gave a boost as well as being over the half way.

The only serious 'low' was in the upper Glen Dessarry when a real 'helm o' weet' caught me and with little food, lost tent pegs, an unpleasant emergency camp became essential. Really nasty. However strawberries and cream at Camusrory (and tent pegs too) sorted that out.

In Skye it cleared, to start a good ten day spell which only broke — for good — at Achnashellach Hostel. By then it was only a matter of time, barring accidents. The champagne on Hope was almost incidental, a very low-key ending. Having lived so long with it, it had become a routine, loved and relaxed, and to stop almost unthinkable.

An excellent discipline for my choleric nature, *having* to progress slowly and steadily and I'm sure a long-term blessing. (I can even face the waiting Income Tax Return with less horror than usual).

A few more notes on equipment may interest.

I wore out two pairs of already comfy boots (Sportiva). Heels at times gave sore tendons from bruising. Norwegian stockings were excellent, swopped to a new pair half way 'because they were there'. Next came string pants and old flannels or breeches. (I had a kilt waiting at Milehouse but had thinned beyond its tightest buckling!). On top an appropriate combination from a thick-long-sleeved Damart vest (keeps back dry and can be worn alone on hot days), thin shirt and thin Shetland pullover. A brimmed hat, two hankies, sheet liner, and either long johns or nylon swimming shorts completed the outfit.

A plastic *junk box* contained: First Aid (some bandages, plasters, aspirin, half tube Savlon, vitamin pills), two safety pins, wee scissors, pencil stub, paper, stamps, lettercards, money, jiffy can opener, coins for phones, two needles, thread and wool, biro and log book (I wrote 40,000 words en route), toilet paper, odd cordage, toothbrush, SYHA card, half tube midge cream, bit of pan scourer.

Camera (7 oz. baby Rollei) and films, paperback reading, watch, comb, map and compass — and I think that is every jot and tittle. Some years back I'd made a list on a similar type of trip of what I had with me, then checked what was not used and pared away subsequently to a practical minimum. I lacked nothing vital. I had one big complaint.

There was never enough time!

The walking could last ten/twelve hours and by the time simple but often long meals were eaten and the day's log filled in, it was time to sleep.

It was a simple existence, often so close to nature it crawled about one a bit. (Drain a carton of milk and spit out the overnight big black slug).

It was a hectic return home, caught by press and BBC. The local press gave it front page headlines: between the beauty queen and a rape case. Later a chat programme with Tom Weir on the radio.

Looking back it struck me again (having missed the Alps) that we in Scotland have a landscape unique, fragile, and magnificent — in a European context. It is just a pity we do not have the overall political foresight and leadership to ensure its best survival. In this restless world the wilderness is valuable beyond price.

Marvellous peace to lie at dawn listening to a deer browsing, or the sandpiper call, to sup breakfast in bed and be off in the gold of day. The sweep of days nested in the sweep of the seasons. Snow fell and snows vanished away. Purple saxifrage flowered at the start and purple heather at the end. The arrivals of April. The clarion chorus of May. The speckled fawns of June. The last calling cuckoo of July.

What is time? What is truth? Can we know reality recrudescent?

from THE SCOTTISH MOUNTAINEERING CLUB
JOURNAL *1975*

The World's Walking Record

DICK CRAWSHAW

It is probably true that for the shorter distances, people set their sights on gaining a world walking record at an early age. I do not believe that anyone under 30 is capable of the physical strain of walking a distance of 250 miles because they lack the mental training necessary to accomplish the distance.

From this it might be obvious that I never thought I would ever break such a record — certainly not until the last few years. It became a reality this year* when, thanks to the support given by a wonderful team of helpers, I was able to walk non-stop for 255.84 miles in 76 hours, 21 minutes.

I had my first encounter with long distance walking in 1956 when I was commanding a Territorial Army parachute battalion. In order to select a battalion team for the International Walks at Nijmegen in Holland, I arranged a 107-mile walk from Goole to Liverpool, in full battle order. We completed this walk in a weekend, as planned. The publicity given to this walk resulted in a number of similar walks undertaken by the Army and others, among whom was the redoubtable Dr Barbara Moore.

Five years ago I was asked to start the competitors in a 52-mile marathon organised by the St. John Ambulance Brigade. I decided to take part as well and managed to come in fifth. Having failed to get either the Government or the military authorities to sponsor an international walking week

* Dick Crawshaw set this record in 1974, at the age of 56.

at some suitable centre, I managed with the help of Toxteth Community Council, of which I am President, to arrange an annual 24-hour walking event which now has hundreds of entrants from toddlers to old age pensioners. One such event is an individual 100 miles in 24 hours. I have managed to complete this in each of the past two years and this is what set me thinking about a world record attempt.

Sponsorship
Pleasant as it is to hold a world record, I do not think that this in itself is sufficient to warrant making the attempt. I have always associated walking with sponsorship for charities and was determined that if I did make the attempt it would be in aid of charity. My wife is chairman of the local branch of the NSPCC and the area organiser is one of my former Majors in the Parachute Regiment. Without the help of the NSPCC the attempt would not have been possible.

Training
A good pair of legs is one of the main requisites but this in itself is not sufficient. It is necessary to ensure that every part of the body is in 100% condition. A strong pair of arms and shoulders can take a lot of the effort off the legs and, of course, a good pair of lungs is essential. This requires daily exercise with suitable spring-loaded bar, night and morning.

The next essential is to make sure that one is carrying only muscle and not excess fat. The scales must become a twice-daily habit — not to be slavish about diet, but to correct any tendency for those extra pounds.

A 25-mile non-stop walk in five hours each Sunday morning has been my only real training apart from about another 25 miles walked in daily stints of 3½ miles from my home to the House of Commons and back each weekday.

Most of my training has been unaccompanied. The advantage of this is that one sets a target in one's own mind. If one can do it on one's own it is easy when accompanied by others. I have always trained the hard way and even if I do up to 40 miles non-stop I don't have anything to eat or drink during this time. As a result I generally suffer greater hardship during training than I did at any time on the record walk.

Because the great enemy of sustained physical activity is cramp, I train in shorts and as light a kit as possible, even in winter. It was only after I had walked for 36 hours and with the advent of the second night that I was persuaded to put on my tracksuit trousers. I never got cramp, although I felt there was a possibility of this happening on the last two circuits, after walking the previous ten laps at an increased speed.

Diet

What diet is necessary to attain peak condition? I must admit that there is nothing I don't eat at some time or other. Basically I rely on milk and eggs and usually drink about three pints of milk a day. For some time now I have had Complan as part of my staple diet. I find it can provide the nourishment one could get from a heavier meal, without the worry of getting overweight. Complan was one of the main ingredients of my diet during the record walk. It is equally pleasant taken hot or cold, and I am sure it provided a great part of the energy required for a walk which lasted 76 hours.

I have frequently been asked what were my main worries about undertaking this walk. The main difficulty lay in the fact that the most I had previously done non-stop was 100 miles. Although I felt that I was capable of doing a much greater distance, it would have been very conceited to have asked for the race track for four days, which was what was eventually required. This meant we had to get extensions to the time we were permitted to remain on the track and I was worried during the walk that we might run out of time before I had completed what I felt was possible.

The Target

It was a great pleasure to have Bob Thirtle, a previous world record holder and European champion, taking part in the walk with me. Unfortunately this also brought its worries. We had decided that provided we were both still walking, we would break the record by going across the line together. Bob decided, however, that as soon as we passed the previous record distance he would stop. I had set my sights on reaching

250 miles — the limit that medical knowledge had placed on human endurance.

For hours on the walk I wondered what to do if we broke the record together. Could I, in all fairness, continue when he stopped? I had not resolved this issue when Bob did, by having to give up after 155 miles.

On the third day I was still feeling reasonably fresh and came to the conclusion that the 'limit of human endurance' must refer to the ability to stay awake. I felt this was going to be the main problem, although at this stage I had not felt this was so. This conclusion brought about a decision which caused me considerable discomfort later.

I decided that in order to ward off sleep I would walk cold during the third night and I did not put on the extra smock I had worn the previous night. As a result I caught a chill on my stomach which was extremely unpleasant during the last 12 hours of the walk. My brain remained so alert that during the last six hours I was able to cross-check mentally the distance I had to cover in order to beat the previous record by 25 miles. As the track was 1.64 miles per circuit this meant that I had to work out mentally the distance to two places of decimals. If anything was proof of my excellent diet, this was surely it.

I had a wonderful team of helpers who not only paced me every lap but saw that I was provided with the drink I required each time I passed the main checkpoint. That there were so many people to cheer me on made my task so much lighter. Many of them, including my medical adviser, Colonel Hobday, for whom no praise can be too great, spent three cold and uncomfortable nights on the track.

The only amusing incident — amusing only in retrospect — occurred on the last morning, when I paid my third toilet visit. By this time I had lost the ability to stand still and keep my balance. As a result I fell in the toilet, dragging the hessian screen with me and almost landing in the latrine bucket. I was unable to regain my feet and had to be helped up. The same thing happened when I tried to get out of the bath at home. Only the arrival of the local vicar retrieved the situation, and I remember thinking as he dragged me naked out of the bath that it was all rather like a Jordan baptism!

Although I did not have one blister or piece of skin off the underneath of either foot, both of the smallest toes on each foot were badly damaged on the top. Those on the left foot had merged with each other and started to rot.

After my bath I took a knock-out pill before getting into bed, as I have found from experience that it is possible to reach such a state of exhaustion that it is impossible to sleep because every nerve in the body is pulsating. I left my feet protruding from the bed and my wife doctored them while I was asleep — thus saving me what I am sure would have been a rather unpleasant and painful session.

After five and a half hours' sleep, I awoke feeling as though I had slept for ages. I read and watched TV for hours before repeating the pill process and a further six hours' sleep. I was up at 7 a.m. and felt on top of the world. I realised some of this was false buoyancy in that the excitement was counter-acting the exhaustion. Later in the week I did feel less lively but part of this was caused by stomach trouble. During the morning I was interviewed by newspapers and radio before going out for a stroll in a local park. On the following day I was able to drive to London.

from THE LONG DISTANCE WALKERS' ASSOCIATION
NEWSLETTER *May 1974*

The Wet Welsh Three-Thousanders

DICK SALE

I had climbed all the Welsh three-thousanders, some many times, but had always resisted doing them in one go, seeing it as a piece of sensationalism. I was always going to do them in winter, or there again not at all. When Jean's call went out for fund-raising activities to help a hospital buy an extra bed for spinal injury patients — like the one Andy, who worked with us, had been on — it seemed like a good time to have a go. After all six of us, 14 peaks, say 1p/person/peak and we could make a few bob, and not feel overly competitive either. It was all well prepared. Campsite at the foot of Tryfan with support team — Jean with her frying pan and pounds of bacon, and her husband Mike to drive us to the start and back from wherever we finished. The weather was excellent, clear and warm, but not hot, with little wind. Time for a relaxing drink. We start from above Dolgarrog at 2 a.m. hoping to finish around 6 p.m. Yes, alright then, just a half and then it's sack time.

The room service was great — Jean gently grabbing hold of my leg through my sleeping bag with what felt like a giant pair of pliers. She thrust a cup of tea into my hand and told me it was "about 2". I thought she was right — I was about 2 as well, about 2 turn over and go back to sleep. Someone else said something through the wall of the tent. He said I was missing the train. It was all very confusing. Half dark, half dead, people telling me I was about 2. Mustn't miss the train. . . .

"Dick, Dick."

"Yeah, what?"

"Get up."

"Yeah."

I crawled out of the tent half dressed. He hadn't said train, he'd said rain. Missing? — well these Londoners sound their "p's" funny.

A headlong dive to the canvas strung over the back of Mike's car revealed a sorry bunch, each clutching a sock and a boot in one hand and a bacon roll in the other. Outside the rain fell continuously.

"What happened to all that clear sky?"

"It got a better offer from the Irish."

The general theme seemed to be that if we started at all then we were a bunch of pillocks and deserved to be rained on and blown about — so the sooner we got started the sooner it would be over.

"Bear in mind that it's only the getting wet that's nasty. Once it's happened you're OK. Then you can resign yourself to the misery of it all and stop faffing about trying to stay dry."

And so, despite the fact that no-one apparently wanted to go, we went. The journey out was a bit hectic. Mike, who wasn't the driver, was concerned because he had no wet weather gear. Mike, who wasn't the driver either, was concerned because Mike had no wet weather gear. Mike, who *was* the driver, reckoned that seven people, six with rucksacks, in a small four-seater was too many. Mike, who wasn't the driver, or either of the other two Mikes, reckoned that everyone should be called Mike to avoid confusion, and that being the case would Mike mind getting his boot out of his ear, and would Mike shut up moaning and get on with the driving. I'd managed to arrange it so I was facing backwards, which at least had the advantage of not having to watch us nearly hit things. My foot hurt, so I grabbed hold of it to move it into a more comfortable position. I gave it a good twist, and there was this animal-like shriek from somewhere over on the left. After that my foot still hurt, but not as much as Mike's.

We left B5106 to climb up the back of the Carneddau towards Foel-fras. Someone, who had sussed it out before, was trying to give instructions using a map and torch, and peering into the gloom. The map was on the roof of the car and he seemed to be having difficulty telling left from right. So was I.

"There's a hairpin bend coming up. Very steep and going

right.''

"We'll never do it. I'm in first now, the engine's boiling.
What's going to happen if something's coming. It's single
track.''

"Oh stop nit-picking. Nothing's perfect.''

We emerged on to open moor to the obvious relief of
everyone who could see forward. I had been joined in looking
backwards by Mike, who looked pensive. Was he considering
the great adventure, considering the wonders of nature as the
sky lightened over the Conwy valley, considering the
possibilities of man's eternal soul? No — he was wondering
how he could break the news that he was bursting for a leak.
Luckily, for him, and us, we banged over a cattle-grid (that
brought tears to Mike's eyes) and came to a halt. Someone
managed to open a door and in an instant the road was a
writhing mass of arms and legs. The mass disassembled itself
into separate beings, each moaning about his aches and
pains, the weather, the driving, the lack of public conven-
iences, the test-match score. Mike was complaining that he
couldn't turn the car around to get out and was on a no-
through road. He seemed to find our lack of concern
shameful. We seemed to think that his idea that we should
care how he got home astonishing. He was still there
contemplating the problem as we disappeared over the edge
of a small valley and down to a stream leading back to Foel-
fras. The rain had eased now, in fact it was almost dry. We
had solved the gear problem. Mike had the better of my two
anoraks, and the better of someone else's two pairs of
leggings. Understandably he was very quiet and walked a
little way away from us. He was, of course, on his first ever
visit to Wales etc. and so needed that bit of extra protection
that we hard men could do without etc., but he also feared
that come the crunch, logic and flattery would not protect
him half as well as borrowed wet gear.

More by good fortune than good management we managed
to get ourselves onto the flank of Foel-fras and climbed it
direct to the summit, rather than by our planned route up to
the Drum/Foel-fras ridge. As a result it was not until the wall
on the summit plateau came into view that our worst fears

about the weather were confirmed. It seemed to be raining in Anglesey, with the rain landing somewhere south of Aberystwyth. It was going over the Carneddau horizontally, driven by a wind which was, we decided, at a conservative estimate at least 140 mph, and so must have been 20 mph at least.

The group made it to the wall and formed a scrum. The ball the scrum hooked about was the 'first big question' — what to do next. Eventually everyone realised that the discussion was essentially futile since there was less than one good alternative. Tony maintained that we should all go over to the trig point, it being all about going to the top of all 14 peaks. He seemed surprised by the reaction the suggestion provoked, and pointed out that since his bike was elsewhere he could hardly get on it. With that he was over the wall with all the bravado of a front-liner at Ypres and sprinting head down for the trig pillar. His feet and legs had already turned round and were running back to the wall when a flung-out arm touched the pillar, and he was back — wet, gasping and with a smug look. All in all it was a nasty trick and he maintained that watching the five of us was five times more enjoyable than us five watching one of him. Nobody spoke to him for a long time.

The wall towards Foel-grach afforded some protection provided you remembered to keep your head down occasionally. It was a fairly unmemorable walk, what with the view having been cut drastically, but there was some entertainment — as the rain hit the wall some drops came through the cracks and emerged like machine gun bullets clattering against anoraks and thumping bare flesh hard.

Eventually the wall ended and there was a short pantomime as everybody tried to walk in the lee of the wire fence, hurrying from post to post. After that it was just keep your head down, hood up and on to Garnedd Uchaf. Here the party was split: one third wanted to go to Foel-grach by, apparently, following the Yr Aryg ridge; one third wanted to go to Foel-grach by following the Foel-grach ridge; and one third wanted to know what they were doing up this cold, wet hill anyway. The newcomers were bucked up when they

found out there was a hut on Foel-grach, less so by the idea
that it would then be two down and four to go on the
Carneddau, before the second breakfast. I managed to get
close to Mike of the 'good anorak' who, with marked
reluctance, told me he was reasonably dry. He didn't seem all
that bothered about how I was, so I told him anyway. He was
about to make some embarrassed reply when he was
disturbed by someone else and shuffled across to them
gratefully. They were interested in how his (their) leggings,
which were, incidentally, even better than my anorak, were
performing. . . .

It seemed a pity that somebody had moved the hut two or
three miles since the last time I had been there, but it was just
as dry and free from wind. Over a brew, stories of appalling
deprivation were swapped — Mike of the 'good anorak' and
'even better leggings' staying strangely silent — and it seemed
that by and large everybody was soaked, freezing, hungry,
hacked off with the whole stupid business, and not too bad
really.

We vacated the hut in reasonable trim and made it fairly
uncomfortably to Foel-grach and then to Carnedd Llewelyn.
It was 'second big question' time — did we go to Yr Elen into
the teeth of the wind or did we, um . . ., how shall we say it,
um . . ., lie about it. Somebody decided after a bit that it was
drier in the long run to go and do it than to stand here jawing
about it for half an hour. So we went to Yr Elen thinking it
might be bad, and it was worse. But at least coming back the
wind was on our backs rather than forcing rain down our
anorak fronts. On the Carneddau in that sort of weather you
clutch what comfort you can. So we clutched our comfort to
Craig Llugwy and then it was ripped from our grasp as we
turned into the weather again to go up Carnedd Dafydd.

About half way between Carnedd Dafydd and Pen-yr-
oleu-wen I suddenly realised that Rog, next to me, was
muttering softly. Until then, since in the rain we were
cocooned in our own thoughts, I hadn't really thought that
anybody else could be in a worse state than me — i.e. wetter
or colder. But he was definitely muttering. I edged closer.
Slowly. I mean, it does funny things to you, and he might

have leapt on me blaming me for incorrect weather forecasts and the state of the exhaust pipe on his Chevette. He muttered on. I listened and snatched a look. He had a fixed stare and he muttered over and over.

"Dry Y's. Dry Y's."

Bloody hell, I thought, he's gone over the edge.

"Pardon?"

"Dry Y's . . . I'd give anything for a pair of dry Y-fronts."

He'd found out what hell really is — when Nature gets your whatsisnames in her icy grasp.

It poured liberally all the way to Pen-yr-oleu-wen and then to show there were no hard feelings it went off when it didn't matter, on the descent to the Ogwen Valley. We came down out of the mist and it even brightened enough for us to start believing we could see Jean with her frying pan at the ready. It's hard work off Pen-yr-oleu-wen and we were tired and dispirited by the time we reached the camp road, but Mike and Jean had seen us coming and there were mugs of soup and bacon rolls and cups of tea. Roger got his dry Y's. Mike of the GA and the EBL gave them back saying he was now Mike of the 'really bad blister' and couldn't face any more. We asked why the blister was on his face and he gestured that we should be on our way in two minutes. So we were.

The weather lifted right up to the top of Tryfan and so the support had good theatre as we wound our way up the path to the north ridge. The going seemed fairly easy, interest being maintained by the bits of rock climbing and the views, and sooner than anticipated we were up. We waved from the top of Adam or Eve, but they didn't see us which was a shame as the weather came down again and they were never to see the top of a three-thousander again all weekend. There was somebody else on Bristly Ridge which was amazing really.

"They must be daft. Only an idiot would come out on a day like this."

"True."

The climb up Bristly was good fun and we were soon among the shambles of Glyder Fach. Since the next bit, to the Devil's Kitchen, was easy enough and we now had eight down and only six to go, our spirits rose considerably. We decided to go over the Castle of the Winds, and set off with renewed enthusiasm. It wasn't to last. Near the Castle Tony disappeared off left saying he was going for a crap. Well I mean if you must you must. So we went over the rubble and waited, and waited . . . Finally someone hollered out in exasperation and Tony answered from up in front in the mist. Seemed he'd said he was going to take the track. After that everybody was in a rotten mood until Glyder Fawr where we chose one of the rock piles — is one the highest? — and sat down. I fished out some dried apricots and passed them round. They had the consistency of boiled feathers and tasted of pond water, and everybody heaped nasty sarcasms on my head.

Somebody suggested we go straight down to Pen-y-Pass and it was obviously 'third big question' time. We talked some, and a little humour returned. Rog asked if I had any apricots left and I said yes and he said good, and he hoped they were heavy, and we decided we'd push on to Y Garn at least. If we'd found the lad looking for the top we might even have said sorry and hoped his rock was highest. As it was Mike and I settled for a race down the steep scree and mud to Llyn Cwn. I won because he hit a really slippery rock and almost achieved man-powered flight. He hit the ground pretty hard and ripped his leggings a bit.

It wasn't too clever an idea really, but he was OK, thank God, and it did mean that sanity, after a fashion, had returned. We were all re-united on the top of Y Garn. The grind up the ridge was my Everest, and I was well tired by the time I reached the top. Luckily there was orange squash, no rain and relative comfort in the shelter.

Since there was no real alternative, we decided to traverse around the top of the Dudodyn valley to Elidir Fawr; we pressed on. The walk round was enjoyable, mainly because it was easy for tired limbs and the weather had improved sufficiently to see down towards Nant Peris. If you strained your eyes you could even persuade yourself that you could see Jean and Mike with cups of tea. Just the thought made the slope up to the top of Elidir Fawr less grinding. In fact the

thought seemed to bring tears to your eyes, but it turned out
not to be tears but the rain again.

By the time we were descending from Elidir Fawr towards
Nant Peris it was pouring steadily. I managed to persuade
everybody I knew where I was going, but since the rain was
making my glasses opaque and visibility was poor anyway the
pretence didn't last too long. Still, it was easy enough to find
the Afon Dudodyn and follow it down to meet the footpath.

During the last descent to the river the steep, wet grass
combined with tired legs and weary minds to drop people on
their backsides. Everybody managed it a couple of times, but
I remained miraculously immune. I was beginning to feel real
proud of my balance, especially when Rog asked me with
obvious envy if I ever fell down. No, I said, it comes of being

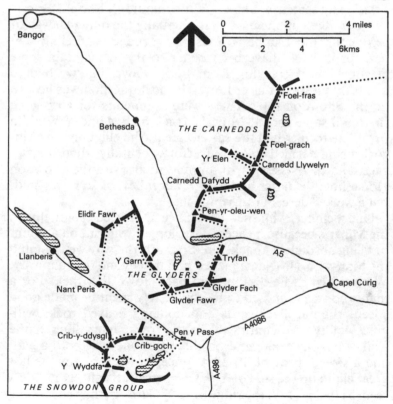

a rock-climber, superb balance. Perhaps coupled, he observed, with being a short-house — low centre of gravity. Slightly piqued, I was about to offer that the 28" inside leg might indeed represent some small percentage, but in the main it was balance and . . . when I was suddenly sliding down the hill feet first on my backside. I was vainly trying to retrieve the situation by pointing out that I was trying a new method of descent — controlled sliding on the anorak, a glissade even — when Rog went past, guffawing loudly.

Nant Peris came and so did Jean. Mike the driver asked if we wanted a lift up to Pen-y-Pass because after all it was only a few yards of tarmac. My spirits rose bird-like into the wet air to be met by the blinding flash of some pikehand saying no thanks, we'd walk the lot. Several of us had trouble offering up sentences like, "No, no, wouldn't be right" etc.

We trudged up the pass — it's actually the only real way of getting up the Llanberis Pass, the Trudge — feeling that perhaps it would have been better to try to maintain some height by back-tracking from Elidir Fawr, but we had to admit that it wasn't clear how. The next question was how to do the Snowdon tops. There were arguments for Crib-goch first, and some for the Miner's Track or Pyg and Y Wyddfa first. The former had the easier ascent, the climbing on Crib-goch being deemed to be less effort, mentally, than the zig-zags, and the possibility of a grand finale with the Snowdon Horseshoe; the latter had four fewer miles, or so it was said, but a wicked descent of Crib-goch.

One member, who shall be nameless, insisted eventually on the Miner's because he needed the longer walk-in, on account of being absolutely knackered. So that's the way we went and the Man-with-No-Name jacked it in up beyond the causeway. We watched as he disappeared back down the track. For a man who was supposed to be completely spent he made good speed, running backwards and dodging heaved rocks with great agility. We continued up the track, marvelling at the skill of anyone capable of producing at one time both a path and a stream bed. Then, all at once, it was time for the last great climb up the side of Y Wyddfa itself. Strangely it didn't seem as bad as, say, the ridge onto Y Garn. Perhaps it was the knowledge that it was the last climb. Perhaps also it was the sheer size of it — on Y Garn the summit was just up there, so frustratingly close. But we were going well, surprisingly well. Despite the drizzle and the tiredness, it was good. Reaching the railway was the usual unpleasant anti-climax. You feel you've done it all, but you haven't. So up again, wishing I had legs that would allow me to step from sleeper to sleeper. And finally the top, with no view at all, but a few hardy types clutching the trig pillar and peering out over the edge of Clogwyn y Garnedd. A couple seemed to be on the point of going down for a better look, oblivious to the fact that not many steps down you reach a step that's a real lulu. But they didn't venture far and then it was back to the café and the waiting train. We thought about the café, but decided that people in wet weather gear, tired, wet and dirty would be a bit incongruous and unwelcome, so it was done again.

By now the general air was euphoria. Crib-y-ddysgl came and went, and even the climb down to Bwlch Coch wasn't as bad as we feared it might be with tired legs. The scent of success was in our nostrils now and we went at the pinnacles all laughs and whoop-tee-doo. The rain stopped again and the visibility improved enough to take the sting out of the traverse. Yes it was wet, but we were unhurried. And then there it was, the point where Crib-goch falls away on (almost) all sides. Not really a summit, but you would have had little success trying to tell us that when we went along the last bit of ridge. Smiles and well-dones. Somebody found a bar of fruit-and-nut. We felt sorry for Mike the Blister, and even sympathy for the Man-with-No-Name, who had got so close. We resolved to do it again in winter, perhaps with a bivouac en route. We marvelled at how much daylight there was left. Then we went down — it was murder, it was everlasting. But eventually there was Jean and she seemed as pleased as we were.

PREVIOUSLY UNPUBLISHED

Author's footnote: Most people paid us the full amount despite the partial success, and we made over £200. There was a sponsored walk over the Pennine Way as well, and that made over £300. Jean kept on organising even after that and eventually she had made £950, and the bed was bought. It was a fine achievement. Jean had every right to be as pleased as we were.

More than Stanes and Watter

ROGER SMITH

"Why, it's nobbut stanes and watter" is the famous remark said to have been made by an old countryman on his first visit to the Lake District. I know what he meant: there's a lot of stone, and a lot of water — but he told less than the full story. There's so much else besides. Long after my memories of the stone and water have faded. I shall remember, with that pleasurable dulling of the agony that retrospect can bring, the heather of Great Calva and the tussocks of Seat Sandal and Stybarrow Dodd.

That's three: the other 39 have their memories too, many of them painful but all of them very special. To set yourself an impossible challenge and then succeed ensures that the experience will be unforgettable. To try to write about it in a way that does it justice, when it involves 24 hours (all but 23 minutes) continuous travel on foot around an area so richly beautiful and so frequently and gloriously celebrated in literature as the Lake District, seems to me now a task harder by far than the journey itself.

The Bob Graham Round

In 1932, Bob Graham, a noted hill-walker of his day, set off from Keswick Moot Hall to walk over as many Lakeland tops as he could within 24 hours. Twenty-three hours and 38 minutes later he returned to Keswick with 42 summits under his feet. This circuit is now known as the Bob Graham Round. For 28 years Graham's feat was not emulated. Then, with the growth of the sport of fell-running, others began to try the Round. Many failed, some succeeded. Inevitably, with our penchant for banding together, a Bob Graham Club was formed: membership open only to those who have completed the Round. Inevitably, too, the number of summits topped in the 24-hour period was uplifted to 45, to 50, to 60. The absolute record now stands to Joss Naylor. The *basic round* is 42 peaks, 72 miles and 25,000ft. of ascent. Joss's record is 72 summits, 90 miles and well over 30,000ft. of ascent, all within 24 hours. One can only shake one's head and marvel at it.

Rules for attempts on the Round are simple: start and finish at Keswick Moot Hall (at any time of the day or night you choose) and touch the cairns on the summits of all the 42 peaks on Graham's list, recording your time at each. You can go either way round (Graham went clockwise, Skiddaw first, Robinson last). Before 9th June 1979 there were 114 full members of the Club — 112 men and two women, Jean Dawes and Anne-Marie Grindley.

Preparation

At 8.30 a.m. on Saturday 9th June a small crowd assembled outside the Moot Hall, getting in the way of the traders setting up stalls for the Saturday market. Six were prancing around like nervous racehorses before the start of the Grand National. Two, Graham and Andrew, were acting as pacers and porters on the first stage of the long day's travelling: the other four were attempting the Round.

For Jack Bloor it was, at 53, his third try. The first time, on his own in bad weather, he got off route and lost more time than he could hope to make up. Last year, he was forced down into Langdale when halfway round by continuous rain and fierce winds (and that was in July). Dick Courchee (40) had been with Jack last year, so this was his second try. Dick did most of our organisation. For Malcolm Cox and myself it was a first attempt. Malcolm is a damn good athlete and orienteer, with some fell-running experience.

And me? As I've said in print before, my problem is that I get ideas above my station. I had known about the BGR for some years, but it was something that other people — supermen — did. Then I started entering, and enjoying, long fell races and challenge walks, though my performances were pretty moderate. Last year I completed the Lakes 3,000ft. peaks walk (46 miles) in 13 hours. Dick and Jack were there, using the walk (much of which we ran) as training for the

BGR attempt. I wished them luck: I wasn't going with them, but it set me thinking.

Wouldn't it be fun to try the BGR myself — a real, personal Everest for me to aim at? And wouldn't it be even *more* fun to try it this year, to celebrate reaching the age of 40? Then I heard that Dick and Jack had failed (though that's a cruel word when they kept to schedule for 12 hours before being beaten off by atrocious conditions) and wanted to try again. That did it. The final little push came in February when Dick rang to say that he had fixed 9th/10th June for their attempt, and that Malcolm was joining them.

"Can I come too?" I asked.

"By all means," said Dick. "Glad to have you along."

That gave me four months for physical preparation. You can take that side of it for granted — suffice to say that I did what I could, not easy in such a long winter, culminating in a 50-mile sponsored walk/run in late May which I finished without strain in 12 hours. The *mental* preparation is probably of more interest.

As soon as I knew the date of our attempt, I fixed it in my mind as a target. I would not be afraid of the challenge, though it was physically way above anything I'd tried before. I would set that date in my mind and try to reach it absolutely ready to go, determined to try my best and to enjoy myself into the bargain. It seemed to me that a very different approach was needed from that of the athlete preparing for an important track race — or even a marathon — though he too may know the date months in advance. He is looking to 'psyche' himself up, to get to the starting line charged with adrenalin, to be able to beat his rivals and reach the tape first.

I was looking for the opposite. Ours was a very long, sustained effort demanding the stamina to travel at 3 mph over rough mountain terrain for a day and a night with only a few brief stops for food and drink. I felt that I should get to the Moot Hall physically at a peak, certainly, but with nervous energy running at a very *low* level. I almost wanted to wake up that Saturday morning and have to think what I was going to do that day, then just go out and do it. This approach, of single-minded determination to succeed if at all possible combined with a relaxed enjoyment of the thing while I was about it, worked better than I could have hoped, despite a few little setbacks.

During April and May we 'recced' the whole route between us, except for the final section (Threlkeld-Keswick). We had decided to go anti-clockwise (Robinson first, Skiddaw last) as with an 8.30 a.m. start this would give us the comparatively easy ground of the Helvellyn range to cover during the night. Dick also felt that to finish with Skiddaw and a long easy run down to Keswick was far better than coming off Robinson and being faced with five miles of roads — murder when you're very tired.

Dick prepared a schedule for 24 hours exactly (psychology again — it would help like mad if we got ahead of it) and Jack, inevitably, prepared his own schedule for 23½ hours. This led to a certain amount of mental agony on the day, as you'll read later. The 24-hour schedule suited me as, romantic that I am, I could see my attempt as a re-creation of Graham's original round (though he was 42 to my 40).

In May, Dick and I did the central section in seven hours against a schedule of eight and a half hours. It was beginning to come together. I did my '50' and had a final note from Dick. "All is ready. Jack completed the Fellsman Hike (61 miles of tough Yorkshire moorland) in 17 hours and has declared himself fit. See you there." On the Friday I packaged up clothing and food to be taken to the various road crossings. I guess the others were doing the same. All our wives were supporting us magnificently and would meet us at every road crossing, even Threlkeld at 3 a.m. (I learnt later that Pat Bloor asked Sue Courchee a couple of days beforehand, "Are you looking forward to this? — I'm not sure I am". It must have been worse for them in a way than it was for us — seeing us arrive, increasingly tired, gobble down some food and struggle off again, not to reappear for anything up to six hours).

We had been lucky enough to get pacers/porters for the whole trip — experienced men who had done the Round themselves and knew what it involved. This made a vital difference in my case. For the last stage, Threlkeld to

Keswick, we had two pacers, as we felt we might be split into two groups of two by then — "or four groups of one" as Dick dryly observed.

I think we all felt, as I did, that given a decent day and a bit of luck we were in with a sporting chance. The weather forecast on Friday evening was highly encouraging — cool and dry with no low cloud and only light winds. That would be perfect. I left my wife and family in the good hands of our friends the Bainbridges and retired to a guest house in Keswick (Acorn House, run by Denise and Bill Booth — highly recommended to all walkers) to ensure a good night's sleep undisturbed by babies. You will not be surprised to learn that I spent most of the night listening to the church clock mocking me with its chimes every quarter. Ah well, who needs sleep anyway?

Rapidly Round Robinson

"How far is it to Newlands?" asked Malcolm. "About 4 miles? That would be 18 minutes normally!"

He could take 18 minutes if he liked — I knew how long I wanted to take! A too-fast start would be disaster. Malcolm knew this too really, and we settled into a nice steady jog as we watched the clouds lifting over Grisedale Pike.

At Newlands we took a quick drink and set off through High Snab and on to Robinson. It was great to have a fell underfoot. The weather showed alarming signs of getting warm but once on the ridge it was just about perfect. Hazy views across to Hopegill Head one way and Hindscarth (our second top) the other, a good path underfoot and a feeling of enormous happiness and well-being.

This section is short, sweet and simple. Robinson 9.52 a.m. Hindscarth 10.10, Dale Head 10.23 and a free swinging run down to the cars at the top of Honister. 10.35 a.m., 15 minutes up on Dick's schedule.

Rock in the Afternoon

I didn't know where we were going when we left Honister at 10.45 a.m. I had better qualify that. I knew the major peaks we would be crossing on this section and that the next stop was Wasdale Head. (I also knew that the schedule had us there at 3.00 p.m., and I wanted to be there by 2.30 p.m.). But the first couple of tops after Honister — Grey Knotts and Brandreth — were new ground to me.

They fell to us pretty easily, and once over Brandreth we could begin to assimilate what lay ahead. All around us were peaks of a rude and awesome majesty, rising, some blunt, some sharp, all hard and uncompromising, out of the valleys. Here were 'stanes and watter' indeed — Green Gable, Great Gable, Kirk Fell, Pillar and Steeple. Glorious names, an inspiration to countless walkers and climbers, and certainly now to us.

For the first time there was cloud on the tops. Getting to the top of Great Gable was not difficult — harder on the feet than on the brain, as the mountain forced its way into our consciousness with the imprint of its rock upon the soles of our feet. Getting off it was even less comfortable. Dick knew the route, and gave us the bearing, and then vanished ahead of us — but then he has been traversing ground like this since he was ten. Jack and Malcolm stayed with him but for a couple of minutes Graham and I were in temporary difficulty and seemed to be suspended on that rocky face, unable to see the others or to follow their route.

Eventually we picked up the line of descent and crossed the col to start up Kirk Fell. Suddenly we were surrounded by runners clad even more lightly than ourselves: we had joined the route of the Ennerdale Horseshoe Fell Race! For the next hour or so these braw lads provided us with much diversion and not a little encouragement as they came by. "On the Bob Graham? Good luck, lads, keep it going," came from many of them. Nice people, fell-runners.

About here I made what I thought was a pretty good joke. "It's a disgrace, leaving all these loose rocks lying about," I said. "Really, the council ought to do something about it." This shot of exquisite repartee was greeted with (dare I say it?) stony silence!

Down to Black Sail Pass and up to Pillar: a hard old climb, rough and steep, but at least our slow progress gave us the chance to savour the views across Ennerdale to the lake, the

Liza and the conifers. We skipped Scoat Fell (not on Bob
Graham's list) for Steeple, the day's first out-and-back. It's a
delightful little peak with a marvellously airy wee col below
the summit, but any dogleg is bound to be resented a bit. Dick
had suffered a bad patch on Pillar but caught us up here, and
we started over to Red Pike (after the others had restrained
me from heading away to Haycock with the fell-runners)
feeling happy to be back on grass and happier to have
grabbed 30 minutes from our schedule, as we wanted.

It must have been around this time that I started looking at
my feet a lot, for I began to notice vast numbers of large sleek
slugs in the grass. I don't remember seeing so many of such a
size before — they were present in great quantities for the rest
of the day, and with the Helvellyn skylarks were about the
most impressive fauna we encountered.

Dick dropped back again on Kirk Fell, but we thought
perhaps he was just taking his own pace, and set off on the
long incline to Dore Head. Our first decent run since
Honister and we made the most of it. Yewbarrow stood
ahead like a big long loaf with a wee bump where the
mountain dough had risen a little extra to provide a summit.

We went up diagonally, teetering on a scratch of a track
and pecking away at the upgrade until we had to breathe deep
and step straight up the hill to the ridge, hands on hips and no
chat. Our route was good and a short final effort brought us
to the cairn. Touch and away, looking for the scree shoot
that would take us down to the road, to Brackenclose, to our
wives and supporters, and to our long-awaited lunch. Food
for our bodies had been much on our minds the past hour or
so: but not enough to stop us from letting the magnificence
of our surroundings feed our spirits. The Scafells ahead and
Wastwater below: the true incomparable Lakeland picture.
Stanes and watter that would fill any man's heart with
gladness.

I got to the bottom of the slope using my patent slow-
motion scree-running technique (take one pace and stop) with
three away ahead of me and Dick a bit behind, and jogged up
to the hut at Brackenclose. 2.30 p.m. as planned. My food
was there, and Sue Courchee, appearing like a vision with hot

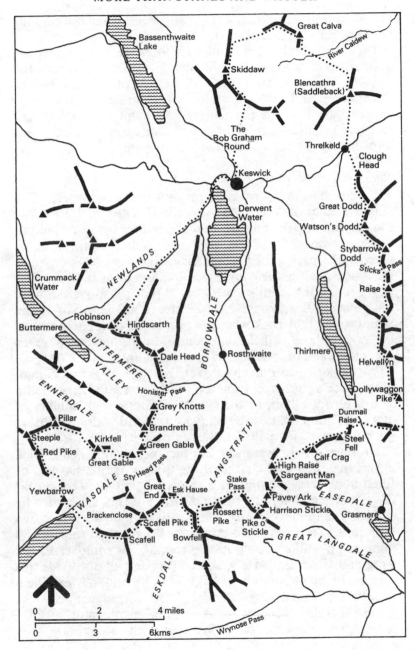

sweet tea (I can't normally stand sugar in my tea but on long walks or runs it's like nectar).

Dick arrived about five minutes after me, not feeling too good, sadly. Malcolm ate a bowl of fruit and cereal too quickly, was sick, and felt a lot better for it. Jack looked undisturbed and undisturbable. After some food (my wife's superb date cake in particular) and a lot of drink I had recovered enough to have my photograph taken. Sue ministered to Dick, who decided to carry on.

Pikes and Peaks in the Evening

We said our thanks to Graham and our new pacer, Mike Gilbert, led us off on the toil up Scafell. The first 1,500ft. we took straight up the fellside: bad enough for the rest of us but obviously worse for Dick, who again fell behind. Once we reached the path at about 2,000ft. Mike went back down to see if he was alright leaving us to plod on upwards.

We touched Scafell's cairn at 4.20 p.m., just over an hour after leaving Brackenclose. Mike met us at the top of Broad Stand to say that Dick was going on at his own pace: he had leg cramps and a headache but thought he could reach Dunmail Raise (our next road crossing point).

We then tipped ourselves over the edge of Broad Stand, under Jack's guidance. I was a bit worried about Broad Stand as it is a rock-climb, of sorts, and I'm not a rock-climber of any sort. But Jack is, the rock was dry, and with his help we got down easily (actually I rather enjoyed it).

However, there was now another problem. Losing Dick meant that Jack had charge of the timecards that have to be filled in at every summit: it also meant that we were on his 23½ hour schedule. The first indication of this came when he suddenly announced on Scafell Pike that we were two minutes down: hard to accept when I'd got used to being 30 minutes up! Mike's reaction was to make us run over Broad Crag and Great End. He was now carrying all our loads (his own rucksack and two bum-bags — as he said, "I feel like a packhorse") and urging us on by giving us frequent drinks of water liberally laced with Accolade, a preparation that replenishes mineral salts lost through sweating — I

recommend it unreservedly. He was a very real source of help
and inspiration to us over this stage, and we owe him a lot.

By Bowfell we were starting to get inside even Jack's
schedule, and I knew that after Rossett Pike the going got a
lot easier and we could hope to pick up more time. There
were plenty of clouds about but no rain and our luck with the
weather looked like holding.

With a last look at the mountains behind us (however many
times I cover them I still find them inexpressibly majestic and
inspiring) we took a direct line off Bowfell to the col above
Angle Tarn — one of my favourite little lakes, and as usual
dotted with tents round the shoreline — and easily up to
Rossett Pike. A delightful little top and I'm glad Bob Graham
had the wit to include it. It seemed to mark a significant point
on the journey. We had been out ten hours, so were nearing
halfway in terms of time: we were gaining on our schedule all
the time: and most of the rough going was behind us. Ahead
lay the Langdale Pikes, the easy run over High Raise and the
long spine of Steel Fell. Dick and I had covered this section in
well under two hours on our 'recce' so it held no fears.

We knew, too, that a bonus was just ahead. Andrew and
his wife had offered to come up to Stake Pass from Langdale
with flasks of tea. I was delighted to find that, thanks to the
recce, I was entrusted with the navigation to the mobile
teabar. The responsibility lent speed to my heels and at 6.40
p.m. we arrived at the Pass to find our refreshment waiting.
The tea was great and we were cheered to be told that we all
looked in fine shape: at that point I think we felt it. I was
almost beginning to let myself believe that I might get all the
way round, but forced the thought away, got to my feet and
followed the others off to Pike o'Stickle.

The party on the Pike admiring the view, which through
360 degrees is admittedly very fine; and probably waiting for
the sunset, obviously thought we were crackers as we toiled
up the last few feet, touched the cairn and skidded straight
off again. Maybe we were: but each to his own madness, say
I, and we were without doubt enjoying ourselves hugely too.

Harrison Stickle, Thunacar Knott (almost a cheat, that
one, it's so flat), Sergeant Man, High Raise. 8.10 p.m. as we

left High Raise and every chance of getting to Dunmail by 9 p.m. That would be an hour up on the 24-hour schedule: I wanted that hour, as I was pretty sure we would need it in the later stages.

Going across to Calf Crag — not difficult country, a bit boggy perhaps, but mostly fair going and not steep either — I found the others moving away from me. Mike saw that I was slowing and came back. Quite suddenly I had almost run out of strength. Thank heaven it happened here and not two hours before. Only Steel Fell (only?) to get over and then Dunmail, a rest, a change of clothes, and some food. Terry would be there too: my dear and constant inspiration.

Steel Fell is 1,811ft., it took me a long time to get there, nor did I enjoy the very steep 700ft. drop down to Dunmail. Just as well I was slow: as I crawled down I saw our car arriving. I wouldn't have liked to have got there before them. It was 9.02 p.m.

I sat wearily on the car's tailboard, feeling like death warmed up. If anyone had suggested that maybe I would be wise to pack up there — give it best — I might well have succumbed to the temptation. Sensibly, they didn't, and it was cheering to find Fred Rogerson there too. Fred is the record-keeper for all BGR attempts and his great labour of love is the Record of Notable Fell Walks in the Lake District which he publishes himself and updates every two years. A real Lakeland character.

Soup and tea brought a vestige of life to my limbs. Jack and Malcolm were pretty quiet, too. I think we all felt that this was a crucial time and had withdrawn into ourselves to help us get through it. I will admit to praying for strength.

Larks Over Helvellyn

After 45 minutes Dick had still not arrived and the three of us decided to set off. Our pacer for the night section, John Richards, stayed behind in case his help was needed. We had heard that Dick was 30 minutes behind us through Stake Pass: we were all worried about him but there was no point in all of us stopping there.

Going up Seat Sandal was the absolute low point of the

journey for me. I was tired, the night was coming on, the slope was steep, and the other two drew steadily away from me. Twice I stopped and very nearly turned and went down. Terry told me later she felt awful watching me drag up there in the gathering gloom — she wanted to come after me and bring me back down again. She also told me however, that if I *had* started back down, Mike would have set off up the fell to give me a kick up the backside and tell me to get on with it!

At length Seat Sandal summit appeared, Jack and Malcolm waiting beside it. They had to wait for me — I knew the best route over the next section! We dropped down to Grisedale Tarn and started up Fairfield. None of us could understand why Bob Graham had included Fairfield — it's not a logical hill to put in, being part of a separate ridge, and it's a bastard to climb from the tarn. The track is eroded, rough, and desperately steep. I don't think any of us want to see that hill again for a good long time!

Coming back down to Grisedale Tarn, as you must, a light flashed below us. On the way up we had seen torches and heard voices on the far side of the tarn (a party camping, no doubt) but this was a solitary light, signalling straight at us. Surely it could only be John?

It was. And with good news — Dick was safe. He had arrived at Dunmail Raise not long after we had left and had decided to retire there. A sensible decision, but we all felt desperately sorry for him — he had done so much of the planning and was not now to reap the reward.

John had joined us at a very good moment, psychologically — the start of the third and final steep climb on this section, up to Dollywaggon Pike. All the way up he kept saying the nicest things, like how well we were going and that we could slow down if we wanted (I felt I couldn't *go* any slower). The top is a way off the path and not easy to find in the dark. We reached it just two minutes before midnight. I recalled Dick's words to me three weeks earlier: "If I'm on Dollywaggon by midnight, I reckon I can do it." Had we cracked it? Don't think about it, lad, just get on.

The walk along the Helvellyn ridge from Dollywaggon Pike to Clough Head is nowhere demanding and we all perked up noticeably from that point on. You knock off summits at a rapid rate, too — ten of them in all. If we could get to Clough Head by 3 a.m. and Threlkeld by 3.30, we would surely get round by 8.30 a.m.?

All along this stretch we were accompanied by skylarks, singing their endless cadenzas above us. For much of the way there was a big bright moon, bright enough to cast shadows. How lucky we were with the weather. How lucky just to be out there in all that great beauty, walking through the night towards what it increasingly seemed would be a triumphant morning.

Physically, this was new territory for me. I'd never been out for more than 15 hours and never walked right through the night before. On the three climbs, especially Seat Sandal, I felt dreadful, and only willpower and staunch companions kept me going. After Dollywaggon Pike I just felt weird: almost disorientated, as if I were outside myself. I voiced this to the others, and they agreed with me. Jack said he was "virtually sleepwalking" and it was a great relief to us to have John doing the navigating.

At Sticks Pass we had a drink stop and for the first time I wondered aloud if we might not be on our way to success. Jack and Malcolm shut me up quickly: chicken-counting was obviously not recommended. Stybarrow Dodd was tedious, not because it is long or steep, but because it's so featureless: a non-summit on the round, whereas Calfhow Pike, a super little top, isn't included (I visited it anyway, it's so close to the route).

Clough Head at 2.50 a.m. couldn't be bad: the descent from there to Threlkeld was far longer than I remembered, but at least John found a route that kept us on grass all the way to the end of the farm road at Newsham. We had been seen coming off the hill and a car's headlights flashed a welcome at us. They seemed a long way away. They were — at the end of the lane in Threlkeld village that leads to the path up Blencathra.

As we came down, the night changed almost imperceptibly to day. Not a dramatic dawn, but one we were all happy to see. We reached the cars at 3.35 a.m., heralded by cuckoos, and I was delighted and moved to find not only Terry but Ronnie and Margaret Bainbridge *and* my elder daughter Becky (aged 2½) there. Having seen me suffering at Dunmail, they were equally happy to find me now in such good spirits.

Happy Ending

Our final section was over Blencathra, Great Calva, and Skiddaw, and back to Keswick. Only three tops, but a long way between them when you've been out 19 hours already. Mike was rejoining us for this section and we had Terry Marsh too. Both knew the ground well, and both were to give assistance without which I, at least, might have been cruelly denied what I had tried so hard to achieve.

I kept my stop at Threlkeld very brief. I didn't want food: plenty of drink and then Terry and I set off at 3.50 a.m. He thought we might not make it back in time (though he didn't tell us that). I felt we just about had enough time.

Blencathra is a stiff pull up from the road (2,300ft. of climb) but at least you hit it on the nose. At the top of Hall's Ridge the summit is directly there. It took us 50 minutes, and as we'd allowed an hour we were pleased with ourselves. 4.40 a.m., just under four hours left. The north side of Blencathra is quite different from the steep and craggy south face — a long gradual slope, mostly grass, going steadily downhill for almost three miles over Mungrisdale Common to reach the River Caldew at the foot of Great Calva. Mike and Terry made us *run* most of it (or at least convert the rapid plod we had employed all through the night into a slightly faster ungainly shamble) and it took us just over half an hour. Wading the Caldew was a bit tricky in our state, but at 5.15 a.m. we set off up Great Calva.

It was misty, and I really was feeling very, very tired. The summit seemed to float away as I tried to get up to it. Underfoot was coarse heather, a lot of it half-burnt; just about the worst thing possible for anyone in my state. Jack and Malcolm had forged ahead with Terry; Mike stayed with me. If he hadn't, I think I would have laid down in that awful heather and expired.

I didn't dare look at my watch, but I felt that time was racing away. I wanted to stop it, but I couldn't. I kept praying: "Please let me get there. Please don't let me fail now".

Great Calva kept its final joke to the end. There are two distinct summits, and it was, of course, the further one that we wanted. I got there. Don't ask me how. I dared to look at my watch. 5.50 a.m.? It must have stopped! That eternity of dragging one foot after the other up through the heather had lasted just 35 minutes. As well as hallucinations (I could have sworn a rock was a large lump of green ice-cream) I was now suffering from time-warp!

All the way up that slope Mike had encouraged me, keeping me going, giving me sips of Accolade, not letting me stop for more than a few seconds. It must have been very tedious for him but it helped me more than he'll ever know. Thanks, Mike.

As we left Great Calva I told him I wanted to be at the top of Skiddaw by 7 a.m. He shook his head. "I don't think you'll make that. Ten past, perhaps." Perhaps this was psychology again — the ascent was long but easy, we could see the summit all the way, and the autopilot had taken over my legs. I knew that if I reached the summit by 7 a.m. nothing could stop me getting back to Keswick by 8.30 a.m. I was now on a 'tiredness high'. The summit was sharply defined despite a lot of haze and from a long way off I could clearly see two figures there. I didn't know who they were but I knew they were waiting for me. Angels, perhaps? As if to support this theory, a cloud started rolling *up* the hill beside us. Have you ever seen that? It's a beautiful sight.

We reached Skiddaw, the 42nd summit, at exactly 7 a.m. The two figures waiting there were Bill Booth from Acorn House and his son. When people are prepared to get up at 5 a.m. and climb Skiddaw just to greet you and say "well done", there's no way you can let them down.

And I didn't — not them, nor all our pacers, nor everyone who helped — and especially not my wife, who supported me so totally and to whom I owe so much. I have rarely enjoyed a descent as much as I enjoyed that jog off Skiddaw. The first sight of Keswick over the flank of the mountain was something I relished then and will remember always. Journey's end. I was going to get there and complete the round and I would become member 117 of the Bob Graham Club: something that I never thought I would achieve.

Malcolm and Jack are members 115 and 116. We were all pleased for Jack: to have done the Round at the age of 53 is a tremendous achievement, especially after two previous disappointments.

At 8.07 a.m. on Sunday 10th June I trotted up to the Moot Hall in Keswick, grinning like a fool. Terry gave me a hug: she knew how much it meant to me. And so I have joined what I had previously thought of as an elite. I see now that it is not; it is a band of people who love the fells and love a challenge. The comradeship extends to helping others, in the way our pacers helped us. I'm sure Dick will try again, hopefully on a better day for him. If a very average fell-runner like me can get round, I'm damned sure he can. Another thing I'm sure of: I'll be there helping him. My Bob Graham Round was an unforgettable experience which has deepened my love of, and respect for, the hills of the Lake District. Dick shared the great moment when I achieved my personal Everest and I want to be there when he joins what is now, to me, the best club in the country.

from CLIMBER AND RAMBLER *April 1980*

Author's footnote: Six weeks later, Dick Courchee *did* try again, assisted by the three of us and John Richards, and got round with 12 minutes to spare — a tremendously brave effort.

The Big Walk

ANON

In early 1960, the 'holiday camp king', Billy Butlin, organised a race from John o'Groats to Land's End — the whole length of the mainland of Britain, a distance by road of about 900 miles. The race caught the imagination of the public in a quite extraordinary way, and nearly 1,000 entries were received, of whom over 700 actually started from John o'Groats on February 26 in very wintry conditions.

The Big Walk is an account of the walk written anonymously by one of those taking part; we have been unable to discover his or her identity and are grateful to the Butlin Organisation for giving permission to reprint this extract describing an early stage of the walk, down the west side of Loch Ness. *Editor's Note*

Shortly after Drumnadrochit, the glen road divides on either hand of a small bay inlet of Loch Ness, the left-hand fork going to Inverness and the right one down the Great Glen to Fort Augustus. It was not too dark to see the outline of the hills, and in this light one had an impression of gigantic size on reaching the lochside proper. Towards Inverness, the water seemed to stretch away into endless distance, giving an illusion of looking out to sea. In this direction, it was as if one was looking slightly uphill along the line of the water, which grew lighter in hue as it neared the imagined sea until it ended in a haze of dawny light.

The other way, between the great mountains on either hand, the loch flowed gently downhill into dark depths of unknown mystery. No doubt this contrast of impressions was due to the hills becoming gradually lower towards Inverness, and higher in the other direction, towards the very heart of the Highlands. The loch weaved an atmosphere of obscure secrecy and fascination about its hidden depths, as it does at all times, but perhaps more so to a person walking its shores alone on a winter night.

There was none of the ice and snow on the road here that we had heard about, and I made good speed for the first two

226

hours, almost catching up with the Yorkshireman. He was wearing steel studded boots, and at one point I could hear their echo in the stillness of the night just half a mile ahead. But that was the closest I ever came to him, for after putting on a spurt my blisters were burning the soles of my feet so badly that I was forced to stop for a break.

Starting again five minutes later was like going through hell. It was as if hundreds of little devils, each with a tiny red hot pitchfork, were prodding my feet continually. I could almost see the wide grins on their ugly little faces as they danced about me. They were quite naked, with flaming red skin, big ears and polished white horns — like those of a prima donna dairy cow ready for a show. On their feet they wore white boots, laced tightly to the tops and glowing phosphorescently in the dark. Standing only half an inch high, they leaped and danced soundlessly round my feet, and I imagined that somewhere behind, a group of reserves were heating their pitchforks in a mobile brazier, ready for their turn to join in the bloodthirsty sport of pricking my feet. The pilgrims of old who put stones in their shoes when they walked cannot have suffered more than I did that night alongside Loch Ness, and I felt that if I had been doing this walk as a penance, I would have been absolved from and forgiven many sins. All the same, I wished that the monster would appear and gather the little wretches with her tendrils into the icy depths. What a sizzling there would have been as their red hot bodies touched the surface! Perhaps the monster knew this, and that the waters of the loch would have boiled and made things uncomfortable for her. At any rate, she stayed where she was and I never had a glimpse of her.

There was little traffic on the road; only two cars passed me the whole night. About halfway to Fort Augustus I met a tramp walking the other way, and passed the time of day (or rather night) with him. He should have been on the walk, I suggested. Yes, he had thought about it. He was used to walking long distances on the roads, but had heard of a job he might get near Inverness. He was on his way there from Glasgow, and his last long stop had been in Fort William. He had seen quite a few walkers in Fort William and had passed occasional ones or groups every few miles since then. He had seen the Yorkshireman just a mile down the road, having a rest.

Some miles on I came to a house on the lochside, and rested awhile in the porch of an outhouse. I was becoming sleepy and thought I could snatch a few winks sitting on the concrete floor. I dozed for a minute or two but was soon chilled and aching all over, so got up to continue. As I was emerging round the side of the house, a voice from the darkness called out: " 'Ullo, 'ow are you?''

Thinking that this was the house owner, I started to explain that I had just used his porch to rest a few moments. Then he told me he was the wee fellow with the bad leg — the one I had overtaken near 'Drum'. I tried to persuade him to come on with me for company, but he said he was all in and would stay the night. As he appeared to be crouching on an upturned bucket, I have no doubt he did not enjoy his rest very much, but he was obviously in great pain and I let him be. I met him again later the same day, as I was leaving Fort Augustus; at that time he had given up the race and was going home. He was very miserable at his failure — not so much because he had not lived up to his own expectations of himself, but rather because he felt he had let down his family and friends. This attitude was not uncommon; indeed, I think we all suffered from the same mental outlook at one time or other, if not all the time. There was no conceit in the perception that those we had left at home depended on us to do well, or at least to complete the journey. The encouragement we received from our home areas, individually, was a very real thing, and may well have been the reason for some of us keeping going long after we knew we had lost all hope of winning any prize.

As dawn broke, a tall young Englishman wearing a duffle coat caught up with me. I had left him asleep in the hotel at Drumnadrochit; he had left at 2 a.m. and had not stopped since, but was now very sleepy. So was I.

We arrived at the hamlet of Invermoriston at 7 a.m. and, deciding we must have a nap before completing the remaining seven miles to Fort Augustus, rested on seats on the verandah of a hotel. We were woken ten minutes later by three lusty youths who arrived for breakfast, and banged on the door for service. When they got no answer, two of them joined us on the seats. The third said he was going on, which he did.

The other two were steel workers from Bradford, good chaps both, and I saw quite a bit of them over the next week. We had all been sitting there for five minutes or so, eating chocolate and biscuits, when someone suddenly realised that the road the other man had taken was signposted to Skye. We tried shouting, but he had obviously gone too far to hear us and no one had the energy to get up and follow him. We all thought this was a hilarious joke and laughed our heads off at the thought of a Butlin walker solemnly plodding his way through Glen Shiel and then finding himself on the west coast.

However, the wandering stranger returned after a while, realising his mistake, and we all set off together. This was much easier than being alone or even than being with just one other. For if one of us eased up a little, the others all bullied the offender into keeping up. We were no longer tired, but very hungry, and the thought of breakfast kept us going at a steady four miles an hour.

I can remember few more pleasing and more beautiful sights than Fort Augustus as it came into our view that morning. Nestling serenely amongst trees at the end of the loch, it seemed that here was heaven after the hell of the night. The little town appeared to be coming to meet us in its image on the surface of Loch Ness, and when we were still a mile away we could almost smell the bacon and eggs.

from THE BIG WALK *1961*

The Warm South

JOHN HILLABY

If I moved fast on that last two-day stage of 60 miles, the journey moved even faster. Far from coming to an end abruptly, as I thought it would, it scampered on ahead from somewhere just south of St. Etienne and I never really wanted to catch it up. The physical details are of small account. The track trickles down through the herb-scented hills by way of St. Sauveur and the Mountain of the Madonna above Utelle. I left it at Levens some 12 miles from the coast and took to the valley of the Var. There on the autoway, beside the river, the rich herdsmen of Europe hooted their way down to what the regulars call the Old Blue Strip, the Cote d'Azur, a modern fringe to an ancient garment.

In that noisy company I walked for three or four hours, mentally turning over the dividends of not just this trip, but also what it meant in relation to others I had made.

> I am part of all that I have met;
> Yet all experience is an arch wherethrough
> Gleams that untravelled world whose margin fades
> For ever and for ever when I move. . .

I have described some of the highlights and shadows of this journey, but they are for the most part the view from the hill or the rural bypath. On the few occasions when, through pressure of time, I took short cuts across industrial areas, I was appalled by what I saw. I am thinking particularly of the abject condition of the Lower Rhine, the Meuse, the Moselle, and the layer of rotting fish on the surface of Lake Geneva. Many of the Swiss lakes are all but done for. They are communal cesspools, almost entirely devoid of any form of wholesome life, and as for the Mediterranean, that mother sea of civilisations, the belt of frothy scum, composed in part of oil and undecomposed human excrement, around many of the holiday centres is frightful to look at. It makes even the thought of bathing abhorrent.

Pollution is not merely confined to sea coast and heavily industrialised regions. It is creeping into Alpine villages where those who have stubbornly stuck it out, such as the oldsters of Gurraz and Ceillac in the High Alps, are bluntly advised to sell out and die somewhere else. They are squatting on an unexploited goldmine of tourism. If they remain they will be obliged to act as servants of that industry, as dishonest mimics of themselves got up in costume their grandparents wore. They will become the lay figures of the guided tour, of travel adventure advertised and sold in packages, guaranteed like processed farmhouse stew, hamburgers, and scampi and chips to be consumed without risk. The price is degradation.

As I see it, we are not much moved by waste, by pollution, by exploitation unless it offends our sight or hurts our pockets. The precepts of land management, of living in harmony with the environment, are as clear as the ten commandments, but until they are written round the walls of junior schools they can't be repeated too often. The first is that the wholly commercial, the industrial way of life, with its ethos of expansion, is simply not sustainable. It cannot last. The rapidly closing circle of enjoyable space must constrict to the point of intolerability within the lifetime of someone born today.

I recall the start of this journey vividly: the cold grey sea, the young people on the beach, the feeling that anything might happen from that moment on. After months of planning I knew I wasn't getting away from it all; I was trying to get *with* something. Essentially, it was the rediscovery and enlargement of a portion of the world of which I have the joy of being a part. That world is what's left of unspoiled land, of land brimful of self-sustaining energy, a community of plants and animals, the ground floor of people and cultures, of changing landscapes which, I believe, can be seen and enjoyed best by striding across its subtle graduations on foot.

In the process of rediscovery many of my preconceptions have been modified or completely changed. Much of western Europe is undergoing social and cultural convulsions so profound and at such a pace that I could only wonder at what point I had stepped in and where it would all end.

The changes are evident in the tide-like drift of people from remote rural areas to the towns and cities, a process which has been going on since Roman times at least, but now at an unprecedented rate. Cultural diffusion is being accelerated by wandering gangs of labourers from Spain, Italy, Algiers, Greece and other places. The peaks of local individuality are being smoothed out by droves of tourists with money to spend on what the city agencies have largely made up for their diversion. "It's not what the customer wants; it's what he needs." Everywhere I went I tried to meet people with most claim to be called natives. Through the barriers of language I knew I should miss a great deal, but I guessed that a lone traveller on foot has a better chance of breaking down those barriers than most.

As for the route itself, rather more than half the distance between the North Sea and the Mediterranean has already been surveyed and signposted indifferently well by national committees of *sentiers* in France and Belgium. Unfortunately, they confine their activities strictly to trails within their own frontiers. There is no co-ordination that I could discover between the French, the Swiss, the Dutch and the Italian authorities, who between them might, if they were interested or encouraged, work out a wonderful international trail with alternative routes. The first major gap lies between the coast of the North Sea and the start of the serpentine *Sentier Ardennais* near Liege; the second is from south Luxembourg to the Vosges by way of Lorraine, and the third from Masevaux at the foot of the Vosges to Lake Geneva where the trans-Alpine trail begins. Hopefully, these gaps will be bridged within the next few years.

The argument that only a few walkers would use a long-distance trail is usually put forward by those who don't want to get involved in the self-centred politics of the organisations concerned. As matters stand at the moment, the map of western Europe is fly-speckled with isolated reserves and sanctuaries with here and there a big park like the Vanoise, a wilderness area in danger of human erosion. Trails are vitally necessary to keep the way for tomorrow open. They are the least we can hope for within contemporary patterns of development. With a little ingenuity they could be used to link up some splendid country in the Netherlands with the Ardennes, the Vosges, and the southern Alps. They can be picked up from most of the nearby roads and cities and relinquished just as easily.

One well-found trail from coast to coast might well become the trunk of an ever-growing tree with outward-spreading branches. It offers an opportunity for striding out for hundreds of miles. It affords an escape from the grey disease of conformity. Certainly whatever remains on those trails of the essential differences between varying kinds of country, of people and their cultures, will resist the smoothing-out process longest.

Long after dusk I reached the lights, the indolent palms, the rowdy manic traffic of Nice, the fifth city of France but for *divertissements en tout genres* second only to Paris. Empty *Gauloise* packets in the gutter. Bougainvilleas and baskets of pink geraniums. Clip joints. Lines of hotels like wedding cakes. Cafés that sell coffee and brandy, eight different kinds of *pastis* and Smith's Potato Crisps. Two Algerian winos, dead drunk, their mouths open, lay near a traffic sign that advocated *Prudence*. High over the Bay of Angels, streaks of rockets burst in scarlet chrysanthemums, briefly illuminating what is claimed to be the biggest supermarket in the world. Crowds flocked round an open-air cinema. They cheered wildly at the news-flashes. "They have got there," they said. Who'd got where? "The Americans," they said. "They are actually walking on the moon." Near midnight I scratched myself trying to cut a corner off the approach to the *Promenade des Anglais* by pushing through the prickly pears around the perimeter of the airport. Then down to the beach, walking among the youngsters sleeping there, not stopping until I had walked into the warm sea.

from JOURNEY THROUGH EUROPE *1972*

Extracts from 'The Rucksack Man'

SEBASTIAN SNOW

In 1973 and 1974, Sebastian Snow walked 8,700 miles from Tierra del Fuego at the southern tip of South America to the Panama Canal — an epic journey in which he survived more adventures and near-disasters than most people meet in a lifetime.

   These two extracts from his account of the walk depict him at the very beginning and at the very end: a telling and moving contrast. *Editor's Note*

Start: Tierra del Fuego

I had spent some considerable time wondering what I should take with me. It was an impossibly difficult task, for I would be travelling through snow and desert sand; in rain and at immensely high altitudes; the variations were extreme. Best therefore to simplify the whole and wear what I was used to and stick to what I walked in at home: some Derbyshire tweed knickerbockers, a pair of long Norwegian mountaineering knee socks made out of pure wool, a heavy double ventile anorak and the usual vest, pants, shirt and hand-knitted sweater. I'd need several changes of clothes but they could all be of the same type and the less I took, the less I would have to carry.

Vitally important were several pairs of contact lenses, my spectacles, a tent and sleeping bag, a watch and a camera. But most essential of all would be several pairs of footgear. I walked in soft light supple Italian walking-cum-climbing boots made of leather. How long would each pair last? How many should I carry?

Would I need something to read on lonely evenings as I did not speak the language, or would I be so tired I'd fall instantly asleep? In the end I took too many books for they were so very heavy. Medicines, maps, a compass and a torch were a must and also a plastic mug so that I could drink from passing streams. Water would be too heavy and awkward to carry and so would food but I'd have to take something for when I got stuck on the way and had to spend the night camping in the wilds. Otherwise I was determined to eat at local inns. If I travelled light then I would need money; money to pay for food and lodgings for months on end. That and my passport had to be thief-proof.

I dithered about, pushing things in and pulling them out. Finally, on 5th February 1973, I started walking due north, carrying a 60lb pack. It was so heavy that I had the greatest possible difficulty getting out of Ushuaia. Within ten minutes I lost all movement in my arms which had become completely numb, as I had fastened the rucksack straps too tight.

Although it was impossible to get lost I enquired of a passer-by the road to Kaiken and was told there was only one

road and I was not on it. As I slowly headed and heaved north I saw the photogenic Mt. Olivia towering 4,000ft. to my right and the peaks of the Martial Massif to my left looking like Gothic spires.

The road was not tarmaced. I found the going heavy; sweat poured off my face and eyebrows in rivulets and every time a vehicle passed I was blinded with dust which infiltrated behind my contact lenses causing agony — an agony that I stupidly put up with for 19 months.

After about nine-and-a-half kilometres of dog-potting through the mountains a Canadian motorcyclist stopped beside me and said, "Poor soul. Aren't you a famous author?"

"No," I replied but he persisted, saying, "Yes, I've got it — your name is Scott".

"My name is Snow."

"Ah yes, I knew it began with an 'S'."

He'd driven from Quebec in exactly three months, which sounded good going.

I wondered how long it would take me to reach Panama City and what adventures would befall me on the way. I had walked and climbed before in South America and had always found walking by far the best way of getting to know and understand a country. You are in touch with the land, palpably through the soles of your feet the entire time, not insulated from it by glass or perspex. You see the landscape unfold slowly before you and come to understand something of its rhythm, its harshness or softness, its sense of space. You see a village a long way off, and approach it slowly as the inhabitants do. By the time you have reached it you are getting to know its silhouette well, you have had time to assimilate it, to work out its plan, to think about its people and to wonder what lies ahead.

You can talk to all whom you meet at your leisure and you have some understanding of their lives, their problems and their attitudes for you too are steeped in the landscape, in the contours of the land, in the feeling of the wind and the rain and the force of the elements.

Walking is man's natural pace, his normal speed of

progress. At this tempo you have time to think, to reflect and to cogitate on what you see around you. It is lonely but then I've always found it a welcoming loneliness. Once a steady rhythm has been established you can let your mind go quite blank or you can be alert, watching for birds or animals. You can amble along in a peaceful relaxing silence or you can indulge in a thought-provoking period, in reflection or private inner arguments. Nobody interrupts.

Walking is a delightfully self-reliant activity, no companions to let you down, no animals to contend with, no engine to fail. If you feel lazy, stay another day. If you feel immensely energetic, increase the speed. It's a hobby in which all can indulge, it doesn't need vast equipment, complex training schedules or other people.

The great art is not to worry or fuss, not to bustle or push but to set yourself a task and to muddle through the pressures at your own pace; ignore physical discomfort, remain amused by complications. Just keep going.

Or at least, that was what I'd always found. Would it be the same walking a whole continent?

As I stumbled along that first day I wished that my preparations for the trip had been more thorough. I had wandered the lanes of Devon for a couple of hours each day in order to get fit, but it had clearly been insufficient training. I only managed another three-and-a-quarter kilometres that day which made it the shortest of my whole trip. I stopped exhausted at a hosteria where cakes and soft drinks were served, only too grateful to rest.

At night the hosteria turned into a nightclub. It was called Monte Olivaia and was crowded out with a bus-load of elderly American tourists who, of all things, had just been to the South Pole. They were all very enterprising, enthusiastic and vociferous, equipped with very expensive cameras that hung — ready for instant action — around their necks, drooping like pendulums over paunchy stomachs. I took my hat off to them. One of them edged up to me and said critically, "You are from Exeter, England, are you not?" "Yes," I answered. "How on earth did you know?" "I can read people's minds" was the enigmatic rejoinder.

A very chic heavy-lidded French dame — rather like Juliette Greco in her younger night-club days — yelled out that I would never make it over the first range of mountains. I made a very rude sign — which she reciprocated with gusto — and passed on.

That night I made my first camp near the hosteria beside a trout stream. I took one and a half hours putting up my tent which a clueless boy scout could have run up in three minutes blindfold in a force ten gale. All I had to do was slip three clips into five holes. I had no sleep, experiencing bloody awful toothache and squitters — until the tent fell on top of me and I had something else to think about.

The End: Panama City

Well, I had made it. I'd traversed the continent of South America on foot and crossed the Darien Gap. The end was hazardous, ghastly, a gruelling nightmare where death stalked. Only willpower kept me going. Underweight by about five stones, two sprained ankles, both swollen and discoloured, my feet and ankles covered with gore, blood and bites, a mass of suppurating sores, stung by a hornet on the neck, bitten by a scorpion, nipped by a vampire bat, ticks under the skin, I looked in the mirror and saw what days in the jungle could do.

I beheld my shrivelled, emaciated body, spotted chicken-pox red with insect bites. I knew I needed to pick off all the ticks and leeches that the dirt hid. I looked down at my feet, scaly, infected, skin just peeling off from lack of vitamins and foot rot. It hurt to try on a size 14 shirt that someone gave me charitably and to find it fitted after years of size 16. But worst of all is to look in someone's face and see: "My God, we have to help this kid", and you wondered who they were talking about and you looked at them from your rotting clothes, stiff, dismal, grey from days of sweat and mud. Nobody could understand why I had come all that way through the jungle. Who knows . . . but I believed in God.

A most hospitable couple called Vaughan (he was the British Airways representative in Panama City) let me stay with them in their apartment on the 17th floor of a high rise block. From the window I could look down on a mini plot of land of less than a quarter of an acre, hardly room for a dog to cock its leg on, which I was assured was to be sold for one million dollars. Inflation seemed to be galloping here, all right. I thought I'd better not stay long but had to decide whether to return to England to recuperate or continue my walk up through North America to Alaska. Or should I walk across to Washington?

But could I go on? I wanted to go on, to accomplish the longest walk in the world and indeed I knew I could. My legs would keep going, my brain would accept it but what about the rest of me? They told me that I was in bad shape and that if I continued I would become a wizened old crock, toothless, bald, emaciated, permanently broken in health. All my teeth would fall out and maybe my liver would pack up. Did I want to live the rest of my life on soup?

Evidently I had lost too many vitamins, too many chemicals to be able to replace them by a few injections. The whole chemical balance of my body was temporarily upset.

The problem was, how long would it take me to get fit and could I afford to sit around in this incredibly expensive place waiting? Return to England to recuperate, they said, and maybe for once they were right. The US would of course be full of vitamins but where would I get them in sufficient quantities in Costa Rica, in Guatemala or in the Mexican desert? Had I contracted the dreaded Chaga disease perhaps on my journey? This was evidently something peculiar to South America and said to be carried by the armadillo. The prospect of imminent relapsing fever getting in on top of everything else made me feel that maybe a return to England would be a good idea after all.

First, however, I walked to the Panama Canal and marched across it so that I had indeed covered the continent of South America in every respect and had clearly set foot in North America too, to prove it. I'd made it, despite all those Cassandras who had cried impossible, despite all those who had feared I would be murdered, run over or hit by typhoid. As I made this last lap, I thought back over all that had happened to me since Tierra del Fuego and decided that the

Peruvian desert had been the worst section of all: that burning asphalt, so hard on the feet. The Gap had only taken about a month which had been less than I had expected: of course, we had zig-zagged about so much, we must have covered about one and a half times the actual straight distance across.

Wade had left a note for me with the film and it formed a fitting epilogue to our successful traverse:

> The luxuries of jungle life: the smoke of the fire that chases away the bugs, a banana almost gone bad sitting in a bin, a thatch hut found in the wood, a rainless night, a fresh kill, whatever it may be, water deep enough to bathe in, a hint of solid shit, a full night's sleep, a lemon tree found in the jungle . . .

It had been a good walk. But should I have done it the other way round, beginning with the hot jungle and progressing slowly towards the Antarctic cool?

Ideally I would like in the future to do it all over again, but next time downhill all the way from Alaska to Tierra del Fuego.

from THE RUCKSACK MAN *1975*

From Desert to Pines

DAVID JOERIS

As we struggled with our packs each of us toyed silently with the same thought: What were we doing with those ridiculously heavy burdens with 2,000ft. of loose rock and cactus towering above us?

The answer, I told myself, was simple enough — we were going to explore the Guadalupe Mountains National Park in the western corner of Texas by going beyond the usual day hike excursion up to the ridge top. For three days, we were going to see the park from the inside, the view you miss as you drive by in the desert below it.

A simple idea, perhaps, but not so simple an undertaking.

The Guadalupe Mountains National Park, formed in 1972, is one of the newest of our national parks, and probably the most rugged and least developed. The trails are rocky, narrow, faded and not maintained. The majority of the high country, 46,850 acres, is being considered for designation as wilderness. Located 110 miles from El Paso, Texas, on US Highway 62-180, the park itself is virtually isolated from civilisation. The Guadalupe Mountains rise abruptly from the surrounding desert plains, which are rich in stories of Indian battles and settlers' troubles, but not much else. Even today, you can look to the horizon 75 miles away and count the signs of human intrusion on the fingers of one, maybe two hands.

The Park occupies the southern tip of the range, including Guadalupe Peak, the highest point in Texas at 8,751ft. It is protected from all but the hardiest visitor who is willing to climb 2,000ft. in a mile to reach the high plateau area that is the Guadalupes.

Once in the high country, the only amenities provided by the National Park Service are a few barely marked trails that frequently have a tendency to become part of the wilderness themselves. Nature provides even fewer invitations to human visitors. The only available water comes from unreliable springs and the weather can change so suddenly that 70mph winds and freezing temperatures are produced with little warning. Faced with this, the average visitor to the park is limited to short day hikes on the edge of the park. Having done this ourselves many times, four of us resolved to go beyond and experience the Guadalupes as they should be — with a backpack.

Students at the University of Texas at El Paso, we planned to use the Thanksgiving holidays to hike some 15 miles across the park. Our route would pass from desert up a barren escarpment, through pine forest, along a wind-swept ridge and down into a green, tree-filled canyon which produces a year-round stream that disappears into the arid country beyond the canyon mouth. Starting in 85°F heat in the desert, we each carried two and a half gallons of water to last for two days. By the time we loaded the rest of our equipment, our packs had bulged to their limits. With camera equipment, my pack weighed 70lb — not the kind of load that facilitates fleet-footed climbing.

Thus it was not without some apprehension that we ventured up the Bear Canyon Trail that starts on the desert floor near an old Butterfield stage stop, the Pinery Station, and climbs to the top of the escarpment in about a mile. The path is well defined by steep slopes of impassable loose rock on either side. For the first 20 minutes we complimented each other on what a fine pace we were keeping until the trail itself suddenly turned upward at an almost 45 degree angle and degenerated into nothing but loose rock. For the next hour we talked excitedly at rest stops as our view of the country below us extended 50, 75, then 100 miles across the desert.

While hiking, though, it was a different story: take two steps, slide back one, squeeze around a prickly pear, then carefully work your way around a hairpin bend with a fifty-foot drop on the side of a two-foot trail. Casual conversation sort of dried up as feet slipped and packs swayed. As we neared the top the trail got steeper; in places there were logs anchored in place to collect loose stones, providing some semblance of a trail in the midst of a huge rockslide. Two hours after leaving the desert heat we could still see nothing but rocks, cactus, the occasional stunted tree and endless desert plains stretching away from the rockface. But there was a difference. In the cool wind blowing down from above we could sense, in the dusty desert air, the fresh smell of pines. Given this added incentive we pushed on faster, revitalised by the thought of escape from the oppressive desert.

The faint pine smell fails to prepare you for the spectacle that unfolds when you finally reach the crest. You are no longer dodging cactus: abruptly, you are standing under the boughs of a Ponderosa pine. Within 20ft. of the crest, you are immersed in a relic pine forest. In the short time it takes you to walk that distance your whole world changes. Your feet go from treacherous rocks to soft pine needles. The sun that has been beating down is suddenly a flickering light illuminating the pine needles. Even the weight of our over-loaded packs could not detract from the otherworldliness of the transformation. We dumped our loads in a pile against the nearest tree and stood there quietly, luxuriating in the splendour of the experience and breathing the pine-smelling air deeply. The trail from the crest descends into the trees and becomes less and less distinct. Because so few people penetrate the 'Bowl', as the forest area is called, you have to watch closely to stay on the trail. We didn't and soon found ourselves following an animal path which subsequently turned into three or four paths. Soon these disappeared among the pines and we realised we didn't know where we were. With just the Park Service map to rely on we would have been lost, but luckily we also had a topographical map of the area. Reaching a clearing, we figured our position by sighting from the surrounding peaks and headed across country in the direction of our proposed campsite. Our route took us a few hours to cover so we connected with the trail again just as the sun went down, leaving us in darkness. With the sun went its warmth. We decided to camp along the trail rather than try to reach the designated campsite two miles ahead.

The next morning we were eager to get on the way again. After a breakfast of fruit and Granola washed down with a little delicious water, we started down the trail, watching it very closely this time.

From the Bowl, the path winds up out of the thick pines to a rocky ridgeline trail covered with cactus and a few hardy trees that have managed to survive the continuous wind. The trail is marked here by small rock cairns. So few people reach this area of the park that the path would be non-existent without the cairns. We found the campsite we had been aiming for the previous day perched on the side of the ridge and paused to admire the view of Sierra Blanca peak, 100 miles to the west.

The hike along the McKittrick Ridge Trail gives you some of the most spectacular views imaginable. The feeling you get from being able to look out across the desert and see no sign of man's civilisation for a hundred miles to the horizon awes the mind. As you walk, the drop off to the right of the path becomes steeper and steeper, ending 2,000ft. below in the brilliant colours of McKittrick Canyon.

We spent all day along this section, arriving at the McKittrick Ridge primitive campsite just before sunset. The campsite is perched below a mountain crest and sheltered by a few windblown pines. Again, we found the area so untouched by man that, had there not been a sign, we would not have known it was a campsite.

That evening we ventured over to the edge of the canyon to watch the moon rise. We found no moon, but in its place a huge thunderhead nestled on the horizon. As we sat there, our legs dangling over 100ft. of air, the cloud began to glow. Soon the whole thing became one spectacular fireworks display. The cloud flashed with golds and oranges, while its silhouetted outline became more and more distinct as the sky beyond it grew light. Suddenly, as the cloud let forth a particularly blinding series of flashes, the centre of it produced a shining white sliver. Almost as if giving birth, the thunderhead contorted itself with lightning, pushing more and more of the moon into the black sky above it. This display lasted a good ten minutes until finally the full moon broke free from the clouds entirely, rising to illuminate the desert floor beneath it. Not one single light could be seen in the desert in front of the cloud; nothing but a vast empty space and the moon.

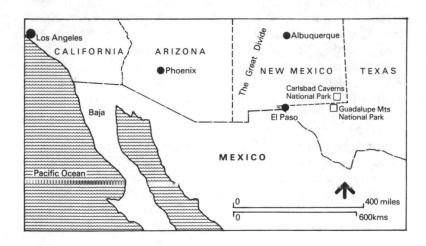

The next morning we were ready to take on the most spectacular part of the trip, the descent to the floor of McKittrick Canyon. This is accomplished by means of a nearly vertical trail which plummets 2,000ft. doubling back on itself endlessly. Half sliding, half walking, we dropped lower with each step. The cactus and rocks of the ridgeline give way to an occasional tree. As you continue, these occasional trees turn into a canopy that enfolds the trail. By the time you reach the bottom you are in a desert oasis. The windswept ridge towers above you, its harsh outline jutting against the sky, but down in the canyon a gentle stream greets you at the bottom of the trail. The Guadalupe Park is a place of contrast and nowhere is this more apparent than in McKittrick Canyon. Open for day use only, the canyon harbours rare species of plants in a uniquely isolated desert sanctuary.

We drank greedily from the stream since our water supply had run out on the climb down, and after a short rest we followed the stream down the canyon. There was evidence of deer all along the trail and so we were not too surprised to come around some trees and find ourselves staring at a group of mule deer in the path some 60ft. ahead. We were delighted when one of the herd, which is protected from hunters, looked at us and started walking up the trail in our direction. Soon another joined him. They came about 15ft. closer, not sure what we were. Then, deciding that we weren't really interesting, they calmly continued on their way across the trail, unperturbed by our presence. Here was yet another reminder of the wilderness quality of the park.

Further downstream, among some trees, we found an old hunter's cabin, the first sign of human intrusion into this wilderness and the first sign of human existence we had seen for three days. The cabin was empty now, but at one time was a remote paradise for guests of the rancher who used to own land around the park. We paused to rest, Bob taking advantage of an ancient rocking chair on the front porch of the stone structure. Across the stream we could see deer moving gracefully along the canyon wall, grazing as they went.

By now the sun was slipping below the canyon rim and the

whole place was in shade. The rest of the trail was easy compared to what we'd gotten used to in the past two days. We covered the three miles to the mouth of the canyon in a very short time. The path gives a gradual readjustment to the desert. As you walk, the stream disappears and resurfaces a few times before going underground to stay. The trees give way to cactus and scrub again and the canyon walls grow less sheer and rocky.

We followed the trail out to the fence at the canyon's end, erected by the Park Service to control visitor use, and there we saw four people, our first in three days. Bob spoke first, greeting them with a friendly Texas "howdy" and they responded smiling, but looking rather strangely at us.

"Where did y'all come from with all that on your backs?" one of them asked. "Did you go up for the day?"

"No, we came over those mountains. Started three days ago."

"Three days! Up there? No way you'd get me to carry all that for three days."

One of the women quit staring long enough to speak. "I've never seen a backpacker before."

from MOUNTAIN GAZETTE 60 *1977*

Sinai

MICHAEL TOBIAS

There is only one way to really experience desert that I know of. That is to walk, naked, for a few weeks, in the wrong direction — in no direction — with too little water, too little food, and nothing else. No matches, no weapon, nothing. A light rucksack. No shoes, not even a loin-cloth. And certainly no sunglasses. The desert is a way of stepping out of the world, of one's civilisation.

Civilisation. With its decors, stale lolls, fanatical shelters, lifeless predictability. Its lack of vision. Its useless origins and laughable edifices. Its ornate euphemisms, neutron bombs and tramways. Its complacent jobs and deaths and burials and fathomless shit which runs on time; the clocks, the payrolls, the newspapers, the sewers. Stepping out into the desert, out of one's pants, is not merely an easy, extreme escape from the society of men, but a rare deliverance. All aspiration and past images are denuded in the giddy, trigger-happy barrenness of sudden self, of life marvellously reduced to the hot instantaneous, to mirrorless monologue, to danger. If civilisation has real merit, it is this; the delectable, half-mad logic — aesthetic — which aspires to escape it, or to understand it anew.

At first I sprawled, careening over roots and boulders, my freedom caving into the discovered vortex of my life. Every action was a *frisson* of paradise, a source of panic, of pleasurable hubris. My thoughts were quickly submerged in stone, reduced to outlines, to words like locust which went screaming out into the void. Shameless, my genitals swaying to each vague suicidal step, the sun pierced my pale white back, consuming it brown with cosmological talons. Ants up my leg. Like swimming in pain, total immersion. To walk into a season-worth of passion, right there, in a matter of minutes, hours, during the course of the night; until, by the pressure-cooker of the desert, the skillet of shipwreck on all sides, by the high voltage of nothingness, my mind should have erupted into the wiry inoculum of itself, the blowtorch, ice floe, legacy, the entire disarray of its being.

Getting lost is the only way to really challenge everything one knows and believes in. To render oneself absolutely vulnerable. To shift, if only by a degree, one's perspective on this trudge we call existence. No one told me of the jackals. Nor of the sun which, by two in the afternoon, covers a third of the white sky. The air wavers. My ribs hurt. My nose and shoulders are blistered. Like bile, something bubbles under the nostrils. Foam prickles the upper lip. My urine is ivory-coloured. My eyes seem to be oozing, weighted down with dust. And the head is dull with fire and throbbing. The sides of myself — epileptic, ongoing — have shrunk in the festering travail. I am out at sea, crossing a stretch with so little feeling that I might be moving in circles for all I know.

But the nights, wherever I am, are irresistible. Sand twinkling with the breathtaking retinal nervousness of crackling stars. Nebulae and chinooks. Wind rushing over the sweet sabra. Rocks suddenly spalling from cliff-sides. Vipers sleeking in the darkness nearby. Jackals howling in a murderous pack. I surround myself with whatever rocks may be near. I pee on them. And start screaming. For hours. Each god-awful shriek whiplashing my brain, accenting my maniacal laughing in echoes of perilous exhibitionism. I keep watching for yellow eyes converging.

At sunrise I am refreshed. I gaze out at some fantastic cliffs. My hair is getting white. I'm limber. Bengali thin. Black. My muscles are alive and aching to move. Never have I felt so topographically physiological. My bones, my sighs and flesh, the ideas raining in and draining out, the hard stub of moving marrow, the light in the iris, the ground edging nearer to some source up my feet — a surface of interior gesture remaking the world of my senses. I haven't the faintest idea where I am. I'm rationing water. Experimenting with whatever plants I come across. Some are bitter. I leave them. Others are only semi-bitter. I swallow them fast. None are particularly suited to my taste. Few delectations other than the night's coolness. But that is enough. The sizzling daytime is a reverie, a contrast, Mersault's blinding moment of murder in Camus' *Stranger*. Like the unapproachable glare of a bomb's rim, I walk into the contagion of skylines riveted with haze and sunburst. Ascending a narrow arroyo, feeling like I'm about to have a heart attack. It must be 130°F. Entering a fabulous spectacle; what Neil Armstrong must have been referring to when he said the Sinai is the landform most akin to the moon. The astronauts had done training(?) here. Idiots!

I come up to some tracks. The vague remains of a Land-Rover. I follow it through an ocean of blankness into ribs of rift, black, burnt siennas, rusts, dulled umbers of dust caking the broiled plates of stone. A narrow, cliff-girt wadi. It narrows and narrows. Suddenly there are no more tracks. Perhaps turned round. The gorge, after several hours and innumerable wends, pinches to a sombre close. Walls 200ft.

high. Sheer. The sun is directly overhead. What a place to die, in the loins of a labyrinth. The sand is up to my knees now. And solid, radiating white. A low humming of electricity, the heat. Trapped in an unrimmed quarry, stubble, hard gravel, conscience in my throat. I am dizzying, stymied, a holocaust burning inward. My eyes granitic, my palms flustered. There is riddled wildness, a mayhem smolt with muscle spilling out its rage, an ardour twisting directionless, a cloaked matador that's been gored.

I assault my predicament with a final logic. Regret, revulsion, and a flinging single idea — to save myself. The body, stripped bare, becomes a gust and hurls itself backwards. There in a cranny of the rock it sees life. A rag, of flesh and ramskin, whitened, stuffed by wind between a bramble clump and dusty shades, without a recall, utterance or marker, lone, mere pestled bones, a shambled, wizened, long forgotten heap of bleach, no meaning. Perhaps a sheep, or a Bedouin boy. . . .

I scream. An eboned surface lost in the sun. Voids of blood and voice admixed in a hot groan. Like a lizard on a steaming binge, I go back. There is a whirlpool, a smooth sculpture of centuries suddenly traumatising my retreat. I am hungry. Dying of thirst. Ready to vomit. I am a straw-dog, a squealing, agitated pig, a battery corroded; I want to rebuke the landscape underfoot. I hallucinate trotting dens of splotched hyena over the angling plains. Oily apparitions

infect my trembling sight. Slurching beings, gold frescoed walls, burning dogwood, driftwood, ocean eddies, and the sun, a huge bloated bulwark, a platinum blood clot settling for good over the jaundiced throe of hills. My mind in white-bald demolition, the heart sick with ruinous sand in its ventricles; sand scorching the frail thoughts; an hourglass in the lungs; a jumble of anatomy on fire. The rock is too hot to touch. The air is asphyxiating. Even the plastic water container is melting. The upsurge of heat has condensed around the pinched face. A deluge of fever slurping on the skin, dissecting the pores, ravishing the death impulse.

I retrace the morning. Slinking through my erosion, I reach the entrance to the gorge and sit scanning my body, my surroundings, until is born against my will the inextricable idea of myself. Etymologies, concepts, predictions come flooding over my rawness. Disaster strikes! The end of the world. My mind backlashes with a grip. Collision of sense and idea, the explosion rips through me. I pour into the velocity of my fate. I see it. Now a thousand reasons for getting out, and fast. My eyes go for the desert's edge. Forty miles perhaps to the vague image of mountains. Then what? Recrimination. Nothing comes. I walked north. That's all I remember. But how many turns, how many days? There is the ghastly ignorance of not knowing whether I am acting or reacting; not knowing or knowing. What difference? I scout out my directions, staring into the sun. Jolted with a temporary blindness, clutching myself, weeping inside with anger, I get up and start walking, hopefully, south.

I am vicious now. I walk as fast as I can, kicking up dust, throwing rocks, screaming at things, slapping bugs on my forearms.

Night obviates the furnace with inverse cruelty. I crawl under a rock formation. My nakedness stings the soul. I hold tight. I hear each thud of racing heartbeat. Waiting for the last bit of water to get cold, I rub myself to stay warm. At sunrise I am off. There are high mountains in all directions. I verge towards an immense lake of white sand. There is some brush jutting from the salt marshes on one side. A glare freezes the other side. Lazars brimming with steam, confusing distance, foreshortening peripheries, taunting me.

I go alert to my excruciating torpor, while the animate sun nibbles voraciously on my dead genitals I am too weary to protect. Minutish, exposed to the drill bit of overhead, I slog on as on some glacier. Half the day goes and the barrier of mountains is no nearer. Panic builds.

The ground is painfully difficult to manoeuvre now. There are sharp rocks and tiny needles of some mica formations. Getting into the blue mountains. A sultry dust colour, like a surface gangrene, runs over the eyes and with it comes darkness, and animals. The incline is steep. Nowhere to hide. Out of water. Is it possible? How could someone die, would he just die or would he lie down or would death lay him down; would he close his eyes, would he fall, or go unconscious; would he scream and scream and the desert take him; I mean how does someone just die? I say to myself, curling up to do something, breathing hard, hearing jackals. I stretch my rucksack into ten angles making of it a mother, a cave, a pillow, blanket, underwear and socks. The stars offer no commiseration. Not that I expected any help from them.

Sunrise. I stand up. My throat won't open. Must be filled with dust. Dull, burning delirium. I move higher into the mountains. Granite ledges. Cracks. Steep dihedrals of encrusted turmoil. Ancient broken stones tortuously lodged in pell-mell unisons.

Suddenly there is a wind that hits me with a vigour from the otherworld. Incense permeates my weakened nostrils. On all fours I shimmy the final outcrops beneath a notch on the summit. Insects are shooting through the slit at high speed coming from one side of the mountain and going to the other. I smell sea. Climbing higher, through the final stratum of barrenness, I am suddenly cut short. Beneath me is the Sinai. It spreads colourfully in all directions. And the Red Sea, the Suez, the East Coast of Egypt. Not the blue Aegean; no green sward, no Appalachian splendour. But the road: there it is! God, if it isn't a road. Leading nowhere. Moses' Canaan.

based on DESERT PART TWO,
MOUNTAIN GAZETTE 56 *April 1977*

PART 5

Fair Summer Trails

The walker's idyll — the sun shines, the trail stretches invitingly ahead, the scenery is beautiful. In a sense, though, it is harder to write about summer walks than about winter epics. The articles in this section, while tantalising with visions of cloudless days, do not attempt to hide the other side of summer walking: the oppressiveness of the heat, and its enervating quality.

Frances Slade's reverie of glorious cliff scenery in Cornwall is rudely and repeatedly interrupted by the noise and bustle of people taking their recreation in ways less peaceful than hers. Livia Visser-Fuch's *North Downs Pilgrimage* is an altogether gentler journey, with a splendid sense of wonderment at the ways of the English.

Malcolm Arney suffers on *The Long Skye Ridge;* John Hillaby has trouble escaping from an inn at Strasbourg on his cross-Europe walk; Ray Shepherd makes it *To Bishop Pass and Back* in the Sierra Nevadas.

Behind all these stories there lies a hint of the walker's awareness that things could have been different, that to be granted a summer journey is a blessing scarce deserved.

Summer on the South Downs Way

BRIAN ATKIN

There is always something unreal about the start of a long distance walk. In spite of months of previous planning, it is a time when one is unable to grasp the magnitude of the task ahead. It is also the time when boots and rucksack seem heavy, cumbersome and uncomfortable. Feet and muscles have to be allowed to get gradually acclimatised to the new conditions. Tomorrow everything will be all right. By the end of the week absence of rucksack and boots will make one feel positively undressed.

For years my sons, friends and I had been walking long distance paths in the north of England. Each one was a unique experience full of pleasurable memories. Then, after what had been a rather reluctant job transfer to London, I had given serious consideration to the Ways in the South for the first time. The choice was a wide one. Ultimately I decided on the South Downs Way, primarily for nostalgic reasons. My first real walking experiences in those long ago pre-war days were with my father along the great sandy littoral of our native East Lincolnshire home, and with my cousin and her family on the Downs around Lewes during summer holidays. I have been walking ever since.

So my eldest son and I found ourselves, on a July morning, climbing the northward-facing steep ridge of the Downs up a deep-cut ancient track enclosed in a tunnel of trees. Only the first two miles of the South Downs Way are in Hampshire; the remainder are in Sussex. As its name suggests, the Downs are the key feature of the scene along its whole length. A little knowledge of their geological history is relevant. In the distant past the whole area of what is now the Weald was under water. The bed of this water was gradually covered by deposits of sand and clay and then topped by a very thick layer of material which was eventually to become the much harder-wearing chalk.

There is a vast difference between the massive crags of the Alps and our own gentle southern English landscape, but geologically they are connected. The earth movements which created the Alps also caused the area of the Weald to thrust up into a great dome. The top of this dome was somewhere above the centre of the present-day Weald. Once weathering action had penetrated the harder chalk crust at the top of the dome, the underlying softer rocks were rapidly worn away. Today only the remnants of the hard crust at the edges of the dome stand out as the North and South Downs. Each range presents a steep slope facing the Weald. In the case of the South Downs there are gentle hills tailing back towards the sea. In the west, opposite the start of the Way, there is a coastal plain between the higher ground and the Channel. This gradually narrows until the chalk cliffs begin at Brighton. Eastwards, the sea nibbles deeper and deeper into the Downs until it is attacking the top of the main ridge at Beachy Head, near the end of the Way.

The First Day

At this particular stage, however, we were more interested in our immediate situation. On reaching the metalled track running up towards Sunwood Farm, the Way proper begins, some four miles out from Petersfield. At first the mixture of arable farmland and heavily wooded terrain was not the Downs as I recalled them, but it was very pleasant walking country. Eventually we came out on to a different scene; the wide open slopes of Beacon Hill, which stirred a few memories. Then we were back in the trees again along an extremely well signposted route (in fact waymarking is excellent throughout West Sussex). In East Sussex it is sparse and the small concrete indicators were occasionally obscured by the summer growth. Ordnance Survey maps of 1:50,000 scale with the Way superimposed on them, together with a compass for emergencies, are all the route aids that are really necessary. However, one compact and moderately priced guide which is full of useful information is recommended. This is *Along the South Downs Way,* published by the Eastbourne Rambling Club. Having described the excellent waymarking I have to admit we lost our way. Complacency and carelessness resulted in our missing a dog-leg turn at Philliswood Down. We were marching briskly down to Chilgrove before the mistake became apparent.

Fortunately the threatening heavy rain held off. Glowering clouds remained above the distant Wealden hills, but to the south-west the sky was alternately light and dark above the Isle of Wight. Towards the end of the day the temperature dropped noticeably. Standing up in the cool breeze at the top of the hill was quite different from sitting back in the comfortable residual warmth of the long grass. It had been a long and energetic day. I dozed happily for a time.

We spent the night at Heyshott. From late evening onwards there was intermittent heavy rain which continued right up to the time we set out in the morning. Down in the village the weather was warm and humid. Only the foot of the South Downs ridge was visible, the rest being completely obscured by cloud. As we ascended it became increasingly dank and cool, and there was a keen breeze at the top. For some miles we were in an imtimate, lonely world bounded by thick woodlands and the enclosing mist. The wind in the beech trees sounded like the distant sea. The only other noise was the plod of boots and the creak of rucksacks. In those drab surroundings the delicate wild roses with drops of moisture on their faces took on a special beauty. The trees ended on Littleton Down, and the way forward was not obvious. For the first and only time during the holiday we were obliged to use a compass to stay on course.

Stane Street and the Arun Valley

Roman Stane Street was soon reached; an eerie place in the mist. A prominent signpost pointed up and down the track towards Londinium and Regnum respectively. In the circumstances it was possible to imagine a time slip. This romantic idea was soon quashed by a stationary car looming up in the adjacent car park! Man has a very long history on the Downs. The Iron Age forts on many of the high points are still very evident. Most of the bronze age tumuli which are meticulously marked on OS maps have been ploughed up and are no longer visible, except perhaps from the air. It is a sobering thought that many historic relics which survived for approximately 3,000 years have disappeared within our lifetime.

The one old feature which has survived, and indeed has had a new lease of life, is the South Downs Way itself. It first became important as a route linking the farming settlements in Neolithic times. The manageable light soils of the Downs were cultivated when most of England was dense forest. The hills were eventually abandoned to sheep walks when progress allowed the heavier lowland soils to be cultivated. In recent times arable farming has returned to the Downs on a very large scale and few sheep are now to be seen. Modern mechanised farming does not require many people, so apart from walkers and other country lovers, these hills are probably lonelier now than they have been since the time of the first farmers.

Occasional solitary barns are a feature of the Downs. In other parts of the country there would be farms in similar locations, but lack of water here was most probably the decisive factor. Lunch was taken seated on farm machinery near one of these lone barns. We did not dally as the mist had given way to rain. For a time we were undecided about caping up — a step always taken with reluctance. Not for the first time were we glad that we had decided to walk from west to east. This is the direction of the prevailing weather and rain on one's back is much less depressing than wet streaking down one's face. Our raingear stayed in our rucksacks.

The Arun river valley came into view. This was the first of several rivers which break through the barrier of the South Downs as they flow southwards to the sea. At first sight this drainage pattern is odd, but it is a legacy of the past. At one time the Wealden drainage system radiated from the high mountain dome at its centre. This same pattern still exists today when much of the Weald has been worn away to a lower level than the South Downs. The extensive river gaps were originally cut by swift flowing streams. Today they are sluggish, tidal and meandering. These gaps were natural lines of communication and small towns and ports developed in them at an early stage. Today they have come down to us as the most picturesque places in this part of Sussex.

It was while we were looking at the panorama that a red deer suddenly reared up in the immediate foreground. It went thrashing away through the ripening barley at great speed, leaving us more than a little surprised. We left the Way at Amberley Station to head for our night's stopping place further down the valley at Burpham (pronounced Burfham by the sensitive!). The lonely track ran through the trees at the edge of the water meadows below the Downs. Our destination proved to be a pretty little village at the end of a cul-de-sac, complete with church, one shop, a castle site and American tourists.

No blisters had developed by the third day so we did not expect to have problems during the remainder of the walk. If the opposite is the case, it generally means that they will gradually get worse in spite of careful and frequent medication. One good trick I have learnt is to rub the feet well with slightly wetted soap before each day's walk. This serves as an excellent lubricant between skin and sock.

The day's walk was short and easy, but we did hurry past Kithurst Hill above the army firing range. There was an interesting feature above Washington. Between a rubbish dump and a pig farm we found a South Downs Way Water Tap. The weather being warm and dry, it was more than a little attractive. The top was of a modern push-button type. The effect of pressure was unexpected, a considerable fountain of water shooting up into the air from around the button! On its way down it gave both of us a shock-cooling. It was the only tap we noted on the whole route.

Chanctonbury Ring
After crossing the busy Worthing road, there was a steady climb up to one of the main features of the Downs, Chanctonbury Ring. A cool breeze had sprung up and we sheltered in the lee of that famous clump of trees. The direct warmth of the sun was luxurious. Time passed. A ground-shaking thunder came towards us over the brow of the hill. We had passed through a large herd of cattle earlier gently

grazing. At first we thought they were stampeding. But no, it proved to be two riders going hell for leather. We had by now got used to seeing very few people. Although a very popular spot and mid-summer it might have been a lonely hill in the north in mid-winter for all the company we had. The solitude was heightened by the obvious presence of the heavily populated coastal strip just a very few miles away. We saw plenty of evidence of use of the Way, but clearly and quite accidentally we had chosen to walk it during the quiet season.

The next river gap through the Downs is that of the Adur. Its entrance is guarded by the small town of Steyning which has a fine Norman church, many wood-framed houses at its centre and perhaps just a touch of suburbia in its outskirts. Superficially Sussex might seem to be real rural England. It once was. The beautiful southern English place names roll off the tongue. Unfortunately it is also within the outer London commuter belt and much of its original character appears to have been lost. People spoke with a variety of accents and there was not one which we could identify as being individual to the area.

The start of the next day was marked by some minor irritations. It was raining again. None of the footpaths which should have led back to the Way appeared to exist and we were obliged to do some road walking. The main road to

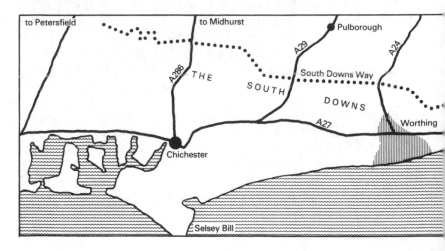

Shoreham was very unpleasant with heavy traffic. In all this bustle, it was ironic to note the blocked-up side aisle of St Botolph's Church, a sure sign that population had fallen drastically at some time in the distant past! It took a long climb up the hill before the noise receded to an acceptable background, and by then the rain had also stopped. A residuum of the morning's irritation remained when I noticed the Chapel of Lancing College. It jarred with the rest of the scenery. It took me a while before I recognised what was wrong. It would have fitted in if it had been attached to the missing remainder of the Cathedral, which was never built.

It was sunny all the way to Devil's Dyke, the first busy place we had come to on the walk. The car park was nearly full, the pub and café were open. Sightseers had something to watch, for novices suspended from their tethered kites were learning the rudiments of hang-gliding, but it was not our scene and we pushed on. There was soon cause to regret leaving the shelter of the buildings on the Dyke. One of the procession of showers which had been glowering away to the North now came in our direction accompanied by ominous claps of thunder.

The scene changed almost in a trice. Now very much alone and exposed we were getting wet in the downpour in spite of

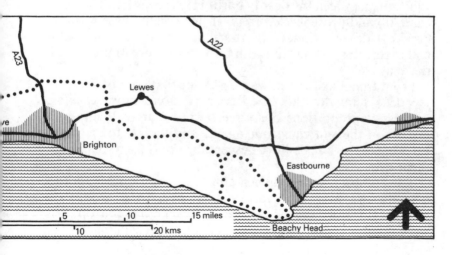

our wet-weather gear. Encased in this bulky extra covering, each of us withdrew into a personal warm, damp and sticky environment. All movement required greater effort, the miles became much longer, access to the map and guide became difficult. In this situation scenery has little importance. Signposts can easily go unnoticed and the route lost. Fortunately this did not happen and the heavy rain ended soon after leaving Saddlescombe, though the weather remained unsettled for the rest of the day.

The soaking had changed the surface of the Way into glutinous chalk mud of a type which I had all but forgotten about. It was not until we were on the thick short turf leading up to Ditchling Beacon that vigorous boot scraping every two or three minutes became unnecessary.

A Confrontation — and a Sea View

This was the day that we had our confrontation. Imagine a bridleway well fenced on each side with new taut and tall barbed wire fences. Two walkers are proceeding towards a herd of cows moving in the opposite direction. But dismay! On closer inspection it was evident that there was a bull complete with ring-in-nose in their midst. Based on past experience, avoiding action seemed the best course. This was only achieved by taking off rucksacks and raingear and squirming between the deadly barbs into the barley. The herd came up and proceded leisurely, if not regally, past without even a sideways glance. In the manoeuvre our rucksacks collected dabs of mud, souvenirs which we wore to the end of the Way.

From Ditchling Beacon we gained our first sight of Seaford Head; a reminder that the sea cliffs were now reaching impressive proportions on our eastward march. In the late afternoon the sun came out again, and we sat for a while listening to the larks before descending the ridge to our overnight stop.

Thus far, our walk had been almost a gentle amble, but the next day we were to cover 19 miles over three groups of Downs. Our start was the usual morning climb to the top. We were now in country which should have been familiar, but

Blackcap did not look as I remembered it. The cap of trees was more extensive and much lower, and there was now a great deal of arable farmland. Only the valley bottoms were unchanged in their wild state. In one of them many years ago my old uncle, in true boy scout style, had tried to reheat cold tea in an old fashioned cream cracker tin over a twig fire. The results had not been particularly successful, but the quixotic memory had remained; a brief cameo of a happy long-ago holiday.

From the top of Kingston Down there is a tremendous view of the large, flat, almost treeless basin of the Ouse Valley. Hills stood all around with the castle at Lewes guarding a gap to the north. The valley narrows considerably at Southease and it was here that we ate our lunch on the banks of the Ouse watching the tide ebb. Afterwards the Way runs up the bare flanks of Itford Hill and over Firle Beacon.

Cuckmere and the Cliffs

On the following day, our last, a short walk brought us to Alfriston in the Cuckmere Valley. There is a choice of routes after Alfriston. The bridleway continues along the crest of the Downs and the footpath makes its way down the Cuckmere Valley and then along the cliffs to Eastbourne. We chose the latter. For the first time, stiles replaced gates as the path made its way through woods to the self-consciously pretty village of Westdean. A short step further brought us to the fascinating and educational Exeat Information Centre.

The lower Cuckmere Valley must be unique in the South of England in that it has not been developed. Although I believe there was a village hereabouts in the Middle Ages, there are now no buildings below Exeat Bridge. The river makes its way along flat meadows to go through a simple shingle bank into the sea. Each flank of the bay is guarded by the white cliffs of old England. Although the day was rather dull, the change in the quality of light at the sea shore was dazzling.

On the eastern side of the valley there is a steep bank up Cliff End, where the river has carved into the hillside in former times. From then on it was up and down over the eight Seven Sisters, an unexpectedly tiring switchback. Gentle valleys and spurs flow down from the higher hills to the north to abruptly terminate in these undulating cliffs. The bottom of each dip is not too far above the sea, and here the turf was scorched brown by spray. Above there were colonies of deep blue wild flowers.

The Seven Sisters end at Birling Gap where there is relatively easy access down to the shingle beach. It is a rather nondescript place. A row of terrace houses are gradually succumbing to the sea. There is a pub and a café. The owner of the latter lamented the poor season as we partook of refreshment. The final climb to Beachy Head starts here, passing *en route* the curiously modified Belle Toute lighthouse. The café business might have been bad in Birling Gap but at the Head there was a milling crowd of sightseers. Below, a procession of full launches from Eastbourne were making a ritual close inspection of the lighthouse. For the first time that day the sun shone, but only briefly. The path turned sharply northwards and we found ourselves descending the steep scarp slope of the Downs for the last time. The sprawl of the town and the long curving flat coastline lay before us.

At the bottom of the hill is a mapboard where the path joins the road: the terminus of the South Downs Way. It was no crowded winning post, just two disinterested people buying ice cream at the nearby kiosk.

In retrospect it had been an unforgettable holiday. Perhaps it had lacked some of the rich incident and personalities of earlier walks. This may have something to do with the more self-conscious South. Nevertheless, we did meet a zealous pyrotechnician, a charming lady who was mad, and a cat who had cat-like owners, but was treated like a dog.

Later that evening we returned to London. The weather was still dull, but it was no longer obvious and it did not matter any more. We were surrounded by multitudes of many sizes and hues jabbering all the world's languages. We were back.

from THE GREAT OUTDOORS *June 1979*

The Cornish Coastal Path: Stepper from Whipsiderry

FRANCES SLADE

On a day near Midsummer, when most of England was piling on sweaters, frantically turning knobs on central-heating systems and re-erecting the double-glazing, Cornwall had one of those gleaming, wind-blown, azure and golden days, with the sea a deeper blue than the Mediterranean and the clifftops a riot of summer flowers. This was my sort of day, and I persuaded the kind friends with whom I was camping to drop me off by car at Trevelgue Head, just north of Newquay, whence I proposed to walk to Stepper Point, near Padstow. About 20 miles in all, not taking into account the ups and downs and ins and outs, but so beautiful that your legs forget to ache until you stop. And probably collapse, but who cares, then?

Looking south towards Newquay from the near-island of Trevelgue (which is a cliff castle, a relic of the late bronze age), distance lent a modicum of enchantment to some of the horrors of our civilisation — the ice-cream parlours and beach cafés, the games emporia and shops selling everything from candy floss to foot ointment. The bays and cliffs looked beautiful and uncrowded, which, at that early hour, perhaps they were. On my other side, looking north, lay Whipsiderry Cove and Flory Island, two examples of the unlikely but bewitching names which Cornwall scatters along her shoreline; and, beyond them, one of those long stretches of the North Cornish coast which catch at the heart, with its beauty and the remorseless nature of its strength and power and changelessness. Grey stone and creaming surf, green clifftops and shimmering sky, wheeling gulls and hovering kestrels, and always the rollers pounding with orgasmic fury against the granite bastions which have withstood their onslaught for centuries. But it has all been said before, and the time had come to stop rhapsodising and to start walking.

Round the golden sands of Whipsiderry, averting my eyes from the hideous modern erections on my right, I climbed gradually up the cliff edge towards Watergate. Here is one of the longest straight stretches of beach in Cornwall, where surfing championships are held, and the spring tides race in over the sea-scoured sands. Two more cliff castles, circular reminders of our far-distant ancestry, and the scene of who knows what bloody battles and fierce defences, in surroundings largely unchanged for 3,000 years. Looking down, I could see the hordes of early seaside addicts pouring down to Watergate Beach from the car park, to settle on the small strip of soft sand untouched by the high tide; cheek by jowl, grandpa from Birmingham rubbing elbows with grandma from Bristol, the middle generation busily erecting windshields and chairs, the youngest waving buckets and shrimping-nets. And from 200ft. above them I could hear the squawks and yells as a shrimping-net caught in and competed with grandma's hairnet, and elder brother snatched a carelessly held bucket or wielded a threatening spade, much as his forbears from the cliff castles wielded their battle-axes. (Or didn't they have battle-axes? — even bronze ones?)

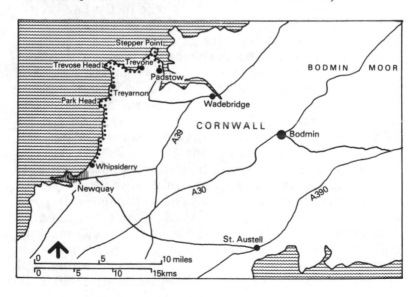

I had to descend to sea-level here, but crossed the car park quickly and started up the steep cliff on the other side of the bay. Another long and glorious stretch of cliff-walking, from Watergate to St Mawgan, round the seemingly inaccessible curve of Beacon Cove, where the path skirts a sheer drop of more than 250ft. to the sand below. But there is a small steep track down, unsuitable for both grandmas and shrimping-nets, leading to an enclosed beach where one can at least hope to find peace and relative solitude. And then the great wedge-shaped bay of St Mawgan emerged before me, the tide out, a vast expanse of golden sand, where even all of Bristol and Birmingham could be lost and scattered if they wished. But of course they don't, and sure enough, there they all were, crammed into a highest corner of the beach, cheek to cheek. Surely these were the identical people I'd left at Watergate? The same windshields, the same cricket bats and shrimping-nets, the same yells and squawks, the same pungent odour of scented suntan oil. Could they have decamped from Water-gate as soon as my back was turned and raced up the coast ahead of me in their cars to settle here? I shall never know.

Leaving St Mawgan, I climbed the path up to Trenance Point, where the heather and thyme and gorse grow in profusion amid a rockstrewn wilderness, a natural rock garden, with the deep blue ocean curling far below. Against the sound of the surf, a baby gull sat on a rock spur, opening and shutting its beak in a silent scream for food, or help, or whatever, its brown baby feathers belying its adult size. I rounded High Cove, where the drop is over 300ft., and saw opening up before me the breathtakingly lovely Bedruthan Steps. Surely for sand and sea and rock there is nothing in the world to beat this; the beaches of Pembrokeshire and of North-west Scotland haven't this shining quality; the Mediterranean coasts — beautiful, mountainous, exotic, flower-bedecked — have very little sand, are marred by man-made amenities, and never display this glory of gold and silver, blue and green. The time- and sea-sculpted cliffs here have an air of immutability, and, as in the high mountains, one is overwhelmed with a sense of the smallness and unimportance of the human race.

But, even here, the human race cannot be ignored. Until two years ago, Bedruthan Steps, where legend tells of the giant who marked each footstep with a mighty rock as he strode up the mile-long strand, was inaccessible to ordinary walkers and beachcombers, although it was possible to scramble down the cliffs of the northern-most bay. Now concrete steps have been built into the cliff, and the car parks at the top are seasonally filled with every kind of vehicle, while streams of toiling holidaymakers struggle and sweat and pant their way up and down. It was here that I heard a harassed mother saying to her toddler on the cliff edge: "If you fall over there, Mummy is going to be very cross indeed."

This is National Trust land, and much effort is being put into preservation and control of the holiday hordes and their litter; and as always, pollution and erosion seem to be winning. But in spite of the crowds, one can still find privacy and solitude among the many coves and inlets which comprise this long beach — all covered at high tide, so the sea must be watched, as the cliffs are vertical and drownings far from unknown.

On, on. Park Head, with the Cow and Calf (rocks, not a pub — bad luck), then down to Porth Mear, a dreary, sandless, seaweedy inlet, the only piece of un-beauty on this walk apart from man-made ugliness. Then up again, beside cornfields jewelled with pimpernel and betony, past Trescore Islands, beloved of snorkellers when, sometimes, the surge of the tide allows safe swimming, and on to Porthcothan. A long deep inlet, this, with more golden sands, and an unpleasant scatter of the ubiquitous beach architecture at the head of the cove.

I crossed the beach and wound my way up to the most exciting — for me — mile of all this coast, maybe because I was approaching home (my tent in a field on the cliff edge); but the cliffs here are more sheer and tortuous, more extraordinarily carved and sculpted and indented than any I know. Following their exact edge would entail several miles of walking, and is a wonderful evening stroll when the sun is going down in a blaze of glory on the western lip of the sea;

but today I trod the coastal footpath, which in places cuts off the spurs jutting out into the ocean, and in others traces the very rim of the chasm, so that a single sidestep would send you plummeting down to the rocks below. There are many fjord-like creeks on this stretch, with deep bottomless black caves, tiny golden beaches accessible only by airy tracks from rock edge to tufts of turf, and a wreck in Fox's Cove, the skeleton of a ship driven on to the beckoning reefs in a winter storm ten years ago.

From Fox's Cove a few steps off the path brought me to my tent, pitched beside a friend's caravan in what must be the pleasantest campsite in Cornwall — a legitimate 'site', but never crowded and with the minimum of those horrors called facilities. Here we sat, and I ate my sandwiches and rested awhile. A family in a nearby caravan noticed us opening a carton of Cornish cream and commented: "Funny stuff that — all clotted and nasty. I prefer Nestles meself." Ah well, it do take all sorts, so they say.

Now down to Treyarnon, and the surf just right. Never bathe for an hour after a meal, my grandmother used to say, but a sandwich isn't a real meal and the surf waits for no man. I am only a belly-boarder, having tried and neither conquered nor been conquered by the joys of malibu-surfing. It's all too much like hard work, and horrible wet-suits, and all that paddling, which is said to develop enormous biceps and cause bosoms to vanish without trace. I love my belly-board, and find the rush of a hundred-yard run, on racing surf, all the exhilaration I could desire.

An hour or so of this, then out to dry in the sun and wind, to towel out the sand-between-the-toes and get walking again. Up over the low headland that borders Treyarnon to the north, and then to one of the most dangerous beaches in all Cornwall, Constantine Bay. Backed by massive dunes, a mile-long crescent of deep-yellow sand, this is a bay where the currents are unpredictable, whirlpools abound, and drownings are tragically frequent, because people will not listen to advice. It was here that my young son was caught in a vortex of whirling water and rescued by a chain of us holding surfboards; and here at low tide, my teenage daughter, wandering along the sea's edge, picked up a drowned child whose parents had allowed it to play unwatched. Will we ever learn?

Past Constantine, to the curiously named Booby's Bay, a mysterious and not easily reached cove, where the surfing can be superb. Then up through the thyme and wild carrot (an unromantic name for a beautiful and multi-coloured flower), to Trevose Head. On this cape is one of the rare red-flashing lighthouses, and from Dinas Head below the Light you can see the whole stretch of the Cornish and Devon coast from Hartland Point to St. Ives. Notwithstanding the car park and the road to the lighthouse, this is a wild region, with a blow-hole a hundred feet deep on the south-west side, and cliffs plunging to the sea on the north, where fulmars and ravens nest.

But the wildness is soon forgotten, for as you round the headland past Cat Cove and Merope Rocks, your nostrils are assailed with an odour even more overpowering and unexpected than the suntan oil — fish and chips. In such a place this smell seems a little surprising, until your eyes are drawn to the shocking invasion of a huge area of beautiful coastline by an army of caravans. This is the Mother Ivey's caravan site — hundreds of white square boxes drawn up in neat rows with military precision, and no regard at all for privacy or room to breathe. Fish and chips, candy floss and ice-cream flourish, but the smell of frying drifts up and down the coast on the shifting winds. Mother Ivey's Bay itself is small and lovely, but so overcrowded at all states of the tide that only late on a summer evening, or out of season, can it be seen and enjoyed in peace. The new Padstow life-boat station, an imposing edifice, stands on a steep but sheltered cliffside to the north-west of this bay.

I hurried round Mother Ivey's, breathing through my mouth in an effort to avoid the smell, and rounded Cataclews Point at a brisk gallop, there to pause, as always, to absorb the magnificence of Harlyn Bay and the shore beyond. The tide was almost high now, coming up to the springs, so not much of the vast expanse of Harlyn sands was visible, and I had to follow the curve of the bay instead of crossing the beach. Then round a series of low cliffs to Trevone, a Victorian village with some hideous little houses and a few lovely gardens. This was the last sandy bay on my walk, but I didn't linger; I had had enough of beaches and their populations, and hastened on to the last lap, the wonderful cliffs between Trevone and Stepper Point.

The last few climbs and descents on the path to Stepper Point seemed long and arduous, but at last I stood on the top, beside the ruined watch tower. (Whom did it watch? Irish or Welsh invaders perhaps — or the French?) The great panorama of the Camel Estuary filled me with renewed delight; the Doom Bar was flooded by the incoming tide, so there was no trace of the sandbank — a death trap for sailors which, we are told, was put there in revenge for a betrayal in love by a despairing mermaid. Certainly navigating the Estuary is never without interest, as the tide roars in and out and the deep channel is narrow, and always there is white water between the Doom Bar and Trebetherick Rocks.

My walk was over. My legs were tired and my shoulders ached, but all I had to do now was to stroll down to Padstow, where a meal and friends and a car awaited me. This is a walk I have done many times, in many moods and weathers, and I shall do it again, for its pleasures never pall. There is always something new and fresh, and there is always the old enchantment; for, long, long ago, Cornwall captured me, and its changing but changeless landscape sealed a love affair which will last as long as I have a heart for loving.

from THE GREAT OUTDOORS *July 1979*

The Long Skye Ridge

MALCOLM ARNEY

If you have come to Skye to climb mountains it is unlikely that you will look far from the Kyleakin — Glen Brittle road. The attraction of the Cuillin Hills is so great that the left turn at Sligachan seems almost obligatory.

But the fact is that Skye would be worth visiting even if the Cuillins did not exist — although in all fairness, by the walker rather than the climber — for, if you can forget for a moment your last memories of the high ridges and corries, you will readily appreciate the splendidly shaped hills rising to the south all the way from the ferry. Further on, if you ignore the Glen Brittle turning and are prepared to overlook the monotony of the next ten miles, you can have hill-walking on a grand scale with magnificent views in unspoilt and infrequently visited country — and, statistically, in drier weather.

We have received many soakings on Skye, both in the Cuillins and in the hills to their east so, for a change, and a chance for frayed fingers to recover, we looked to the north.

The arm of land pointing to the Arctic is Skye's largest northern peninsula and is known as Trotternish. It is circumnavigated by a road which runs along the east coast through Staffin and Flodigarry (home of Flora MacDonald for several years), cuts across the tip of the peninsula to reach the west coast at Kilmuir, and then continues southward through Uig, and then ultimately back to Portree. However, the vast interior of the peninsula is dominated by an almost continuous basaltic escarpment facing the Scottish mainland and providing an impressive barrier to the east-west traveller. Only in one place along its 19 mile length has it been possible to force a road, and the average walker would be unable to cross it in more than a handful of other places.

Not only is the escarpment impossibly steep, with cliffs of up to 500ft. along its entire length, but in several places bizarre groups of pinnacles rise amidst surrealistic terrain, the result of ancient landslips.

The crest of the escarpment is entirely different, being the culminating point of the gradual rise in the moors to the west — the only barrier from this direction being the miles of trackless bog! There is little bog on the crest, however, where there is delightful walking on well-cropped greensward, in many places as smooth and firm as a putting green.

Varying in height between about 1,000 and 2,400ft., the crest boasts 11 named summits and a few unnamed ones. To traverse the whole length would necessitate ascending 7,500ft. and covering 22 miles, allowing for the distance to and from the first and last tops. We solved the transportation problem by having access to two cars and, with the seed sown by the SMC guide, the fine spring sunshine did the rest and we left the road two miles from the northernmost top at 9.15 a.m.

This hill, Sgurr Mor, is really a flat plateau at about 1,500ft. and fairly obvious steep grass slopes breech the otherwise impregnable crags which present something of a miniature Lost World in appearance. Leaving Connista croft the top seemed very close but the map should have warned us, showing little net gain in height for more than a mile. The going was the worst of the day, not on account of the bogs but because of the thigh-deep heather covering the undulating and deceptive moor. We were facing the sun, as we would do more or less throughout our trek, and even wearing nothing but shorts and boots we found it uncomfortably hot.

Nevertheless the first summit was reached at 10.30 a.m. — or at least I think it was the summit; we spent some time arguing over which was the highest point, rushing to a mound that looked supreme only to find the one we'd just left looking higher. It was too hot, and we had too much left to do, to stop and build a cairn — and anyway there was a noticeable shortage of stones. Maybe in my declining years I'll make the pilgrimage again and start the route off with a distinct landmark.

Landmark we had as we headed for what appeared to be a

radio mast on the summit of our next hill, Meall nan
Suireamach. Although only a few hundred feet higher, its
huge bulk blocked out all views to the south. It seemed a pity
that we would be denied the moment of contented achievement that comes at the end of a long ridge route when
looking back over the summits traversed. Still, we strolled
easily up the gentle gradient and before long we were at the
top. We started to pick out the tops we had yet to traverse,
only just convincing ourselves that we could see The Storr —
nearly 15 miles away and the highest summit of the day, but
concealing the final top, three miles further on.

We said little, feeling a bit discouraged, but it was a fine
day and we were fit so we quickly carried on, detouring left to
obtain a bird's eye view of the Quiraing. Unique in the British
Isles, it looked to us as if some malevolent giant had savaged
the east slopes of Meall nan Suireamach and left a
nightmarish landscape of pinnacles, gullies and crags, either
decayed or decaying. The only direct access is from below,
following a narrow, and at times exposed path running
beneath the cliff and starting at a lay-by near the road pass to
which we now turned.

The only people we saw all day were encountered here, and
after attempting to put them on the Quiraing sight-seeing
path we headed south and up to the next top, Biod Buidhe,
overlooking a curious, Stac Polly-like hillock called Cleat — I
wonder how many people have stood on *this* summit.

It was getting more remote now as we descended to an
indeterminate bealach. And then up; the biggest continuous
pull of the day — 1,000ft. to the summit of Beinn Edra which
just breaks the 2,000ft. barrier and, from some vantage
points, looks like a Brecon Beacon. A long haul this, but still
enough determination to knock-off one more top before
lunch at 2 p.m. Lunch? Quickly away within 15 minutes,
knowing we were half-way between the two cars and four
boggy miles to the nearest road.

On and on; up and down; keeping to the crest as far as
possible where only the semblance of a sheep track existed.
Why is it that these animals insist on walking such a tightrope within inches of crumbling precipices? Still, the views

were impressive, even though we may have been getting a bit
blase about the verticality to our immediate left. Further left
we could just make out the road along which we had driven,
what was it, seven hours ago. And then the sea — but that
was all; the impressive Scottish coastline, on a clear day
almost incomparable from the north of Skye, was blurred by
the haze.

Progress seemed slower than it really was; talk desultory.
Some argument over whether we had seen an eagle or not,
possible in these parts, but in this case I suspect it was a
buzzard. Discussion passes the time until it gets too steep to
talk, then we separate to find our own rhythm up into the
sun. Stripped and dripping — our extravagant purchase of
sun-tan lotion somehow getting into eyes and mouth — not
recommended for taste!

Another halt at 4.30 p.m. on a short spur blessed by a
magnificent top with cliffs on three sides. This was Sgurr a
Mhadaidh Ruaidh, the romance of the Gaelic enhancing it
still further — how much more prosaic the (fortunately never
used) English — peak of the red fox. Still sunny, but the
breeze at 2,000ft. soon chilling the sweat, so rucksacks
quickly on and back to the main route.

Easy going for nearly two miles, then, just as we think
things are becoming straightforward, a jolting descent over
unstable scree and broken rocks. Then up again to an
unnamed top followed by a long descent to Bealach a Chuirn.
Every downward step makes the bulk of The Storr more
intimidating. Separate thoughts now with 18 miles behind us,
both knowing that after the next 800ft. rise we've more or less
finished. 800ft. is only a matter of time and you pass the time
by calculating how long it will take — 20 minutes, 25 at the
most. Zig-zagging on the steep bits but keeping going; his
stride shorter than mine, his choice of angle more direct — he
will get there first. Or perhaps I'm getting old. Step by step,
ignoring the sheep ridiculing you. Step by step — and then
the summit, the highest point of the day. But no elation:
looking inaccessible and distant the final top is at last in view.

It's only three miles you tell yourself as you press on down
the steep, uneven slopes. But still taking care — a twisted

ankle now could mean failure. And then it's level; well, more or less; rabbit holes abound and every incline defeats your attempts to find the easiest line.

On and on, the road closer now to the left; The Storr slowly receding behind us. On and on and up and down and then the final 'few hundred feet' identified the night before, rears up before us as a 500ft. scree slope. What a finale! We have to stop several times, the first slope during the whole day that makes us capitulate to its gradient.

We arrive at the summit of Beinn a Chearcaill at 7 p.m., the sun still strong in the west. No lingering, back to the road, summoning up the last reserves, the long stride. Running down the sheep track, following the stream that leads miraculously to the road and the car. Boots off and fast to Portree to relax with a pint of lager.

Looking back, not a great problem for fit and strong walkers, but the aesthetic nature of the route and its solitude, added to the splendour of the scenery, made it a very special day.

I'd like to do it again, perhaps after a fresh north-westerly has cleared the air, or when the snow is crisp underfoot. But then, there are so many hills. . . .

from CLIMBER AND RAMBLER *July 1979*

Peaks and Waves

DENNIS DRABELLE

If you look at a map of California and follow Route 1 north out of San Francisco, you will see that it hugs the coast for about 175 miles. Then, just above Rockport, the highway veers 30 miles inland. It doesn't swing back to the coast until Eureka, 75 miles farther north. In the rugged country in between — country that defeated the highway engineers — is the Burea of Land Management's [BLM] King Range National Conservation Area.

I had heard of the King Range while working in Washington D.C. at the Department of the Interior. I was intrigued by its combination of 4,000ft. peaks and the Pacific Ocean a half-day's walk from each other.

I was also eager to explore some BLM backcountry. The BLM is a multiple-use agency. Unlike the National Park Service and (with a few exceptions) the US Fish and Wildlife Service, its sister agencies in Interior, BLM permits utilisation of its resources. BLM lands are mined, logged, and grazed. They are also, increasingly, preserved as 'primitive' or natural areas. The 25 miles of mountains and beach that we would hike is not wilderness yet, but has been designated a primitive area — no roads, no vehicles, no new development. With Jim Coda, a friend from Washington days recently transferred to Interior's San Francisco field solicitor's office, I decided to make a circuit hike through both of the range's worlds.

The range is in chain-saw country. We drove by a billboard extolling Echo brand saws on the way to our embarkation-eve' campground at Wailaki Recreation Site. In the morning, driving to the trailhead at the northern end of Saddle Mountain Road, we heard a saw nagging away at some tree. But once we were on the King Crest Trail, all we heard was the wind soughing in the trees.

The trail rose towards King Peak through forests bulging with brush: manzanita, Pacific rhododendron, tanbark oak,

277

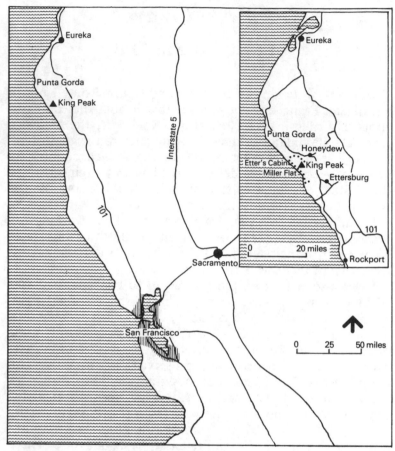

whitehorn, and scrub live oak. To the west, beneath hump-
backed slopes of Douglas fir and mountain hemlock, the
ocean was calm. But the wind had shoved fog to shore and
backed it up in the coves. To the east stretched the Mattole
River Valley and the parallel blue ridges of the Coast Range.
We almost always had an unobstructed view of either the
ocean or the mountains. But on top of King Peak, we had
both at once. We could glance from breakers rolling nearly a
mile below us to hawks riding mountain thermals just over
our heads.

We walked north-west along the crest, toward the Smith-

Etter Road, which would take us down to the beach. What
had started as a wide, pebbly path deteriorated into a thin
ridge of talus along a steepening slope. At one point the
terrain assumed a 45-degree angle across the trail. I had to
lean into the slope, using one hand as an anchor, and walk on
the sides of my boots. I inched along like a bowlegged tripod.

When the trail shaped up again, it led us through a glade of
sugar pines, whose cones are the largest of any American
tree. I picked up one at least 14 inches long. Just past the
glade, we stopped at the edge of a canyon to peer at tortured
striations of sediment in rock that had been uplifted and
flung on its side.

At several points the trail signs confused us. Some, though
still standing, had been battered and wrenched until they
pointed the wrong way. Others lay splintered and rotting. We
had to disregard them and stick to our maps. (Back in San
Francisco we asked the BLM managers about this. They said
their signs in the range are constantly being vandalised — by
bears).

We camped in a clearing beside the gravel road. In the
afternoon the wind in the trees had made a sweeping
cleansing sound. But toward sundown the wind rose, and the
gentle cleansing sound became a scouring roar. We staked the
tent deep and taut, and all night it flexed and relaxed in the
gusts.

We suffered through a dry morning. The map showed a
few springs along the trail. But by the time we realised we
were short of water, we were a mile past the last one and too
tired to backtrack. After eating a breakfast of cookies and
oranges, we grumpily stumbled down the road, which wound
— no, coiled — its tedious way to the beach.

The fog had slipped out to sea, where it hung in a long
rampart. The air was clear and gold-tipped. The sea breeze
mingled with the pungent smell of pine. And BLM had
assured us that even in this second consecutive summer of
drought the creeks were still flowing to the ocean. We knew
our discomfort was only temporary.

The last mile of road presented us with a dark-sand beach,
strewn with gray logs and driftwood and bisected by a jeep

trail. Just before hitting the sand, we stirred up a dozen sheep munching the dry yellow grass of the lower slopes. We hustled south to Kinsey Creek and exulted in our first drinks in 13 hours. The water was cold but not shocking, warm enough, in fact, to serve as habitat for undetermined tiny creatures which we didn't bother to worry about swallowing. After reconnoitering the logs at the creek's mouth (BLM had warned they are favourite haunts of rattlesnakes), we sat down to drink more water and rest.

When we were juicy again, we followed the jeep trail along the coast. Underlain by concrete for a while, in places no more than faint grooves, it took us through a grassy field and past Etters Cabin. The cabin is not, as it sounds, a rustic log structure, but a damned house that looks as if it were dropped on the beach from some celestial suburb. It resides on a small triangle of private land whose hypotenuse is the sea. Above us a sparrow hawk sniped at a circling raven. "The hawk is protecting its territory," explained Jim, who is a wildlife photographer.

At the edge of an expansive plain called Big Flat (the site where BLM plans to reintroduce elk to the King Range), we came upon myriad bits of shell heaped along the trail. Jim noticed that the heaps were always near animal holes and theorised that something — probably a rat — was getting take-out food from the sea. The flat was also home for dozens of western bluebirds, which perched on decaying fence posts left over from some long-ago farm.

We crossed Big Flat Creek and went on to Miller Flat, through shin-high blonde grass flattening and undulating in the breeze. We made camp at the flat's edge. This was a little short of Shipman Creek, our goal, but as far as we could see down the coast the beach was crowded by cliffs, and we weren't about to pitch the tent in sand.

After dinner the wind died down. The tide rolled in over the beach pebbles, rattling them like all the dice in Las Vegas. The setting sun highlighted pink and gold crests on the breakers. A bat flitted overhead, sheep came to graze on a slope above us, and a black-tail deer scampered across the flat not 20 yards away. It was as though we had wandered

into the Pastoral Symphony sequence in Walt Disney's
Fantasia.

The tide was out the next morning, and the beach was
littered with hoses of kelp and fronds of seaweed. All traces
of the jeep trail had disappeared at Big Flat, but dune buggies
had made tracks along the beach early in the morning. We
had taken BLM's advice to keep the wind at our backs by
hiking south along the beach. Now we stepped on pebbles or
stayed inside the dune buggy tracks, rather than plod through
boot-gripping sand.

We rested at Buck Creek, at the foot of the rough road we
would follow inland. A Chevy Blazer drove up from the
south. Two men got out, and we struck up a conversation.
Both worked for the US Geological Survey (another branch
of Interior), and one had actually drawn the topo map for
this area. In 1969 he spent two months there, fleshing out
aerial photographs taken at 15,000ft. He hadn't seen a single
vehicle on the beach the entire time, he said. (The BLM
managers are aware that vehicular use of the beach is a
problem. Despite recent regulations forbidding vehicles
between Gitchell Creek and Punta Gorda, dune buggies have
been reported going there anyway). It was only after we had
said goodbye to the surveyors and gone too far up the road to
turn back that I realised what we should have done: pull out
our map and ask its draughtsman to autograph it.

A thick row of grass grew along the middle of the road.
Suddenly the row was alive with cheeping dark chicks:
California quail. Their mother, realising the folly of having
built their nest in a road, screamed at them to abandon it.
They followed her into the brush in a tumbling hurry.

The road was relentlessly steep. Jim had a bad knee, and I
carried a lot of his gear, so both of us were hurting. But the
views eased the pain. This is the one I want to remember, the
one that best unites the two worlds of the King Range: a pair
of Douglas firs frames a tawny ridge topped by a serrated row
of pines. Beyond spreads the sea, cobalt blue streaked with
white vectors. And beyond that you have to squint to make
out the fuzzy line where the sea meets the sky.

from BACKPACKER 27 *1978*

To Bishop Pass and Back

RAY SHEPHERD

The first sound I heard on waking at dawn Saturday morning was the rushing water of Bishop Creek. We were camped in a secluded site in Bishop Park Camp at about 8,000ft. of elevation. It was the approach to the Bishop Pass Trail on the eastern slope of the Sierra Nevada, high above the Owens Valley.

I slipped on the parka I'd used as a pillow during the night. Though it was August, the chill mountain air was in the low forties. My hiking partners, Stu Guttenplan and Howard Strauss, were still asleep when I wormed out of my sleeping bag. We had driven five hours from Los Angeles the night before and had slept under the stars. I wandered down to the creek and watched the sun shine through the cottonwoods, but decided to wait for it to get a little higher before taking pictures. "Get up, you lazy so-and-sos. Do you want to sleep the whole day?"

We each cooked up our own breakfast. Mine was simple — coffee, cheese and a store-bought apricot pie.

After breakfast I took photos of the sunlight coming through the cottonwoods along the creek. I was glad Stu and Howard are used to my picture taking and weren't bothered by being delayed while I got my shots.

After packing our gear, we tossed it into Stu's pickup with its camper body and drove the remaining eight miles to the trailhead.

We had decided to make the weekend hike in the eastern Sierra since there you can start hiking at a much higher altitude and climb much higher, quicker, than in the western Sierra. Our trailhead was at 9,700ft. By comparison, approaching Bishop Pass from the west you'd have to start hiking at about 7,500ft. of elevation, and it would take that much longer to get to the tree line.

The South Lake trailhead is one of the most spectacular in

the eastern Sierra. It begins just below tree line. Looking southward, we saw the granite bulk of Hurd Peak towering over the lake. Behind the peak and to the right, the spires and peaks of the more distant Sierra crest enclosed the large basin.

It was 8 a.m. when we shouldered our packs and started up the trail. We hiked along the east side of South Lake through aspens. One mile later we came to the trail's first fork. We stayed on the left while the right fork headed west to the Treasure Lakes. I had hiked in to Treasure Lakes on a winter hike in April, three years ago. I'd decided to return in the summer to climb a peak. Thus, when Stu and Howard asked me to pick a place for a hike, the Bishop Pass area was the first to spring to mind. A little farther along the trail, we broke into the open and stopped for a drink from a mountain stream. It felt good to drop our packs for a few minutes. While Stu and Howard rested, I took a few pictures of a meadow. Since companionship is so important to the success of any hike, I was very pleased at how well Stu and Howard were hitting it off. This was the first time they had met. And it was particularly important to me that they liked each other because both were special friends. Stu had been my hiking partner for three years, until he'd gotten married a year before. He had lived across the street from me, so it was really convenient for us to put together a hike. Then he had moved to another part of town, and we saw each other less often.

Howard, another neighbour, became my hiking partner after Stu moved away. Stu and Howard are different types of people — Stu very extroverted, Howard normally reticent. I had counted on their outdoors enthusiasm to be a bonding element. It was a relief to me, of course, to see how well they got along.

Passing some ponds on our left, we switchbacked up the South Lake Trail and in another mile came to a second fork. The main trail, which we followed, continued south between the brown and white slopes of Chocolate Peak and past the blue waters of Long Lake.

The beauty of Long Lake was reason for another stop for

pictures and a drink of mountain water. I took some shots of the view across the lake to Hurd Peak and the Sierra crest to the south.

We started gaining elevation as the trail switchbacked up to the basin cradling Saddlerock Lake. At the three-and-a-half-mile mark, we reached a high vantage point and stopped for a view back down the valley toward South Lake. Ahead of us were the clear waters of Saddlerock Lake, with the granite wall of the Inconsolable Range to the left.

I started looking for a campsite. Most areas around Saddlerock Lake were too rocky or brush covered. Passing by the lake, we saw better terrain south of it, near the smaller Bishop Lake. After some exploring, we located a sheltered site at the 11,200ft. level between the two lakes.

Howard and I each use bivouac bags instead of regular tents like Stu's. I had used my bivy sack on several backpacks and was quite happy with it. Mainly, the light weight, one-and-a-half pounds, is easy on the back.

It was one o'clock by the time we set up camp, so we decided to have lunch. While eating, we noticed a basin high up next to 13,000ft. Mt. Goode. Since we planned to hike to Bishop Pass after lunch, we decided to explore the Mt. Goode basin the next day.

On the trail to the pass we overtook a girl with a gigantic pack. She told us she was hiking the John Muir Trail by herself. She didn't look as if she weighed more than 100lb. and appeared to be carrying 75lb. She had already travelled almost half the 250-mile route. I've met several girls hiking by themselves, but I've never met one who was hiking such a long distance with such an impressive load.

With our light day packs, we quickly left her behind. Switchbacking up the steep trail, we marvelled at the sharp spires and talus slopes of the Inconsolable Range to the east. One of the three notches on the skyline was Jigsaw Pass; we speculated about which one.

Finally we broke over the edge to the pass at 11,900ft. There the views were spectacular south to Dusy Basin and the Sierra backcountry, and north back down our route. Stu was bothered by the altitude — headache and woozy stomach.

While he rested, Howard and I decided to climb a nearby unnamed peak. After a 500ft. scramble up rock and snow, we reached the summit. Howard climbed the 12ft. boulder on top and straddled it. From the map we attempted to identify various peaks and lakes within view. We admired 13,890ft. Mt. Agassiz to the east and Isosceles Peak to the south. After half an hour it was time to leave. We found an easy way down and returned to the pass. Stu was feeling better, and we descended to camp.

The sun dropped behind the Sierra crest; the air began to chill. We put on our parkas and heated water for dinner. I ate freeze-dried stroganoff, Howard ate freeze-dried chicken and rice, but Stu had no appetite. For dessert we had fig newtons and some brandy. By the time we finished eating and cleaning the dishes, it was dusk and the temperature had dropped to freezing. Even though it was only 8 p.m. we decided to climb into our sleeping bags.

Howard was first to rise the next morning. After a breakfast of hot chocolate, cheese, and sausage, Stu and I walked down to Saddlerock Lake to take a few pictures,

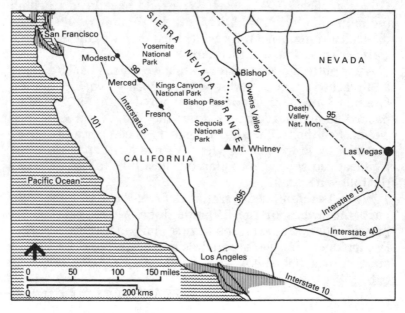

which is one of the main reasons I go backpacking. I use a Canon F135mm single lens reflex camera with a 35mm lens. I also carry 24mm and 85mm lenses. I shoot about two rolls of Kodachrome 64 (36 exposures) per day. The early morning light is the time I like most for taking pictures. Stu also had his camera with him, but he is not a fanatic like me; he shoots only a couple of photos. But he was not in any hurry, for during the night he had been up a couple of times with nausea. If we'd had sense enough, Howard and I would have taken him back out.

After about an hour we wandered back to camp. Stu decided to stay there that morning because the altitude was still bothering him. So Howard and I loaded our day packs and headed for the Mt. Goode basin we had noticed the day before.

We worked our way around Bishop Lake and a small pond and started climbing a steep slope to the west. An hour later we were high enough for a good view of the basin where our camp was located and the Inconsolable Range beyond. Another hour brought us just under the summit slopes of Mt. Goode at the 12,300ft. level. We would have liked to climb the mountain itself. With ice axes the summit would not be difficult; without them, forget it. Next time we go there, we'll start earlier and take our ice axes.

After puttering around for awhile we started back to camp and reached it about noon. We ate lunch — cheese, apples, Granola bars, and lemonade flavoured with ERG — then packed up and headed back down the trail. At three o'clock we reached the trailhead. We loaded the camper and started the long drive to Los Angeles. Stu had felt better since the trailhead, so we began to plan our next hike to Mt. Whitney the following month.

We still couldn't get over that 100lb. girl carrying the 75lb. pack the length of the 250-mile John Muir Trail, all by herself. That was the most amazing thing about the trip. And lest anyone think we are male chauvinists, we'd be just as amazed by a 100lb. *boy* with a 75lb. pack making the same trip.

from BACKPACKER 33 *1979*

North Downs Pilgrimage

LIVIA VISSER-FUCHS

In 1979, Livia Visser-Fuchs and her husband came from Holland to try their first British long-distance path. They followed the Pilgrim's Way from Box Hill in Surrey to Canterbury Cathedral, and in this article Mrs Visser-Fuchs gives her impressions of the walk and the people she met. [Editor's preamble from *The Great Outdoors*]

A pilgrimage, of course, should start at one's own doorstep, but owing to the complexities of geography and family life we began this one with the stretch of sandy beach between the Hague and the Hook of Holland and after some careful use of public transport we continued from Boxhill/Westhumble station near Dorking. Untrained and with 30lb. on our backs we thought we could get from there to Canterbury comfortably within our allotted five or six days. Moreover I especially wanted to use the stepping stones across the river Mole and ignored the RA footbridge as if it did not exist. The climb of Box Hill immediately set us wondering why we had come to England at all: the GR57 path last year in Belgium had been equally bumpy and Holland is so nice and flat. The problem is that in our country you will mostly have the same view for hours and there hardly ever is a place where you are allowed to have a sudden revelation, sink down upon the grass and say "we did it".

Having looked our fill from Box Hill to the South Downs and meeting the first party of fellow North Downs walkers (we never got rid of them again, nor they of us and they kept losing members of their original party of four or picking them up again, it seemed), we went on our way again in the heat of the afternoon. An elderly gentleman rigorously pruning his lilac, when asked for some water, filled our bottles (even put ice in them) and invited us in for a most welcome tea. Was it because we were backpackers, or obviously foreigners, or did we look so very hot and tired?

At the end of this first half-day we were allowed to camp in an absolutely quiet, level grassy spot with only rabbits and a real tap with unlimited water for company. It seemed unbelievable after three weeks' bike-packing with our children in our own crowded, over-regulated country, dotted with trampled, noisy, many-coloured commercial camping sites, to find such a place right by our path.

Next morning we had the pleasure of meeting (and not for the last time) several stiles, kissing-gates and public footpaths (all three almost unknown in Holland), but by the end of the day we got rather bored with the North Downs Way and the docile following of a marked path, so we wandered off in search of the remains of a Roman villa in Titsey Park, which we never found. Somewhere around here our fellow-walkers came up behind us (two at that time) and apparently slightly irritated to find us there before them again, they asked if we did a lot of walking. We don't, but we should have explained to them that camping *without* our two fairly small children is so wonderfully simple, so refreshingly easy, that our own small pains and cramps and occasional boredom on indifferent stretches are absolutely negligible, even enjoyable in comparison. The quick, efficient pitching of your one tent, the undisturbed cooking (or not cooking) of your evening meal and the perfect freedom of movement and conversation guarantee an ideal holiday even if it lasts only a few days. People who have ever been backpacking with their children, pleasant and rewarding though it is in other ways, will perhaps remember and know.

A smiling farmer offered us a place for the night. There was even water to be had in the field, he said: the water supply of the cattle-trough was only screwed on by hand, too. Three quarters of an hour later, wet from head to foot, muddy and scratched, we still found ourselves struggling with a recalcitrant jet of water that would not be tamed, by no hand of ours at least. We would not have slept quietly, knowing that through our fault the Kent/Surrey border was being slowly flooded, so we trudged back to the farmer again. He was still smiling, laughing rather, and politely said it was an excellent opportunity to mend the leaking water pipe at the same time. We could only retreat, pitch our tent and restore our self-confidence with the contents of a small bottle brought along for just such a purpose.

On our way to a pub next morning we were confronted for the first time with the LDP-syndrome: someone accused us of 'cheating' because we were taking the metalled road. Our unsportsmanlike behaviour saved us, as we had hoped, from our first real shower and rewarded us with a large cup of fresh coffee. It was almost the last coffee we had in any public house. To us the way in which British publicans try to prescribe what one shall eat or drink at each hour of the day is very confusing and irritating. We do not want a 'pint' on a cold morning after a wet walk, but sometimes we do like to have one in the middle of a sunny afternoon. An English tea, too, is very difficult to find these days except along the motorway or in some tourist-infested beauty spot.

We kept cheating or rather walking the real Pilgrim's Way and found a footpath right through Chevening Park with fine views of the house and on to Chevening Church, where the only other Dutch pilgrim in the whole of the visitors' book had passed only the day before. Because of the regretful tendency of the North Downs Way itself to pass all churches and villages at a distance (and we rather like to arrive somewhere and leave some place behind us again) we cheated all next day, visited several lovely churches and crossed the Medway by the beautiful bridge at Aylesford (no tea).

The evening was spent at a farm high on the Downs, talking with the farmer and his family about interesting, international things like strikes and prices, the common market and the folly and wisdom of governments. We slept late, aware of the continuous sound of rain on the tent and the cloud-wrapped hills around and when we were ready to go at last the ancient people who chose the dry Pilgrim's Way seemed wiser to us than the moderns who made muddy long-distance footpaths. We went from village to village pursued by scurrying clouds and intermittent sunshine and we constantly wrapped and unwrapped ourselves in rainproof clothes. We had lunch on the hillside in a nice thunderstorm that attacked us from three sides and, as always, made us slightly afraid of our own frame-packs, but rumbling and echoing it passed harmlessly by. This time it was the North

Downs Way itself that gave in: it joined us again above Lenham and led us through endless jungles of wild roses, brambles and immense nettles, described as 'leafy paths' or 'slightly overgrown' in our guiding leaflet. We went far that day and it was a sombre evening with a western wind blowing us on: the tent, once pitched, and the light of the lamp were especially comfortable and so were all the un-dehydrated delicacies brought from Charing.

The valley north of Westwell and the surroundings of the Eastwell Park were remarkably fresh and beautiful next morning in the new sunshine. As a Ricardian, I was curious to see the reputed tomb of the supposed son of Richard III in the ruins of the church of St. Mary at the edge of the lake. It turned out to be a lovely spot, one of those, to me, typically English places where the mellow-coloured, roughly-shaped ruins of an old building contrast so finely with the orderliness of a scrupulously kept garden and the straightness of a well-mown lawn. But the road goes ever on: leaving a white rose upon the grave, we made our way towards Challock Forest and up there had our first view of Canterbury Cathedral, catching the sunlight far away across Godmersham Park and the Stour valley.

Beyond Chilham (tea/tourists) the countryside, lovely though it is, seems to get more crowded and man-made, and

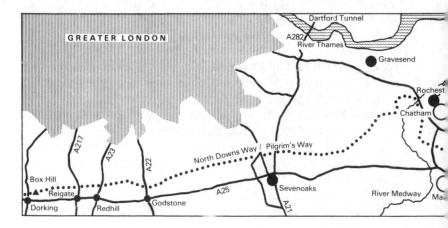

one's last illusions are left behind in the grey mud of the Harbledown bypass. The sight of the West Gate, however, the half-timbered houses and the cathedral itself, just visible above the heads of the crowd, may do much to restore one's happiness. We did as pilgrims should: we booked at a hotel, washed, rested, spread out our belongings to dry, attended evensong and finally went shopping with abandon. Being in the mood we acquired the Lives of the Saints in twelve volumes at an antiquarian bookshop and at once did penance for our extravagance by having to carry them all and arousing the suspicion of the customs men with our heavy cardboard box. We survived though, and so did the Saints, right through all the traffic, the trains, the crowded boat and through all the noise and press of holidaymakers, and got home safely.

Every now and then in the midst of the complications of everyday life we pause to say "if only we were walking down that path again or sitting on that hill again when life was simple" and we would like to urge all ramblers, wanderers, tramps, pilgrims and backpackers to thank their special saints for the unique possession of public footpaths and pray that they may be preserved.

from THE GREAT OUTDOORS *December 1979*

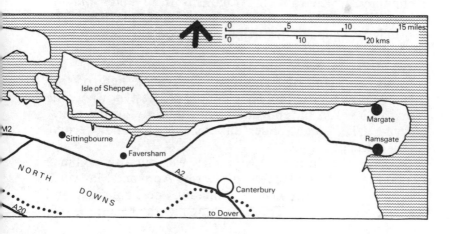

Departure from Strasbourg

JOHN HILLABY

For the long-distance walker few moments in life are more exhilarating than setting out after an enforced delay. It's necessary to dress up, carefully, like a bullfighter. There must be no loose straps or badly-tied boots. Adjustments can be made when you get under way, but for the take-off the need is to swing forward with all lashed down, the muscles tingling in anticipation and the spirits high. For these heaven-sent occasions I stock a few marching tunes. I don't often sing them aloud, but from memory I can call up a complete orchestra and let the themes whirl through my head. A few are by Sibelius. When there are clouds ahead or I am unsure of the way I can make good use of the scherzo from the First Symphony, but it's stern Nordic stuff. You've got to walk fast. The percussion is furious and there's much torment in the air. I've had some good send-offs from Britten, Dvorak and Janacek, but of all composers give me Prokofiev for a fine day.

I strode down the *quai Turckheim* accompanied by that mischievous tune from the second movement of the Fifth Symphony, which contains fragments from *Peter and the Wolf*. The clarinet skips along pursued by the bass. The footfalls are light and irresistible. They contain the very stuff of motion, of controlled unrest. There is a gait, a going-forwardness in every phrase. The clarinets took me out towards the Island of Fishermen. They made light of that great highway to Selestat. They danced off west, down a little lane to Lingolsheim, and on I went, burning up the miles, glorying in larks and wonderfully clean air, for I had become a walker again.

Skylarks sing through most of the year, but after a climax in mid-March the gabble falls off during April and May when the pairs are preoccupied with mating, nest-building, and keeping off intruders. The June song may be reckoned a *Te*

292

Deum or, in more prosaic terms, an assertion by the cock bird that he has done his best, that the youngsters are being provided for, and he has time for song. And what a song!

The birds are afraid of trees; they even shun hedges and overhanging rocks that might harbour enemies, but with the sky for a watch-tower they sing:

> In crisps of curl off wild winch whirl, and pour
> And pelt music, till none's to spill nor spend.

The last I saw of Strasbourg was the tower of the cathedral, a rose-pink finger of stone in the sunlight but changing in colour with every cloud that passed. It slipped from sight near Entzheim, where that walk back to the Vosgés so wonderfully begun became a miserable affair, since by chance I strayed into country where military aircraft are put through their paces at a height perilously close to the ground.

For two hours I walked on amid the mind-bewildering noise of engines and supersonic bangs. They came from jet-black fighter aircraft with swept-back wings. On the ground they screamed petulantly as if chafing at restraint. And then with an exultant howl they leaped into the air in groups of three, rising almost vertically. Once aloft they turned over on their wing-tips, banking and diving through cloud-rack, becoming more and more minute until nought remained but sound, the sound you might expect to hear for all time in the very depths of hell.

I made some ear-plugs out of moistened bread, but the sound got through. The planes came back at me fast, at ground level. I scurried along nervously, looking round, never knowing where the next would come from. I likened those furies to Valkyries. I tried to admire the way they were flung through the sky, but at heart I cursed them, feeling angry that human beings were obliged to endure that noise without being able to do anything about it. I remember thinking that if ever I came across one of those pilots I would give him a talking-to he would never forget. But that was before I reached a little tavern near Obernai where half a dozen pilots lounged over the bar. And what did I do? I bought a drink and said nothing.

They were very young-looking men with the grave expression of seminarists, though from the sinuous gestures they made they seemed to be talking about girl-friends. I caught the word Odette and how Marcelle would have behaved, presumably in similar circumstances. But when one of them described a loop with his finger, it became apparent that the names were those of their planes and the gestures had to do with how they performed in the billowy beds of the sky.

The warmth of that company completely defused my indignation. They invited me to take a drink. They were amused that I had thought of them as Valkyries and explained that, to avoid scaring livestock, they only flew low over certain parts of the plain. They asked me where I intended to walk. I said up to Oberhaslach and then, hope-fully, down the spine of the Vosges, but everything depended on the weather. If it looked as dour as it did that evening I should head direct for the Höhwald.

They knew the Haslach intimately. They had lost a rocket there. There had been a court of inquiry and it took search parties nearly a month to find it. Heavily forested, they said. As for the weather, they thought it promised well. A high ceiling from 8 a.m. the next morning. Perhaps a bit of *brume* on the hills at dawn when, as they put it, the trees began to breathe. But I should have confidence, for they had seen a weather report that very afternoon.

Outside, the hills were covered by a dirty tablecloth of cloud, but encouraged enormously by expert opinion I struck out for Haslach with a packed supper of rye bread and cold roast partridge.

from JOURNEY THROUGH EUROPE *1972*

PART 6

Hard Winter Trails

There is a streak of adventure in all of us though for many it lies dormant, or surfaces in only a mild form. In a few it will not be denied; these are the winter wanderers, the men and women who extend their explorations into the hard cold months and reap the special reward given to those who dare and achieve their dare.

A characteristic of such people is their modesty: their explorations and achievements are shrugged off as nothing special. This feeling comes through in much of the writing in this section, yet underneath the words are hints of unexpressed emotions, perhaps too personal and powerful to be shared.

W. H. Murray's account of a new year camp on Ben Nevis summit is a magnificently taut piece of writing that cannot fail to enthrall and inspire the reader. Margaret and Bump Smith face, and overcome, the Appalachian Trail at its wildest, Chris Godber dices with death in Wales, and George Schaller treats us to an excellent account of walking in the Himalayas.

I have to confess that my favourites in this section are the two Alpine pieces. The anonymous *An Eventful Day* is typical of its period, a perfect vignette of Victorian/heroic mountaineering, and E. F. Knight's *The Lost Valley* really sums up what the winter adventurer gets for his trouble: hardship, hostile conditions and, at the end, a simple reward — survival.

The Pennine Way in Winter

BOB HANKINSON

Several hundred readers of *The Great Outdoors* will have trod the Pennine Way last summer. Probably many more of you intended to but one problem or another prevented you, and you have postponed your idea to this year. But why wait for summer? A winter walk on the Pennine Way is in my view far more satisfying than a summer stroll, when two of the enduring memories will probably be crowds and quagmire.

In summer you can anticipate following dozens of other walkers along a broad black squishy highway, but this congestion is not because of a sudden increase in the traffic of Wayfarers. Certainly there will be considerable effort in walking the Way, and a sense of achievement at the end, for nobody can walk 250-odd miles without feeling something, but it is as devoid of adventure as a stroll up the A1. You may think that a major part of the enjoyment is in meeting other people during your walk, and you may be just as happy on the South Downs Way. But to me and mine it is sadly ironic that the Pennine Way is no longer wholly representative of the wild moors through which the walk was planned. There is a path, well marked and signposted except on Kinder, and though a map and compass are essential safeguards to complement your green-backed Wainwright's, you will see the route as the backs of walkers; a line of diminishing specks on a line leading over the horizon. You will not be alone, certainly not at weekends. You will be one of hundreds who sign their names in the book kept in many of the cafés on the Way; there were six pages of entries for August 1978 at Gargrave.

There is another way; only 15 names were entered in that book between October 1978 and April 1979. That does not mean that those 15 were the only people who did the Pennine Way in that period, but whilst we were walking we didn't hear of any others doing the full distance. Indeed, most people we met in the villages thought we were mad. We did see three other walkers on the route: one who had cut through the Army ranges above Cronkley Scar; one on Cross Fell; and one curious American with a bag full of Hershey bars who was wandering near Hadrian's Wall. Encountering people at the rate of one person every four *days* was, to our mind, preferable to one every four *yards*.

We set off northward from Edale on 11th December. We chose the easy method, staying in Youth Hostels as often as we could. Nevertheless, this was only six nights; this was the best permutation of Hostel closing nights at that time of year. Some of the facilities available in Summer are closed after September, and this is the major penalty faced by Winter high-Way-men.

There are certainly other features of a Winter transit; water freezing in water-bottles between breakfast and mid-morning is common in the Scottish Winter, but rather rare in Yorkshire. Dawn to dusk walking gives only from 8.30 a.m. till 3.30 p.m. at the end of December, and a lot of walking has to be fitted in to those seven hours. We aimed to start walking at 8 a.m. each day, just as dawn was breaking, and we finished in the dark on 11 of our 13 days walking. In each case, however, we were on the easy finishing stretch, except for the long days: Edale to Marsden and Malham to Hawes.

We would have preferred to take 15 days, so as to split the two long days, but we were constrained by circumstance — we could not miss an annual reunion party in Scotland on December 9th, and had to start back for the Christmas festivities at Braemar before public transport ground to its' seasonal halt. Consequently, we had to accept this penalty. The prospect of finishing in the dark was an important factor in choosing our night stops, and when we knew we faced a navigation problem towards the end of the day we were particular in pressing on through the day after an early start. It was difficult to get an 8 a.m. start — Youth Hostels do not really cater for starts before 8.30 a.m. Despite this, the facilities of Youth Hostels are excellent and we all agreed in retrospect that it was worthwhile to take the Warden's dinners (which we always did) and breakfast (which we did

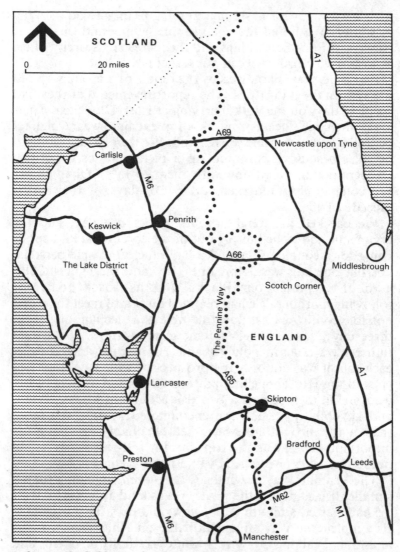

only once). Self catering breakfasts are easy, but they seem to eat into the available time. Breakfasts under open skies are far more time-consuming yet.

From Middleton the frost hardened the sodden paths and turf like concrete. It also broadened the smiles of the local people we met, who all seemed to think us mad to do the Way in winter. We noted the changes in flavour and quality of packets of Pork Scratchings and the increasing scarcity of ice as we moved North — ice in pubs, that is!

At Lothersdale Farm we saw the report of a group who did the Way in the mid-fifties. The report revealed that they had spent 18 days on the walk, carrying at least 47lb. each. Their loads included jackets and ties for evening wear, blanket bedrolls, and a portable wash stand. We were greatly amused by this, because it conjured up a picture to us of British Officers taking everything with them to the Afghan Wars. We could understand them taking 18 days, if their loads exceeded 47lb.!

We checked the weight of our packs one day, and the arguments about the sharing out of the communal kit kept us going for a couple of days. We had much the same personal kit, but one bag was 33lb., one 31lb. and the lightest 30lb. Two of us posted our Blacks' Anoraks back home the following morning. We had planned our kit to meet the worst possible contingencies; duvet as well as a sleeping bag each; three days' food as well as emergency rations. We would rather have taken a polybag and YoHo card and a wallet each, but it was not only the prospect of winter weather and gaps in the Hostel opening pattern that made us take more; we were all members of a Scottish Mountain Rescue Team, and anybody in trouble we encountered would need more than a thermos of lukewarm tea. Probably reckoning as important was having the capacity for self-rescue; we could not let ourselves be rescued by an English Team!

The Pennine Way in winter is far more demanding than a summer transit even if the weather is as kind as it was to us. If we had started a month later, we would only have been able to complete the Way on langlauf skis, and this is still a vague ambition. Walking the Way in winter is wholly different, and would provide a challenge to a strong walker who might have thought the Pennine Way a boring trudge. If you don't want to be part of a 250-mile crocodile, don't go between Easter and September — try it in February or March!

from THE GREAT OUTDOORS *January 1980*

An Eventful Day on an Alpine Pass

ANON

Like other hard-working people, I enjoy a holiday; but a real holiday to me must have two excellent qualities: one, a total absence of responsibility; the other, it must be amongst mountains; and whether these be Scottish mountains, the Alps, the Pyrenees, or any others, I do not mind very much, so that I can get up somewhere as far as possible out of that world of encumbrances which pertain to a literary man's life — to wit, pens, papers, ink, pamphlets, books of all kinds, letters, and worse than all, these obtrusive barbarously brown telegram envelopes and all their contents. But these form what I may call still-life. There is something worse, if the oppressive cares which are in reality the graver part of life, must be handed over to a deputy who has possessed himself of your probable route. To be in a perpetual state of uncertainty as to what a day may bring forth, when you really want nothing, is only a mild alternative to doing the thing one's self. But if you want to gain tone and elasticity of body, of mind, and of feelings too, and really enjoy perfect freedom, get away out of the ruts of life, as far as you can from all beaten tracks, and as high up as you can, and every day will make a difference.

Again, tastes vary considerably in another direction. The last travelling companion I had was on the continent nearly twenty years ago. He thought, after some weeks of travel, that mountains were made for mountain maniacs, and that he had had his fill. Moreover, he could not walk more than a score of miles per day; nor did he care much about the 10,000 beauties of nature which enchant a lover of botany, geology, entomology, and the like. Ever since then, I have gone alone; besides, there are times when even the most desirable companion is a little too much; I mean, during those supreme moments of life such as are so wondrously expressed in many of Wordsworth's poems.

I was enjoying something of such a holiday in the Pennine

Alps, a few years ago. Of course, I was alone. If any contrast were needed, there was one offered in the abominations of the Rhone Valley, where anyone with a sensitive epidermis understood very soon the qualities of the gnats, mosquitoes, and the rest of the flying plagues. After this, to go to a quiet place outside Chamonix for a week or two, avoiding the noisy hotels, and enjoy the charms of the Monarch of the Alps and his environs, is a different matter altogether.

On the particular occasion referred to, I started from Martigny at 7 a.m. and intended to traverse the 30 miles to the Hospice of the Great St. Bernard before night. As I was following one of my holiday pursuits of butterfly-catching, it need hardly be said that, as those 'winged flying flowers' had a considerable choice of route, my journey was correspondingly lengthened. Frequently, some beauty tempted me to run a few hundred yards exactly in the wrong direction, then dodging over some inaccessible spot, was lost to me. The day was a scorching one; even the rocks reflected the intense heat, and combining with the white dust of the roads, made the first 20 miles unpleasant travelling. Time being of consequence, I thought it prudent, so as to get to the summit of the pass before dark, not to stop for a meal to be cooked at Orsières or Liddes, but pressed forward to the last place before the snow-tramp commenced, the Cantine de Proz. There I met with a young nobleman and his guide. After an interchange of inquiries, and an offer on my part of some chocolate and biscuits to the other travellers, as the Cantine was hard up that day in eatables, we set out together, and had crossed the Plan de Marengo without any presentiment of what was going to happen. The first indication of something wrong was the peculiar appearance which my surroundings seemed to assume. Everything looked hazy to my vision — even the snow and the rocks lying about looked as if enveloped in a fog, although the afternoon was beautifully clear. Then I felt that I must sit down and enjoy it; but the guide's flask of Kirschwasser set me going again. Very soon, however, the former feeling returned; but the same treatment temporarily recovered me. At last I took to stumbling along, fell down several times, and at length could not help myself. My companions urged me in vain to arouse to one more effort; but it was useless.

The guide's experience was now of the utmost service. Divining the exact state of the case, and what might happen, he took a very sensible course. Leaving the marquis to see to me, he hurried forward to meet the two monks who always came down from the Hospice at a particular hour each day, so as to obtain their efficient help. On their arrival, the marquis either went on, on his own account, or was requested to go forward with the news. Anyhow, I was informed the next day that his report was, that "Monsieur le — had perished in the snows". In the meantime the two monks and guide took me in hand, and shaking me up, made my hands clasp a belt round the guide's waist, and each of the monks took an arm. The former acted as a substitute for horse-power, and the two latter as wheels. As for myself, I was fast becoming a dead-weight. Between the Cantine and the Hospice there is a space of seven and a half miles of very rough walking, uphill of course, and with a depth of several feet of snow where the cantonniers had not cleared a path. I suspect that my deliverers had a very difficult task, over at least five miles, to keep me from getting into that sleep from which there is no waking. The sensations of that journey during occasional gleams of consciousness will never be erased from my mind. Is there such an essence of ecstatic delight as *elixir mortis?* If there is, it must have been something like it, or the very thing itself, which I enjoyed that day. No words can possibly express the surpassing desire which I felt to sit down and enjoy my felicity — and sleep. But my inexorable friends knew that sleep meant death; and though my repeated appeals of *"Doucement, doucement"* were plaintive enough, they were met by redoubled efforts to force me onwards even when my own legs would not move any longer. The collapse was complete. After the long hot day, the additional distances which the butterflies had added to the 30 miles, and the abstention from a good meal since 5 a.m. it can easily be understood how the intense cold, which immediately follows after the sun is lost to view on the other side of the giant mountains, seized hold of every vital muscle and nerve, and very nearly claimed the victim beyond recall. I may add that, though the month was July, the frost at night was so great as to send the thermometer down nearly to zero.

During the sustained efforts of the three men, I had but momentary glimpses of consciousness. I remember seeing two somethings, black, one on each side, but very indistinct. These of course were the friendly monks. The one over-whelming idea that filled my mind then was how to get to that sleep, that blissful euthanasia which poets have sung about, but which my companions were doing their best to rob me of, just when I had got it within my grasp.

Another lucid interval occurred just as we approached the door of the Hospice, for I saw two or three of the dogs; and then I was lost again, till I found myself in the large room, surrounded by several of the canons. One administered some Extract of Orange Flowers, and that was followed by some warm broth. Then another tugged off my boots, socks, etc; and between them, somehow or other, they got me into bed. (This particular room would not have been mine, if I had gone as an ordinary traveller usually does. I am under the impression that it was looked upon as the best bedroom, being the one used by Napoleon Bonaparte when he stopped at the Hospice en route to the Italian campaign). In the night, I woke, breathing very quickly and very hard. The room itself had the appearance of being one mass of cotton-wool. Congestion of the lungs had got hold of me now, and I felt very ill indeed. But, however, the next morning I did what the monks had ineffectually tried to impress upon me the night before, and I made an effort. My first duty to others was to see the excellent guide and make him a due acknowledge-ment; and as the noble and heroic monks, who live only for others, would not hear of anything but thanks, I had recourse to the *tronc* of the church. To the three men, I am, humanly speaking, indebted for my life. A grateful heart never need be ashamed of its precious burden.

Then, curiosity drew my steps outside the Hospice to visit the Morgue. I expect that very few have had such weighty cause for looking at that very strange building with such peculiar feelings as I did on that occasion; for there, in all

probability, I should have been consigned to keep company with the many other members of that unburied guild of death. It is not essential for me to describe what has been so frequently written about; everybody knows about the weird sights of that remarkable habitation of the dead. But when I saw it, those standing figures, men stricken with death as if in the act of listening to a possible sound of voices, or straining to get another glint of an approaching light, had only been put there a few months before — they, and the sight of others huddled up with their heads on their knees, and any quantity of remains, bones, and clothes, are engraved on my mind most vividly. It is all realistic enough to the very last degree.

At all times, the touch of a hand that is still in death is like nothing else; and though I have seen other Morgues and other awful sights, the one on the Great St. Bernard Pass had fitted itself to my memory as distinctly as scenes only of yesterday. Even the trivial incidents are here at hand again — Turco with a bone; what bone? and Pluton growling at him; the pretty little Soldanella trying to push its little lavender-coloured parachute through the snow, to keep company with the cushioned Gentian and the graceful Arabis. And can I forget the old cantonnier, who, when strength had returned to my limbs, and I had wielded his pick and shovel removing snow, thankfully received my coin as I paid for my invasion of his duty, on purpose to teach him some other and higher truth? Or that half-witted kineherd who had not a shred of intelligence about him till I gave him a few centesimi, and for the same purpose? But chiefly, yes, above all, the transcendent kindness of the clavandier of the monastery deserves record? His personal attention was unremitting — in fact, it was from him that I learnt more than I knew before what an unusual case mine had been, and that recovery had but seldom rewarded their efforts under similar circumstances. Hence the day in my holiday notes is rightly headed, 'an eventful day'.

from CHAMBERS' JOURNAL *1888*

I Know! I Know!

CHRIS GODBER

O, you rash men who go out on the Glyders,
Not one of you ever considers,
The women you leave behind,
As widders.

I had walked countless miles over the Derbyshire hills, climbed most of the peaks in North Wales and the Lake District and because of this, assessed myself, without actually being asked or saying so, as 'experienced'.

And so, on the Thursday night before Easter when it started to snow, my friend Dennis and I gave little thought to weather conditions. Why should we? We had camped in snow before so these few flakes were not going to put us off our four-day holiday in Wales.

By the time we reached our site, not far from Idwal Youth Hostel — between Bangor and Capel Curig — everywhere was covered with an extra thick white blanket. Indeed, we had been lucky to get there at all by the local bus, for the snow ploughs were fighting hard to win the battle.

All day Friday it snowed; sometimes so heavily it was impossible for our eyes to penetrate through it. And the wind — I had heard with disbelief that in certain parts of the world it is possible to lean against it — we just could not fall over, no matter how hard we tried.

On Saturday, both the wind and snow eased off, and we were able to spend an enjoyable day climbing Tryfan, from whose summit we gazed with awe at the extent of the snow and marvelled at the unearth-like features around us sculptured by the icy wind.

Sunday looked even more promising — a clear blue sky. Our object today was Glyder Fawr (3,279ft.) by way of Devil's Kitchen. For anyone unfamiliar with this district it is impossible for me to describe how we attained the summit. Looking back, I don't really know myself. I can only say that at one point we walked across a quarter-mile long snow-drift

306

with at least 60ft. of tightly packed snow beneath us.

From the top of Glyder Fawr, our intended route looked so hazardous that we decided to call it off and return to camp. But, like climbing a tree, going up is quite often far easier than coming down and our way down was not apparent at all. To go back the way we had come was out of the question; it looked too precarious from this new angle and we certainly didn't want to cross that drift again.

After discussion and a lot of searching, we found a gully with enough snow-free rocks on which to hug our way slowly down. Alas, these rocks quickly ran out and we stood at the edge of a wide, even, thick expanse of snow dropping away from us at something like 85 degrees. It looked a very long way down. The bottom of a sheer cliff went away to our left and it was agreed that I should traverse along this to find out if there was any place at all where the snow was thin enough to find solid ground below and so afford us a way down.

To this day, Dennis does not know how it happened. I looked back to see him sliding on his bottom in an upright position down the gradient at an ever increasing speed. There was nothing I could do (which shows how experienced we really were) or thought to do, for his dignified descent was almost comical and I probably did laugh out loud. Only when he became smaller and smaller did it register that it had not been his intention to get out of our predicament in this manner. Somehow, he maintained the same almost statue-like posture until he very nearly disappeared from view. Only just could I see the distant Dennis take a sudden turn to the left, circle twice and come to rest.

I shouted at the top of my voice several times but getting no reply, assumed it was too far for him to hear me. "What's the silly blighter doing now?" I thought, or words to that effect. The graceful way he had gone down that near vertical slope had not given me any real cause for alarm; he was down and I was still stuck with the problem of getting down. I shouted again but seeing that he wasn't moving, muttered to myself that I had better get down to him.

The only way I could see of doing this was to lean backwards and kick out steps in the crusty snow with my heels; we had done a similar thing going up Tryfan the day before. As I have already stated, the angle was steep and my 'experience' should have told me that it was too steep. It didn't — it allowed me to kick out two steps only. The action of bending one knee to kick out the third step, threw me completely off balance. I like to tell myself that my heel must have hit a rock for there is a strange gap at this point of my descent which I cannot account for. I was not aware that I had fallen until the breath was forced out of me by my back hitting the snow. Had the snow been soft, then the force with which I must have hit it would have embedded me in it and possibly held me. But it wasn't, it was hard enough to bounce me straight back off again, somersaulting me head over heels time and time again.

My past life did not come rushing back to me — the only thing I can remember is swearing every time my body made contact. But now, somewhere in mid-air, I glimpsed real danger. Directly in my path was a large, bigger-than-me, rock. For a second, I was the right way up and it was there — straight in front of me. At the speed I was travelling, my only thought was "This is it!" for I knew without any doubt at all that my next bounce would splatter me all over it.

I opened my eyes (I can't remember closing them) and could see clearly down the Ogwen Valley. The horizon was vertical. I watched it slowly right itself and wondered why two deep gashes on my left hand were not bleeding. The watch on my wrist was splayed out like one of Emmet's gadgets so I took it off and tossed it away. I felt no pain whatsoever so stood up quite easily. Looming up behind me was the large rock, and I will never know how I came over it instead of through. From where I stood, it was about 30ft. high and I could see that it was only about half that height round the other side where it faced the slope I had just rapidly come down. I looked up to the point where I had started; the distance I had fallen I will not give for no-one would believe me, I don't even believe it myself. I do, however, believe in Guardian Angels and no-one will ever convince me that they don't exist.

A short distance below me, the ground was flat and I could

see where it had been trampled down into a path. Dazed but still feeling no pain despite the fact that I had wiped quite a lot of blood away from my forehead, I staggered down and came across a group of people — rock-climbers at the foot of Idwal Slabs. What I said to them I can't remember but from the looks on their faces I must have appeared a sorry or horrifying sight. They gathered from me that Dennis was still up there somewhere and it seemed only a short time before two of them came back with him. He was pale but hadn't a scratch on him.

The rock-climbers (I wish I knew who they were) helped us back to the road where they wisely guided us into the Youth Hostel rather than our tent. I insisted that I would be alright but the knowledgeable warden sat me in a chair where I promptly passed out.

The staff at Bangor Hospital (where the pain from previously unseen injuries revealed itself) treated me marvellously and my scars today are a credit to their skill and patience.

Although I have looked for that particular rock several times, I haven't found it. Without that amount of snow the whole area looks entirely different but I have only to close my eyes at anytime to see it, vividly, about to obliterate my life.

I know, as does Dennis, how lucky (if that's the right word) we were and I hope that this story will not deter anyone from enjoying the mountains but please, please don't assess your 'experience' like I did — your Guardian Angel might not be as alert as mine was.

from THE GREAT OUTDOORS *March 1979*

New Year on Ben Nevis

W. H. MURRAY

There is more than one way of observing the New Year in Scotland, and it may be that the devout pub-crawler alone knows true wisdom. Wherever the truth may lie, R. G. Donaldson, G. R. B. McCarter and I, in a fit of ascetic resolve on Hogmanay, severed all ties with the triumphs of 1939 civilisation in order to mortify our flesh on the icy summit of Ben Nevis.

On 30th December we met in a black frost at Bridge of Orchy. There we decided to pitch a tent on the Nevis plateau. A preliminary reference to the Scottish Mountaineering Club guide revealed that winter hurricanes on Nevis could reach a velocity of 150 miles per hour. It seemed too much to hope that we should enjoy the privilege of such an experience; but in midwinter all things are possible on Nevis. Our imaginations leapt to the conception that our tent with ourselves inside might be uprooted at midnight and hurled through Cimmerian darkness to the 2,000ft. contour in the Allt a'Mhuilinn. Therefore, we planned to countersink our tent in the snow-cap by excavating a two-foot pit and building a two-foot wall above. As insulation from the snow we procured light sponge-rubber mats (not a success), four single sleeping bags, and one double bag. Our tent was a high-altitude model, weighing 10lb., with sewn-in groundsheet.

We proceeded to Fort William, and at noon on the last day of the year sallied forth from Achintee. Our rucksacks weighed 35lb. each. We followed the path for 2,000ft., and thenceforward snow lay heavily. The sun shone from a cloudless sky and tempered the freezing air to a choice crispness, so that we could walk slowly and breathe deeply, drinking the cool air as the thirsty climber drinks his beer. After three and a half hours we arrived on the summit plateau, where the great snowfields were surfaced with an icy crust, the whole awash with the fire of sunset until we

310

seemed encompassed by seas of live flame, as though not only Nevis but every summit of Scotland had reverted to red-hot lava. The sky had become a riot of all colours from palest green to scarlet. The beauty was agonising, yet there was no feature describable. We watched, hardly breathing, until the colours began to fade. We felt dazed, as though the eyes of the soul had been blinded by too great a wonder.

"I'd rather be here," said Donaldson, "than have done the best rock-climb on Nevis."

He meant so much more than that — but what more, or what less, could one say?

The weather was now so settled that we abandoned our plan of excavating a pit, and without more delay pitched our tent south of the Observatory ruins, whose walls projected six feet from the snow. Therefore the snow-cap must have been six feet thick. From the door of the tent the snow-slope dipped sharply to Glen Nevis, so that we could look straight across the twisted spine of the Mamores to Glencoe, past the Blackmount and the hills of Crianlarich, until the eye came to rest on the dim outline of Ben Lomond, 71 miles south.

The cold was now intense. There was not a breath of wind. With three of us there was no tent-space for rucksacks, so we left them beside the Observatory and took into the tent only food and sleeping bags. Before tying up the door I took one last look out. The horizons were everywhere dull and dark with night, but far out to the west there lingered one long, thin, and blood-red streak.

Both the doors and ventilators had been completely sealed, so that after preparing a meal we found it warm enough inside for sleep with only one bag. But we paid dearly for this comfort later in the night. The temperature in the tent was too high in relation to the extreme cold outside, with the result that condensation of body moisture reached enormous proportions. The sponge rubber mats on which we lay gave poor insulation; water-vapour condensed in such volume on the groundsheet that our sleeping bags were soaked right through. We roused ourselves towards midnight and drank in the New Year from a communal mug filled with "Mummery's Blood'. The moon was up by this time; we could see it shining through the tent fabric. We put on our boots and went out to the open snowfields — out into such a splendour of moonlight as one sees but rarely in a lifetime.

I took my axe and wandered alone toward the North East Buttress. My shadow moved thin and black along the glistening snow-crust, which crunched quietly underfoot. For 20 miles around me the world was a storm-sea frozen, inundated by a pure, even light, the heavenly grace outpoured to earth. The sky was crowded, shining with stars that were steady and did not twinkle; and 4,000ft. below in the depths of the Spean valley, wrapping the foothills in a light transparent vapour, hung a fine white mist, which the moonbeams pierced.

I cannot believe that any human could look long and alone upon that pale-faced night and not be stirred by awe — stirred if with naught else by despair at his insufficiency, by the sternness of the trials that must lie ahead before it be possible for his mind to contain the true beauty; by awareness that for such attainment no sacrifice could be too much. And should thought be confused, none the less he will know that Masefield was right, and that beauty, the intangible, can take a man by the throat.

Donaldson and McCarter joined me. From the top of North East Buttress we admired the rock scenery of the cliffs, then separated and prowled about the plateau in silent delight. After a while each went to the summit cairn, returned to the tent, and slept uncomfortably until 8.30 a.m.

The darkness was noticeably lessening when McCarter opened up the tent to get snow for breakfast. He looked out and gave a shout of astonishment. "Another damned dawn," I thought. But sleepiness vanished and cold was forgotten when I saw the sight for myself. Across the entire length of the east horizon, from farthest north to south, ran a broad crimson bar, fading to orange in its upper fringe, then melting into pale-blue sky, which darkened and deepened toward the zenith and became navy-blue in the west, where night still hung over the frost-bound land. Very long, very thin, unsubstantial streamers of cloud hung about the sky, and these were caught and fired by great beams of light which radiated from a central point in the crimson bar. The whole made a perfect geometrical pattern like a vast cobweb, of which the threads were jets of orange and pink flame suspended across the vault of the sky.

The mountains of Wester Ross, incredibly wild and icy, dominated the north. They looked like the original Alpine range of 10,000ft. from which they are reputedly descended. Now the most aged mountains in Europe, and but the stumps of their former selves, they still display their old nobility in the sharp lines of ridge and peak. Farther east the Cairngorms bulged against the sky in huge rolling domes, like 'frosted cities of infinite sleep'. But the absorbing subtleties of this northern panorama were soon swamped by the stirring crudities of the eastern skyscape, where like a cannon-ball white-hot from the forge the sun came flashing, streaming, blasting up in a glory of blinding light; higher, higher, until we could no longer with level eye look squarely into its face. The colours vanished from the sky, which became an even blue; the icy sparkle of the snow-peaks changed to a growing glare.

Between us we travelled over 1,000 miles to reach Nevis at the New Year; we carried 115lb. of equipment through a vertical height of 4,400ft.; we spent an uncomfortable night on the snow-cap; our car was frozen when we returned to Achintee. For all this work and unpleasantness we have, say the Philistines, nothing to show except one gully climb*. Nothing to clink in our pockets, so to speak. Nothing but a memory. A memory of the wide, silent snow-fields crimsoned by the rioting sky, and of frozen hills under the slow moon. These have remained with us.

from MOUNTAINEERING IN SCOTLAND *1947*

* After an epic climb of Gardyloo gully, the party regained the summit of Ben Nevis at 5 p.m. on New Year's Day. *Editor's Note*

White-out on Foel-goch

SHOWELL STYLES

One of the most distinguished novelists of the early Twentieth Century, E. H. Young, has a poem about Y Garn that begins:

> She sits in splendour, great against the sky,
> And broods upon the little ways of men.

It conveys the impression of aloofness, of superior contemplation, which you receive as you look up at the mountain from Ogwen or across at it from the slopes of Tryfan. Possibly this impression is due to the lofty brow bent as in meditation above the shadowed cwm; or to the two ridges curving down and round like folded arms. The ridges enclose a small lake, Llyn Clyd, which the poet calls 'a secret tarn like the dim eye of God', so well hidden that only a mountaineer or a careful student of the Ordnance Survey map would know of its presence. E. H. Young was both, for in her non-literary capacity she was Mrs Daniell, one of the earliest woman rock-climbers and participator in the first ascent of Hope, on the Idwal Slabs, in 1915.

But great and splendid though Y Garn looks from the Ogwen side she is only half as fine as she looks. The photograph, in which the mountain is seen from the western flank of Tryfan looking across Llyn Bochlwyd, hints at this. The crags, the cwm, and the sweeping ridges are all on view in their bold and massive sculpture, but the left-hand skyline sloping so gently and evenly away from the summit tells of the even more massive monotony of Y Garn's hidden side. Like W. S. Gilbert's actress, she is 'round behind'. There is probably no duller mountainside in Snowdonia than the bald flanks that sweep down between west and south to Nant Peris, 2,700ft. of uninteresting sheep-run whose only graces are the two mountain streams that form its boundaries to north and south. These are both charming, and the little Afon Las, which rises only a very short way from Llyn-y-

314

Cwn above the Devil's Kitchen, enlivens the path of descent when you cross the range from Ogwen to Gwastadnant.

Having once referred to the photograph of Y Garn and its neighbours, I may as well make all possible use of its topographical clarity. The mountains we are looking at are (from left to right) Y Garn, Elidir Fawr, and Foel-goch, and they stretch away north-westward from the sharp angle made with the Glyders. The main ridge goes on over Foel Goch, which is not quite in the picture, to cross two other summits which are out of it altogether; Mynydd Perfedd and Carnedd-y-Filiast, the latter being the northern terminal of the range. Elidir Fawr's notched whaleback stands out to westward of this main line of tops, projecting towards the Llanberis valley as Tryfan projects towards the Ogwen valley from the Glyders; invisible between its crest as seen in the picture and the nearer ridge below it there is the deeply-cut glen of the Dudodyn stream. The right-hand cwm of the two in the photograph is Cwm Cywion (this, too, has a small lake) whose name means 'the cwm of the chickens'. The black-shadowed ridge much nearer on the left above Llyn Bochlwyd, is the end of the Gribin that descends from the summit ridge of the Glyders; it is among these calcareous outcrops that the choicer 'alpines' are to be found. The deep trough of Cwm Idwal thrusts in between the Gribin and Y Garn, out of sight and nearly 1,000ft. below.

To a mountaineer's eye the most attractive feature in this photograph is the horseshoe of Cwm Clyd — the two ascending ridges curving to meet at the summit of Y Garn. Up by the left-hand ridge, down by its brother, gives a short but exhilarating expedition in summer and a rather more serious exercise under good snow conditions. The shattered buttresses of the left-hand ridge give short sections of easy scrambling. Their rock is not sound enough for rock-climbing, and Y Garn's main attraction for users of the climbing rope is a winter route up its north-east face, where the shadow lies in the picture. Good hard snow may endure for weeks here, but the final obstacle is usually a big snow cornice jutting from the summit ridge and overhanging the whole route, a potential danger because warm southerly

winds may have crept up those gentle slopes on the other
flank and softened the snow of the crest. There has been
more than one bad accident here due to the unexpected
falling of the cornice.

Though an ascent from the north-east, by taking Y Garn at
its face value, makes the most of this two-sided mountain, I
would not begin my 'recommended route' by either of the
ridges. The walk has to include Elidir Fawr, an awkward
mountain to fit into any circular route and nearer to
Llanberis than to Ogwen — though for more reasons than
one it is usually climbed from Ogwen — and I would make
Elidir my main objective, gaining height by the easiest route I
could find to place me on the main ridge. From Ogwen by the
path up Cwm Idwal, then, and up past the Devil's Kitchen to
the saddle near Llyn-y-Cwn. The long slope to the cairn of Y
Garn (3,104ft.) has its compensations in good views if the
weather is clear, and when you have descended 600ft. on its
northern side there is very little up-and-down for the next two
miles, until you begin the short climb to the top of Elidir.
Bwlch-y-Brecan is the name of the saddle under the south
flank of Mynydd Perfedd whence the long spur of Elidir
Fawr shoots suddenly out west-south-west from the main
northward ridge. From the sharp crest where you look down
to a big lake, Marchlyn Mawr, on the right hand, the narrow
but easy ridge rises ruggedly to the summit cairn at 3,030ft.,
just 700ft. above Bwlch-y-Brecan.

For the return to Ogwen, go down again to Bwlch-y-Brecan
("persons troubled with giddy heads can keep on the right of
the ridge" says an old guide-book helpfully) and back by the
same route as far as Foel-goch, whose undistinguished table-
land was crossed on the outward journey. If you keep the
edge of the Foel-goch cliffs in view on your left, you can
hardly miss the slope of descent into Cwm Cywion to south-
eastward. There is a good diving-place in little Llyn Cywion;
on the April afternoon I used it the more important thing was
a quick-getting-out place, which is also provided. It is much
easier to follow the stream down to the old road than to
traverse round into Cwm Idwal, and when you strike the old
road you are little more than half a mile from Ogwen

Cottage, the youth hostel, and the A5.

The paths are well marked on all this route except the descent from Cwm Cywion, where there is in any case an easy-to-follow stream. In a mist it might be possible to miss the point of descent from Foel-goch — to be more honest and positive, it is possible, because I have done it myself, with a somewhat unusual result.

It was early spring and I had been storm-bound in the Club hut at Ogwen for two days. Snow lay above 1,500ft. and the rain that lashed the valleys ceaselessly was snow or sleet or hail on the tops. On the third day I resolved to defy the weather and get on the crests; a traverse of the range from Foel-goch to Glyder Fach was my plan, no less. I had no companion, but I had an ice-axe and I knew that part of the hills 'like the back of my hand' (how many people could draw the back of their hand with any pretence at accuracy?). Naturally I carried map and compass, but I did not expect to use them.

The saddle of Bwlch-y-Brecan lies just north of Foel-goch and I got up into the snowy cwm beneath it. In summer there is a steep but practicable ascent to the saddle, but the slope I now began to climb — in lightly-falling snow — was a hard white wall where only the ice-axe, properly used, could give security. I kicked steps at first; soon I was cutting them with the adze of the axe, in much harder snow. Two-thirds of the way up the snowfall thickened, just as I reached a steepening of the slope, a fold or short wall running across the incline as far as I could see on either hand. As often happens, this steeper section was frozen more solidly than the rest. It was ice, where a slip could not be checked with the axe — and a slide from that height would be the end of me, even if by a miracle I had nothing worse than a broken leg. No one, you see, knew where I was.

For a minute I stood in my snow-steps at the foot of the steep bit, considering it. The wise thing was to turn back. But it was not yet noon and I had still to reach the start of the traverse I had planned — the grand battle with the elements I proposed to indulge in. And the icy section was plainly not more than 15ft. high, with what looked like easier stuff above it. The rim of the saddle overhead was hidden by the whirling flakes but it must be quite close now. I began to move up, cutting large steps in the ice and balancing with care. Just short of where the angle became easier a gust of snow like a small whirlwind upset my balance and for an instant I thought I was certain to fall. I didn't, though, and a few more hewn steps brought me to easy-angled snow where I could move more quickly and leave my momentary fright behind.

The steep bit seemed to be the place where the eddies of snow in the cwm connected with the real snowstorm raging on Bwlch-y-Brecan above. As I climbed up the air became thick with snow, and when I came over the rim of the saddle it seemed that the snow that drove at me had no interstices where air could be. I couldn't breathe. I couldn't see, I could hardly stand up. And it was deathly cold. I was not such a fool as to imagine I could survive even a short battle with the elements in conditions like these. The aim of any sane mountaineer would be to get down below that snowstorm as quickly as possible, I told myself; and immediately decided that the quickest way — the route by which I had come up — was out of the question. The alternative was to contour round the back of Foel-goch and go down the easier slope into Cwm Cywion and so back to Ogwen.

I started off at once, heading to the left across the white mountainside and holding to a horizontal course that should bring me (I thought) to the Cywion descent. To get out map and compass in that storm of snow was almost impossible, and unnecessary anyway; I knew these hills like the back of my hand.

It was like walking blindfold, for I could see nothing through the driving snow. But everything happened just as it should do according to the picture of the mountains I had in mind. There was a kind of shoulder — impossible to say how broad or long — and then a sudden steepening of the snow underfoot, downhill. This, of course, was the dip into Cwm Cywion. In my mind's eye (my bodily eyes were veiled and blinded with snow) I saw myself descending rapidly towards the little lake, coming soon below the snowstorm and down the sheltered flanks to Ogwen. I could picture the map, and the compass points clicked into place: south down on my right front, north somewhere behind my left ear, south-east straight ahead down the invisible slope of snow.

I stamped my way down for five minutes or more, defeated but secure in the wisdom of my retreat. The blinding snow abated very little as I lost height, and I soon realised that I must be heading straight down towards the Nant Ffrancon, bypassing the little cwm. Then the spinning snowflakes began to slow and thin and through the dingy screen I discerned the loom of the Ogwen mountains — Tryfan, that would be, over to my right. The shapes stood suddenly dark and bold through a gap in the drifting snowfall. They were where Tryfan should be but they were not Tryfan. They were not like any mountains I knew. Their outlines were sharp and straight, triangular or severe rectangular; Impressionist mountains — mountains not of this world.

I knew then that I was dead. I *had* slipped and fallen from that little ice-wall. The rest had been the blind crossing between life and death. This was my first glimpse of the 'Undiscovered Country'.

I knew this with certainty for perhaps two seconds, the time it took my mind to erase that other certainty about compass directions. As soon as I could twirl my preconception through 180 degrees and see myself heading north-west instead of south-east I knew where I was. I had passed below the Cwm Cywion shoulder and missed the descent on the Ogwen flank altogether. I was halfway down the slopes to Llanberis, and the pointed other-worldly mountains were the silhouettes of the giant slate tips in the Dinorwic quarries.

from THE MOUNTAINS OF NORTH WALES *1973*

Beinn Ime by Moonlight

ROBIN LLOYD JONES

It was one thirty in the morning. The road, an empty ribbon of snow, unfolded before our headlights. Helensburgh, Gare-lochhead, Arrochar — the red mini hummed in and out of people's dreams.

A winter climb by moonlight — I'd waited a long time for this. I had wanted a full moon, snow on the hills, a clear sky, a free weekend. I'd waited 18 years. Hardest of all was the finding of a companion who shared my brand of madness. Once I had set off to do it solo, but in thickening cloud, with rain on the way, I had abandoned the attempt.

We topped the rise. Ahead, pale shrouded Beinn-an-Lochain haunted the skyline. Loch Restil lay in frozen trance as Martin engaged a lower gear for the descent into Glen Kinglas.

In the lay-by opposite Butterbridge Burn I consulted the map. The height given for Beinn Ime was 3,318ft. The brown contour lines and black-hachured cliffs bore no resemblance to the blue-robed monarch at whose feet we sat. I opened the car door. The air bit sharply. More intense even than the cold was the silence. The mountains held their breath; the rushing burns were iron-gripped.

The glimmering, spell-bound landscape, the feeling of unreality, of time suspended — was it all a dream?

Martin whacked the roadside snow with his ice-axe. There was a metallic ring.

"Crampons!" he said, clouds of vapour issuing from his mouth. We strapped the twelve-pronged frames to our boots. Without them we would face hours of step-cutting in the hardened snow. Usually the crampons didn't come out of the rucksack till well above 2,000ft. To don them at the roadside was a rare event, but then, this was the coldest spell Scotland had known for 40 years.

In the small hours of the morning an empty car in a lonely

spot could trigger off a search party. I wrote a note and stuck it in the rear window: BEINN IME BY MOONLIGHT. BACK FOR BREAKFAST.

"Ready?" I asked.

Through scarf and balaclava, Martin gave a muffled "Yes."

Steel-shod boots clanked over the ice-bound burn, then crunched firmly on the mountainside. Ahead, smooth slopes were shimmering like silk. Our shadows flitted before us over the illuminated snow. We crossed wind-rippled, moon-dappled surfaces of sheer delight. We ascended pearl-encrusted, frosted acres which sparkled in a way never seen by day. Above, the hypnotic moon continually drew our gaze.

On Beinn Ime's flanks the sweat usually pours, the clothes come off — even in winter. Not so this time. Although I was wearing long-johns, breeches, windproof over-trousers, and knee-length canvas gaiters, I felt only a gentle glow.

Where our twelve-clawed marks met the tracks of a mountain hare we stopped. Martin grappled with frozen fastenings and produced coffee from a flask. The chocolate was too hard to break, but the rum fudge was exactly right. The coldest hour, the coldest spell, and well above 2,000ft.! I thought about my warm bed. No! It was here, in this silent realm awash with moonlight, under the stars, that I wanted to be.

Was I imagining it, or did the moon seem yellow-tinged? And was the light now dimmer?

The gradient steepened. Between black cliffs long tongues of ice angled towards the summit ridge. The blade of Martin's axe rose and fell. Glittering chips cascaded down the slope. An hour passed. My turn at cutting came and went. It was definitely darker. In the excitement of starting out I had forgotten that the moon would set! It slipped below the hills of Inveraray and suddenly the mountain was a grimmer place. A chill wind sprang up. 300ft. above us the ridge was silhouetted against the sky, while Martin, a few yards away, was barely visible. Secretly, I was glad to be spared the sight of the lengthening drop beneath my heels.

Breathing hard, we gained the ridge. Almost imperceptible differences in the quality of dark hinted at precipices on either side. Close by, but how close we couldn't tell, the northern edge would be heavily corniced, overhanging the emptiness by six feet or more. My luminous compass pointed where the summit ought to be — but we were going downhill!

Instinct cried, "Bear right!" But experience said, "Trust the compass every time!" And soon the ground took an upward trend.

That cornice worried me. I probed forward with my ice-axe like a blind man with a stick. A pale shape loomed up. Was it the summit still far off? Or perhaps another peak miles away? Ten paces and we bumped into it — a hummock no higher than my head! We knew then it would be foolish to go on. We must stop and wait for dawn.

To escape the wind we dug a hole and cut slabs of hard-packed snow for walls. Inside our plastic survival bags we shivered and waited. Eastwards there was a faint radiation of purple light. We debated whether it was Glasgow's distant halo or a forerunner of the coming day. Due south, Greenock, Gourock and Dunoon were twinkling bracelets on a black velvet coast. The Cloch Point Lighthouse blinked steadily, and far, far down the Firth of Clyde, Ailsa Craig's beam made silver pinpricks in the dark.

The last of the coffee; cold prowling; numb toes. A blush in the sky. Over the shoulder of Ben Lomond crept delicate hues of pink. Slowly, night's dead ashen shapes rekindled in dawn's fire.

We stretched stiff limbs, stamped our feet and wandered in disbelief over fields of crimson snow towards our blood-red peak.

It was too cold to stay more than a few minutes at the top. The wind penetrated to the marrow. As we hurried down, range upon range of snow-clad hills were catching the first rays of the sun. We came upon our footprints of those moonless hours. The chill of fright shook our already cold bodies as we saw that they approached within a yard of the corniced edge, then veered away.

Descent was swift. A huge ball of orange-red thrust

between The Cobbler and Narnain, driving the shadows before us, down the valley. I stumbled; then stumbled again. It was 24 hours since I had slept.

The last splendorous phase now began. With crampons biting the glinting ice, we walked down the Butterbridge Burn; down cascades frozen into opaque and lumpish shapes; down dense black ice and glass-smooth sheets which shone like gold.

The car was in sight. It was 7 a.m. I thought of hot porridge, mugs of coffee, sizzling bacon and slabs of bread. We turned, Martin and I, and gazed for a long time at where we'd been. Then we were mere mortals again, with weary legs and one last snowfield still to cross.

from THE SCOTS MAGAZINE *March 1979*

Cold Night in Nantahala

MARGARET and BUMP SMITH

There were about 1,850 miles of trail behind us now and we slept easily under any circumstances except concrete floors. On logs, boughs, boards, chicken wire, the ground; alone in the forest or jammed in a shelter like cordwood with a dozen other people; in stifling heat, sky-ripping thunderstorms, or foggy chilling cold, we slept. This soft bed wrapped us in comfort and we slept as though tomorrow would never come — but of course it did, and with it, more rain. Rain, *rain*. There was still no money at the post office so we asked that it be forwarded to Suches, Georgia, when it did come. The cabin cost $13; there was an additional cash outlay for supplies, and more for breakfast. We had really splurged, eating like mad, filling our packs with all the food and every last candy bar we could carry. We left Fontana with $3, and laughed like fools in the spattering rain because there was no place to spend it in the woods.

Entering the Nantahala National Forest I remembered

reading somewhere that Nantahala was an Indian word meaning *Land-of-Noon-Day-Sun*. How I wished we might see a little sun at noonday — or any time. It was miserable to be wet all the time. We went up and down over the steep Yellow Creek Mountains, and even though we had covered only about five miles when we reached Cable Gap lean-to at noon, we called it enough, and got under cover to dry out and stay dry for a while. Sometime in the night the rain finally quit. We left before daylight, but were slowed in our attempt to recoup yesterday's lost mileage by the steepness of the Cheoah Mountains.

On November 1 the weather turned cold as we went over Swim Bald, Tyre Top, and Flint Ridge, then crossed the Nantahala River bridge and went south along Wesser Creek. In the distance we could see an elusive fire tower that appeared, disappeared, and reappeared as we zigzagged from one mountain to another. At last we zeroed in and climbed Wesser Bald's 4,627ft. to the tower. Then we climbed the tower to take pictures. It was a clear day and we could see far out over the Nantahala Mountains, their thick spruce and fir interspersed with the strange balds. We climbed down from the fire tower to follow the crest to Tellico Gap and on to a lean-to. Rain dimmed the autumn beauty of the walnut and maple trees. We walked across a half-dozen balds and wondered about their origin. The rain stopped and we kept going over Sheep Knob to Panther Gap, to Swinging Lick Gap, to Winding Stair Gap, to Rocky Cove Knob, to Buck Knob. I found these names intriguing and tried to imagine how each place had earned its name. At Rock Gap lean-to it rained again. Besides being wet it was cold and the temperature was still dropping. There was very little wood and fire building was discouragingly difficult. We shivered as we blew on the fire with smoke in our eyes; we were hungry and longed to be *warm*. Eventually, after several false starts, we had a blazing fire. What had been dismal and wet became warm and cheery. Reluctant to let the fire die, we tended it spasmodically through the night. In the morning we were glad we had made the effort. It was *cold!* As we walked along that morning we plucked icicles from ledges and sucked them. The day was clear and it warmed up a little. We made about 20 miles, climbing Big Pinnacle, Albert Mountain, the Ridgepoles and Little Bald. Below Standing Indian there were banks of clouds that made the other mountaintops look like islands in the sea. The lean-to and its nearby brook were all ours. It was cold, but there was plenty of dry wood, so we settled in comfortably. Tomorrow we would be in Georgia.

In the night I had a dreamlike sensation of discomfort, of cold. I fought my way up through layers of sleep, and saw *snow*. Snow everywhere! It actually was *snowing!* I poked Bump, and he reared up, the snow flying off the foot of his sleeping bag. "What?" he began, but the "what" was grimly obvious. We were caught in a blizzard.

Our boots were frozen stiff. Our hands felt the same way. The thin cotton of our gloves and our pants gave us little protection from the snow and cold. Bump built up the fire, piled on wood, and set our boots close to the fire to thaw out. We covered ourselves with the space blanket, but the wind was blowing hard and driving all the heat out into the snowy darkness. Our boots thawed enough so we could get them on. My shoes had been too close to the fire and the laces had burned. With numbed fingers Bump replaced them with pieces of our clothesline. I cooked some oatmeal and we ate, standing over the fire with snow blowing all around us.

We were afraid that if we stayed we would surely freeze to death, so we threw the dirty dishes into our packs and started hiking. We were at an elevation of some 6,000ft. If we could work our way down we might be able to walk out of the storm. It was almost daylight now but we could see very little. We crept along, hair and eyelashes caked with snow, boots like chunks of ice. The soles on Bump's boots were worn smooth and he kept slipping and half-falling. I was terrified, afraid he would fall and injure his already weakened back. We had said we would finish the trail or drop trying. I began to get angry. In frustration I shouted to Bump, "If we die I'll come back and haunt this damn Standing Indian!"

For hours it seemed that we barely moved over the slippery snow-covered trail. However, we gradually made our way down out of the wind and blinding snow, and off the mountain. Finally, a long way off, we could see buildings and smoke curling into the frosty air. Half-frozen, we moved toward that smoke. It was a farmhouse, and when we reached it we met Willard and Elva Rogers, who get our vote for being the best people in the world. Willard took off our packs; we couldn't. Elva took care of our wet jackets and boots and huddled us around the stove. They listened to our story and told us we were to stay with them until we could buy warmer clothing. We agreed wholeheartedly with this idea, but we had no money. We started making phone calls, but no one was home — not Steve, not Bump's parents or his sister, not my mother — *no one!* Them Bump remembered Howard Bridges, a friend who had said, "If you run into trouble, just call."

Howard was at home. "No problem. I'll wire the money. It's as good as there."

We were in Titus, which was a very small place. The nearest town was Hiawassee, and Mr. Rogers said he would drive us over in the morning. The Rogers fed us a hearty supper, and bedded us down with an electric blanket! I was too weary to think about the extremes of our fortunes. It was enough that we were under cover, warm, dry, and fed.

from HIKING THE APPALACHIAN TRAIL *1975*

Return to Jumla

GEORGE B. SCHALLER

The three porters are anxious to leave in the morning because, they say, we must make our way through a canyon before 11 a.m., before the meltwaters from the snows raise the stream too high, even at this season, to make passage difficult. Moving along the gravelly river bed, we cross and recross the stream on brittle ice bridges. The hillsides are terribly overgrazed by livestock and deeply eroded, deterioration hastened by the fact that the animals are now largely cut off from their traditional winter pastures in Tibet; villagers also pull *Lonicera* and other bushes out by the roots to serve as fuel.

The canyon cliffs are up to 3,000ft. high on the eastern side, and we hurry through the depths, facing a bitter wind under a frozen sky. Finally the walls give way to wide rolling hills. It is 10.30 a.m. Punctually at 11 a.m. a rush of grey water floods the dry channels and sweeps over the ice. At noon Phu-Tsering collects yak droppings for a fire and makes tea. The valley soon divides, the junction marked by a stone cairn on which are piled the skulls of about ten Tibetan argali and a few bharal. One of our guides tells us that he shot an argali near here last summer. A pack of three or four wolves had preceded us up the valley by only a few hours and I am pleased to note from the tracks that one is a pup. It is only 2 p.m. when the porters stop, saying that it is too late in the day to cross the first of the two passes ahead. I feel uneasy, and to find an outlet for my tension, climb a high hill to look for argali. All I see is a low dark wall of cloud rolling towards us in the distance, and soon after I return to camp it begins to snow.

An awful night. The wind eddies fitfully around the tent, piling snow against it, and in the other tent the Sherpas and porters argue, undoubtedly about tomorrow's plans. The morning is but a thin solution of the night as, still in cloud and swirling snow, I join the others. The porters refuse to go on because even if we get across the passes, more snow may prevent them from returning home until spring. With all landmarks obliterated, we have no means of finding the route by ourselves. But one man, a traveller who has attached himself to our group, agrees to take us as far as the first pass, the Raka La, without a load, in exchange for any items we may have to discard. Knowing that we must condense seven loads into four, his profits will be considerable. We repack our loads: out goes all food except a three-day supply of tea, tsampa, sugar and rice; out go an old tent, buckets, most pots and pans, and other kitchen equipment; and out go even such unessential scientific specimens as rock samples, fossils, and bharal droppings (which I wanted to analyse for parasite eggs). I hand over all my extra clothing to the thinly clad Sherpas. Gyaltsen is in shorts and tennis shoes, like a schoolboy on a picnic. I tell him to put on his boots, but he replies that he has no boots, that the money I gave him to buy a pair in Kathmandu was spent on other things. To cross passes nearly 18,000ft. high in midwinter in tennis shoes is a good way to freeze toes, I note dourly, and hand him my last clean pair of wool socks.

When at 9.30 a.m. the clouds thin a little, we shoulder our packs and begin the ascent. The first part is steep and the slope slippery with a layer of fresh snow on ice, and we fall often and heavily, robbed of all agility by our 70lb. loads. After only a few hundred feet our guide stops, vaguely waves one arm at the clouds, saying the pass is somewhere ahead, and flees down the mountainside. We trudge on, wholly lost in this featureless and formless expanse. As the clouds engulf us again, it snows harder and the force of the wind increases. And then, just as we despair of finding the route, we hear above us the ringing of bells and the whistling and calling of men, *oo-oo-oo*. Out of the clouds, out of the grey nothing-ness, evolves a caravan of 50 or more yaks. In a single undulating line the animals plough downhill, shaggy dark creatures, their coats encrusted with driven snow; the men are just as wild-looking in sheepskin *chubas* and long wind-tangled hair as they urge the beasts on with waving sticks and hollow cries as if dispersing a gathering of mountain spirits.

Soon they all vanish in the mist as if they have never been, and after a few minutes their tracks too have drifted over. But at intervals we now find frozen yak droppings, and using these as trail markers we toil towards the pass. Clouds scud along the slope and winds scream, whipping snow horizontally in gusts so savage that we must stand with our backs towards them until their force is spent. With visibility only a few feet, we remain close, seeking security from each other in this raging wilderness.

Shouting above the howls of the blizzard, I suggest that we try to make a bivouac. Just then we hear bells again, coming towards us from below, and soon a ghostly caravan of six yaks driven by two men and two teenage boys emerges from the snow. The leader agrees to carry one of our loads on his yak. Our packs lightened by about 15lb. each and with yaks to break trail, we ascend with renewed vigour to the pass. A cairn surmounted by a gnarled pole marks the summit. One of the men takes from his snow-encrusted *chuba* a prayer flag and ties it to the pole as a votive offering; as I pass it, whipping in the gale, I also give my quiet thanks to the mountain gods.

We drop into a high broad valley, and farther on follow a canyon flanked by cliffs shadowy in cloud. At dusk we camp beneath a rock overhang. The Dolpo men unload their yaks and turn them free to find whatever meagre forage exists beneath the snow. A bit of tsampa mixed with sugar and water is our dinner. Before falling into a weary sleep I note with satisfaction that the snow has ceased to fall and a wan moon shines through the thinning clouds. However, the weather remains unsettled the next morning and the Dolpo men inform us that they will be ready to go on after it has warmed up but at 9 a.m. they are still beneath their blankets. No, they say, they will not continue today after all. We ask for a guide through this maze of peaks until the route to the next pass becomes obvious. After much vacillation and haggling one of the men, a young one in his twenties, agrees to come with us for an exorbitant price, to be paid in advance.

After an hour of travel our guide walks so slowly that,

suspicions aroused, I watch him carefully. While we drink at a rivulet, he walks ahead and falls purposefully afterward moaning and rubbing his leg as if injured. Jang-bu hurries up to help him, but when I tell him of the deceit, his concern changes to fury. Jang-bu demands our money back, and when he finds out that it has been left in camp, his frustrations with the unreliability of Dolpo men erupts. He kicks the fellow in the legs with his heavy boots until I point out that if he does not stop the imaginary injury may well become real. Thereupon Jang-bu punches him in the head with his fists until he lies sobbing in the snow. Jang-bu orders him to pick up a load and carry it to the pass. His wind-chapped cheeks wet with tears, the man replies that the path to the pass is deep in snow, very difficult, but that the route down the Deokomukh Khola to Phoksumdo Lake is easy. I look at the canyon of the Deokomukh just ahead and know the descent is far from easy and that we will be away from a travelled route in case of mishap. But then I remember Gyaltsen in tennis shoes. With the weather clearing and temperatures dropping, Gyaltsen is hardly dressed for a high pass; tough and uncomplaining, he might not tell me if his toes are freezing. We discuss the pros and cons of each route. All three Sherpas vote for the Deokomukh and I concur with misgivings. Well, if the route is so easy the Dolpo man surely does not mind showing us the way and carrying a pack for a few hours. Prodding him to his feet, we begin the descent with myself in the lead and the three Sherpas in the rear to prevent the escape of our reluctant porter.

The canyon narrows almost immediately and in it a turbulent stream, covered with ice bridges, ricochets from wall to wall and leaps over precipices. Snow covers every boulder, and near the water's edge, everything is glazed with ice, making all footing treacherous. To cross the stream we must use the ice bridges. "You first, sah," urges Phu-Tsering. "You biggest." The logic of his suggestion is overwhelming; if the ice supports me, then the Sherpas can march across safely. Inching ahead, ready to leap back with the first hollow cracking, I barely breathe during each tense crossing. Most bridges ring solidly beneath my boots but a few rotten ones collapse with the first tentative tap of my foot. There are also questionable ones that groan and grumble yet seem strong, and sometimes they hold and sometimes not, only a desperate leap saving me from an icy immersion.

During one crossing, the Dolpo porter suddenly drops his load and scrambles back up the canyon. No-one tries to stop him; we have no more use for him. Soon after, the gorge narrows to the width of the stream, and there is a 20ft. waterfall, a magic fall whose tumbling waters have been turned to clear shining glass. Water continues to flow between its ice-covered surface and the rock. I descend cautiously over the ice bulges, partly supporting my weight on a rope tied to a boulder. The others first lower the packs to me, and then descend too, hoping that the fragile shell of ice does not break. Farther on, a rocky slab slants from the stream. While traversing it, my boot slips and I fall into the water, soaking myself from the chest down. My clothes begin to freeze almost immediately, but we can now see the first birches and pines ahead, and I hurry on, trying to keep warm until we can find a good campsite and build a fire. Although a trail is now visible for the first time, I soon wish for rotten ice bridges and slippery boulders. To circumvent an impassable part of the gorge, the path climbs up the canyon wall, and, for a short distance, crosses the cliff face on a narrow snow-covered ledge, sloping outward. With bare fingers digging into frozen cracks of the wall and heels hanging over the abyss, I shuffle sideways, scraping with my toes little platforms on which the Sherpas can tread. But after this perilous path the canyon widens and in a copse of pine and birch, I build a fire. Soon my pants steam and as the warmth flows into me the strains of the past two days have already become memories. The worst part of the gorge is behind us; Phoksumdo Lake is near. A tawny wood owl hoots at dusk as I wait for the Sherpas.

The next morning we finally emerge from the dark canyon into bright sun. On a small plain covered with brush and grass, a snow leopard suddenly bounds away, across a stream, through a thicket, and into broken cliffs. For five weeks I sought a meeting with this species at Shey and was not once granted even a glimpse; now, on our last full day in the cat's mountain home, with my physical and mental energy sapped by altitude and hardship, I have this fleeting encounter. I drop my pack and search for its tracks on patches of snow, not following it into the cliffs, but retracing its path to discover what it had been doing before our arrival. I note immediately that not one but two medium-sized snow leopards have been here, one having vanished unseen. After coming down a hillside near Phoksumdo Lake, the two animals travelled up the valley along the banks of a rivulet, one usually behind the other. One made an occasional detour to investigate a boulder or the trunk of a downed tree, and depressions in the snow show where they reclined for brief rests. A leisurely morning until disrupted by our arrival.

There apparently being no path to Ringmo down the east shore of Phoksumdo Lake, we must loop around the north end. A livestock trail ascends the steep slope for 2,300ft. before following its contours. A snow leopard has travelled here too, a male judging by his large pugmarks. In the manner typical of his race, he marked his routes with scrapes and faeces, placing these on or near promontories. Full of delight, as if on a treasure hunt, I hurry along the trail collecting faeces, old and fresh, and taking notes. Three snow leopard visited Shey and now I have evidence for three around Phoksumdo Lake, making at least six in about 200 square miles.

The naturalist Rodney Jackson was in Namlang Khola, just west of Dolpo, between December 1976 and February 1977, and there he estimated three to five snow leopard in 160 to 200 square miles. But local hunters killed two of the cats during his short visit. His report to the Nepal government describes the intensive hunting in that area:

> The hunting of musk deer, blue sheep and snow leopard by Dolphu villagers is rampant. Sale of musk at 1,000 to 1,200 rupees a tola represent the primary source of hard cash for many of the families in Dolphu. Some 30 hunters, operating from about seven base camps, spent November, December and part of January hunting the Namlang Valley and Kanjiroba Himal. Hundreds of poisoned bamboo spears were placed in

the birch/juniper zones for musk deer, and along trails leading
to water for blue sheep. Other spears were placed along rocky
passes for the snow leopard, while stone deadfalls were used
to kill rodents, martens and other mustellids.

We arrive at the western arm of the lake in mid-afternoon,
too late to continue to Ringmo. I erect my tent on the same
spot as on October 25, and with this act I mentally complete
my journey.

from STONES OF SILENCE — JOURNEYS
IN THE HIMALAYA *1980*

The Lost Valley

E. F. KNIGHT

On leaving Genoa I zig-zagged back to the town of Paesana on
the Po and thence proceeded to cross the frontier into France
by the Mt. Viso. On leaving Paesana I had no intention of
visiting the Vaudois Valleys which lie to the north of this
town but I was fated to see them. I followed the Po through
its upper valley; very interesting indeed and always very fine
with Mt. Viso always in the background. The pass I wished to
cross by is called the Col of Traversette, a pass of great height
passing from the valley of the Po to that of the Guill or Val
Queras; the *sentier,* only practicable for a few months, very
often disappears altogether for several hundreds of yards and
I often had difficulty in recovering it. It follows the Po to its
source and the scenery is magnificent. The Po forms several
very fine cascades.

At last after a rough scramble over stones and snow I
reached the Italian *Douaniers* crouching under a wall of flat
stones, rolled up in their blankets, for it is always bitterly cold
up here. On leaving them, the path soon disappeared
altogether and a great field of snow and glacier lay before me.
Directing my steps to what appeared to be the col I ascended

for some time when suddenly I was enveloped in clouds and the most fearful thunderstorm I have ever seen commenced, also it began to snow and the wind blowing from the north-east was intensely cold. As I could now see nothing I was completely lost, but pushed on for to halt would have been to freeze, so I kept mounting till at last the storm partially ceased and I soon discovered I had missed the way entirely.

The view from this point, for I had reached the summit of the Alps and was probably some 11,000ft. above sea level, was magnificent, when I caught a glimpse of it through the clouds. Beyond the snowy ranges of the Alps I saw the plain of Piedmont stretching out like a great blue sea, but in the direction I was going I saw nothing but a great confused mass of rock and ice. Having lost the pass I was determined to make one for myself. So scrambling with great difficulty, rolling stones slipping, and constantly having to keep a sharp lookout for large masses of rock and ice which were rolling down from above being dislodged by the storm, I at last reached a point whence I looked on what I supposed was France. A deep ravine ran out from my feet in a north-easterly direction; beyond the snow and stones I perceived pastures; just at my feet lay a lake half frozen and surrounded with snow. I descended to this lake and cautiously passing round it found it fell in the most magnificent cascade I have ever seen into the abyss that lay beneath. The most difficult feat of my tour was the descent of the precipice over which it fell, my boots being very slippery I took them off, and nearly got frost-bitten in consequence. After much trouble I descended and then found that the ravine descended in a series of steps over which the torrent fell in cascades; as each of these steps was nearly perpendicular and in height equal to the *Côte* at *Honfleur,* the descent was difficult. After continuing through this gorge (the most utterly desolate and terrible I have ever seen) for some time, night came on and I bivouacked under a rock and slept well notwithstanding the bitter cold and the fact of my being wet through. The next morning, after more scrambling by the banks of the torrent I reached pastures sprinkled with glaciers and snow banks, here I found a shepherd's cabin where I procured black bread, milk and cheese. After devouring an enormous quantity I gave my host half a franc which he refused and said a sou was enough, at last we effected a compromise, he taking the half franc but on condition of loading my pockets with bread and cheese and drinking several more bowls of milk. This shepherd was very astonished to see me, for he said in his remembrance, and he was very old, no one had descended the mountain by that valley. From him I made out that I had crossed not the main chain of the Alps but the still higher branch dividing the valleys of the Pellice and Po, and thus I was still in Italy.

He told me my best plan was to scramble over a mountain he pointed out to me to get to Pra on the Pellice and thence cross into France by the great pass of the Vaudois, the Col de la Croix. I followed his advice, but on reaching snow, a storm came on again and I was again in an unenviable position of cold. I at last descended into the bed of a torrent flowing often under snow banks which I descended knowing in time I should reach the Pellice. Nothing could be more awfully desolate than the upper part of this torrent, enormous mountains hung over it utterly bare, and so steep that even snow could rarely find a footing. An avalanche of rock, earth and snow fell from above with a terrific roar into the torrent while I was there. This valley is utterly unknown even to the inhabitants of the neighbouring valleys, for there is nothing to entice them, no wood for the charcoal burner and no wild beasts for the hunter. To descend I had often to walk down the torrent itself up to the waist in water, holding on to the rocks to prevent myself being washed off. I at last reached another torrent which received the waters of the first, after some time this became more civilised, pine forests, pasture, at last a mule path then a village appearing where they were very astonished to see me for they said you have come down a road that leads nowhere, only into the mountains. I found this second valley is called la Combe de la Charbonniere. By a good mule path along the banks of the torrent I soon reached the Pellice and the village of Bobbio, one of the largest in the Vaudois Valleys. I may here remark that of all the people I have seen in France and Italy the Vaudois are the nicest, always very hospitable to an Englishman, for they are very grateful to England and several spoke to me of Oliver Cromwell. I slept here for the night, and my host, an old shepherd, gave me many interesting details about the valleys.

LETTER TO C. S. JERRAM *1872*

PART 7

Trail Philosophies

As I hinted in the Introduction, the pace of walking tends to encourage reflection, and the pieces in this section are all the result of that reflective thought that runs with the rhythm of the stride.

They should all be read several times to get the most from them. Many readers will find themselves in sympathy with Hugh Westacott's *Listening to the Silence:* our world is so full of noise that silence, instead of being the most natural of qualities, has become a sought-after rarity, divulged to the walker as much as to anyone.

Nicholas Howe's *Boots/Roots* is very American in tone, though the ideas are gaining ground in Europe, as the erosion from lug soles becomes more noticeable on popular trails. Showell Styles' *Lament for the Wayside Fire* is both evocative of the 1930s and perhaps a foretaste of future decades; who knows what will happen when the oil runs out?

The 'rogue' here is Graham Newson. I almost put *The Art of Coarse Walking* into the next section with the humorous pieces but, reflecting on the problem during a walk, decided it should stay here to provide a lighter touch and balance the more serious soliloquies.

Notes on Vagrancy

ISABELLE EBERHARDT

A subject to which few intellectuals ever give a thought is the right to be a vagrant, the freedom to wander. Yet vagrancy is deliverance, and life on the open road is the essence of freedom. To have the courage to smash the chains with which modern life has weighted us (under the pretext that it was offering us more liberty), then to take up the symbolic stick and bundle, and get out!

To the one who understands the value and the delectable flavour of solitary freedom (for no one is free who is not alone) leaving is the bravest and finest act of all.

An egotistical happiness, possibly. But for him who relishes the flavour, happiness.

To be alone, to be poor in needs, to be ignored, to be an outsider who is at home everywhere, and to walk, great and by oneself, towards the conquest of the world.

The healthy wayfarer sitting beside the road scanning the horizon open before him, is he not the absolute master of the earth, the waters, and even the sky? What house-dweller can vie with him in power and wealth? His estate has no limits, his empire no law. No work bends him toward the ground, for the bounty and beauty of the earth are already his.

In our modern society the nomad is a pariah 'without known domicile or residence'. By adding these few words to the name of anyone whose appearance they consider irregular, those who make and enforce the laws can decide a man's fate.

To have a home, a family, a property or a public function, to have a definite means of livelihood and to be a useful cog in the social machine, all these things seem necessary, even indispensable, to the vast majority of men, including intellectuals, and including even those who think of themselves as wholly liberated. And yet such things are only a different form of the slavery that comes of contact with others especially regulated and continued contact.

339

I have always listened with admiration, if not envy, to the declarations of citizens who tell how they have lived for 20 or 30 years in the same section of town, or even the same house, and who have never been out of their native city.

Not to feel the torturing need to know and see for oneself what is there, beyond the mysterious blue wall of the horizon, not to find the arrangements of life monotonous and depressing, to look at the white road leading off into the unknown distance without feeling the imperious necessity of giving in to it and following it obediently across mountains and valleys! The cowardly belief that a man must stay in one place is too reminiscent of the unquestioning resignation of animals, beasts of burden stupified by servitude and yet always willing to accept the slipping on of the harness.

There are limits to every domain, and laws to govern every organised power. But the vagrant owns the whole vast earth that ends only at the nonexistent horizon, and his empire is an intangible one, for his domination and enjoyment of it are things of the spirit.

Listening to the Silence

HUGH WESTACOTT

This article is likely to offend a lot of people. My great delight is to walk alone and on the whole I find my own company the most stimulating. I have now mortified the Editor, Showell Styles, Mark Richards and Tim Pridgeon who are but a few of the delightful people with whom I have walked during the past year. Mr. Wainwright has remarked that many walkers seem to regard the practice as not only dangerous but downright immoral. He remains unrepentant and so do I.

It is not my intention to persuade anyone to walk alone but merely to give an indication of some of the pleasure it gives me. If like me you subscribe to the aphorism that hell is other people and believe that the most poignant biblical prayer is the

Pharisee's "Oh Lord, I thank thee that I am not as other men are" you will get no pleasure from walking in a crocodile of ramblers and waiting your turn to cross every stile.

The toes of the Editor are probably curling in their boots with anxiety and so I hasten to utter the obligatory 'dire warning'. The moors, mountains and fells of the British Isles can be dangerous. Although by the standards of Europe and North America the mountains are not high, the northerly latitude and the unpredictable weather conditions can make the upland areas of Britain very dangerous. The warm wet westerly winds which normally flow over the country keep our climate generally mild but the weather pattern only has to change slightly in winter time for northerly winds from the Arctic to sweep in. These will be bitterly cold and the temperature in mountainous areas can soon drop to well below zero.

Even in summertime the weather can change dramatically. When I lived in Airedale I was sometimes teased for carrying a cagoule, compass and map even when out for an afternoon stroll in fine weather on Ilkley Moor. But on one occasion I was standing looking up the dale when suddenly I saw a thunderstorm approaching with the speed of an express train. I was the most conspicuous object on the top of the flat moor so I lay down in a drainage ditch to avoid being struck by lightning. It was all over in a few minutes but I have seldom been so frightened and after the storm had passed there was sufficient low cloud about to make me thankful I had a compass with me to help me find my way down.

Never go onto the hills, however well you think you may know them, without being properly clad. Carry with you a map and compass *and know how to use them* and an emergency supply of food and drink. I always have with me an emergency space blanket which remains permanently in the pocket of my day pack. Never go onto the hills alone unless you are a very experienced walker. In this context 'experienced' means having walked for several years on the fells and in particular to have been responsible for planning routes and navigating in all weathers. There is all the difference in the world between being led in adverse conditions and actually leading.

The Solitary Wayfarer

During my teens I became an enthusiastic cyclist and discovered the joys of cycling alone. This happened because I loathe all organised sport and will do anything to escape from it. Whilst I can just about comprehend the pleasure some people derive from a contest between individuals, team events are beyond my understanding. I took to playing truant from school on Wednesday afternoons which were, according to season, devoted to the follies of rugby and cricket. Instead of donning shorts or flannels I stuffed my blazer, cap and tie into my saddlebag and disappeared into the leafy lanes of Surrey to explore the North Downs and the Greensand Ridge. Here I visited churches and explored some of the hilltop forts which I found more valuable and interesting than singing rugby songs in the school showers. At seventeen I drew my life savings of £16 from the Post Office and cycled alone across France to the Alps. The following year I bicycled to Assisi to explore the hill towns of Umbria and to begin a life-long love affair with the art of the Italian Renaissance.

My parents were indefatigable walkers and I accompanied them until I was of an age to be seduced by more carnal pleasures. I did not resume walking until after I was married and living on the outskirts of Sheffield, but a few hundred yards from the boundary of the Peak National Park. One glorious November day I determined to introduce my wife to walking and we set off to explore Stanage Edge. The sun shone brilliantly over a thick frost and after lunch a cold wind sprang up. It was then that I discovered that my woollen hat was not in my rucksack, so to prevent frostbitten ears I wore on my head the paper bag in which our sandwiches had been packed. And that is probably the reason why, 20 years later, I walk alone.

Nevertheless I have made a virtue of necessity and find that solitary wayfaring suits the introspective side of my nature. However often I go walking I always savour that magical moment when I pull on my boots, shoulder my rucksack, climb the first stile and head for the hills, leaving the grosser aspects of twentieth-century life behind. Before long a feeling of joy suffuses my being, any problems which may have occupied my mind seem to evaporate and all my senses are concentrated on the walk. The physical effort and the rhythm of my gait heightens my awareness of the surroundings like a drug affects the addict.

The Witching Hour

There is no exciting scenery near my home in Buckinghamshire to send my spirit soaring but I find that even dull countryside can be transformed by the beauty of the sky. The cloud pattern is always changing and the fascinating shapes that the different kinds of cloud assume are a constant source of delight. If the cloud cover is not too thick, the sky is at its most interesting just after dawn and before sunset. The evening sky is more familiar to most because, outside the winter months, more people have leisure to enjoy it. This is when the sky is at its most dramatic with vivid and startling colours but I prefer the subtlety of dawn.

Rosy-fingered dawn, as described by Homer and echoed by poets from time immemorial, is the most witching hour of the day. I am one of those insufferable people whose senses are most alert early in the morning. My eyes open every day at 5 a.m. and instantly I am awake and ready for anything, so I have seen many a dewy-eyed dawn from my tent doorway whilst drinking the first cup of tea of the day. I love the way that hedges, walls and trees gradually become less blurred and mysterious and assume their familiar shape. If the conditions are right the sun's rays reflected on the clouds produce a wonderfully complicated pattern of pinks and blues which blend and change, strengthen and decline as the sun slowly appears over the rim of the world to suffuse us all in light.

It is at such moments when camping near a stream that I feel particularly in tune with the more primitive promptings of humanity and closest to the Old Gods which have haunted the western world in one form or another since the dawn of history. I half expect to see a water deity chuckling at me as I fill my bucket and should not be surprised to see the Horned One moving through the grove of trees. I can well understand what compelled our pre-Christian ancestors to worship the

Great Earth Mother at the shrine of the swelling breast and the upright phallus. Swinburne was right when in his most memorable line of poetry he cried "Thou has conquered O pale Galilean, the world has grown cold with thy breath".

The Full Experience

It is the solitary wayfarer who has the best opportunity to appreciate the landscape. Walking speed is so slow, at most three miles an hour, that the countryside gradually unfolds and new vistas and perspectives slowly come into view. Walking is about the only form of locomotion which does not require constant attention to steering or surface conditions so the wayfarer has ample opportunity to gaze about and immerse himself in the experience of the countryside. He can admire the pattern of hedgerows and stone walls; he can note the limits of cultivated countryside and speculate why the fields end where they do; he can observe the field drainage system which connects with some distant river and ultimately the sea and he can take an intelligent interest in the crops and stock on the land he crosses.

Two minds impose a discipline upon each other and it is not always possible to pursue a line of thought with single-minded purpose when there is a constant need to consider the feelings of a companion. When I am walking I want to be able to stop when I feel like it, to eat and drink as my appetite demands and to burst into song when my heart is overflowing with joy. If I am wet and miserable I do not wish to inflict my suffering and ill-temper on a companion, nor do I want to jolly anyone along.

Solitary backpacking has its own special delights. It is a marvellous feeling to set off one morning with a week's supply of food knowing that the whole of Britain lies waiting to be explored. A long backpacking trip puts modern life into perspective. Even when dining on accelerated freeze-dried *Chicken a la King* it is possible to share some of the feelings of the backwoodsman and explorer who set a snare or bagged something for the pot with his fowling piece. In most men there is a latent desire to prove that they are self-reliant and can exist successfully in a hostile environment and I always enjoy the moment when I snuggle into my sleeping bag at the end of a long wet day when I had to employ all the skill and cunning I have learned over the years to erect my tent in a howling gale and keep my gear dry.

Small disasters can tax the ingenuity of the backpacker. A broken rucksack strap or a lost tent peg means the need to improvise. I remember one wild wet night when an impurity in the fuel line of my stove blocked the main jet and I had to crawl out into the darkness and hunt around until I found the gorse bush which I had noticed as I erected my tent. Gingerly, I broke off a small twig and returned to my tent to clear the blockage with one of the thorns.

Listen to the Silence
Backpacking alone gives me the opportunity to refresh myself spiritually and to re-establish contact with the things that really matter. I vividly remember the long descent from God's Bridge on the Pennine Way to the A66. I had been walking alone for a week and when I first saw the A66 several miles away I could just make out tiny objects moving slowly along it. As I drew closer they grew larger and identified themselves as lorries. The noise increased with every step and when I reached the road I thought the whole world had gone mad and that no sane society could tolerate the thunder of these behemoths hurtling along the road. But then I had to acknowledge ruefully that busy roads were probably the inevitable consequences of advanced technology (the current jargon 'high technology' always makes me think of a nuclear power station on top of a mountain) and that I should probably not have the leisure to enjoy walking for pleasure were it not for some aspects of modern society which I often deplore.

Solitary backpacking also helps me to evaluate some of the more lunatic intellectual pretensions of our age. One winter night I lay in my tent in the Brecon Beacons listening on my pocket radio to two BBC exquisites discussing the aesthetic implications of an expensive pile of bricks which the Tate Gallery had recently bought and placed on exhibition. One in particular in whom, despite his careful diction, I detected the rhythms and cadences of a South London street market, seemed to think that this work was the Tate's greatest acquisition since the Turners. I fell asleep laughing at such absurdities.

The next day I set off in a grey drizzle to explore the Afon Twrch. I navigated by compass as visibility was very poor until I reached the stone terraces of Ffrydiau Twrch. Here I found a natural stone seat and sat eating my lunch musing on the previous night's broadcast. Suddenly the atmosphere brightened, the clouds rolled back, a patch of watery blue sky appeared and below me was the gorge. For a moment I wished that I had the Director of the Tate, the artist, *and* the critics with me so that they could share the experience of the landscape and blow some of the cobwebs from their minds. Then I dismissed the thought and settled down to absorb into my being what lay before me; and to listen to the silence.

from THE GREAT OUTDOORS *June 1979*

Boots/Roots

NICHOLAS HOWE

Aunt Harriet always wore sneakers. Her brother, on the other hand, favoured moccasins or brogans. That was about the extent of the choice in what I think of as the classical age of White Mountains hiking — from the final years of Victoria's reign to the outbreak of World War II. Occasionally one would encounter on the trails an advanced specialist wearing hobnailed boots, somebody who had been to Europe and brought back a pair of boots affected by the gentlemen climbers of the Alps. For the rest, though, it was sneakers, moccasins or brogans. The brogans were 'stout walking shoes'. The moccasins were shin-high, lace-up boots of soft leather. The sneakers were made of canvas and rubber. Aunt Harriet's were white, and they looked insubstantial to me.

On my own earliest perambulations, I was shod with none of

these. Children my age wore leather sandals with a little strap that buckled over the instep — hardly the thing for even mild hiking. Furthermore, after graduating from sandals, I developed an eccentric but deep aversion to sneakers, a prejudice firmly rooted in family history.

Since late in the nineteenth century, the Howes had spent their summers in Jackson, New Hampshire. Large throngs of relatives and loose connections gathered there each year and gradually filled black photo albums with the record of their exploits. These albums were stacked in the big living room of the houses and were standard rainy-day entertainments during my formative years. In them my cousins and I studied the fading images of elders being vigorous in the mountains. Those age-stained photographs revealed a time not only before the introduction of special hiking boots but before the introduction of almost everything in the mountains that we now take for granted.

Gentlemen went hiking in white shirts with neckties, accompanied by ladies in ankle-length skirts and blouses with leg-of-mutton sleeves, with straw hats firmly pinned to their elaborately coiffed hair. For more demanding treks, three-piece suits, plug hats, and even overcoats were worn by the men, and the ladies added serge jackets with tea party cuffs and collars. Packs were not much more than small canvas satchels with shoulder straps. For overnight hikes, woollen blankets were made into bed-rolls; a rubber ground cloth formed the outside layer. Spare clothes and provisions were rolled inside them, and the arrangement was slung over one shoulder and the ends tied at the opposite hip. These were the standard equipment of the rising generation, the *fin-de-siècle* company of my father as he led his friends onto the heights.

Several album pages later, as these aunts, uncles, and friends matured, the approved fashion for ladies became long stockings and knickers or bloomers with the omnipresent middy blouses. (Some of the practical-minded girls would drop their luncheon sandwiches into the voluminous folds of the bloomers). The men, more resistant to change, acknowledged the new age of freedom by taking off their neckties. And their moccasins and sneakers carried them to epic climbs.

Since they had no easy access to automobiles, a hike from the house in Jackson might be preceded by a five-mile hike on the road to make connections with the train at Glen Station to reach the mountains on the other side of Crawford Notch. Returning in the evening, they would take sponge baths in cold spring water, eat supper, and then walk back down the hill a mile and a half to the village to dance the night away at one of the big summer hotels. Remembering a phrase from Sunday school, I realised that there were giants in the earth in those days.

My mother was different. She had spent her childhood summers at her family's house on Cape Cod, and somewhere I had seen a picture of her family on the beach. All the women and girls were wearing black blouses, black bloomers, long black stockings, floppy black cloth bathing caps, and what I took to be black ankle-high sneakers. It was the standard 'bathing costume' of the day. I was fascinated by the outlandish outfits. Clearly, anyone who went into the water swaddled in all those yardgoods would be dragged straight to the bottom. But her modesty, from neck to toe, would be perfectly preserved. Teddy Roosevelt might have been proclaiming the virtues of the strenuous life from the White House, but it was obvious to me that the message had not reached the proper Bostonians at their seaside frolics.

Ankle-high sneakers in the mountains were one thing (although in combination with long stockings, bloomers, and bedrolls they led me to harbour private doubts about the accumulated wisdom of the ages). But to wear ankle-high sneakers, long stockings and bloomers while swimming seemed to me to be symptomatic of serious derangement. I concluded that sneakers were the symbol of a regressive approach to outdoor sport, and I would have nothing to do with them. My cousins and I wore moccasins when we went hiking. They were the low kind, not laced, but kept tight by a complex pattern of rawhide which ran over the instep and tied into the thongs that ran along the sides. To master that lacing system was the sign of advanced prowess in woodcraft.

At that time, around 1940, my older brother and his friends almost always wore sneakers when hiking. The design had progressed; the sneakers were still ~~ vas and rubber, but they were black with round patches over the ankle bones. It was obvious to me that Aunt Harriet had gotten to my own generation and subverted their adolescent ideas about proper mountain footwear. I vowed it would never happen to me.

After the war, the first real hiking boots appeared on the trails — the first design that clearly could not be used for anything else. Like almost all the outdoor recreation equipment in the late 1940s, these were army surplus: the standard issue boots of the 10th Mountain Division. They were meant for year-round use and had two distinguishing characteristics. For one thing, they marked the introduction of lug soles, a blocky pattern of composition rubber that looked as if someone had nailed dominoes to a canoe paddle. And then there was that immense rigid square toe. This was necessary to accommodate the type of ski binding in universal use at the time — the 'bear trap' toe iron, with its high steel side-plates. The total effect was impressive, even monumental. It looked as if the owner had bought the boots and then thrown them away, keeping the shipping crate to wear instead. But they were durable. From time to time, a pair can still be seen in the mountains, and 35 years of wear makes up for a lot of ugliness.

I never had a pair of that fabled example of army engineering. By the time I got serious about boots I was starting to work in the Appalachian Mountain Club's hut system, and GI surplus equipment had become passé among the hutmen. Work in the huts made extravagant demands on footgear. A hutman had to make a pack trip every few days, and the round trip would be as long as 11⅔ miles. The trails were rough. At Lakes of the Clouds, every step is over flinty granite, and other pack trails are a combination of ledge, loose stones, root-laced dirt, and mud. Such terrain puts maximum wear on every part of a boot, and boots had to bear not only the hutman's weight but that of the load.

This last factor was an important consideration: in those days, competitive packing was in vogue. Loads were as heavy as 331lb. for packers working on construction sites, where dense materials like nails and cement reduced the volume to be tied on. Loads among regular crews varied from hut to hut and from one individual to another, but 100 to more than 200lbs. was not uncommon. (Since then, the Appalachian Mountain Club has put strict limits on packing weights). Added to this strain on footwear was the mileage of far-flung hiking trips during our two and a half days off every two weeks.

With this kind of use, the few brands of boots on the market would quickly wear out or fall apart. They were designed for the week-end 'tramper' most often seen on calendars, sitting by a campfire with his pipe in one hand and patting his faithful Irish setter with the other. A bottle of scotch would be on a stump at his elbow, a canoe in the middle distance, and the moon would be painting a silvery highway on a lake in the background. We encountered few people of this type on the high ridges of the White Mountains.

To meet their needs, virtually all hutmen wore hobnailed boots and had evolved a standard practice to create them. Each would find a boot or work shoe that suited his fancy. Choices were highly idiosyncratic and often hotly debated. I favoured the J.C.Penney work boot, which I thought was cut from superior leather and assembled with more care and better stitching than any other. It was also two lace holes higher. Other hutmen heaped scorn on me for this choice, but I never wavered.

The boots would be taken straight from the shoestore to a cobbler to have the bottoms ripped off. Almost all of them came with rather soft soles made of composition rubber mixed with what looked like cut-up string. These were invariably replaced with triple-layer leather soles and heels.

Then the ritual of nailing would begin. Each hut, and the Appalachian Mountain Club's headquarters at Pinkham Notch, had a shoemaker's anvil — a steel pedestal topped with an inverted iron foot. Putting a boot on this foot, we would hammer in the hobnails according to personal formulae of Byzantine complexity. The nails had ribs on the shank to make them stay in better, and a high, rounded head with a sunburst of ridges. Marvellous combinations of nails were invented, with different patterns for the toe, the edge of the sole, the middle, the instep, and the heel. Some individualists would work their initials into the nail job, reversed so the imprint would read correctly on a soft trail.

When the nailing was finished, layers of sole and seam sealer were painted on, and still more coats of various greases and oils applied to the uppers. A local cobbler once warned a hutman about the use of a certain commercial preparation on the stitching because it would, he said in his heavy accent, "rot the t'reads." This became a catchphrase, and the uninitiated would wonder how a mere waterproofing could dissolve steel hobnails.

The finished boots were a wonder to behold. Some enthusiasts achieved a thickness of more than an inch of leather and steel in the sole, and the entire boot gleamed from layer upon layer of carefully rubbed unguents. The boots were also so heavy that one had to develop a fairly advanced physique to lift them. Their highly artistic effect was soon lost, however. They became scuffed and dented from rocks, and every trip would knock out several nails. Then the repair sessions would begin, as we filled the empty holes with glue and wooden match sticks before hammering in the longer nails we used for replacements. Even with such careful preparation and maintenance, a set of hobs would wear smooth in one summer, and planning would begin for next year's model.

In use, the boots were a mixed blessing. The traction was good on rough rock, not so good on smooth ledge, and terrible on roots or the peeled logs bridging wet places. They were very noisy, and the rocks of the Presidential Range will probably bear their scrape marks until the next ice age. But they really came into their own indoors. It was the custom in the huts to scrub the kitchen floors with powerful solutions of boiling water, ammonia, and lye. Traction was good on the resulting open-pored surface. The dining room floors, on the other hand, were treated with an oil finish. With a good start from the kitchen, an experienced hutman could slide the entire length of the dining room on a pair of hobnailed boots.

I was very proud of my hobs. On visits to the family house in Jackson, I'd clump around indoors much longer than necessary before taking them off, chipping paint and varnish on the floors of every room. Aunt Harriet would invariably look at them and say, "Aren't those boots awfully heavy for climbing? I always wore sneakers."

Flood tide in this era of metallic artistry was the European nails: tricounis and quintounis. These were beautiful pieces of geometry, with three or four heavy teeth serrating a steel L-bar base. They were fastened to the sole by an intricate arrangement of nails, screws, and rigid wire which required a master cobbler to install. There were different designs for different parts of the perimeter of the sole and heel, and another for the inner surface. The finished boot was imposing indeed, and no regular hutman I knew had a pair; boots with such expensive fittings would cost most of a summer's salary.

Then in the mid-1950s Vibram burst upon the scene, and almost overnight the clatter and scrape of hobnails disappeared from the mountains. My well-connected brother-in-law got me my first Vibram-soled boots, a pair left over from the special order for the Italian expedition that made the first ascent of K2. They were truly beautiful creations, with carefully engineered foot support, D-ring lacers, and the first padded, double-leather uppers I had seen. The material and craftsmanship were beyond compare, and I used them for 19 years before the original soles wore out. On that sad day, the uppers were as sound and pliable as they were on the day I bought them, but I was unable to find an American shoemaker who could rebuild the sole. I concluded that the bootmakers must have thrown away the recipe after they made that original batch of Italian Vibram.

These marvels of longevity were succeeded by a pair of the Molitor 'Wanderhorn' model, the lighter version of the 'Eiger'. The choice was dictated by my long affection for leather Molitor ski boots, which fit so well they seemed to have been constructed on a last fashioned from a cast of my own foot. (I still wear a pair of the last all-leather ski boots Molitor made, despite the incredulous stares of partners on double chair lifts, encased as they are in plastic half-way up to their knees). The hiking boots fit just as well as the ski boots, and I wore them for a year and a half. But then I noticed a change setting in. My legs began to tire on long hikes, something that had never happened before. I was not ready for this onset of old age, and I quickly looked for causes elsewhere than the calendar.

On a hunch, I tried kletter-shoes for hiking. They were a well-made pair of lightly padded boots meant for rock climbing, strong and durable, but weighing about a third less than the Molitors. The fountain of youth once again flowed undiminished, and I stepped off 20-mile days without a pang. Still not certain that it was the boots that had made the difference, I tried an experiment. I took a hike wearing one Molitor and one kletter-shoe. This lopsided outing produced symptoms so bizarre that any hypothesis in any field of research could have been instantly confirmed, so I judged the test to be inconclusive. But I stayed with the kletter-shoes.

My physical rejuvenation was not gained without a certain psychological cost. For the preceding 25 years I had been the willing slave of the heroic ethos in boot design. Year by year, I had seen more material added to the uppers of boots on equipment store shelves. Layers of support padding and insulation proliferated. Concurrently, boot tops crept higher. Hinges then became necessary to flex this mass of leather and synthetics, so complex assemblies were installed forward of the ankle and above the heel. Welt design kept pace as more and heavier rows of stitching appeared over the sole. Finally, the bootmakers went all the way and offered 'expedition' models featuring one and then two inner boots that could be removed and worn as snug bootees around camp or in the tent.

While these developmental prodigies followed one upon another, I had remained steadfastly faithful to my old Italian K2s. As much as any other design, these had blazed the way for all that followed, but they began to seem positively primitive. Still, as the years went by, they showed no signs of aging, and my budget showed no means of access to the latter-day wonder boots. I kept wearing the K2s, but I secretly lusted after the behemoths in which other hikers stumped along the trails.

And now, after my fling with the Molitors, I was wearing the diminutive kletter-shoes. They were hardly more than slippers compared with the fashions of the day. I sensed that passing hikers would charitably avert their gaze from my feet. I was thankful for this small blessing, but I strained to overhear the condescending remarks that I was sure would follow me down the trail.

Then I got to thinking. I couldn't deny the salutary effect of the kletter-shoes on my legs, and I found myself filling the miles with mental arithmetic as I worked on an idea that I'd been unable to shake since reading an article on marathon running. The author described how big-time runners get superlight shoes and then work them over with razor blades and sandpaper, trimming away every possible sliver to further reduce the weight. Then the author debated the wisdom of wearing socks. The cushioning and absorbency are valuable, but each sock weighs an ounce, and how many times is each foot lifted in 26 miles, 385 yards? It adds up.

I also knew of a study made by the British Army during the African campaign in World War II. Concerned with the logistical problems of moving supplies from Alexandria to the highly mobile front lines, the army had focused on a variable which, though obscure, was at least more easily controlled than Rommel. They ran tests to discover how much sand a soldier scuffed into the tops of his boots in a mile of desert marching. Then they weighed the sand, calculated how much it added to the burden sustained by the soldier's nutritional allotment, and calculated how much this increment added to the weight of the rations that had to be transported cross-country to feed each man in the field. It came to 250lb. of rations per man per six months. The high command passed word down the line that the men should empty the sand from their boots at frequent intervals, and the British won the desert war.

As the kletter-shoes began to wear out, I continued to study the matter of weight. What were the real dimensions of the problem? There must be a point at which the benefits of lightness failed to balance the risk of a broken ankle, I reasoned, and that point was presumably somewhere this side of going barefoot. But where, exactly, was it? I decided to make another test. I did not replace the kletter-shoes when they wore out; instead, I surveyed the running-shoe market.

I hike more than a thousand miles a year, and I assumed that my ankles were reasonably strong and that my feet were chiropodially sound. It seemed that a well-fitted pair of running shoes should be the next stage in my research. Thus it came to pass that I took counsel with an experienced White Mountains hiker who was also a shoe salesperson with a vast stock of brands and models under her command. I selected a pair of Adidas 'Country' running shoes and put them to the test with a hike up Castle Ravine to Mount Jefferson, and down via Castellated Ridge. It turned out to be the lightest and most fantastic trip yet. Another decade of aging slid from my legs.

My euphoria was easily reducible to weights and measures. The Molitors weigh 3.25lb. each. The kletter-shoes weigh 2lb. each. The running shoes weigh 0.75lb. each. I take about 2,000 steps in a mile (somewhat more, by actual count, but 2,000 is a handy figure for multiplication). At that rate, an average day hike of ten miles needs 20,000 steps. With the Molitors, this means that I lift 65,000lb. of leather; by wearing the kletter-shoes the weight is reduced to 40,000lb. Changing to the running shoes, I cut the weight to 15,000lb. I place my feet more carefully on rough trails, but that is a small price to pay for the 25 tons that I leave in the closet at home.

So now I've converted to sneakers. The design is a little more sophisticated than the despised high-cut black canvas models with the round rubber patches on the ankles, but that's a mere quibble. Aunt Harriet was right, after all.

from BACKPACKER 29 *1978*

Coarse Walking

GRAHAM NEWSON

The steady increase in Challenge Walks, regularly advertised in *The Great Outdoors,* cuts no ice with the Coarse Walker, for whom large distances covered in short times hold none of the true pleasures of the sport. Whenever I mention in conversation that I have 'done' the Lyke Wake Walk, I am by no means ashamed to add. "Not in 24 hours though, our expedition took three days."

Great fun — camping at the end of Day One outside the pub at Blakey Howe, and on Day Two outside Wheeldale Youth Hostel, leaving a final stage to Robin Hood's Bay. Unfortunately, after two days of glorious sunshine the weather broke with a vengeance and, in driving rain, the military fence and globes of Fylingdales loomed eerily out of the mist as we squelched past. Even that had its charm, although arriving at the large hotel on the cliff top proved a sad anti-climax — it was April and the place was closed until May!

That's the sort of tactical error to avoid in future. When I lived in Devon it was almost a standing order that Dartmoor walks should take in (or better still finish at) the Warren House Inn. One of the best ridge walks I know is Widecombe-Hameldown-Grimspound-Warren House and if done on Boxing Day morning this particular walk had the extra bonus of free sandwiches at the Inn (is this splendid tradition still maintained?).

The Three Peaks Walk in Yorkshire is fine, but can I present the *Three Pubs Walk* for consideration? Starting at Buckden at the Buck Inn, a pleasant footpath along Buckden Rake and down to the White Lion at Cray, then down the lanes to the George at Hubberholme on the banks of the Wharfe for lunch, returning along the river to Buckden.

This makes an excellent lunchtime walk (though it must be one of unseemly haste on a Sunday with our archaic licensing hours) and no doubt would be equally attractive on a warm summer evening. Total distance three miles: total climbing about 300ft.!

The Merrills, Hillabys and Browns of this world command our admiration but they are in a different class from us lesser mortals (am I the only reader, by the way, to find Hamish Brown's habit of reading on long stretches of his walk quite mystifying?).

A friend and I once began to formulate some Rules of Coarse Walking but never got beyond Rule 1: *Start at Pub A to walk to Pub B: if Pub A is better than Pub B, remain at Pub A?*

(We must have remained at **Pub A**). A local rule in the Appendix for Pennine Way walkers would certainly read: *Start at Edale. Climb up Grindsbrook to Kinder Plateau. Look at view. Return to Edale. Arrange transport to Gargrave. Restart walk.*

Coarse walkers have problems in plenty, without clock-in times and food pick-ups to worry about. Four of us did part of the Offa's Dyke Path in its infancy (when the Shell guide was more or less the only one available) and there were numerous detours and ambiguities on the route. Finally we came upon an electrified fence right across the Path — it couldn't be electrified, we agreed, not on the Offa's Dyke Path. Someone tried it; it was.

Doubtless it's now full of people racing up and down it, setting up records for North, South, backwards and sideways on a path suffering from severe erosion and destined to be 'conserved' with wooden planking. True Coarse Walkers are those of us who can go up Crinkle Crags in fours and unanimously come off the top 180 degrees off course (it *was* misty!); or stay in a Youth Hostel in Wales and have to knock up the Warden at breakfast time as he'd overslept. Are my companions and I the only ones to whom this sort of thing happens?

from THE GREAT OUTDOORS *May 1980*

A consideration of bipedal progression

The Art of Walking

SHOWELL STYLES

"Early man's gleeful achievement of balance on one
foot out of four." *C. E. Montague*

It is, when you come to think of it, a remarkable achievement.
On a flattish piece of flesh and bone measuring some eleven
inches by four, an ungainly edifice six feet high and weighing
160lb. is perfectly balanced for half-a-second, carried forward
a yard, and perfectly balanced again, in unending progression.
In a 20-mile walk this feat of balance and forward movement is
performed nearly 36,000 times. And when you look at that
figure again, picturing the complicated mechanism of muscle
and tendon that operates with each stride, it becomes plain
enough that method is of some importance.

"A 20-mile walk." I suspect that ninety-nine persons out of
a hundred, reading that phrase, would regard the distance as
quite formidable; they have never walked 20 miles at a stretch
and never will. And it may be that a much larger percentage of
us are in this category. Even the average tramper, the Youth
Hosteller or walking-tourist, thinks of 20 miles as a pretty
heroic day's walk. Yet it is only within the last 100 years or so
that human legs have begun to lose their powers and the
ordinary man to look upon walking as an unpleasant labour
only undertaken when he misses his bus. Ladies were not
expected to walk any distance — indeed, their peculiar garb of
100 years ago forbade it — but men walked 12 or 14 miles to
work and back without thinking anything of it, and gentlemen
of leisure walked long distances with less mercenary motives.

At dinner they met again, after a five-and-twenty mile walk,
undertaken by the males at Wardle's recommendation, to get
rid of the effects of the wine at breakfast.

That passage from The Pickwick Papers (1837) nowadays
makes us re-read it to see whether we have read it correctly. But

358

Dickens was reporting accurately on his times, though his characters were fantastic, and it is noteworthy that those 'males' who undertook the sobering stroll (it was after a wedding-breakfast) danced energetically until midnight the same evening. As for the men who went on holiday walking-tours and therefore correspond to the modern Tramper, 40 miles was a day's walk for them. Edward Whymper of Matterhorn fame wrote in 1861 that he would consider no one as companion for an Alpine tour who could not walk 50 miles a day without being fatigued.

So it does seem that the practice of walking is quickly falling into decay. From the front door to the garage is the longest walk undertaken by large numbers of us, and more than one Utopian writer has prophesised a complete atrophy of the human lower limbs by the year 2956 or thereabouts. It will be a bad lookout for the spacemen if, when they arrive by rocket on Mars or Venus, they find that transport on those planets has not developed to the same extent as on Earth and they are required to walk in order to explore the new world. Perhaps by then the Tramper will have become the sole preserver of an ancient art, and his week-end tours — two miles out and back on a specially-laid walking-links — regarded rather as we regard Morris-Dancing today. In that hypothetical future Walking will have become as strict an art as Pole-Vaulting, and its practitioners will have to learn the correct placing of the foot and poise of the trunk which will enable them to take several consecutive steps without falling over. Even today there is something to be gained by examining one's own method of walking.

The kind of walking done by the Tramper, whether by lane and field-path or by mountain and moor, has little in common with Pedestrianism, or the racing walk. To cover a distance on foot as quickly as possible without running is not usually the aim of the Tramper. If he does have to cover the last mile of his journey at top speed in order to catch the homeward bus, I recommend alternate running and walking, 50 paces each — but it is an exasperating exercise to run with a rucksack on one's back. You could, if you liked, try the racing walk, which is done (according to one authority) as follows:

The body should be kept upright, with the shoulders well back and the arms across the chest, swinging with the loins at each stride. The outside of the back of the heel should be well dug into the earth, the body being brought forward over the heel, almost before the toe touches the ground. The ball of the foot and toe should hardly remain on the ground for a perceptible space of time, but the progression should consist as much as possible of a series of quick, firm steps from heel to heel. Dwelling too long on the foot, and especially on the ball or toe of it, develops a tendency to bend the knee, by putting an immense strain on the toe, which is unable to bear it. The right arm should go well over the left shoulder, in unison with the right leg, and the left arm similarly over the right shoulder

This is what those exiguously-clad men we sometimes see wiggling their way along our streets are doing, and all honour to them. To attain good speeds they have to undergo a severe preliminary course. "In all cases of training for long distances," continues the authority already quoted, "at least five or six hours a day must be spent in walking and running, changing from one to the other as a relief during the early part of training." But we are not here concerned with this sort of walking. The Tramper's aim is to be able to walk for an indefinite distance at no particularly fast rate with the minimum of fatigue, and if he tries to do this on "the outside of the back of the heel" he will certainly fail. For the secret of good walking is *balance*.

A small minority of folk are born good walkers. If they have the good fortune to live in the country or the opportunity to walk freely and often, they will probably remain good walkers. But town life seems to spoil the leg and foot action, possibly because the constrained and interrupted progress along crowded streets does not permit a balanced stride to be maintained and causes a certain flinching from the straight-footed walk. The good walkers are known by the placing of their feet. On a level sandy shore the foot-prints of a good walker would show a perfectly straight line — if he was making straight across the sand — each print being directly behind the one in front and the toes pointing neither to left nor to right. A slightly in-toed walk is not a bad thing, but feet splayed outward is the sign of a bad walker. All the primitive races who are famed for long and tireless walking make these straight-line tracks, which are due to unconscious but perpetual control and perfect balance. The Red Indian of the great American forests always excited the admiration of the Palefaces by the ease and swiftness with which he covered long distances on foot. Here is what a hunter who lived with Indians for some years writes of their walking:

> If the Indian were turned to stone while in the act of step-ping, the statue would probably stand balanced on one foot. This gait gives the limbs great control over his movement. He is always poised. If a stick cracks under him it is because of his weight, and not by reason of the impact. He goes silently on, and with great economy of force. His steady balance enables him to put his moving foot down as gently as you would lay an egg on the table.

Trampers are not, of course, greatly anxious to move silently; many of them, indeed, like to make a good deal of noise of one kind or another while walking. The two points worth noting from the Red Indian's walk are the controlled movement and the economy of force.

Fatigue in all forms of exercise comes on doubly fast when muscular energy is being wasted. To obtain economy of movement, so that every ounce of energy goes just where you want it, control is necessary. The people who tire most quickly on a tramp may be fit enough in wind and limb but wasting half their strength in careless use of their muscles. It is well worth doing a bit of consciously-controlled walking by way of self-education; it very quickly becomes habit and can be forgotten. Take a backward glance at your footprints sometime when you are walking across the sands, and see how far they conform to the straight-line walk. If the prints are a foot apart laterally and the toes pointing 45 degrees from your line of march, it's time to do something about it.

The straight-line walk is an effect, not a cause, of good walking action. The townsman's method of walking differs from the Tramper's or the shepherd's rather as a soldier's differs from a sailor's. The townsman walks with an up-and-down knee action, hips rather rigid, toes pointing outwards and heels striking the ground first. He carries himself erect, his movement is fairly springy, and the whole effect is graceful and efficient so long as he is walking on level ground where no alteration of balance is necessary. It is an ill-poised gait because his weight falls first upon the heel alone, and at that instant he has little control of his balance. An inequality of the surface, a loose pebble — above all, a banana-skin — and his balance is gone. Serious and even fatal injuries from falls are not very uncommon among town-dwellers, and the uncontrolled walk is a main reason. By contrast, the good walker's action — the ideal for the Tramper — appears less military and more lounging. He had a slightly rolling action, his hips swaying a little towards the stepping side, giving a long stride. His step is much more flat-footed, so that the centre of gravity is supported by the whole foot and the poise is as secure as that of a tightrope walker. The toes are pointed straight forward, even a trifle inward, so that the inside of the heel, the outside of the ball of the foot, and the smaller toes, all take a fair share of the work and assist in balancing. Exaggerated pushing with the toes is not a good thing; forward progress is achieved by an even distribution of effort, not by thrust and jerk. The knee action is resilient, with a 'give' at every step, particularly in going downhill. And rhythm of stride is the final touch.

To sum up, then, the sort of walk a bad walker must strive to acquire if he is to enjoy tramping: a slight forward swing of the hip; the foot pointing straight ahead; the weight carried forward smoothly over the whole of the gently-planted foot; the spring of the knee during this action; the even and rhythmic stride.

Tramping over rough ground, open mountainside for example, will be found immensely easier if the action detailed above has been acquired. The bad walker, who may have held his own with the good walker along the metalled road of setting forth, will have begun to lag and stumble occasionally when the lane leading to the hills is reached; over the tussocky bog, rocks, heather and steep turf of the mountainside he will be hopelessly slow and will probably be thoroughly fatigued after an hour's going. The control which the good walker's action

gives him over his legs and feet enables him to receive the
inequalities of surface as they come and absorb them in the
resilience of his stride. He can maintain a regular stride while
his companion is continually hesitating and catching his foot
against obstructions. A stumble and recovery entails as much
effort as 50 sure and controlled strides, so that the stumbler
quickly grows tired. There is a moral here which should not be
missed by the Tramper contemplating a walking holiday with a
companion: be sure that your companion has walking powers
approximately equal to your own — and remember that equal
physical fitness is not the same thing.

It cannot be sufficiently emphasised that downhill going on
a steep hillside requires a very resilient knee. More damage is
done to leg muscles by stiff-leg downhill going than by any
other kind of walking. Try all the time to avoid the jar of the
straight unsprung leg. The action to cultivate is that of a man
carrying a heavy burden, who lets his knees sag and recover at
every step. Even more than in climbing a hillside, descending it
demands quick pre-selection of the spot where the foot is to be
placed. Running down long stretches of mountainside is
extremely unwise unless the leg muscles are in perfect trim.

The Tramper will also find that Control is the key-word to
success in the beginning of a week's or a fortnight's tramp. It is
commonly said that the second day of a tramping holiday is the
worst. The first day passes with delightful ease in the exhilaration and novelty of travelling on foot. On the morning of the
second day muscles long unused are in revolt and the novelty
has worn off; truly it is unlikely to be a good day. But if the
Tramper sets his teeth and doggedly persists in covering as
much ground as he did the first day, the third day will be worse
still. See to it that the second day of a tramp is by far the easiest
in distance and time of walking. Take it gently, with frequent
halts. These halts should be short, not more than five minutes
(except the halt for lunch) and the rucksack should be slipped
off at each halt. Note, however, that when you are in good
tramping trim and wish to make a long day's journey, short
halts are a bad thing. Long hauls, long halts, is the best rule
then.

Trampers who are naturally good walkers, reading the foregoing pages, will probably opine that a great deal of fuss has been made about nothing. They have only to spend a day in the open with a bad walker to find their mistake. There *is* an Art of Walking, and it can be cultivated. Art, according to Sir Thomas Browne, is the perfection of Nature. In paying some little attention to the art of good walking we are merely assisting Nature to recover for us that perfection of free movement on foot which is the heritage of every man and woman and the key to a thousand delightful journeys.

from THE CAMPERS' AND TRAMPERS' WEEKEND BOOK *1956*

On Walking Away

MICHAEL TOBIAS

Some day a Turner will paint such scenes; a novelist convert them into his own; a poet insist upon their essence. Glacier beggars come once in a while. The youngsters shiver compulsively from habit, the women are beautiful but sickly, their goats hearty, cowled in thick, white furs. These goats, yaks and vague herdsmen come and go. During migrations in Bhutan, throughout the Hindu Kush. And without much belabouring of basics they live on, propagate, and vanish, surrounded by the mountains they have learned to live with. It is not so much a difference of angle — separating in degrees the horizontal from the vertical — but a cultural distinction which makes it difficult for us to disabuse ourselves of the notion that all people find mountains beautiful. It is difficult to fathom the casual symbiosis by which these people live among their mountains.

The difference between climbers and hikers is an interesting one, for it smacks of the difference between cultures. The former is more goal oriented, more Western in the aggressive sense. While the latter seems to retain the patience and long-distance scope of Kalihari hunters, Chinese apostles, Inca couriers. The climber expects more from his ordeal, and manipulates the circumstances, as best he may, to achieve ultimate gratification, and the thrill of the instantaneous. The climber asks, what would be the worth of the long march home if not for the mountain? The hiker, conversely, says, what is home but the long march to discover it, the effort to get there?

Lichen of gold, rust, grey, umber, gold rock, bristling white glacier, swallows whistling maniacally through the crisp etherium. Seduced into lavish disarray, the climber's ruminations hang suspended over un-utterable vastness. Dozing at belays, the body hugging itself. Moving in enshrouded, tandem silence with his partner. Conscious of the parody they're formulating up there. Mangled happily in the fear, the race of adrenalin, the self-effacing, self-confronting consciousness.

Small and breathing, undressed and dwarfed, by mildly hallucinogenic response, the climber cuddles the exposure, the whole life of his mind distilled, yet fraught with the living legacy of itself, sprawled out on nubbins, asleep on ledges, autobiographical, and relentless. The rope's shadows bob back and forth. Parka sleeves pulled up, the nose daubed with zinc, muscles on edge. Amidst the nerves and reveries, the bleeding knuckles, dishevelled, speck-larded hair, flooded veins, bronze skin, hard lips and cracking eyelets an evolving mythology. The lambent, sun-splattered noon-time. A heroica of private details, dreaming their depths into a lore of himself, the climber, despite all his abandonment to 'intensity' and risk, is more self-conscious than the backpacker, and stands to lose more.

'Vulnerability to landscape' is an ancient proposition of the wilderness sage. But it is not risk in the dangerous sense. In spectator sports, such as figure skating or gymnastics, there is no risk-substitute for grace, no amount of nerve that can better honed and simple majesty of movement. The virtuoso 5.12 climber, if we are able to witness his ascent, or view his portfolio of photographs, must strike us with awe, with a fabulous allegiance to the momentary, but with nothing else. In that respect, his route, his fierce and plunging musculature has little significance. The risks committed by Han-shan, however, teach us something about human nature, about the meaning of commitment. Han-shan, remember, was the legendary poet of Cold Mountain. He disappeared there some time in the late eighth century. He wrote poems, scrambled along the cliffs, befriended neighbouring monks, and disappeared. A legend, a simple old man, with timeless verve and a poignant understanding of Taoism and survival. In a sense he was a climber. But in a greater sense he was not.

An epic burden, like electricity, buffeting the face, parching the throat, congealing snot in the nostrils, hampering blood flow to the toes. It is an eccentric collaboration of space and self, mountain climbing. Yes, it transcends metaphors. It *is* ineffable. As much as we try to convey it, we are stopped short of our goal. Danger, writes Paul Zweig, was the original subject matter worth talking about. Mastodons had to be dragged down and it was risky. Pain and discomfort were the earliest catalysts of consciousness, say neuropsychiatrists with anxiety; meaning and risk are easily confused. Like other religions, climbing gets confused at a certain altitude, it loses its grasp on pertinence. Perhaps a meaningless world is more easily enjoyed. Throughout Zen intellectual history it is silence, that vertical koan, which ignites the really profound sentience. But I doubt there are very many climbers around able to forego the applause, that is, the homecoming of their various forays. Without Penelope, Odysseus would have never made a career of his adventures, and the loss would have been ours. The only possible locale of meaning is *home*. The Charlie Porters* and Milarepas aside, we were not meant to live on a cliff. If such cliche is platitudinous, it is also a fundamental variety among the Sherpa, the Bolivian coal miners, as it was among the Inca. The Inca climbed to 22,000ft. on Lluillailaco, built shelters on snowy summits, worshipped mountain gods and left mummies, but always they went down to their jungles and forested bastions. The Himalayan caravanserai following the Tibetan borax trade routes cross over 20,000ft. passes, and cross them quickly. They are mountain people, the Tibetans. Not one of them that I know of has ever expressed the slightest desire to go climbing around unnecessarily in the snow. The Russian scientists in Nepal studying the Yeti believe he is the

---

* American climber noted for his multi-day, often solo, big-wall ascents.

last vestige of Neanderthal alive on the planet. Doubtless, were it not for the tourists encroaching on his territory, forcing him even further back into the glacial penitralia of Asia, his species would prefer the lowlands.

One can walk carefree there. The forests of the world are nearer our disposition, our genetic calm, than is a cliff. As one walks one loses thoughts, is more relaxedly immersed. The very meaning of woods is this loss, this stunning, gliding serenity of entry by foot. There is no entry on a mountain. One is suddenly there, pinned, or exposed to the volatile impingements. And then comes the aerial anxiousness, the dire weighing of stratagem, and that wavering apostasy which transforms subtle possibility into fantastic danger. Similes of risk compound fantasy; the wilderness of the wall assumes a character, an archetypal personality which is fanciful, introspective, but dangerous. Enraged, almost desperate, the quiet ego maims itself with worry. It can no longer see things. It construes them instead, stacking cairns, falls, piton placements, loose flakes, and storm into a lethal perspective which self-aggravates, and dextro-amphetamizes all beauty.

The backpacker can afford to be philosophical. His route does not demand his hands. But the artisan of ascent is committed, often times against his will, his better instincts, to an all-out grappling. The graphic alliteration of air around him, a constant likelihood of falling, procures no grandiose conviction, no better marriages. Nor has there ever been a brilliant book written about mountains, to my knowledge. Climbing courts a pantheon of hapless reactions charged with the overpowering sense of self-importance. And when alpinists refuse seriousness, they become ludicrously banal instead. Nerve-wracked, even pitiful in middle age. The pleasures to be derived are those of an escaped convict. He is fraught with a paradox which molests him on the condition of movement. His fondest ideals lack substance, in the end, for they are always construed, arrested on the edge of the imagination. A purple-shadowed mountain on the horizon all too quickly becomes the tedious, steep and undistinguished talus slope. That hypnotic spire is suddenly a point of rock under one's bottom, like tens of thousands of others. What counts is the world below.

But climbers have a penchant for obstinacy. Herman Buhl did. Barbier and Patey and Haston did. Call it love, dedication, intoxication, or just rotten luck that they got wiped out. Certainly backpackers have their own problems. Grizzlies, mean natives, ants . . . but I'm pretty sure, statistically, more climbers disappear than walkers. Walkers have none of the mental masochism turned physique of mountaineers. They know when to stop (or I do anyway). The climber misses out on much of his environment because he cannot fall into it. But the walker defers nothing. Beethoven, Basho, Airmatov — they embrace their forests. Stendhal sauntered to Moscow and back, notebook in hand, musing, relaxing at inns, chatting with other wayfarers and all the while conceiving new books. There are no John McPhees in the climbing world, no Ed Abbeys.

The climb distorts sensation into superstition, while a hike promotes the senses, revealing them in their natural turn. The energies of enjoyment are diverted on a wall, its aesthetics concentrated like a knot of apprehension allowing for no swoon. A hike can be awash with the thought diffusing levity of uncommitment. But inherent in this leisure, the hiker confronts his own shortcoming. He may swoon for trekking duration and still go home empty-handed. Here is the insistence, the Mallory-22, at the essence of the mountaineer's own eternal return. As Geoffrey Young remarked, mountaineering hindsight has the inevitable habit of forgetting pain and remembering pleasure. In the vague recesses of his past, the climber remembers something akin to a totality of response, which he finds nowhere else. In his book *The Challenge* Reinhold Messner agrees that this memory promotes the ultimate selfishness. But it is an essential component of living, with no guarantee of consummate adventure. The climber risks more than mere injury. Forgetful in the aftermath which has converted desperation into rapture, climbers pursue their phantom summits, expressing new facets of themselves if only in the solitude of their sling belays. The line between habituating to danger, becoming numb by it, and thriving with its mysterious invigoration, is the vehicle for describing this vertical landscape of thought.

Horizontal perception is at ease. It has a composure, an excess of self-awareness. The climber on the other hand experiences something akin to a vertical dark night of the soul. His hyped-up frenzy is like continuous revelation for he sees himself clearly caught between two possibilities and it is up to him to manoeuvre the outcome. Having trespassed on the no-man's land of himself, he is in a sense freer than the walker, for he had touched the live wire, has tasted the limit. A walker can go forever and never know limits.

The distinction is a mental one. The body moves, regardless of its surroundings. But it is precisely the mountaineering consciousness which awakens a recognition that is unique to its enterprise alone. The prize of frailty. It is a kind of emotion which does not lend itself well to literature. It eludes details — the countless expedition, or macho log books — and refutes philosophical glorification. It is friendless, but desirous of friends. And though it plays with humility, by the strength still pulsing in its limbs, it can't believe it.

For this reason, hikers are more apt historically to produce works of art than are climbers. Two millenia of Chinese painting; the poetry and landscapes of Romanticism in England, America, France and Germany; known as the Abhidharmasastra, a metaphysics of walking; the exaltations of Da Vinci, Hsu hsia k'o, Gessner, Thoreau, and Gauguin. Mankind has always walked its world. While climbing is certainly no modern phenomenon, its impulse stems from walking. Our epics attest to this. Gilgamesh, Beowulf, Tristan, Jason, Dante — the notion of ascent is inexorably wound up in the ideality of *dangerous walking*. The mountain may be a heaven of metaphors but it is also the one enduring link which offers the walker his definition, his elegant extent, primitive man's cyclical cosmos. To attempt to go beyond that limit would seem to repudiate one's self perception. But the perception — bound by greater laws than reason — tenaciously upholds its origins, its security, and consequently the beginning of a journey, the valley, the first mile, will constitute the grammar to which all subsequent feverishness is indebted.

The language of walking defines and moulds the expression of climbing. Such walking is the leaven of mountaineering, its sole substenance, the trek in and the same trek out. For John Muir, this was 'practical immortality'. The Fourteenth Century founder of Soto Zen, Dogen, struck deep this chord when he averred, "He who would understand his own walking must also understand the walking of the blue mountains".

from CLIMBING *July 1979*

Silence and Sounds

LAURA and GUY WATERMAN

> Heard melodies are sweet,
> But those unheard are sweeter
>
> *Keats*

Most people think of the attractions of the backcountry in terms of sights: striking mountain vistas, the rolling green carpets of hillsides that flame into orange and red in the fall, lovely waterfalls and cascades, intimate miniatures of moss and fern.

But the *sounds* as well as the sights of the backcountry attract the perceptive visitor. And the principal sound to treasure is that of silence.

True silence — not just the avoidance of major distracting noises, but that absolute absence of *any* sound, 'the eternal silence of these infinite spaces', is rare even in the backwoods. The soft, sweet sounds of the natural world, principally wind and water, are very often present, not to mention birds, animals, and those articulate observers and commentators, the trees. We'll talk about these in a moment. But for now reflect on how rare is true, absolute silence.

The city dweller rarely hears the sound of silence. Houses and apartments abound in a diversity of sounds that we normally take for granted and scarcely 'hear' with our conscious minds: heating systems stopping and starting, clocks ticking, refrigerators ruminating the way refrigerators do, radiators clucking nervously, air conditioning units muttering and occasionally expostulating, outside street-noises of traffic, children, doors closing, dogs barking, airplanes passing overhead, somewhere a radio. Offices are noisier yet, and libraries possibly noisiest of all.

One of the frustrations of modern life is the impossibility of escaping noise. Even that highest creation of the Muses, music, has been debased by being droned into our ears perpetually in offices, stores, supermarkets, elevators, everywhere. The quietest places in modern society were formerly the anterooms of dental surgeries — so quiet you could hear the soft whine of a drill in the next room, remember? — but even here piped-in, innocuous music is now supplied. Few of us command the position of George Bernard Shaw, who was told in a restaurant that the orchestra would play "anything you like — what would you like them to play, Mr. Shaw?" His reply: "Dominoes".

C. S. Lewis, devilish author of *The Screwtape Letters,* wrote (30 years ago):

> . . . Noise, the grand dynamism, the audible expression of all that is exultant, ruthless, and virile — noise which alone defends us from silly qualms, despairing scruples, and impossible desires. We will make the whole universe a noise in the end. We have already made great strides in this direction as regards the earth. The melodies and silences of heaven will be shouted down in the end.

Getting away from civilisation's cacophony is one major reason why people value the backwoods and fly to it as to a sanctuary, "gone far away into the silent land".

Back in 1869, the Reverend William Henry Harrison Murray, writing of a sojourn in the woods of the Adirondacks, observed: "It is the silence of this wilderness that most impressed me". Ever since, people have been seeking that silence in the wild lands away from man's noisy works. We can recall many moments, on still days when the wind was silent, far enough away from any brook, unnoticed for the moment by birds, when we sat perfectly still to hear that rarest of sound, its absence. It is a void, almost as awesome as being on the rim of some vast, bottomless canyon. Into this immensity of soundlessness, you could drop a whisper and it would seem to float interminably through the abyss. "Speech is of Time, Silence is of Eternity", wrote Carlyle. There is indeed a timelessness, a suspension of events in true silence.

The backpacking boom has brought more people into the woods and hills, and increased the noise level, but the land is large enough to absorb an awful lot of us. You can still find perfect quiet up there on the less travelled ridges, the hidden valleys. You can even get it in the popular, oft-visited places, if you're there at the right time. The President of the Mount Washington Observatory, Alan A. Smith, told us of doing some mapping on Washington in November: "There were a few hikers on top, and some were scattered over the northern peaks — we could see them as we did our triangulation from the summit. Later, however, working our way down the road, there was *nobody* — we could stand and listen to the silence!"

The New York chapter of the Appalachian Mountain Club regularly schedules a unique kind of excursion, known as 'silent walks'. They are hikes whose itinerary may be like that of any other hike, but during which the group periodically walks for 20 minutes without anyone saying a word. It may sound goofy: a dozen or more people lumping along the trail without speaking to each other. Those who have been along, though, say that once you grow accustomed to it, your eyes open wider to the world around you, you tune in to the wind and water, and to the sounds of the woods, and a sense of oneness both within the group and within the natural world as a whole is felt. We prefer our silence in smaller numbers, but the idea sounds intriguing.

from BACKWOODS ETHICS *1979*

Lament for the Roadside Fire

SHOWELL STYLES

Browsing again in the lush pastures of Hugh Westacott's admirable *Walker's Handbook,* I checked at the bitter herbage — one small patch — in Chapter Seven:

"Walkers must never," says Hugh emphatically, "light fires in this country." And he adds: "Lighting fires in cultivated country is unforgivable and is done only by the ignorant and stupid."

That is a hard saying. The dictum, from such an authority, must of course be sound, and should be adhered to. And yet . . .

There was a time, not so very long ago, when the fire by the wayside was the chief sign and emblem of the hardier traveller-on-foot. The term 'backpacker' was unknown in Britain then, and this sort of journeying was generally called 'tramping'; but the Tramper answered the Backpacker definition well enough carrying all the means of existence — including a box of matches — on his back and travelling by sequestered lanes and wilder hill-tracks. For him the end of the day's journey, the proof that he was at home wherever he went, was the wayside fire. Stephen Graham in *The Gentle Art of Tramping* devotes a whole chapter to The Fire. "It is part of the very poetry of the tramping life," says he with perfect truth; nor stays to debate whether there is any poetry inherent in a stove. A winter's wandering across Europe and back glows in my memory with the light of 51 campfires straggling across France and Italy and Switzerland, for though there were nights in barns and hovels and even in a tavern or two these were unmemorable lapses from the independence of the roadside fire. A bramble-grown ruin on a hilltop in Auvergne still glimmers with firelight across the years. The gale "plies the saplings double", rain drives horizontally out of the November night, but I am at home there with my tent slung cunningly from the briars and my little fire blazing hearteningly in the one corner still standing. No doubt a stove would have heated my Maggi soup as speedily and less smokily; but it would not have warmed my heart as well as my belly, or pleased the lizards that peeped from the crannies with their eyes glinting like tiny rubies in the fireglow.

That Auvergne fire was bigger than most wayside fires because it had to warm and dry a drenched wayfarer. And yet it was only a small one. No two synonymous things could be more different than the traveller's campfire and the Camp Fire with capital letters — I mean the roaring conflagration around which Scouts and other hearty souls spread themselves at a safe distance to sing and carouse on cocoa. Ordinarily, the tramper's fire is the smallest compatible with the production of enough heat to boil a billycan of water. Since the diameter of the billy's bottom is likely to be no more than six inches, and it will rest its edges on the stones of brickends forming the fireplace, the size of the fire is pre-ordained, as also is the necessity of having a great quantity of small dry twigs — twice as many as you think you will need — ready before lighting it, for its maintenance.

All the skill and craft of a genuine art go to the making of this kind of fire. Twigs of yew, ash, larch, or birch are the best for it, with beech, hawthorn and hazel as a triple-tie second. On a dry day the pyramid of dry twigs will blossom into flame from a kindling of withered flower-stalks, or from the screws of newspaper you have prudently carried in your breeches pocket. Observe a niceness, now, in the placement of the next twigs to catch the wavering yellow blade of fire; a vital, a breathless moment, conducive to silent prayer. It catches! The first of the larger sticks goes gently on above the rising flame, the billy settles into position, and the rest is a matter of loving care and judicious feeding.

If the dry-weather fire is an achievement, the fire in the rain is a triumph. It is the foot-wanderer's certificate of competency as a full-blown Tramper — or Tramp, if you prefer it. I wish someone would tell me the author of four lines that have haunted me since I was old enough to make journeys on foot:

Change is his mistress, Chance his counsellor;

Love cannot hold him, Duty forge no chain.
The wide seas and the mountains call him,
And grey dawns know his campfires in the rain.

It is the last line that is so evocative of the sort of life some of us would like to live — for a time, at any rate. But the morning fire on a rainy day is customarily a somewhat perfunctory business; you are impatient to get breakfast over and the subsequent unpleasantness of packing-up wet, and be on your way into a happier climate. The fire at the day's end is more important and less dispensable. You are road-weary and the rain is helping dusk to come early when at last you find a place for your tent among the dripping thickets. Both soul and body need the restorative of a fire.

Those screws of newspaper, children of forethought, are in your pocket, dry and indeed already warm; but where are you to find dry wood? Among trees or bushes of any size the answer is "In the branches that are clear of the ground". Dead twigs and sticks that have ledged there take some time to gather but it is time well spent, for they will only be surface-wet at all and will dry in a twinkling — in the first twinkling of your ignited newspaper-screw, in fact. And now comes the crux, the moment of Yea or Nay, more breathless, more prayer-compelling, than with the campfire of a dry summer evening. Not only your supper, but your spiritual well-being also, depend on the confident uprising of that struggling flame. And when its small bright fingers grasp the wood and draw it up into expanding flamehood, how great the victory! I doubt if there is a more genuine satisfaction in life than this of opposing and conquering cold and darkness with warmth and light of one's own creation; and I think it is so partly because it was one of the earliest victories of Man.

There comes, with usage and proficiency, a kind of hallowed ritual into the making of a campfire on a journey. The adept wishes to be solitary before his altar, and when the sacred flame is burning rejects testily the unworthy offerings brought to feed it by his companions; he alone, having raised the god, can act as server, it seems. But when the meal is cooked and the ashes are still red-hot this tension — in wild country — can be relaxed. In the Pyrenees, where four of us eschewed stoves and used fires on a month's backpacking, an American of the party waxed daily more impatient with my minimal fires and yearned to show us what the term 'campfire' implied in the States. In a high glen of the mountains where the crags stood with their feet in dark pine-trees we gave him his wish, and the little cooking-fire grew into a pyre of blazing boughs that would have roasted an ox whole, or at least an isard. That, however, was not a roadside fire.

My first genuine roadside fire is the best-remembered of them all, for in its flames the dross of a spurious 'respect-ability' was separated from the true gold of freedom. It was near Châteaugirons north of the Loire in a drear-nighted October. Each night of the journey across France towards the Mediterranean I had asked permission of farmers to camp in field or orchard and it had been freely given; but on this particular evening two farms refused me, and at a third (it was already dark) the door was banged in my face and a voice threatened to set the dogs on me. Dispiritedly I went on along the road and found a roadside space that had been used to store road-metal, an ugly weed-grown place flanked by scrubby trees that loomed like ogres in the darkness. It was hard pitching for the tent and only a pace from the highway — but there was firewood to be had for the picking-up. As soon as the fire was lit the place was transfigured. The ruddy circle of firelight became my rightful domain, the uncertain darkness a stockade, the thin cotton tent a dwelling as solid as a house. I was at home, not this time in some hedged and sheltered corner of private land but right on the verge of the road that was to be companion and guide for the next five months. After that I camped no more by permission but set up house by the wayside. Well indeed did Lavengro observe, making his first camp in the dingle, "Housekeeping without a fire is a very sorry affair".

Scarcely less memorable was the campfire in the thickets close beside the Dolgellau road, a fire so small (though a billy-boiler) and so smokeless that no passer-by noticed it. Nor could I forget the delectable fire in the snowy fir-wood above Corran Ferry. Nor, certainly, the campfire on the summit of

Crib Goch, made from old juniper roots gathered precariously from the rockface, on which I cooked porridge and boiled an egg; hardly a roadside fire, this last, though the map-distance to the road over Llanberis Pass was less than a mile. And there was the magical fire beside the lane in the Chilterns, that charmed away footsoreness.

But here is only a sequence of Paeans when I am ostensibly engaged upon a Lament; and they are paeans in praise of a thing past and done with. For, you will tell me, these old campfires of yours may have been very well in your heyday but nowadays they are unnecessary, impracticable, an unforgivable indulgence. Well, I shall have to concede it.

I must lament the passing of the roadside fire and be content to warm my hands at its memory. "How quick bright things come to confusion!" After all, its passing was inevitable. The road itself, the wanderer's Road to Anywhere with its illimitable divergences and byways that might lead a man to Roundabout or the Rockies, is now a thing to be avoided by any traveller afoot except the ignoble hitch-hiker. As for the roadside, it is lined with the plastic jetsam of passing cars, and the only roadside fires are the blazing carcases of crashed automobiles. Even the wide and bushy verges of the winding lanes are gone, buried under the extra width and road-metal demanded by farm vehicles. The walking venturer has been crowded off the Queen's Highways and crowded onto Long-Distance Footpaths which — unlike the Open Road — lead only to one place, and that the terminus. Yes, Stevenson's "fine song for singing" is an old song indeed.

> Of the broad road that stretches, and the
> roadside fire.

But though so much is lost, it may not be lost forever. When all is said, the roadside fires of journeying men twinkled along the darkling roads of Britain and Europe for 20 centuries and more, while the automobile headlights have swept them for a mere half-century. Some turmoil of strife in the Middle East, some error of prognostication concerning the treasures of the North Sea, and the speeding Juggernauts of the roads could grind to a halt, perhaps for good. And then — then, at night-fall across a quiet countryside, may be seen a twinkling line of red stars throwing a fitful glow on the grass that sprouts in the fissures of a deserted roadway: the travellers on the M6 have lit their roadside fires.

from THE GREAT OUTDOORS *December 1980*

PART 8

Tall Trail Tales

A sense of humour is an indefinable thing. I would imagine that most walkers possess it in some degree, yet very few seem to be able to *write* humorously about walking.

This section is therefore a mixture of amusing pieces and strange stories. One of them, Sydney Smith's intriguing pseudo-ghost story, has elements of both. The pieces by Alasdair Borthwick and Walt Unsworth have much in common, though the former is youthful fact, and the latter is fiction (but surely based on some dark experience?). The most joyous of the links between them lies in their ability to make us laugh — and if we laugh with them, we are laughing a little at ourselves, which is perhaps not a bad thing.

The pieces by John Barr, Tony Foxlow and Showell Styles all contain an element of the inexplicable. It appeals to some strange corner of my being that there are odd happenings in the hills; I keep hoping something like this will happen to me. It hasn't yet — perhaps if I keep walking long enough.

Quest in a Haunted Glen

JOHN T. K. BARR

For nearly 20 years, the strange happenings of that dark night had been etched in my memory, and I had long intended to return.

It was during a wet and windy week in July 1958 that I first encountered Bynack Lodge, in the upper part of Glen Tilt. With a party of Scouts from the 7th Paisley (JNI) Troop, I had taken refuge there from a storm, but mysterious movements had caused us to abandon our shelter and camp out. The story of these events had passed into the folklore of our Troop, and had been handed down over the years as a real live ghost story.

The opportunity to go back and examine the lodge presented itself in October 1977, during a school holiday. With the four present patrol leaders of the Troop, I turned off the A9 in Blair Atholl to leave the car just beyond the Old Bridge of Tilt.

Advising a local farmer of our plans, we set off up the track to the east of the River Tilt, carrying tents and supplies for three days. Our idea was to camp in the upper part of the glen, make for the lodge on the second day, and return to Blair Atholl and the car late on the third day. The first day proved one of those marvellous days all too rarely experienced in the Scottish hills. The autumn colours on the trees in the lower part of the glen were outlined against a clear blue sky, and with conditions dry and hard underfoot, we made good progress past Croftmore and Auchgobhal farms. By the time we passed Marble Lodge and crossed to the west bank of the river, we had left most of the trees behind, and the bare valley sides were beginning to close in, with slopes rising steeply for 800ft. or so on both sides. Beyond here, as far as Forest Lodge some three miles further up the glen, the almost pastoral scene of lower Glen Tilt, with its glimpses of Blair Castle, gave way to the more rugged landscape of the upper glen, with little evidence of Man's presence. Groups of deer could be seen on both hillsides, following our progress into their domain, and their snorting and grunting echoed up and down the valley.

The steepness of the valley sides, and the almost direct line of the valley in a north-east direction noticed right away by the boys, is attributable to the fact that the glen has been carved out along a small fault line, and that it marks the geological divide between two main groups of rocks. Along this line of weakness, the river and then the ice have carved what many people regard as one of Scotland's finest glens.

Half a mile beyond Forest Lodge, we found a sheltered spot among some trees near the remains of Dail-an-eas Bridge, and set up our three small tents just beside the river, which was swirling among large outcrops of rock to form deep pools and disturbed areas of white water among the rapids. As we tidied up after our meal, two large salmon began jumping in the deep pool just below us, while some sheep crossing a large patch of scree on the other side of the river dislodged pieces of rock which rattled and clattered down the slope throughout the evening. These sounds, plus the continued grunting of the deer above and around us, seemed to indicate that we would have a disturbed night, but before turning in, our new generation of patrol leaders asked me to recount the weird happenings in the glen on that earlier visit . . .

It had been our plan, that wet July in 1958, to walk through Glen Tilt to Braemar, and then cross the Lairig Ghru as far as Aviemore, taking a week to complete the trip. Apart from the weather, things had been going according to plan as we plodded up the cloud-filled valley of upper Glen Tilt. We were looking for a suitable spot to pitch our tents and start making our evening meal, but it did not look as though we were going to have much luck because of the atrocious weather conditions. The heavy rain of the previous two or three days had made the going heavy and marshy underfoot, and as we approached the ruins of Bynack Lodge, it seemed an obvious place to spend the night. Darkness was beginning to close in as we reached the lodge, picking our way through a half-fallen clump of trees which moved slightly and sighed in the wind. Behind them, the dark bulk of the lodge loomed up out of the mist and darkness.

It had been a two-storey building, but most of the roof had

gone, and much of the southern end of the house had collapsed. The front door opened easily to the touch, and a quick inspection revealed that the ground floor room to the right (the north) of the small entrance hall was dry, and offered us the shelter we sought.

A fire was soon blazing in the grate, and as we dried out and cooked our meal on our small stoves, we had a chance to look around us.

Apart from a low table facing the fireplace, and a large black trunk against the back wall, there was no furniture at all in the room, which measured about 15ft. by 12ft. In one of the shorter walls facing the front of the house was a boarded-up window. Facing it, along the back wall, lay the large black trunk, which on investigation proved to be empty. The fireplace lay in the centre of the longer wall — the outside wall — facing north, and between it and the rear wall was an alcove, containing a small shuttered window. Fixed to the remaining wall, opposite the fire and above the low table, was a shelf about six feet up, holding nothing but a couple of rusty tin cans.

We were sitting drinking coffee and discussing the sleeping arrangements, when things started to happen. First, an empty bottle holding a candle toppled over on to its side on a small shelf above the fire. It was broken right through, in an almost perfect straight line, about four inches above its base. We had no sooner begun to comment on this, when a rusty tin can bounced on the floor behind us in the centre of the room. It could only have come from the high shelf above the table, and thinking some small animal had dislodged it, we clambered up on to the table to investigate. There was an inch of dust on the shelf, but no animal tracks. There was a clean cut circle in the dust where the can had been, and although this was ten inches from the edge of the shelf, there was no other disturbance visible, and the second can had not moved. The first can had not been upset by an animal, it had not rolled off the shelf as if blown by a wind, but looked as if it had been picked carefully straight up out of the dust before being dropped on to the floor.

The strange possibilities of this had just started to sink in when, with a crash that shook the whole building, the shutter on the small window beside the fire burst open inwards and clattered against the wall.

That was enough! We grabbed our rucksacks and made for the door. Outside, the clouds had cleared, and a bright moon bathed the lodge ruins in an eerie glow. We pitched our tents some distance from the building on the edge of the small copse of trees, and settled down to a rather disturbed night's sleep.

The next morning, in bright sunshine, we examined the lodge in detail, but could find no explanation for the events of the previous night. As we headed off down the valley towards Inverey and Braemar, I made up my mind to return some day . . .

And so here we were, nearly 20 years later, once more camped in Glen Tilt, and only some ten miles or so from the ruined lodge, I could see that my listeners were impressed with the story; they quizzed me on the details for nearly an hour before we turned in. It was a long time before I fell asleep that night — the events of that earlier visit kept turning over and over in my head, and I wandered if the lodge would have changed.

The morning dawned dry and bright, although there was a suggestion of changes in the weather in a thin veil of very high cloud. We were eager to reach the lodge, and set off from our tents at about 9.30 a.m. From now on, the glen became even wilder, but we continued without stopping till we left the main track to take a much fainter path near the river which would lead us to the bridge over the Tarf Water. This bridge, built in 1886 in memory of a walker who was drowned trying to cross the river, afforded us some shelter from the strengthening wind and light rain now in the air, as we munched our lunch. A quick detour for ten minutes up the tributary valley allowed us to view the Falls of Tarf, and then we pressed on. The path now lay in the bottom of an almost gorge-like valley, and this was our route for a further two miles before emerging on to a level area of indistinct and poor drainage. This was the watershed between the Allt Garbh Buidhe flowing south-west into the Tilt, and the Allt an t-Seillich flowing north-east into the Geldie and then the Dee.

The path became difficult to follow, and cut up to the left to avoid the worst of the peat bog. Visibility was very poor, and the rain was getting heavier, but we plodded on for another mile before deciding to return to the tents. It seemed that the lodge would keep its secret, and we were disappointed.

We reached the tents again about 6 p.m., and retired early after a good meal. On the morning of the third day, we packed up and set off back down the glen. Although not successful in our main aim, we agreed that the journey had been well worth while — this part of Scotland always lives up to expectations.

However, I determined not to be beaten, and the following Saturday, one of the patrol leaders and another adult leader joined me in the long drive north to Braemar. We left the car this time near the Linn of Dee, just beyond Inverey, and set off up Glen Dee to try and reach the lodge from the north.

Our route took us over the White Bridge, with tantalising glimpses northwards into the Lairig Ghru and the Devil's Point, before we turned south along the banks of the Geldie. There were young forestry plantations in this valley, and around us the land was being drained for new plantings, but we could still see beyond the trees into the upper part of the valley where we knew the lodge would be. Crossing the Geldie by stepping-stones, we continued for a mile and a half along the banks of the river before coming in sight of Bynack Lodge, still surrounded by its clump of trees.

Even before we crossed the Bynack Burn, it was obvious that most of the building had gone. The roof had disappeared completely, and both the downstairs rooms were open to the sky. Most of the walls were in an advanced state of disrepair, and I was able to point out where the shelf and the alcove window had been. The alcove window now gaped out to give a view back down the valley, and the shelf, the table, and the black trunk had all gone. Grass grew on the rubble-strewn floor of the room where once we had sought shelter.

It was a sad and disappointing end to a quest, and yet, as I stood quietly in the doorway remembering my previous visit, I decided that it was perhaps a fitting conclusion. The happenings of that first visit would now remain a mystery forever, and the story can continue to be told round camp fires and cooking stoves wherever our Troop finds itself in the future.

from THE GREAT OUTDOORS *December 1978*

Hunger March

ALASDAIR BORTHWICK

Some day a poet will do justice to the railway journey from Glasgow to Mallaig and end the matter once and for all. Until then it is a subject to avoid. The theme is noble, inviting a great heaping up of metaphor and adjective, a pen splashing purple ink, for it is the most beautiful journey in Britain; but the pens of so many prose writers have splashed only an anaemic blue in its honour that I feel prose is unequal to the task. Let us say, simply, that the train arrived at Fort William, picked up Sandy Mackendrick from the platform he had reached by the through train from London, and continued on its way to meet the mid-day boat at Mallaig. Sandy was excited and a little puzzled. For a month he had been receiving relays of letters, couched in lyrical terms, on mountains and other matters which seemed remote to one who earned his living in London. What, he wanted to know, was all this about? He had obeyed instructions and bought boots. He had joined the Scottish Youth Hostels' Association. He had bought a rucksack. But why this sudden rabid enthusiasm? And who was Hamish?

So we told him all about it, chapter and verse, from Fort William to Mallaig, and from Mallaig by sea to Broadford, where we left the boat and set foot for the first time on the Isle of Skye. There were four of us — John, Sandy, William Makins, and myself. William was a tall youth whom few people ever seemed to call "Bill". He had a high forehead and a weakness for economics, and he was managing to maintain his customary air of dignity despite the fact that he was wearing a pair of breeches made for his uncle 40 years before, when cyclists, sartorially, were cyclists. These objects had been resurrected for the occasion from some obscure cupboard: he had seen our knees when we returned from Arrochar.

Sandy and William had been friends since childhood, and were utterly unlike in most respects, as many such couples are. William argued from precedent, Sandy from his own fertile ideas. William was patient, Sandy impetuous. William saw a thing, studied it, liked it, kept on liking it; Sandy spent his life in a hurricane of enthusiasms which died as suddenly as they began. To this partnership, when I joined it, I added much voluble and irrelevant argument; and John, who came to know us later, contributed wit and the ability to pin down most of the hares Sandy and I started. We were a curiously assorted quartet.

We walked into a shop and bought postcards.

"So you are going to Sligachan?" said the old man we found behind the counter, a benign old soul with a soft, liquid accent which flowed through a tangle of white beard.

We said that that was our intention.

"Chust so," murmured the old man. "Chust so. And what 'bus would you be catching?"

The one that met the boat, we said.

"Dear, dear!" The ancient was perturbed. "Do you tell me that, now! That is a fery great pity, indeed it is, a fery great pity. Why? Because the 'bus did not bother to wait for the boat, and I doubt if you will get another one before nine o'clock."

"Just like that," I said. "It didn't bother to wait."

"No," said the old man.

We absorbed this information in silence. Then Sandy produced a map, started a council of war, and roped in the old man as an expert witness.

"It's four o'clock now," said Sandy, leaning over the map, "and we're here." He jabbed a finger at Broadford. "At nine o'clock a 'bus arrives and takes us north to Sligachan, here. Say it takes an hour. Ten o'clock. And after that we've to walk nine miles south-west in the dark to Glen Brittle, over a moor we've never seen in our lives, to a hostel where they go to bed at eleven. Not likely! What's to prevent us cutting across country, and going north-west direct to Glen Brittle?"

"And sleeping out," said John. "We have the tent; but all the blankets bar one have been sent on ahead. Still, we could make do for the night."

"Sleep out by all means, if we need to," said Sandy, "but I don't see why we shouldn't walk right through the night and fetch up at Glen Brittle in time for breakfast. It doesn't look more than 30 miles at the outside, and I could do with some exercise. It's better than kicking our heels here for five hours, anyway."

"But," said William, "what's the path like?"

"Road for ten miles or so, then a path," said Sandy. "Doesn't look too bad." He looked at the old man for confirmation, and received an affirmative nod.

"Yes, yes," said the old man, "the path will be all right."

And so it was agreed, though our decision would have been different had we known two facts, first that in Skye everything "will be all right" because the natives are so polite that they will agree black is white rather than contradict a stranger; and second that, thanks to the atrocious state of the path we had to cover, the journey could not be done in a single night. Two and a half days were to pass before we reached Glen Brittle; and our total supply of food was eight sandwiches and a slab of chocolate.

We covered 12 miles that night, becoming increasingly conscious as each mile went by that our last square meal had been eaten on the train early in the morning, and that our chances of crossing the moor in darkness were slender. When, at 10 p.m. we reached the point where the road ended and the moor track began, we were ravenous and the night was so dark that we could not find the track. We did the only possible things. We pitched the tent and ate the sandwiches. It was a silent night, without wind. The sky was overcast, so that little of the ground was visible; but there was still some light on the horizon, throwing one of the Red Hills into profile against the sky, a slope so straight that it might have been drawn with a ruler. In the foreground it was reflected in the shallows of Loch Slapin. And something told me that soon there would be frost.

At this stage it is necessary to describe the odd and inept

collection of equipment which filled the rucksacks of the expedition, because it was our equipment as much as our sad lack of training which brought us to grief in the end. The loads we carried were enormous. We intended to stay in Skye for a fortnight and to climb all the time, first of all from Glen Brittle Hostel, and later from our tent, which we proposed pitching among the outlying peaks of the Cuillin. Both climbing and camping are wet games. They involve ample reserves of clothing, for one cannot rely on drying wet clothes overnight in readiness for the next day, especially in camp. So our rucksacks were crammed with clothes, primus stoves, boots, a rope, a tent, and much else besides, to the tune of 40lb. apiece. The only things they did not contain were the two vital ones — food and blankets. Food had not seemed necessary, and the blankets had been sent on ahead. In John's rucksack was one small travelling-rug, and in William's two-thirds of a ground-sheet, an ancient thing, pock-marked as the face of the moon, with threadbare patches from which the rubber had long since fallen.

We balloted for positions in the tent, which was a small affair designed to accommodate in comfort a maximum of two people. By this time the warmth of walking had left us, and a cold mist was creeping up from the loch. There is no warmth in sandwiches. We crammed on every stitch of clothing we had (William wore pyjamas on top of two full sets of clothes) and bedded down, shivering, like Babes in the Wood beyond the robin country. John and William had the inner berths, Sandy and I lay on either side of them, clutching the fringes of the rug, which was stretched taut as a drum. The mist was beginning to condense on the blades of grass by the door. An owl hooted. Somehow, we slept.

At 4 a.m. I woke, feeling as if I had been drowned and later revived by the primitive method of being rolled on a barrel. I was stiff, and sore, and miserably cold. Nor was my case unique, as I discovered as I stretched over to recover my end of the rug, stolen by Sandy in the night, for John spoke when he knew I was awake.

"This is awful," he said.

"Have you been awake long?"

"Half-an-hour. And I'm getting colder and hungrier every minute. How much food have we?"

"A sixpenny block of chocolate. But I think there's a village four or five miles away. Camasunary, it's called. It's on our way. We could get breakfast there."

William groaned and grunted his way to wakefulness.

"I feel like death," he said. "What was that about breakfast?"

We explained.

"Camasunary? Never heard of it. Anyway, there's a moon now, and anything's better than this ice-box."

We punched Sandy awake, ate all the chocolate, struck the tent, and started. We were stiff, and the start was painful. The owl still hooted. We lost the path almost immediately, and had to set a course across the moor by map and compass, stumbling in the moonlight through coarse grass and clumps of heather. But soon we were warm, and for a time saw the whole affair as a joke. We made quite good speed at that stage, laughing at the discomforts of the tent, and dreaming of ham and eggs at Camasunary; but the way was rougher than we had anticipated, and our pace grew slower. By 6 a.m. it was light enough to walk with freedom, though the sun was not above the horizon; but depression had set in again, and we were feeling sorry for ourselves. The moor was a bleak, monotonous grey, a level stretch of bog, and grass, and heather stretching endlessly in all directions, except that which lay ahead of us. There it tilted upwards a little, and beyond was the sky. A deep glen apparently lay beyond the rise.

Sandy was 100 yards ahead, skirting a rocky bluff on the edge of the moor, when suddenly he shouted and began to run, an absurd little figure, all eagerness and joggling rucksack. He was wildly excited. He was cheering. We ran, too, and as we came round the bluff and looked out across the glen we stopped dead in our tracks and gaped. No one said anything.

The whole vast chain of the Black Cuillin, from Gars-bheinn to Sgurr nan Gillean, was stretched out like a curtain before us, with the sun, which had not yet dropped to our level, lighting the range from end to end. The mountains seemed close enough to touch. The morning mist was rising from them, softly, effortlessly, revealing first one buttress, then another, of the 20 peaks which stretched for miles, linked in a continuous whole by high ridges, scored by gullies, turreted, pinnacled, heaved up to the sky; rock, rock, and more rock as far as the eye could see. And, Black Cuillin or not, they were blue, the pale, delicate blue of a spring sunset, matt like a butterfly's wing. As the mist dissolved, more and more peaks took the skyline, more and more pinnacles broke the ridges, until only the gullies smoked. Then the last puff dissolved and broke, and they, too, were clear. The Cuillin were ours.

William began to sing. We slung on our rucksacks and lunged downhill to Camasunary.

We lay on an immense slab of rock, roasting in the sun and trying to snatch some of the sleep we had lost on the previous night. The sun was pitiless. All morning the heat had grown; and now, at 5 p.m. when some respite might have been expected, it was worse than ever, for the sun was still high and the rock was releasing the stored heat of the day. Though, as Sandy pointed out, we were like four fried eggs in a pan, no escape was possible: at the place we had reached nothing grew. We were lost in a wilderness of bare rock which was hot to the touch.

William groaned at the casual mention of eggs. Eggs were a sore point. We did not talk about eggs. When we had reached Camasunary nine hours before in what we then imagined to be the last stages of hunger, we had found, not a village, but one house; and the owner of the house had not relieved our hunger by frying ham and eggs, for the very good reason that he was not at home, and had locked the door behind him. We were, therefore, acutely conscious of the fact that our last real meal was 33 hours behind us, and our next one, to the best of our knowledge, 13 miles ahead. We were lying on a wide terrace overlooking Loch Scavaig, hoping against hope that a small dot on the map, representing a spot three miles ahead, might be a house. Hoping was energy wasted. When we reached it, hours later, we found only scattered stones where a house had once stood. To eat, we had to reach Glen Brittle.

The view, from the point where we lay, was magnificent. Bare rock walls, on one of which we were perched, plunged down into Scavaig, a sea-loch. We were looking over and beyond it into the heart of the Cuillin horse shoe, where naked cliffs sweep 3,000ft. to the shores of Loch Coruisk, a fresh-water loch whose bed is far below the level of the sea. Still the butterfly blue dusted the rocks. There was no wind. Every-thing was calm, and vast, and still. And in the middle distance was a patch of gold and translucent green where the waters of Scavaig broke on a little beach. We looked at it. We looked at each other, and were unanimous. We should bathe.

But between us and the beach was the Bad Step, "on which" says the Scottish Mountaineering Club's Guidebook to the Cuillin, "there is not the slightest difficulty if crossed at the right place. Most people who get into trouble here attempt to cross too high up." Perhaps we tried to cross too high up. Perhaps we did hit off the proper route, but were too inexper-ienced, exhausted, and heavily laden for an easy passage to be possible. I do not know which of these alternatives is the true one, for in those days all of us had an exaggerated idea of the difficulty of the climbs we undertook, and none of us has seen the Bad Step since; but I do know that on that occasion the Bad Step lived up to its name.

To those who have confined their walking to England or the milder parts of the Highlands it may seem incredible that such a thing as the Bad Step can exist, for in these places there is never any natural difficulty which cannot be avoided without much trouble. If a boulder blocks the path, you walk round the boulder. If a river cannot be forded, you look for a bridge. But the Bad Step cannot be avoided: anyone following the south-west coast of Skye from Loch Slapin to Glen Brittle must cross it. The wide, easy terraces which make progress along the wall above Scavaig a simple matter are cut by a great rock buttress which falls straight into the sea from a point high on the cliffs. Like much of the rock in the district, it is black and utterly smooth in outline, so that it looks like an enormous whale with its tail in the water and its head far up the mountainside. Two parallel cracks slant across its back, about five feet apart, for 20 or 30ft.; and the only method we could devise, rightly or wrongly, for crossing it was to place our toes in the bottom crack and our fingers in the top crack, and shuffle. With 40lb.

rucksacks dragging us outwards, this was exciting. Sandy was the only one to acquit himself well: he put on rubber-soled shoes and almost ran across it. I took 20 minutes, John and William gave it up altogether, toiled hundreds of feet up the mountainside, and crossed by a route which I suspect was considerably more difficult, thereby giving us the pleasure of watching them while we lolled at our ease, up to our necks in the sea and jeering the while.

We slept a little after that, basking like seals in the golden bay, subconsciously delaying the evil moment when we should have to move again. I have never seen a more barren spot. We might have been on a volcanic island, upheaved from the Pacific, 1,000 miles from anywhere, so naked and deserted was the picture of green sea, black rock, and the filigree of gold dividing them. Scavaig was remote from the world. It was good to lie there in the sun; lying still, one did not feel so hungry.

But by 6 p.m. some sense of responsibility had penetrated to our sun-drenched minds, and we realised that further delay would mean another night in the open. This was unthinkable. During the afternoon the way had been so rough, and the sun so hot that we had stopped every ten minutes, and to avoid this we now fell back on the ancient army plan of walking for 50 minutes in each hour. How we came to believe that we should accomplish this over the abominable acreage of rock stretching before us it is difficult to understand; but believe it we did.

"Six-fifteen," said Sandy with great conviction. "Next stop, seven-five."

"Seven-five," we said and meant it.

Five minutes later, still overloaded with pride and fine intentions, we came upon the brambles, a great, tangled bed of them, rich and fat and purple, contriving somehow to draw life from this howling wilderness. And they were ripe. We wavered and halted, but did not dare to drop our rucksacks. Sandy looked at his watch as if to assure himself that 50 minutes had passed, and seemed surprised when he found they had not. We all stood looking at each other, and, casting sidelong glances at the brambles, attempted to stem sudden and overwhelming springs of saliva. Sandy cleared his throat nervously, and fiddled with a tie which was not there.

"Eh . . . 45 minutes still to go," he said miserably.

I made a shameless dive. The rest followed.

One hour later I drew away from the rest and sat down pensively by the edge of the loch, purple to the chin, feeling like the worst sort of Channel crossing, and certain that to my dying day I should never eat another bramble. Brambles are a snare and a delusion, drawing blood with their thorns and giving worse than nothing in return. Brambles are all pip and no nourishment. Taken in bulk, and we had eaten pounds, they settle in a cold mass and remain so, impervious to the digestive processes of man. The others joined me.

"We had to eat," said John, "but that was a mistake."

We sat gloomily, spitting pips; and as we sat, the sun dropped below the horizon and we knew that we should not reach Glen Brittle that night. It was then that I discovered I had dropped the tent-pegs as we crossed the Bad Step.

Hunger will lead men to desperate expedients, but we were not sufficiently desperate to touch the villainous brew which John graced with the name of breakfast. He had, he said, thought of it as he dropped off to sleep on the previous night. The problem was to render palatable our sole source of food, the bramble-patch beside the loch; and in an attempt to solve it he had boiled on the wood fire (the primus, he discovered, had no paraffin in it) half a pound of brambles. He had found the wood on the beach. The result was revolting, and reeked of smoke. Had there been sugar to flavour the mixture we might had overlooked its appearance; but without sugar that was impossible. It was of the consistency and bumpiness of the paste with which posters are stuck on hoardings, and was of a virulent purple which left the pot discoloured for weeks. I shook my head. I could not touch it. John ate one tentative spoonful and decided that the recipe was perhaps not such a good one after all. William embarked upon an elaborate discourse on the origins of Tyrian purple: the lost dye, he said, had no connection with boiled mussels as modern scientists claimed, but came from brambles gathered and boiled upon the beach of Scavaig. Sandy dumped the brew in the sea.

We were all hungrier than we had ever been in our lives: but we had slept well. Though the news that I had lost the tent-pegs had been greeted by groans, the accident was the best thing that could have happened, for it prevented us from erecting the tent. Instead we were forced to gather a pile of heather several feet deep and to spread the tent over it like a blanket. This bed, as well as being comfortable as a spring mattress, was really warm. Most of the cold in camp comes from below. The heather dealt so well with that, that the rug and tent were ample protection against the frosty night air. We slept in comfort for eight hours.

But hunger had become a serious problem. We had not eaten from plates for 48 hours, and even our miserable ration of sandwiches and chocolate was a memory of 24 hours ago. Glen Brittle was only eight miles away; but by this time we had no illusions about either the nature of the ground or our own staying power. People have fasted for a month or more before now; but they have taken care to do so at their ease, generally in glass cases at seaside resorts. They have not had to carry 40lb. over rough country with the temperature at 75°F in the shade, a process which, we discovered, left the knees strangely weak.

The sun was as hot as ever. Any thought of walking for 50 minutes in each hour was unthinkable, for none of us could keep on his feet for more than 20 minutes without a long rest, and this despite the change which had taken place in the outlook of the party. Until the previous night the journey had seemed to us a glorified picnic, lightly undertaken and lightly to be carried out. In our innocence, which did not admit of starvation in civilised Scotland, we had taken no precautions and made no plans, thought nothing of our inexperience and lack of condition, but had muddled happily along, secure in the belief that, however unfortunate the start had been, we should reach Glen Brittle and food that night. We had bathed and slept, admired the view, argued, stopped when we felt inclined. But now we had learned our lesson, which was that we could not take liberties with a wilderness. There was nothing of the picnic about that final day, but a slow, determined grind towards Glen Brittle. Hunger, we discovered, was not the localised pain we had imagined it to be.

Once our stomachs had abandoned hope of attracting food by the conventional messages they were wont to send out three times a day, they ceased to be the seat of hunger. We were hungry all over. Our finger-tips were hungry.

By noon we were walking on heather, on the lip of the cliffs where the southern Cuillin drop into the sea. The sea was a pale, transparent green, deep and abnormally clear. When we rested, we did so on the edge of the cliffs, and lay face-down, peering 100ft. to the water and through it into green, silent under-water Cuillin where fish swam. There were seals, too, basking where the Atlantic swell broke against the cliffs; and sea-birds flung themselves like white stones at the water and the fish below. Southwards were the Inner Isles, Rhum, Eigg, Canna, fading into a blue haze.

Sandy was the first to drop out. We were five miles from Glen Brittle on a steady, heart-breaking heather slope which dragged slowly to an upper moor. The slope was a mile long, and the heat was intense. Half-way up, Sandy dropped and refused to move.

"I just can't," he said, "I'm done. Leave me alone."

We said we could not leave him there.

"It's all right," he said; "this will pass off. You carry on, and I'll follow when I'm able."

No one was feeling particularly noble. We took him at his word, and left him. As it happened, it was the best thing we could have done, because my turn came next, and Sandy had reached me before I recovered. We carried on together, and a few minutes later found William stretched out beside a burn. John, who held out until we reached the hostel, waited for us at the top of the rise, so that we finished together.

It was a curious experience, this feeling of weakness which suddenly took command of us. After more than two days of continuous heavy exercise, the brain and the body were functioning independently, so that the brain was left free while the body worked automatically. We were conscious, of course, that we were tired and hungry; but misery appeared to have reached a level just above that which the body could endure and below which it seemed impossible to go. There seemed no reason, we thought, why this state of affairs should not continue in the same dull rhythm of planting one foot before the other for the few miles which remained. Yet suddenly and conclusively, within the space of half-an-hour, three of us knew that we could go no farther until we had gathered strength. It was mental rather than physical, for the reactions of our bodies were numbed. Nor was it an ordinary rest. We just sat down, and, having sat down, knew we could not get up. Our legs refused to support us, and half-an-hour passed in each case before it was possible to go on. I remember thinking how odd it was, as I lay too weak to move, that I had £9 in my pocket. It seemed all wrong.

We had not seen a living soul for two days, and were only a mile or two short of Glen Brittle when we did. We had all recovered, and were resting on the moor below Coire Lagan, an immense rock amphitheatre which opens into the mountains above Loch Brittle. I was lying, gazing idly at Sgurr Alasdair, which is the highest mountain of the Cuillin, pure rock and immensely sharp, when I thought I saw something move. The sky was clear blue and cloudless, so that the final razor-edge of ridge below the summit was thrown up in sharp relief. And as I watched I saw four tiny figures crawl out on to the skyline and scramble slowly to the top. I was excited. I was tired, and thirsty, and hungry; but I still had it in me to be excited. We hoped to be up there soon.

Our imaginations broke all bounds on the final mile, and, nourished on starvation, reached heights of cruel and unwonted vividness. We thought of food so intensely that it seemed almost real. We took a delight in self-torture. Roast beef wrung my heart, roast beef slightly underdone, with Yorkshire pudding and thick gravy. The gravy, I insisted, must be thick, flowing round the rich brown flanks of roasted potatoes. What potatoes those were! They were real enough to touch, they and the French beans which lay beside them. Sandy swore he could smell the roast duck and green peas which filled his mind; and John was haunted by a complete seven-course dinner.

"My lords, ladies, and gentlemen" he kept saying, "dinner is served."

We had not seen real food for nearly three days.

All this was rather pathetic, for our hopes exceeded our performance. We were too hungry to eat when we reached the hostel in the late evening. After a very moderate meal we tumbled into bed and slept for thirteen hours.

from ALWAYS A LITTLE FURTHER **1939**

A Moorland Mystery

TONY FOXLOW

"Beware of the silent man and the dog that
does not bark." *Old Yorkshire quotation*

I completed my first crossing of the Lyke Wake Walk in September 1972 as a member of a party 15 strong. The walk captivated me completely and I resolved to cross again the next year. For different reasons my two associates cried off at the eleventh hour, and I decided to go alone, but supported *en route* by two friends.

The month was August 1973, the exact date escapes me but it was a Saturday evening and there was a full moon in a patchy sky. I had made reasonable time, arriving at Ellerbeck Bridge at 8.30 p.m. Having been fed and watered, I left at 9.00 p.m. with instructions to my support crew to meet me where the Stony Marl Moor path strikes off the Whitby to Scarborough road for the radio beacon.

I followed the path up by Eller Beck and then, losing it during a patch of cloud cover, I struck off for the Early Warning Station fence. I followed the fence for some time, picking out Lilla Howe on the skyline slightly off to the left, until I came to the point where the fence strikes due South. I stopped, took out my compass and orientated myself until I was facing down the line of the fence.

The sky had cleared and the full moon made visibility excellent. I took time to admire the beauty of the moon and then by way of an exercise re-orientated myself to face Lilla Howe and read off a bearing given in Bill Cowley's guide to the walk. Having one last look around me (this is important) I set off walking towards the Howe but after only having gone about 100 yards the strangest feeling overcame me: an overpowering feeling of someone or something watching me. I stopped and turned round, and this is what I saw.

Standing about ten feet away from the fence, in fact just off the stone laid base of the Early Warning Station fence, and no more than 20 or 30ft. from the very corner where I had been standing only seconds before, was a man and a dog.

My first thought was 'security patrol' and I hailed him, saying something like "I'm doing the Lyke Wake Walk". There was no reply. I closed the distance between us by about half and hailed again, "Did you hear me?" No reply again. I closed the gap to some 25 to 30 yards. The sky was still clear and I could distinctly see a dog sat by the side of what I took to be a man. The man was wearing what appeared to be a long overcoat or, on reflection, it could have been a cloak, the bottom of the material flapping gently in the light breeze. The head had no patrolman's cap on but was rather a shapeless lump, possibly a balaclava or a helmet. The dog looked like an Alsatian.

By this time I began to wonder if fatigue was playing tricks on me. I looked away and closed my eyes but when I re-opened them it was still there. I said words to the effect of "Aren't you going to answer me?" at the same time taking off my rucksack and getting out my torch. There was again no reply and I shone my torch at the 'apparition'.

Immediately I saw the green glow of the dog's eyes but I could not make out any features on the man's face.

More to reassure myself than anything else, I shouted "Well, please yourself" then I turned and walked back towards the Howe, looking back six or seven times. Each time there it was. I reached the Howe and my nerve snapped. Looking back at the motionless "silent man and the dog that did not bark" I ran as fast as my tired legs would carry me and I didn't stop till I reached Jugger Howe ravine.

I decided to forget the incident for fear of ridicule but it did, in fact, disturb me to such an extent that in 1976 I did the walk again with two companions and during the walk I related my story to them. We searched the spot in question for any object such as a boulder or boundary stone that might have resembled what I saw, but the moor is featureless at that point.

Laugh if you will but I am sure of what I saw, and it was exactly as I have told it to you.

from THE GREAT OUTDOORS *December 1978*

How to Become a Ghost Without Really Trying

SYDNEY SMITH

The story begins in Glen Affric. Many years ago I was staying in the youth hostel in the Glen. It is, or was, a delightful spot. A small burn ran between the buildings and in this one could wash if one felt the need. Few did. A roaring fire in the common-room made all other light superfluous.

For those so inclined there were mountains all around. That year I was not inclined, but just enjoyed the constantly changing company and hoped for any food left so that my stay could be prolonged. Eventually, all food gone, I shouldered my pack and strode on up the Glen to Ratagan.

That year I had on my kilt, though despite what is said to the contrary, it is not ideal for cross-country work. There is barbed wire, and scraping one's legs on stone dykes on a cold morning, not to mention the feeling if you slip downhill on wet grass or nettles. However, it is ideal for road work, with the swinging of the seven yards of material. Also, with the swish of the pleats, it never gets wet, and the freedom of the bare legs is something to revel in.

As the day was not too advanced I decided to do the ridge walk along the Five Sisters of Kintail and come down to the hostel at Ratagan by evening. Crossing the water, I was soon on the hill, but the going was harder than I had bargained for

— steep grass with a lot of little rock outcrops. Eventually I reached the first top and stopped for a bite to eat and a rest. Going on, I had not been walking for long when I noticed the more distant hills disappearing and the air getting heavier. Soon a fine rain started and the air grew decidedly muggy. I put on my cape but this made me more uncomfortable than ever.

Eventually I reached the end of the ridge and started down. The presence of midges told me that I was getting lower, but did not soothe my temper. Exasperating is the word. Midges, sweat, fatigue, clammy clothing, all combined to make me forget that I was supposed to be enjoying a holiday. By now my legs were a mass of scratches and bloodied in places where I had been driven frantic by the bites. I took off my cape and hung it over my shoulder. My shirt was open to the waist and where my almost invisible enemy had been at work there were scratches of blood there also. My hair was tousled (it was rather long that year). My stockings were down at my ankles, as my legs were too warm. Altogether I must have presented a sorry sight.

The mist cleared for a moment and I caught a glimpse of the road, much nearer than I had thought, and began to make my way down. This was as tiresome as the climb, for it was frequently necessary to detour round the outcrops. Just after that the mist cleared again for a few seconds and it was then I saw one of those pictures where in a moment every detail is taken in. On the roadside was a party standing by a car, obviously in two minds about going for a walk, to judge by the flaying handerchiefs of two girls in the party against the national pest. Beside the car were a row of broom bushes, then above some steep outcrops of rock were three girls standing on what appeared to be a grassy knoll, looking rather lost. Near them ran a path or sheep-track down to the road.

Just then one of the girls looked up and in an instant I pointed with my walking stick to the track away to their right, and at that moment the mist again covered the scene. When I eventually reached the road I was in no mood for casual chat so I passed the car by going behind the bushes till it was hidden by a turn in the road. Just before that I saw the three girls talking to the car party — at least they were safely down.

A year or so later this incident was brought back to me in a most interesting way. I was on my way back home to Glasgow by train and after leaving Fort William I retired to the dining car to enjoy the luxury of a meal set down with all the trimmings, while the scenery unfolded before me. Having cycled up that road many times in wind and rain, I never tire of seeing it from the comfort of a train. My meal was almost over when my attention was drawn to a party of American girls at a table behind me. Each was trying to tell her story and the one with the loudest voice eventually held sway. What she said ran something like this.

"It was in her paper, and she had it with her, showed it to me, suppose she wrote it herself, these hick dumps will print anything. Well, she knew that her ancestors came from Kintail sometime after the rising and she says they still have a family bible to prove it, isn't that something? Anyhow, some uncle or brother was killed at Culloden and she came over last year to see the place her ancestors came from — some place called Ratty or something — what she expected to see we don't know, but she sure was hell bent on the trip." Before any of the other girls could get in a word she was off again. "Well, this is what she wrote. She was on the hills with her two pals to do some climbing, and the mist came down, and they had wandered all day without seeing anybody or even a track, and Sue had hurt her ankle. Now for it: just then the clouds parted and Gillian looking up saw a kilted figure with bloodstained legs, a torn shirt also with blood on it, and with a plaid over its shoulder, and with its sword it pointed down to where a path led to safety, then the cloud closed in again".

By now the others were interested in the outcome of the story and kept quiet. "So they found the way down and were soon on the road where they met a party in an automobile, and what do you think, the mist cleared and the hillside was bare, and the family in the auto hadn't seen anyone either! Gillian got this bug that some ancestor of hers had come back for a moment just to help them to safety. You see it was in the place where her people had come from and then this spook came along just at the right moment. She says he must have looked like that when he was killed all those years ago".

It was too good a story to spoil so I kept silent. Back in Glasgow I was waiting for a bus when a friend, seeing my rucksack, asked if I had had a good time. "Sure," I replied as the bus drew up. "I fell on Culloden Moor, then came back to save one of my descendants from death on the hills!"

from THE GREAT OUTDOORS *January 1980*

A Pleasant Country Bramble

RICHARD WILSON

A psychologist could probably make a convincing case to the effect that I have a subconscious longing to be scratched to pieces, especially if the scratching agent be a bramble bush. Let us consider the evidence.

First, I regularly travel up to 100 miles, and sometimes even more, on Sunday mornings, and having reached my destination, spend one or two hours charging wildly about a forest, with patent disregard for the paths and tracks so thoughtfully provided by the Forestry Commission, thereby ensuring the maximum of contact with undergrowth, of which a fair proportion will be bramble, with bracken and brashings for good measure. Of course, my own explanation for such apparently strange behaviour is that I enjoy orienteering, but psychologists are trained to peer round the conscious self-justification which their subjects employ to rationalise their more eccentric activities.

The second line of evidence for my self-destructive tendencies comes in the form of another of my spare-time pursuits which, like orienteering, involves the use of a map. This is rambling in the countryside around my home (the agricultural area between Cardiff and Newport in South Wales) avoiding, as far as possible, all surfaced roads, by using Public Rights of Way.

The relationship of rambles to brambles may be unclear to those who have never attempted to walk along the course of one of those red dotted lines which are liberally and, as will become apparent, optimistically scattered far and wide over the Ordnance Survey's 1:50,000 maps; it will require no explanation to anybody who has attempted to walk the field-paths in those few areas of Britain where I have done so.

The District Councils in this corner of Wales have been most conscientious in discharging their duty, imposed by the Countryside Act of 1968, to erect signposts wherever a Right of Way joins a metalled road. For that we must be grateful, since it tells us, in the absence of other visible evidence, when we have reached that point on the map at which the red dotted line commences. It is usually at this moment that problems begin to arise.

Even the most car-bound of road-users can hardly have failed to notice those 'Public Footpath' signs which point straight at dense hedges, with nothing that looks like a stile anywhere to be seen. But when one considers that in most agricultural areas, the average footpath crosses many hedges apart from those at its extremities, one can begin to appreciate that what is seen from the road is only the tip of the iceberg. It is for this reason that I have learnt that I cannot rely solely on the 1:50,000 map for navigational purposes: though it is ideal for following paths of whose existence there is some evidence on the ground, such as stiles or a well-worn trail, I have found that it requires supplementation by the 1:25,000 map, with its much greater amount of information, in order to follow accurately the course of a path across fields between one non-existent stile and the next.

As I have already implied, it is open to debate whether that which motivates me is masochism, or dedication to the cause of footpaths as an amenity. Whatever it is, it must be powerful, as anyone will testify who has fought his way through a bramble hedge, six foot high and six foot wide, has been playfully released by that hedge with just enough momentum to carry him headlong into a ditch whose bottom consists of a six-inch layer of evil-smelling slime, and has emerged therefrom to find himself nose-to-nose with an exceptionally fearsome specimen of Hereford bull, who leaves no doubt that he regards this smelly, brown, tattered, gibbering object which has appeared in the corner of *his field* as a potential threat to his heifers. As a result of many such experiences, I hope that I can claim that my use of such footpaths for recreational purposes is a trail-blazing one, though not in a literal sense, for the resilience of bramble is such that the only evidence of my passage to be seen on looking back at a hedge is usually a variety of pieces of my clothing scattered among the thorns. If anyone else feels that the retrospective pleasure of having 'done' a footpath may exceed the actual discomfort of 'doing' it, he or she is welcome to follow in my footsteps!

What is behind the degenerate state of the footpaths? It is probably a great many years since those to which I refer were used regularly, and if I were a farmer, I should find it very hard to justify to myself the expense of maintaining stiles and gates throughout a period when nobody used them. When the idea began to emerge that Rights of Way could be a recreational facility for the weekend refugee from urban civilisation, the existence of Rights of Way over their land had probably been forgotten by many farmers, and the absence of any attempts by the public to use the red dotted lines which appeared on the map could be interpreted as justification of an understandable reluctance to go out and renew stiles which had for years been hidden under a mass of vegetation.

However, when the economic situation of the farmer is as difficult as it usually is, he is likely to ignore the possibility that the vicious circle: (a) lack of use, therefore (b) lack of necessity, therefore (c) lack of maintenance, therefore (d) disrepair, therefore (e) lack of use, might, in the 1970s, start at (c) rather than at (a), where admittedly the fault lay when the degeneration of the network began, years ago.

While I can sympathise with the farmer whose sins are only those of omission, there is another species which actively discourages the use of footpaths over their land. In fact, the majority of my conversations with farmers begin when I am halfway across a field, with one eye hopefully scanning a distant hedge for the slightest evidence of a stile, and the other on my large-scale map. The conversation usually begins with the bawled monosyllable "Oi!" followed by an enquiry into what the . . . I think I am doing. I have found that an accurate and truthful answer does not seem to suffice; neither does a bold brandishing of the map. The subsequent verbal exchange is usually unrewarding, repetitive, and, at a distance of fifty yards, rapidly tiring. It ends when I turn my back and resume my original course, at the same time praying for deliverance from a backside full of buckshot.

I often wonder whether my tendency to extrapolate the conclusions which I cannot avoid drawing from my own experience, to all parts of England and Wales, is a fair one. Whenever I find myself in an untried area, I am drawn, as if by a magnet, towards those magical signposts pointing down leafy lanes, regardless of whether they declare a destination (a remarkable number of footpaths in Wales seem to lead to *Llwybr Cyhoeddus,* though I haven't actually managed to reach the place yet!) or a distance, whether in miles or kilometres. One day, though each new walk leaves me more doubtful of the possibility, I may perhaps take the enchanted path which leads to that Ramblers' Paradise, the Land of Stiles. Until then, one can but hope that the recent Government decision to divert the Nation's Funds Available for the Financing of Footpaths, from those which cover Long Distances, to those which lie within easy reach of people who dwell in conurbations great and small, will achieve in farmland what the Forestry Commission has achieved for the Rights of Way which are its concern, and thus convert the walking of fieldpaths from a considerable feat of navigation and endurance, to the leisurely relaxation which I enjoy so much — but oh, so rarely!

from THE GREAT OUTDOORS *June 1978*

The Glyders Ghost

SHOWELL STYLES

The dip that separates the two Glyder summits is less than 250ft. below them but is dignified on the one-inch map by the resounding name of Bwlch-y-Ddwy-Glyder; if it is ever used as a *bwlch* it must be by people who don't mind steep and rough slopes on both sides of their passes.

It was here that I saw the only ghost I have ever seen on a mountain. It was on a heatwave day, a noontide of absolute stillness when the brassy glare of the sun seemed more like Arabia Deserta than Cambria. There was not a breath of wind at 3,000ft. as I sat panting just above the saddle of Bwlch-y-Ddwy-Glyder and sweated at the mere thought of the slog up to Glyder Fawr summit. Far down the southern slope Pen-y-Gwryd shimmered in the haze. I could see (I thought) a hillwalker coming up that slope, a man or woman dressed in brown. A moment afterwards I perceived that the brown shape was not only too big to be human but also moving too swiftly up the steep boulder scree. It was more like a bear — except that you can't see through bears, and I could see through this thing. And I could hear it. The low roaring or rushing noise it was making swelled as it surged smoothly up to the crest of the pass, twenty yards below where I was sitting, and vanished over the edge of the steep northern side as though it had hurled itself into infinity. I had been able to see, before it disappeared, that it was six or seven feet in diameter, a rapidly whirling mass composed of bits of dry grass. There was still not the slightest stirring of the air near me and the whole ridge appeared utterly windless.

from THE MOUNTAINS OF NORTH WALES *1973*

Rough Shoot

WALT UNSWORTH

We sat at our usual table in Sullivan's Café, idly eating lumps of sugar from the bowl, and ignoring the malevolent glances of Sullivan. He was a bit put out because his wife had returned unexpectedly from London one evening a week back and had caught Fanny Cranshaw doing overtime. She cut up dead rough about it, too, by all accounts; but she always did strike me as a narrow minded bint, and anyhow, as we pointed out to Sullivan, who was to say what she herself had been up to in the gay Metropolis? He asked us not to mention it.

The last lump of sugar had gone and Big Harry was just about to lean over to the next table for another bowl, when the swing door opened to admit two of the roughest characters in the business — any business — Louis the Bum, and his dark familiar, The Bat.

In the normal way of things, I am the last person to criticise the failings of my fellow men, but I have to admit that Louis and The Bat were a couple of uncouth sods.

For a start, they looked uncouth: small with dark greasy hair which tumbled about their ears and ferret-like faces which even a magistrate wouldn't trust. They looked like brothers, terrible twins, for they dressed alike in black leather jackets decorated with brass studs, and black jeans of an outrageous slimness, in the pockets of which they invariably hooked their thumbs. In point of fact they were in no way related, except in spirit, although they had shared many vicissitudes and several mistresses together.

A gentler age would have called them louts, and I always felt that had they lived in medieval times they would have been the boon companions of Richard Crookback, and had a hand in clobbering those kids in the Tower.

They were not prepossessing and young coppers were known to avoid them. Yet Louis and The Bat had their shiny side like most human beings: joined together by a nylon rope, they were one of the finest rock-climbing teams in the country. Because of this they were tolerated, and their opinions carried great force.

"What you been doin, then, Louis?" asked Harry. Meaning we hadn't seen them around for a while.

"Me and the Bat ere, we been walkin these last few week-ends. S'right, ain't it, Bat?"

"S'right," confirmed his shadow.

Harry looked shocked, as did we all.

"You don't mean *walking* — on foot as it were?" he demanded incredulously.

"S'right, mate."

"Stone the crows!"

We all sat stunned at the thought that two of the best rock-climbers ever to disgrace the bar of the Pen y Gwryd should have spent their week-ends walking when they could have been performing miracles of balance on rock faces. Not that we offered any open criticism, mind you, because Louis the Bum is averse to criticism, and The Bat, too, for that matter, and it pays to stay friends with both.

Fortunately for the conversation, Louis offered to enlighten us.

"It were all on account of this book, see?" he began.

"You ain't been readin again, Louis?" chided Sorrowful Jones, very much as a mother might scold a child for stealing jam tarts from the pantry.

"Belt up will yer?" Louis replied sharply. "An let me try and knock some faggin sense into that dim ead of yourn."

"Like I were saying: I got old of this ere book on moun-taineerin by some famous bloke or other — can't remember is name, anyhow you ignorant sods wouldn't know him — an in this book it said as how walkin were an essential part of mountaineerin."

"It were all wrote down," confirmed The Bat, who couldn't even read the four letter words in Lady Chatterley.

"Yeah, well. This bloke reckoned proper walkin were very important; and he ad a lot of little pictures showing ow it should be done, like."

"An we was doin it all wrong," said The Bat. "Funny ain't

it? I been walkin ever since I were a kid, and then after all these years I find I been doin it all wrong.''

Louis gave The Bat a withering look and asked who was telling the tale? The Bat said Louis was, so Louis requested permission to continue, and added that if he had any further interruptions he would place a well aimed boot in The Bat's groin. The Bat, who valued that part of his anatomy, fell silent.

"There's just as much skill in walkin as there is in climbin," Louis the Bum continued. "Only it's different, of course. It's a question of rhythmical balance an conservation of energy, an all that balls. Once yer gets the ang of it, yer can do bloody long walks an set up records and things.''

"Ow many records ave *you* set up then, Louis?" asked Sorrowful Jones, tongue in cheek.

"Well, we ain't set up any as yet," admitted Louis, "cos we only been at it a few times, see? And anyhow, it's the technique I'm interested in, mate, not bloody records.''

Sorrowful nodded in mock sympathy. "Competition don't do nobody any good, mate," he said.

Personally I thought Sorrowful was asking for trouble, taking the mickey out of Louis the Bum like that, but Sorrowful knew his man. Louis never rumbled. The Bat pointed out the time on Sullivan's plastic clock.

"What about them two judies, then, Louis?" he asked.

Louis looked at his own watch and nodded. "We're off," he announced. "Gotta see a coupla tarts. See yer.''

"See yer," we replied in chorus.

"Did you ever ear such a load of bull in all your life?" demanded Toddy, when they had gone.

Big Harry looked thoughtful and stroked his voluminous yellow beard. "I dunno," he said slowly. "I reckon there's summat in this walkin racket.''

"Come off it! It's a load of balls. Who can't walk up to a crag and back? Apart from which, who wants to walk at all?" Toddy looked disgusted at the thought.

Big Harry shifted his bulk back on his chair so that the legs creaked ominously. Like Sullivan said: he wished Harry would sit somewhere else for a change because no one chair was designed to take such a constant hammering, but Harry pointed out that he couldn't move because Sorrowful Jones and Toddy had a side bet of five bob as to when the chair would collapse.

Big Harry said, "I been thinkin about this for some time: Louis the Bum has just brought to a head the whole problem, as yer might say."

"An what problem is that?" asked Sorrowful Jones, who was something of an expert on problems, being one himself.

"Our attitude, that's what mate; our attitude. We reckon we're mountaineers, but we're nothin of the sort — just bloody rock technicians. We do bugger-all but climb rocks an even then its rocks what are near a road like Borrowdale or Llanberis. I tell you this, mates: we've been turnin the cathedrals of the earth into soaped poles!"

"You read that somewhere," accused Sorrowful Jones.

"So what? It's true ain't it? Ow often do we pause to consider the beauty of our surroundings? Never, mate! We get stuck on some bit of rock and all we sees is dirty cracks and grooves, lengths of rope and metal pegs. Do we ever think of the Eternal Hills? Do we faggin hell!

"All we thinks of is how the next pitch is a layback and we wish we'd never started the bloody climb in the first place.

"So we end up as bloody good rock-climbers, maybe, but somewhere along the road we lose our real purpose."

Harry's outburst shook us rigid. Sorrowful Jones said, "You gone all philosophical, ain't you mate? Been watchin BBC telly, or summat?"

"Then there's the other side of it," continued Harry, ignoring him. "What about when we go to Skye? Walkin and route findin become major problems in a wild place like Skye."

If Big Harry's professed love of natural beauty cut no ice with the lads, his last remarks went home. The fact was, we had all agreed to take a few days off work at Whitsun, and by combining them with the Bank Holiday, arranged to have a full week in the Cuillins; that northern mecca of British climbers.

None of us had ever visited the misty Hebridean island and

it was an omission which was keenly felt; partly because of the reputation of the place but mostly, I think, because of Piss Eyed Pete. Pete had been there — once — and he never missed an opportunity of telling us so, since modesty is not Pete's dominant characteristic. We had only to mention some obscure crag or mountain for him to say, "Well, it's alright I suppose, but it don't compare with the Cuillin of Skye. You lot ain't never been to the Cuillin, ave yer? Believe me, mate, the Cuillin are the only *real* mountains in Britain."

The inference being, of course, that anyone who hadn't been there could in no way be regarded as a real mountaineer.

So what with the visit to Skye on our minds and everything, Big Harry's point was well taken.

"You may be right an all," Sorrowful Jones conceded. "The Cuillins is a pretty rough place. I remember Paddy the Wop once come down on the wrong side o the main ridge in a mist, and he ad to walk over 20 miles back to is tent. He were bloody ungry and all by the time he got back, seein as ow e dropped is butties down the Cioch Slab in the morning."

Harry welcomed the support. "Well there it is, ain't it?" he demanded. "I reckon we ought to practise this walkin caper."

Between you and me, there are walks and there are walks, when it comes to a question as to whether one is a good walker or not. Like Toddy said, anyone can toddle up to the foot of a crag and back, if it isn't too far and the weather is right, and nearly everyone can reach the top of a hill without undue peril. I base these surmises on the yobs one encounters from time to time in such elevated positions as the summit of Ben Nevis and the Snowdon Hotel. But not everyone can do a walk.

Walks, in these present times, have become things of contest between man and mountain, and man and time. It is no longer sufficient to stroll around the hills: today a walk — a proper walk — is a challenge as stern in its own way as the stiffest rock climb.

There was a time, and not so very long ago either, when the admission of inadequacy in the mountains was contained in the phrase, "I'm only a walker", meaning that the speaker felt himself unable to comment on the mad rich world of the mountains in the same way that the more romantic rock-climbers did. Rock-climbers tended to look down on walkers (although they would never admit it) and say, "Well, each to his own pleasure old chap," when what they really meant was "The poor sod. The poor *inferior* sod."

But times change. The bloke who goes clanking up Borrowdale with a hundred krabs dangling from his waist and two miles of rope round his shoulders is probably a novice out to climb Brown Slabs, whilst the youngster in training shoes, who looks as though he hasn't yet begun to shave, is like as not the newest hard man. You just can't tell.

So when a bloke today says modestly, "I'm only a walker", you look at him sideways, because his idea of a quiet week-end is likely to be a double traverse of the Welsh Three Thousand Footers or a quick run along the main ridge of the Cuillins. There are more walkers today than climbers, it seems to me, and you meet them everywhere — on top of Napes Needle, for example.

They are a remarkable breed these modern walkers, with adhesive feet and the stamina of a yak. Never under any circumstances offer to go for a walk with one, or you are likely to be convalescent for the following two weeks. They concentrate on accepted routes done within acceptable times, the records for which make you feel slightly sick.

We decided to make our first serious attempt at walking one cold February day, when there was a sprinkling of snow on the Pennine moors and the clouds drooped like veils of lead.

Big Harry knew a bloke who did a lot of walking — a little chap called Amen Smith, who was as bandy as a cowboy and looked as though he couldn't walk across the road, let alone the hills, although in fact he could move like a chamois with a thunderflash up its arse. He had told Harry that one of the best walks was over the moors between Marsden in Yorkshire and Edale in Derbyshire. It was on Amen's recommendation, therefore, that we rolled into Marsden at 8 a.m., cold and sleepy, with Sorrowful Jones moaning away and a whole hunk of wild moor between us and our ultimate destination.

There is something about the hills of Wales or the Lakes which makes them seem friendly to man, so long as he doesn't try to mess them about. Even in Scotland, where things are on an altogether bigger scale, there exists an atmosphere of muted challenge, as though the hills knew that man wanted to play on them and were not altogether averse to the idea. But in the Pennines — in the bleak, wind-swept, grough-riven peat hags of the Pennines — man is an intruder.

These are hills without emotion, without compassion. They have neither form nor beauty and they don't give a damn. Their sombre grit-begrimed faces betray no trace of the eternal challenge between man and mountains and yet you get the message alright: their vastness mocks and says "Put one step wrong here, mate, and we'll kill you". And they would, too.

Our own route for the day ahead lay over three identifiable lumps of moor: Black Hill, Bleaklow, and Kinderscout, separated by deep valleys. At one time, there existed four pubs, equidistant along the line of march, and some do say that it is for this reason that the walk was originated — that the whole thing was nothing more nor less than a sophisticated pub crawl. Such is progress, however, that the first two pubs have been pulled down; not surprising really, when you learn that they were owned by the local water board and therefore in direct competition, as it were.

The first few miles from Marsden lay along a good cart track by the side of reservoirs and we made very rapid progress. Even Sorrowful Jones ceased to complain; the air was crisp, the incline gentle, and we exerted ourselves just sufficiently to keep warm. It was a piece of cake, we said, and we liked walking, we said.

Then we hit Black Hill. The track vanished and there was nothing but the white, snow-speckled acres of moor rising to an indefinite summit. The going was rough and boggy, and we were bothered by the deep groughs where surface streams had cut into the peat. Our speed slackened, and we cursed as we stumbled forwards and up.

The summit never seemed to get any nearer, and to cap our

misfortune, the leaden sky turned a deep violet.

"I don't like it, Arry," gasped Sorrowful Jones, crawling out of a grough. "It's gonna snow."

And for once he was dead right. Hardly had he spoken when the first fine flurry of white needles came swirling down and within minutes we were trapped in a white-out.

I don't think any of us had ever been in a white-out before, and the experience is not one to bolster self-confidence, especially if, like us, you haven't got much idea of your exact position. The world as we knew it simply vanished. Land and sky blended into a diaphanous whole so that you could not tell where the one ended and the other began, and we stepped forward into a never ending wall of vapour. It was a dream-world, a nightmare, where there was no future and no past, where the only substance was self and the rest was the white dawn of nothing.

We stopped, huddling together into a tight group, the snow falling with sinister gentleness all round.

"Ere's a fine how d'ye do," complained Big Harry, blowing into his gloved hands. "What the faggin hell do we do now?"

"We get off these faggin moors a bit sharpish," replied Sorrowful in a gloomy voice, "before we all dies of exposure. Where the hell are we, anyhow?"

That, of course, was the nub of the matter. We had concentrated on picking our tortuous way through the peat hags towards the summit of the hill, and we had never thought of checking our location on the map. Apart from the knowledge that we were somewhere in the vicinity of Black Hill, we were lost.

Big Harry pulled out a map from his anorak pocket and Toddy surprised us all by contributing a compass which he had pinched for the day from his kid brother who was in the Cubs, and we tried to combine the two with our inadequate knowledge of navigation. But without landmarks to guide our futile efforts it was hopeless from the start. We gave Toddy back his compass, telling him what his kid brother could do with it, and Harry put back his map, all soggy and wet with snow.

We had been standing still for five minutes and our feet had begun to freeze. We decided to press on, regardless.

For ages we trod the Slough of Despond which is the summit of Black Hill. It is aptly named: black ooze, positively primeval in concept, squelched over our boot-tops at every step until in the end we didn't care anymore. Then, joyously, the land began to descend.

For better or worse we seemed to be entering some kind of upland valley; whether or not it lay in the right direction we neither knew nor cared. All we wished for at that moment was escape from the cursed moors and the white-out. I think we panicked.

Soon we were walking along an ill defined sheep track in a narrow defile. The white-out vanished as we descended, although it still continued to snow, and even though our vision was limited to a few yards it restored our self confidence to be able to see again and regain contact with reality. The track improved at every yard, and a quick check with the compass showed us that it did indeed run in the right general direction, which was a piece of good luck.

"If only the snow would stop, we could see where we was," Harry shouted over his shoulder at us. "I reckon we must be in one of them side valleys near Holme Moss."

Toddy agreed. "The compass sez we're headin south," he affirmed, "so I reckon you're right, mate. This track should lead us down into Crowden."

"The compass don't mean nothin," said Sorrowful Jones gloomily. "This valley could bend in the next half mile, an then where are we?"

"Up the creek without a paddle, mate," replied Harry, effectively ending the conversation.

The valley began to widen until we could no longer see the opposite bank because of the snowflakes which were still swirling down. It was obvious, though, that it was a vale of some size, for it boasted stone walls and fields. It had about it a faintly familiar air.

"I gotta feelin I been ere before," Big Harry commented, with a puzzled air on his face. "Ello, then. What's this?"

Through the snow-mist there had loomed up before our

30 Camp near Loch Coruisk, Skye, on the Camasunary to Glen Brittle path. *Photo: John Allen*

29 (previous page) Clogwyn du'r Arddu and the storm-capped Snowdon massif from Moel y Cynghorion. *Photo: Ken Wilson*

31 Winter trekking across the Tarmachans in the Southern Highlands of Scotland.
Photo: Ken Andrew

32 The ridge leading to Stoney Hill in Alaska's
Mt. McKinley National Park. *Photo: Kevin White*

*Some of the
writers whose
work appears
in this book*

33 George Borrow

34 John Muir

35 Michael Tobias

36 E. F. Knight

37 Alasdair Borthwick

38 Peter Keleman

39 Brian Atkin

40 Hamish Brown

41 John Hay

42 Phillip Gribbon

43 Frances Slade

44 Kev Reynolds

45 W. H. Murray

46 Malcolm Gwyn Thomas

47 Ray Shepherd

48 Dianne Bullard

49 Dick Crawshaw

50 John T. K. Barr

51 Malcolm Arney

52 George B. Schaller

53 Hugh Westacott

54 Dewi Jones

55 Laura and Guy Waterman

path a mound of earth some six feet high and stretching away into the dim distance. It was bordered by a trench as deep as the mound was high, and containing some rusted wood and iron contraptions. It was not the sort of thing one expects to find on the Derbyshire moors, or anywhere else, in our experience.

"Maybe it's for catchin rabbits wholesale," suggested Sorrowful Jones, pondering the enigma. "One thing's for sure though — some poor bastard will fall into that trench one day and break is bloody neck."

We walked along the side of the trench and entered upon a country straight out of Alice in Wonderland. All about us, for as far as the snow would allow us to see there were more of these strange constructions, arranged in roughly parallel lines. The valley looked as though it had just witnessed a convention of mad archaeologists.

Then the snow stopped, suddenly and without warning, as snow does in mountains. We stopped too, in amazement.

Bang! Bang! Ping!

It's a funny thing, you know, but even if you've never heard the sound of small-arms fire in your life before, you still know when some bugger is firing at you. And somebody was firing at us. Simultaneously, we all four dived into the nearest trench and lay there quaking.

"The bloody rifle range!" exploded Harry, when we eventually picked up enough courage to sit up. "You know — the one in the valley that leads up to Laddow Rocks. The Army uses it every Sunday; an we've walked right into the bastard!"

"No wonder the valley looked familiar," said Toddy. "We must ave passed the Range undred times on our way to the rocks." A sudden thought struck him and he grinned. "Anyhow, the old compass was right lads: this valley leads straight to Crowden."

"If we ever get out alive," added Sorrowful Jones.

After the first, frightening fusillade, the firing stopped, although none of us volunteered to peer over the edge of the trench to see why. Instead, we sat tight and began to prepare some Nescafe. The idea of looking for a better hole did not appeal to us, one bit, and anyway, our hole was comfortable enough as these things go.

In fact, we were just beginning to feel at home when the officer in charge of the shooting party arrived. Apparently he had spotted us through his field glasses; too late to prevent the first burst of fire by his trigger happy platoon, but not too late to give us a bollocking. He was very annoyed, you could see that at a glance, but he was wasting his breath on the lads.

He was a young twat of about 20 with a little moustache and a Sam Browne belt you could have seen to shave in. He stood on the edge of the trench looking down on us and he had a little cane which he flicked angrily in his leather gloved hands, for all the world like a schoolmaster who has discovered some juniors smoking in the toilets.

"What do you people think you are doing down there?" he demanded aggressively, in that peculiar accent which seems to afflict all regular army officers.

"Shelterin from you lot," replied Big Harry.

"Don't be impertinent! I want to know what you are playing at." His cane flicked violently in tune with his temper.

Big Harry stood up and eyed him severely. "*We're* not playin at anythin, mate," he replied. "It's you lot what are playin soldiers. Is there a war on or summat?"

The subaltern went livid. "Get out of there!" he stormed. "This is War Office Property, and you are trespassing. Get out! D'ye hear!"

"Keep yer shirt on," Harry said quietly, packing away the petrol stove. "We're goin."

We scrambled out of the trench. Big Harry towered above the officer and smiled down at him sweetly.

"There's just one thing, mate . . ." he asked.

"And what's that?"

"Which side is winnin?"

The subaltern lost all control over his emotions. Waving his stick around like a demented bell-boy he let fly a string of oaths which even Sorrowful Jones thought was first class. "Get the faggin hell out of here or I'll report you to the Major!" he ended.

"And I'll tell the vicar," added Harry.

We ambled away, with his curses still ringing in our ears.

"He's only a young bloke, ain't he? But he ain't alf got a marvellous command of English," commented Sorrowful Jones, wistfully. "I wonder what he is?"

"That mate," explained Big Harry, "is an officer an a gentleman."

We walked down into the Longdendale valley, where the huge reservoirs flashed in the new found sunlight. Our misadventures on Black Hill and the rifle-range had cost us remarkably little in the way of time, and although we were well behind our original over-optimistic schedule, we felt confident of success. Black Hill lay behind us: all we had to do now was cross Bleaklow and Kinder, and with the weather markedly on the mend, we felt that the job was as good as accomplished.

At Crowden railway station we paused to eat our sandwiches and make our postponed brew of Nescafe. Before us, Bleaklow rose in one great two thousand foot sweep of heather, with the sun glinting on the wet rocks of the numerous gritstone tors which are such a feature of the hill. Away on our right, a fine ridge of grit was etched against the winter sky and pointed the way to the top.

After the ordeals we had suffered that day, the ridge came as blessed relief. Here was something which we understood — rock — and although it wasn't steep enough to be called climbing in the proper sense, after the miry wastes of Black Hill it was a sheer delight. It could have gone on forever, that ridge, but it didn't; within half an hour it debouched us onto the summit plateau of Bleaklow.

"Hell fire!" ejaculated Sorrowful Jones, meaning who would have thought that there could be a place so vast and utterly barren as that which stretched ahead? As far as the eye could see there was nothing but miles of undulating moors rising to a whaleback of a skyline. No hummock of curious shape, no startling tors of gritstone, nothing to break the awful monotony of the great plateau. It was truly the most God forsaken piece of country we had ever seen.

"Well, it's flat, at any rate," said Big Harry. "We should zoom across this lot."

But it wasn't and we didn't.

What from a distance looked all smooth and level turned out in reality to be as rugged an area as you could find in the whole of Britain. The entire plateau was as riven with groughs as a gorgonzola cheese is with blue veins. Some of these ditches were large, some were small, but all contorted and twisted like a million snakes, crossing and recrossing each other every few yards.

There was nothing for it but to push forwards, in and out, up and down, like poor bloody infantry of the First World War scrambling to the attack across the shell holes of No Man's Land.

Time and our energies wasted together, yet the skyline seemed to grow no closer.

As we advanced the groughs seemed to get bigger. There were some, I recall vividly, which seemed 30ft. deep: great canyons of peat, the crossing of which was extremely laborious. In the end, we abandoned all pretence of method; simply falling down one side of the grough and scrambling as best we could up the other.

Conversation was at a discount, but we all had a feeling of panic; a feeling that we were trapped on that labyrinthine moor. The walk we were supposed to be tackling was utterly forgotten; degenerated into a frantic struggle to escape from Bleaklow, lest we leave our exhausted bodies forever in some unknown grough.

The short day of winter began to draw to a close and as the light faded the air grew cold. The peat, once soft and cushion like, started to crackle beneath our steps as it was gripped by the night frosts. In desperation we quickened our pace — if pace it could be called — although each and every one of us was dead tired. How long had we been on that cursed moor — two hours, three? It seemed a lifetime.

Then the groughs ceased, suddenly, and we knew we had at last breasted the crest of the hill. As the final rose tints of the sun died on the skyline we struck across a narrow, deep valley, and inside a quarter of an hour we were free of

Bleaklow, standing on a metalled road.

We leant against a small stone bridge, buggered.

"Well, we made it lads," gasped Harry. "This ere's the Snake Pass."

"All we gotta do now is cross Kinderscout," said Sorrowful Jones gloomily. He got no reply.

When at last we were sufficiently rested we set off down the pass towards the point where a small track leads off it over the great massif of Kinder. We were now hours behind schedule and dog-tired. Nobody spoke, all our thoughts being concentrated on the agony ahead.

We had gone rather more than a mile along the road when we saw a blaze of lights in the trees which fringed the left hand side of the road. It turned out to be an attractively lit white building with big lattice windows through which we could discern luxury, warmth and the magnetic clink of ale glasses. We had reached the Snake Inn.

Big Harry halted. We all halted.

"It's another four or five mile over Kinder . . ." Big Harry began, his voice uncertain.

"We'll never do it in the dark," added Sorrowful.

Big Harry sighed as he pushed open the door to the Bar. "They didn't ought to put a pub in a place like this," he said savagely, "it weakens a bloke's resolution."

We sank into luxurious chairs, pints in our hands, and just let the ache drain out of our tired bodies. For five whole minutes we just sprawled there, eyes closed in sheer bliss, and then we took good long draughts of the excellent ale.

"Why do we do it?" asked Toddy, stretching his legs against cramp. "Why do we bloody well do it?"

"Because we're faggin stupid mate, that's why," replied Big Harry. "But it don't half make the ale taste good, don't it?"

from CLIMBER AND RAMBLER *November 1978*

The Conversion of Ol' One-Pocket

MALCOLM GWYN THOMAS

"Convert him!" said the rock climber's fiancée.

"To what?" said I.

"Backpacking, of course."

"Yes, and why not?" said the rock climber.

The climber's fiancée obviously felt that her future as a married woman would be more assured if her loved one was restricted to plodding harmlessly about the countryside rather than clinging precariously to rock faces.

The climber, though, had me puzzled. I couldn't see beyond the twinkle in his eye. Nevertheless, there we were, climber and backpacker, in Capel Curig, about to embark on a four-day 'reconnaissance trek' around the mountains that he knew "like the back of his hand". 'Reconnaissance' because, despite my name, I'm as Yorkshire as they make 'em and it's to my shame that never before had I set foot on a blade of grass in Snowdonia, let alone a mountain. 'Trek' because I'd emphasised that in no way was I to be confused with a climber, preferring to think of myself as a mountain *walker* or just a backpacker. To be associated with the climbing fraternity would be to disgrace their ranks, as even at ridiculously safe distances from precipices my nerves start jangling.

Trouble is, I wasn't sure the message had got through as I saw him standing there in cotton shirt, breeches, braces, Berghaus and boots. The Berghaus bothered me for a start — it bulged, and seeing as how I hadn't yet divided up the tent, stove, canteen, fuel, water and food, I could only imagine it containing pitons, karabiners and the odd rope or two. And those boots. . . .

"Fifty pounds when I got 'em," he said. Was that the cost or the weight? They looked capable of *levelling* mountains, let alone climbing them.

"Put these in your pack," says I, giving him the lion's share of the dividables. (He's stronger than me.)

"Don't think they'll fit!"

Lesson 1: Choice of Equipment

"As a backpacker, you'll probably find it handier to have a pack with pockets."

With that twinkle in his eye again, he dived in the boot of the car and came up with a massive pocket which he attached to the side of his pack. Now it's not for me to tell Berghaus their job, but I do think they ought to insist that their detachable pockets be worn in pairs or not at all. Having a one-side-pocketed-pack is bad enough, but with my spare Karrimat stuffed between pocket and pack, it's even worse. Apparently, climbers don't have the tidy minds we backpackers do.

Away we went, straight up the concessionary footpath, literally. There must be no word for *zig* or *zag* in the Welsh language. The order of march quickly established itself. Bracing myself so as to utter a sentence without betraying the fact my lungs were sucking in air like a demented vacuum cleaner, and conscious that the reputation of the backpacking fraternity rode on my shoulders, I shouted up at ol' one-pocket:

"How long are your legs?"

"Thirty-three inch," he shouts down.

With a three-inch advantage over me, it looks like I'm going to have to convert him from the rear.

At last the walking is easier, the view magnificent, and again I'm enjoying the best pastime in the world. This must surely be the long-sought-for alternative to my beloved Lake District which for most of the year has got too busy even for me. We listen to the barking croak of ravens — never seen so many at one time. Beneath my boots passes the tiny yellow flower tormentil, which together with the marvellous insect-eating sundew, so abundant in the wetter patches, symbolises the mountains and moors which I love.

The conversion of ol' one-pocket fades from my mind only to come flooding back as I realise I'm using hands as well as feet to go uphill.

"What's happening?"

"Don't worry, there are plenty of holds."

"How d'you mean, holds? I'm a backpacker not a climber. It's me that's converting you, remember. Where are we anyway?"

"The Castle of the Wind."

"Why do they call it that?"

I should never have asked. A gargantuan hand picked me up, rattled my teeth and tried to rip my pack off. Goodness knows what would have happened if I hadn't already been on my hands and knees.

"That's why," drifted back the reply.

Within a few hours I left behind more blood and flesh on the Welsh mountains than I have in a decade of roaming the Lake District. With my hands and knees throbbing we reached our destination for the night.

Lesson 2: Choice of Site

"We'll pitch up here somewhere," I shouted.

"Bit far from the water, isn't it?"

"Nonsense, it can get cold and damp near large bodies of water at night. Warm air at night flows downhill. We're better off up here."

Lesson 3: Life Support

"Any well-informed backpacker has a brew under way before he even considers pitching the tent, then when pitching's completed there's a hot drink to hand. So, who's fetching the water?" One look told me I was.

Lesson 4: Pitching

"This is a backpacker's tent. A Saunders Dalomite. It'll sleep us both and permit us to sit up in the entrance and cook under shelter if necessary. Just a few simple rules to follow. We put the narrow tail end into the wind, the doorway uphill so the blood doesn't rush to our heads, and we align the whole lot so it faces the rising sun. It cheers our breakfast and dries the tent." Half an hour, and several grumbles about non-standard mountains later, we settle for the doorway into the wind, our heads uphill and the sun can please itself.

I've more on my mind than pitching tents. I read somewhere that prior to summit bids, mountain climbers tend to
drink a lot to prevent dehydration. Admittedly, I was reading
about summit bids in the Himalayas, but perhaps they'd
adopted it as a universal ritual. Ol' one-pocket had downed
five pints of liquid, not including that used to reconstitute our
dehydrated food. My fears were confirmed when with only
his nose poking out of his fibre-pile sleeping bag he muttered
something about going for the summit tomorrow.

At dawn, lessons five and six followed in quick succession.

Lesson 5: Clothing

The cotton shirt proved itself totally incapable of keeping
him warm. It's one thing warming up something that heaves
itself up precipices all day and returns to the hostel at night,
it's quite another keeping it warm around camp. An insulated
vest can be the difference between enjoying 'about camp'
activities or being in a rush to get away so as to generate some
heat walking. In the evening it can mean the difference
between shuffling into the sleeping bag early or enjoying the
surrounding delights. So, with him wearing my vest while I
wore the matching sweater, we headed out.

Lesson 6: Emergency Procedure

Despite having a secure reputation, his braces broke, and
he grabbed at my spare guyline like a drowning man grabs a
lifeline. Now he knows at least two good reasons why backpackers carry a spare. With dire threats about what would
happen if he dared cut it, he wrapped it ceremoniously
around his waist. Whilst this arrangement proved effective, it
wasn't as efficient as the support it had replaced, with the
result that during the course of the morning his breeches
slowly worked their way down his leg, effectively reducing his
33″ to my 30″, and I found myself walking shoulder to
shoulder with him long enough to ask as nonchalantly as
possible, "Which summit?"

"Snowdon, of course."

Of course. You don't come to Snowdonia for the first time
without ascending Snowdon, and if they can get a railway up

there's hope for me. With relief, I asked, "How do we get up there?"

"There's the Miners' track, the Pyg track, the Railway track, and *that.*" 'That' proved to be the most horrendous-looking ridge I've ever seen (Crib-goch). "You mean people walk over *that*?" "Some do, others go across on their bottoms."

Was he talking about people in general or just him and me? "Which way are we going?"

"Dunno, depends on the wind. If it's not too bad we'll go over the ridge."

Rarely has a rising wind been more welcomed by a back-packer, and we duly dropped in line behind the mothers and babies on the Pyg track.

Despite having been close to Snowdon for two days, we hadn't yet seen it. Apparently it spends a lot of its time hidden in mist. The first suggestion we were near the summit was a smell I associate with British Rail, the second the appearance of a railway track, and lastly, an unbelievable number of people crowding into a building in which I had been assured there was a pint of lager waiting for me. For the first time I forged ahead.

Safely seated alongside a window through which could be seen nought but mist, I was introduced to that game which appears unique to Snowdon — "Spot the Walker". It is apparently best played shortly before a train begins its descent. Then, following the hurried departure of its clientele, you can check your score.

Spot the *mountains* appeared out of the question, when half an hour later we walked the few yards to the summit to pay our respects. The noise, the smell and the gloom all made me regret that our boots could be counted among the millions that are wearing Snowdon away. There didn't appear to be much for the backpacker, let alone the climber up here. Sadly, I dropped into place behind Ol' one-pocket as he headed for the South Ridge.

Thirty paces, no more, and the mist was whipped away to reveal as magnificent a mountain landscape as you'll ever see. Along with the mist went the mood. Ol' one-pocket, in his element, pointed out the summits, the ridges, the landscapes and even the seascape. In imagination I climbed, contoured, traversed and ascended snow gullies — digging in with crampons and ice axe as he relived countless previous trips. The mountains had worked their magic. Having a doubting Thomas on the summit, Snowdon had chosen to reveal itself a queen among mountains.

The magic was still present that evening as we pitched in Rhyd-ddu. "Curry and Rice or Vegetable Stew?" said I, clutching our dehydrated rations.

"Chicken and chips," said he.

"They don't make 'em."

"There's a pub around the corner."

"They'll not let us in like this."

"I shouldn't think *you'll* have any problem."

"How do you mean, me, what about . . . ?" All was revealed. The mystery of the bulging Berghaus was no more. He was standing there dressed up to the knockers. No longer the climber, but a personable young man about to spend an evening in the pub.

"You mean to tell me you've been carrying all that around with you?" I shrieked.

"Yes, and why not?"

Why not indeed?

"You're crackers!" Feeling very much the guest who had arrived at the party in the wrong clothes, I followed him into the pub, insisting he did all the ordering while I hid in the corner.

The following day we wandered off the beaten track and enjoyed solitude that was only disturbed (and that pleasantly) on the summit of Moel Hebog, and again later when I was introduced to the Vale of Gwynant. There are others who are better qualified than I to describe that experience. Suffice for me to say it seems a perfect place to introduce children to the joys of backpacking, or even a reluctant wife, so easy is the walking, so numerous and quiet the campsites and so beautiful the scenery.

The highlight of the day was to be:

Lesson 7: Application of things learned

It was his turn to select the pitch. He paced round the site, peered over walls, and finally with an expression on his face that must have been akin to Newton's when he discovered gravity he indicated where his fifty quids' worth of boots were nestling in some sheep turds, and exclaimed, "Here!" Dutifully the tent was pitched.

I awoke hazily next morning, conscious only of the warmth of the sleeping bag and colour of the inner — was it Sunshine Yellow or Sunlight Yellow, I couldn't quite remember? I sat upright. Could it be? I frantically unzipped the inner, the outer, it was, the sun was shining straight into the tent! I ran my fingers down the inside of the fly — no condensation. I looked at the ground. We were on a slight incline, heads uphill. The wedge end of the tent was cutting into what was left of the night's wind. In disbelief I prodded the sheath of fibrepile that enclosed Ol' one-pocket. His nose withdrew from its breathing hole, and was replaced by an eye.

"'S up?" he said.

"It's a perfect pitch, we've done it."

"Oh, we have, have we?"

The significance of that remark was lost on me as I set up the Trangia for breakfast, whilst basking in the warmth of the sun.

It was the last breakfast. Just a few more hours, and we'd be back at the car. During the past days I'd learned to use a whole new language.

In future my mountain walking would include traversing — contouring — cwms — buttresses — cols and many others. I'd also spent long enough behind Ol' one-pocket to appreciate that even when a climber backpacks his movements are deliberate, and a place for the feet (and hands) is well chosen. But what about him? Was he now a backpacker, or was I to face the wrath of an enraged fiancée?

Within sight of the car, he deigned to slow down and allow me to close the gap.

"What's that backpacking magazine you get?" he asked.

"*The Great Outdoors.*"

"Hmmm, think I'll order it. I'll not be doing much

climbing in the future. Who makes that tent again?''

At the time I was jubilant. The backpacking fraternity had gained another devotee, Bob Saunders would sell another tent, Roger Smith's circulation figures would increase, and I had a personal triumph.

But as his wedding day approaches I'm riddled with doubts. Who influenced his decision to backpack, me — or his fiancée?

from THE GREAT OUTDOORS *March 1981*

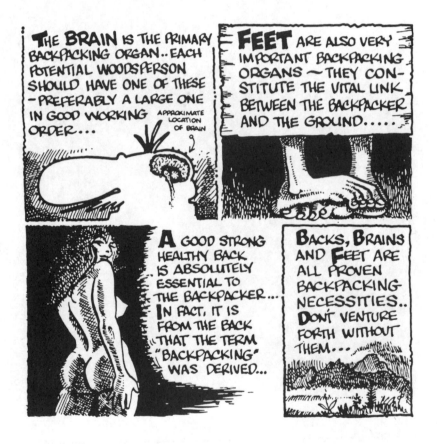

PART 9

Off Trail

When I had finished categorising the pieces in this anthology, I was left with a number that didn't really fit into any of my groups. So I adopted the obvious solution of lumping them all together at the end.

That's too glib, really. These are all fine pieces of writing and, in a way, an assortment like this makes a good culmination to the book — a kind of liqueur after the meal.

Here the eminent climber and explorer, F. S. Smythe, writes about a long tramp over the Surrey hills; Kev Reynolds makes a sensitive plea for the conservation of all wild places, and Laura and Guy Waterman do much the same in a rather more forceful manner.

Kersley Holmes, a Scots writer less well known nowadays than he deserves, rightly gets a place, and at the end Michael Tobias is . . . well, just himself, *Walking Away*. An appropriate note, perhaps, on which to end the book.

The Last Green Valley

KEV REYNOLDS

Man has a voracious appetite for domination of his environment. Progress, the justification for exploitation and the reshaping of a landscape, is an unruly machine that, once set in motion, is exceedingly difficult to check.

Mountains, for so long considered little more than hostile obstacles to trade and communication, are now seen in a completely different light; as a means of trapping wealth, either through tourism or industry. Development takes over. Once-tranquil lakes are dammed to harness hydro-electric power, acres of seclusion become sacrificed to commercial recreation, roads are scored through 'lost' valleys and over passes where mules once journeyed, and regions of wilderness grow ever more scarce.

Fortunate is he who stumbles across one such corner and has the opportunity to appreciate it before the inevitable occurs.

This, then, is a story of our time.

I remember that bright summer journey by the valleys in which we walked and camped, by the mountains and the flowers and clear running streams. I remember, too, the rain that fell as we entered the valley of the Esera, and the soaked wild raspberries that brushed our legs as we steadily gained height through a sparse woodland scented with that uniquely Spanish fragrance that is a mixture of mule-dung and box trees warmed by southern breezes. We came to the stream that had no bridge by which to cross, and we had to wade thigh-deep through the glacial waters. But once around the sharp bend we knew that it had been worthwhile.

The rain gave up then and the sun came out to set the pastures steaming, the big mountains ahead shimmering through the dappled light, dazzling on stream and cascade alike. Snow lay in shallow pockets of hollow corries, and the granite peaks loomed so invitingly ahead. It was a valley to answer the dreams of lowland men, but three days later we ran out of time before we could fully explore its potential. The vision of that valley of rare perfection remained to haunt me through the long winter nights. It was another two years before I could return.

The Second Visit

Spring was a late arrival to the flanks of the High Pyrenees and summer had lost its direction. We climbed out of the hut by way of the window. Avalanches had poured from the heights to engulf all but the eastern side of the hut, and the door was completely hidden, but now in the crisp early morning the snow slopes were glazed and safe, and with the aid of crampons and ice-axes we were able to mount the final steep section that would lead to that valley once more. It seemed impossible, as we crunched our way towards the vague gleam of sunlight showing through an indistinct notch in the frontier ridge, to believe that in summer — only weeks away — energetic tourists would wander up the path from the Hospice de France to gaze at the view from the pass.

And then we emerged from the shadow imposed on us by the constricting mountain walls to a vista of sheer enchantment. Directly before us, and separated by that green and fertile valley, rose the Maladetta massif, the highest lump of mountain in the Pyrenees, all snow and ice and ribs of granite. James David Forbes, the influential young Scots professor of Natural Philosophy at Edinburgh, had stood at this same spot 130 years earlier and was equally impressed.

> . . . the mists cleared away so as to let me have a complete view of this giant mountain, with its prodigious glaciers, which seem to me to rival those of Mont Blanc, and to vie with the ice-fields of Grindelwald. The valley of Venasque is a fitting foreground to such a scene: bare rocks with only scattered pines, savage in the extreme.

Nothing had changed in those 130 years, save perhaps man's concept of 'savagery'.

We descended in the sunlight, across iced tarns and down the shrinking snows to a glorious terrace which was to give the most idyllic campsite of my 20 years' involvement with mountains. The lower hillside levelled onto flat turf alight with trumpet gentians and dogstooth violets and the just-opening blooms of a yellow-headed elder orchid. There was the scent of damp turf and juniper. Dwarf pines struggled for existence and gave off the heady, rich, resinous fragrance that comes with bright sunlight. Streams danced down the hillsides, sprayed into a small tarn and then drained away in lazy curlings beyond our chosen site.

We pitched our tent beside the stream with views which stretched up to the glaciers of the Maladetta and down to the distant acres of the Esera with its carpets of flowers and pine-topped hillocks, out to the sudden bend below more fine mountains where the river forged southwards, the route of my first approach. In unaccustomed contentment we lazily unpacked the rucksacks, and this done I bent to the stream for a billy of water, only to be startled by a movement not 50 yards away downstream. A pair of isard — the chamois of the Pyrenees —had come down to drink, sharing our stream . . . or we, theirs.

For two glorious weeks we remained within the sanctuary of the upper Esera Valley, walking, climbing, studying the vast profusion of flowers, watching the izard. We would begin our day, sometimes, in the pre-dawn darkness, the grass and gentians white with frost, greeting the dawn from verglas-covered rocks, crossing glaciers and iced gullies in that exquisite period when all sound is hushed and an orange glow seems to permeate the light. There were summits where we sat in sunshine, gazing at the maze of peaks jostling all around and below our lofty perch. There was a high ridge where we were met by a vagrant butterfly, wondering by what stray breeze it had risen to 11,000ft. There was another peak upon which ants scurried amongst the snow; another, a frontier summit, where the only sounds to find us were those of low, moaning waterfalls from Spain, and the distant buzzing of a chain saw from one of the vast French forests that lapped against the foothills like a great green sea.

It was by no means an unknown valley. Moating as it does the highest mountain in Europe outside the Alps (with the exception of Mulhacen in the Sierra Nevada) it would attract

numerous climbers during the summer months. There was a
hut, the Renclusa, below the Maladetta, a busy hut in the full
season, but empty now. And during those two weeks we shared
the valley with no-one, no climbers or walkers, not even a
shepherd. On days when we traversed the peaks and bivouaced
in high, hanging valleys, we left the tent and our equipment
unattended, without concern. For all appearances our valley
was as remote and deserted as any Andean cordillera.

As the days multiplied so the season matured and the snow
level advanced up the hillsides. Freed from the burden of
winter, masses of new flowers appeared to flood the valley
with fragrance. Streams and cascades drained the heights and
marmots emerged, blinking from their long period of
hibernation. In those two weeks we saw the full
transformation from winter to full summer. And we gloried in
it.

The Third Time
The following year we returned. It seemed the natural thing to
do. The Esera held all that we sought in mountain scenery, and
again we were not disappointed. But the following spring,
when we set out yet again to revisit the solitudes of upper
Aragon, we were defeated by avalanches, unable to breach the
frontier crest. For full two weeks we attempted pass after pass,
making long and tedious diversions, but each time appalling
conditions and storms, that lasted as much as two and a half
days, denied us the pleasures of that tranquil camp. We
returned home, dejected.

September came and chance for another attempt, this time
with my wife and two children, and I longed to share the secrets
of the Esera with them. We approached through Spain,
travelling slowly from valley to valley, savouring the many
pleasures of the High Pyrenees, and gradually working our
way nearer, drawn by memories and the deep satisfaction of
anticipation.

Ruined Wilderness
There was a road pushing north from Benasque. It had been
there before, since my first visit, but it didn't go far, only to the

dammed lake, and no further. A track which replaced the road led us northwards.

In 1897 two Englishmen came down the valley of the Esera from its source among the glaciers. In their account of the journey they mentioned this 'road'.

> . . . we passed the baths of Venasque . . . and a little below came across some Spanish workmen employed on a road in a desultory fashion. Whether that road will ever be finished is a matter that must rest on the knees of the gods.

Now, as we came to the Banos de Benasque — the baths of Venasque — I saw that the gods had made their decision. Below, on the broad river plain where cattle had grazed last year and for so many years before, contractors' lorries droned and sent out clouds of diesel smoke.

It was growing dusk by the time we turned the bend into the upper sanctuary — still on the bulldozed track that had not been there before. It led us ever higher into the valley and with every yard gained my heart fell into deeper dejection. Tyre tracks scored through the dried mud where before dwarf rhododendron had blazed in spring bloom, and the occasional pool of oil coloured the way.

The rough track came to a halt 50 yards from the site of our idyllic terrace camp.

Three cars were parked there. Cardboard boxes lay strewn amongst the shrubbery, rotting after a shower of rain. Wine bottles had been smashed against rocks, toilet paper fluttered from the gnarled branches of stumpy pine trees, tin cans were rusting in the stream.

"Urban motorised man," writes Fernando Barrientos Fernandez, "has no responsible conservationist regard for nature."

I walked sadly up to that tranquil hillside terrace only to find a metal roadworker's hut positioned exactly where we had pitched our tent for those delectable days and nights of great mountain beauty. And mid-stream on the boulder where I used to sit to wash and draw water there were obscene paint daubs where a workman had cleaned his brushes.

It was too dark now to think of leaving and I pitched our tent without enthusiasm. Darkness swallowed the ugliness of the intrusions, and on the Maladetta's slopes a shepherd's camp-fire glowed like a dim beacon. The glaciers were barely perceived, but a shadowy profile against the distant snows reminded me that the mountains were as yet undefiled. In the night I awoke from a disturbed sleep as a wind came from the west, picked a sheet of polythene and sent it flapping from the tent guys.

Where," I asked myself, "will the isard go to drink now?"

from THE GREAT OUTDOORS *September 1979*

Sgor Thuilm and the Corrie of the Birches

W. K. HOLMES

It would surprise me if many readers could at once place Sgor Thuilm on the map, though it is one of the noble company of hills above 3,000ft. in height, being actually 3,164ft. Definitely it is off the beaten track, and no special distinction can perhaps be claimed for it. Amongst my recollections, however, it figures as the pretext for one of the grandest tramps I have ever had in the Highlands. Every circumstance contributed to make it so, including the weather and the company.

Our expedition took place in May, one year when that month had the still and brilliant warmth that we fondly expect from July. So hot and windless it was that returning from Morar when the weekend was over, I saw the deer standing on the tops of knolls quite near, disregarding the noisy smokey monster rushing past, for the sake of some breath of cooler air.

On the morning fixed for our tramp over Sgor Thuilm I left Fort William by an early train, and found my two friends awaiting me at Glenfinnan station. Both were soldiers on leave, and both belonged to a unit famed for its physical fitness, so I knew I had to be on my toes.

Not taking time even to have a near look at the Prince Charlie monument standing at the head of the Loch, there quite close to the station, we set off up Glenfinnan — and I still seem to be sensible of the strength of the morning sun on my back. I will not spend words on describing the glen, or even the climb to our selected summit; anywhere in the Highlands in May, and in such weather, is as nearly perfect, surely, as anything terrestrial can be. The heat was oppressive, I suppose, till we got above 2,000ft.; beyond that the sun never seems too hot, and the air, diamond clear, almost always has a bracing quality.

Drifts still lay in crannies and other sheltered spots. All day we saw no other human beings. The sheep we encountered suggested by their shyness that our species was a rarity in the neighbourhood; deer and ptarmigan were commoner. (And what a picture of wild nature was shown to us for an instant as a hind shied in her easy canter when a ptarmigan got up close to her feet!) It was surprising, to me at least, to raise a heron right amongst the tops. It was the only time I have seen one so high.

Our aim was to cross the mountain and such ridges and switch-backs as presented themselves, to descend into Glen Pean, walk down it to the head of Loch Morar, and then, by a track indicated on the northern side, to make for Morar, expecting to reach a hospitable house there by perhaps 7.30 p.m.

Our estimate of the time required was almost exactly five hours short, and the extension certainly was not due to lingering by the way.

For one thing, the hill-tops were a good deal more rugged than we had anticipated; for another, the drop into Glen Pean was very much steeper. Perhaps I should be justified in saying it was precipitous, and we were glad of handholds offered by the countless little birch-trees clinging to the rock. Birches, those lovely trees, were characteristic of the surprising gorge in which, after our scramble down, we found ourselves — and was not this named on the map Coire a Bheithe, the Corrie of the Birches? We had descended about the top of the Corrie, which is rather a glen running west to the head of Loch Morar.

At the eastern side of the watershed starts the real Glen Pean, with its tiny lochan Leum an t-Sagairt, 'the loch of the Priest's Leap', whence runs the river Pean to empty itself into Loch Arkaig. The precipitous hillsides above the head of Glen Pean are remarkable for rock-masses rounded and smoothed by glacial action — typical examples of what the geologist calls *roches moutonnées.*

Well, we had scrambled down into that profound cleft, not without caution and many detours, thinking that its attainment would mean that the day's rough stuff was over, and that all we had before us was a longish tramp into Morar. One look round was enough to demonstrate that we should have to think again. I doubt if I have ever been in a wilder-looking place. The glen or pass is quite narrow; to right and left soar hill-sides, everywhere almost precipitous, and here and there consisting of smooth perpendicular slabs. From these heights rocks of all sizes have fallen into the gorge. At its narrowest point it is almost blocked by one mass certainly larger than some modern houses. Inevitably into my mind came Scott's words as a suitable description — "rude fragments of an earlier world". The older masses were clothed with thick, close-growing moss; between them yawned crevices and chasms, and all around, on the sides of this savagely beautiful cleft and amongst the strewn debris with which it was half choked, flourished the fairy beauty of the birches, then in their new tender emerald foliage.

As for the track indicated by the map — all we could find to suggest that a human being had ever passed that way before was an occasional indication on one of the rare patches of turf, a scratch on one of the jumbled rocks. To me it would not have been surprising to catch a glimpse of a wolf, or some other supposedly-extinct wild animal, in that wild and fascinating place. What did meet us was more beautiful than a wolf — an owl, unexpectedly a-wing at that time of day. Perhaps my friends ahead had disturbed his noon siesta, so that I had the benefit. A big bird came towards me, flying almost noiselessly; it was a tawny owl, and its round face with great solemn eyes was within a few yards of me before it banked and swerved away, wonderfully displaying the soft pale colours of its underwings with the sunlight shining through. A fitting tenant for the Corrie of the Birches.

The gorge seemed endless, to men now in a hurry. In the heat that constant scrambling, balancing and jumping amongst the rocks would have been wearisome had not the spell of the place and its untamed beauty kept us interested and astonished.

We emerged at last to the tranquil water's edge at the head of the Loch, and sought the path along the northern slopes. Again we felt a grievance against the cartographer. Either we never found the track indicated, or his ideas of paths are akin to those of the mountain goat. Here again there was little sign of 'traffic', but questionable marks, few and far between; and the rocky, heathery slope is so abrupt that the dark water seemed almost straight below us.

We were tired by this time, and hungry, but we made our forced march through the hours of an evening of the most heavenly beauty. The gloaming was luminous with the sunset's afterglow, and with that afterglow presently merged the golden light of a full moon. The surface of the loch over 100ft. below us reflected all the soft colours of the tranquil sky, and held another golden moon; and from the other side a belated cuckoo called time after time; and — the man in front of me was seized with an attack of hiccoughs, as persistent as the bird. The moon, the serene sky, the cuckoo, and that hiccough, are all revived in my memory every time I see or hear the name of Loch Morar.

There really is a road into Morar from Tarbet, about half-way down the loch.

The walk, as we did it, I do not recommend to any but those in particularly good form; it calls for a considerable amount of stamina, and is not one of those expeditions which can be curtailed by some short cut from half way.

The easiest way to visit the Corrie of the Birches would be to sail to the head of Loch Morar and then walk into the gorge as far as you fancied. There is a cottage called Oban at the head of the Loch, a fact worth remembering if it is inhabited when you plan your exploration.

Perhaps it is worth mentioning that we all three spent the following morning — another perfect one of blue and gold, a real Morar morning — paddling with some youngsters in the warm shallows over the white sand. It was the ideal sequel, from every point of view, to such a day as the one we had spent on the hills.

from TRAMPING THE SCOTTISH HILLS 1946

Camping Out

RANDY THOMAS

After dinner I sat on a stump in the snow and looked at the mountain. Three peaks: one at each end of a banana-shaped ridge and the Black Tusk, a towering rock pinnacle, in between. I sipped my tea. The gain in elevation: 2,500ft. If I got an early start in the morning it looked like an easy walk up.

I was hiking by 6 a.m. The frozen snow ran like a sidewalk to the lower slopes but, once on the incline, my boots scrabbled for traction. Clinging to branches, kicking steps where necessary, I lurched upward in an adrenalin frenzy and made good time.

Better time than I had expected. Soon I was above the treeline, crossing the last snow fields into the rising sun.

At the base of the final rock section I began traversing right across a steep ice slope. After a dozen steps my legs ached from scratching a grip. I slipped twice in 200 yards, so instead started climbing loose rock toward the summit.

The small slabs shifted and collapsed as I moved up, causing minor slides that rumbled and crashed toward the valley far below. Suddenly the air was full of noise and shifting rock. I abandoned that line of attack, 60ft. from the top, and went back.

Blood was splashing on my leg, greasing my aluminium monopod with warm lubricant. I was surprised to see a deep gash in my right hand. I mashed it into the snow and tied my bandana around it, digging the whole thing. The bleeding stopped. I traversed back along a line of goat tracks.

Then I followed another, more stable slide of boulders up, staying near the snowline just in case. The final pitch was a vertical 40ft. chute with good holds. A short stretch of snow later, and I was there.

A sea of tree-dotted white stretched over 100 miles to a horizon rimmed with peaks. Garibaldi Lake looked like a dinner plate frozen in time. Behind me the anomalous Black Tusk thrust its thumb-like bulk into an unearthly sky that ranged from aquamarine on the horizon to deep cobalt directly overhead.

The view through the Superwide was staggering.

Tense and excited, I descended to the ridge and made my way to the opposite summit, along the crest of a giant cornice. If anything, the view was even better here. I could see fresh avalanche activity on nearby crests. In the basin every clearing looked the same.

I crossed over again to the first summit at 9.15 a.m., glissading quickly down the slopes that had cost so much energy to climb. There was no evidence of my earlier trail, but parallel lines of giant tracks (Snowshoes? Sasquatch?) ran off the mountain and into the valley like the quickest route down. I followed them.

I was off the mountain in minutes, angling back toward my campsite. I picked up the outline of Taylor Creek under the snow and knew I was almost there.

Minutes passed. Something was wrong. I had been following the creek for too long and was far down the valley. Behind me, the three peaks had shifted into an alien perspective. I turned back up the creek.

I covered my tracks twice in an hour, seeing no sign of the half-buried shelter or the tree with my pack leaning against it. Looking at my crumpled map again, I saw that I hadn't been following Taylor Creek at all, but an unnamed runoff from the mountain.

The snow was softening. I floundered up the far bank and set off directly down the snowbowl. 'Meadows', my map told me. I was walking through a trackless white void stretching miles into nowhere.

I spotted a series of orange flashers and followed them until they ended, back at the stream.

By now I was badly shaken. I knew I was lost and only growing more confused. I stopped in the middle of a clearing to take stock.

I had lost my wool hat on the mountain. I was wearing a watch, sunglasses, shorts and a red t-shirt. In the pockets of the windbreaker tied at my waist were gloves, map, compass, film and a book of matches. A plastic bag held a Brownie and some dried apricots that would have to be dinner if . . .

No, don't give up, don't even think about it. Stay cool, devise a new plan, stop wandering in crazy vectors.

I was determined not to panic. I had eight hours of daylight left and was probably within two miles of my camp. But I was scared. I had been up and down the valley three times without seeing anything familiar. No matter which way I walked I could not get the three peaks to line up correctly.

The sun was dazzling, and I knew I was frying. I rigged my bandana over my head and draped my jacket across my shoulders.

It was impossible to keep my feet dry in the wet snow. During my next stop, I found a large blister on one toe and wrapped a piece of plastic around it. I also discovered one glove was missing.

By 2 p.m. I realised that I would have to spend the night in the open with little protection. I thought I could tunnel a snow cave at the base of an evergreen when the time came. Temperatures at night were only a shade above freezing — it would not be pleasant. In the morning, I'd move on to the flats and signal an airplane with the slide from my Hasselblad magazine.

My body was holding up very well, but I was gobbling snow under the relentless glare of the sun. I was afraid of sun-stroke and extreme dehydration — and of drinking too much snowwater.

One possibility remained before I surrendered to the long night. I didn't want to consider it; I didn't even know if I could do it. But the alternative was worse. I started back up the mountain.

The snow slopes continued upward forever. It didn't seem

possible that I could climb another foot. I would take a few steps, talk myself out of stopping, and climb a few more before sprawling in the snow. When cold water soaked through to my skin, I'd get up and go on. I kept looking back and was shocked at how far I had climbed. Ahead, there was no hint of the top.

I plodded upwards, first one foot, and then the other. I was sucking on snow continuously now. I tried thinking of other things — sailboats, milkshakes — but it was all crazily irrelevant; comic fantasies. I concentrated on climbing.

When the three peaks finally came into view close at hand, I didn't recognise them at all. Which one had I climbed first? Was that low rise still another peak? For a wild instant, I thought I was on the wrong mountain.

I decided to calm down and eat one of the apricots. I pulled out the film bag. It was the only bag in my pocket.

By 3.30 p.m. I was as orientated as I was going to be that day. There was the line of Sasquatch tracks running like a freeway across the lower slopes, directly away from where I should have gone before. There was the treeline leading down into the maze of woods. There was the notch of my bearing peak on the horizon.

It was the best I could do. I was very tired, had dozed off once already before a family of Whiskey Jacks awakened me with their squawking.

My feet were freezing at last. For the first time I heard the sound of the wind moaning across the snow. I felt that I needed a miracle as I started down.

This time I stayed on course, even found an old bootprint where I knew it would be. Then I was descending through thick woods, angling hard toward my bearing peak, terrified that I was cutting over too far.

I was nearly off the mountain when I knew I had blown it. I did not know where I was, but it felt wrong, made no sense at all. I didn't remember seeing so many trees before.

A floatplane flashed low overhead, engine roaring, and was gone before I could react. I slid the last feet to level ground and began calling in carefully modulated tones. "He-e-lp. He-e-lp. He-e-lp," allowing each cry to fade into silence.

It grew very still. I was no longer afraid. Nothing mattered very much.

I followed the indented track of a stream down into the basin. There was nothing else to do. Once or twice I thought I was near camp and ran panting up the bank to peer into clearings. Each time I saw nothing but trees and snow.

I saw footprints coming toward me in the snow, and I didn't give a shit . . . but there were no cleat marks in these tracks, and I had seen some just like them when I was exploring Taylor Creek the evening before.

I sprinted up the slope and ran into a clearing. Nothing! Wait — the metal roof of the shelter, 100 yards away; and close by, my pack, just as I had left it against the tree.

When I awoke on the couch, two days later, I felt like the survivor of some bizarre catastrophe. My arms and legs still burned. My lips felt like blimps, two canvas bubbles cracked and fused on my face.

I was hungry, having been too tired to eat the big meal I'd prepared on my return.

Re-entry. Doors were slamming up and down the block, kids were yelling, dogs were barking, owners were barking back. Somebody was *hammering* for Godssake!

Giant Pontiacs crashed into my consciousness. A chain saw began buzzing. Jesus! I had passed out of some heavy wilderness narrative straight into civilisation and could not handle the trauma.

I got up and threw on some clothes. It was cold in the house, and I didn't even want to think about being cold. My scalp felt like it had been tattooed. When I had finished typing last night, the den was in almost total darkness. I hadn't noticed. I took the pages into the next room where a light was burning and read through them seven or eight times, not quite understanding the relationship between myself and the character called 'I'. Was that really myself trudging across those virginal pages! Already, the horror was fading . . .

from MOUNTAIN GAZETTE 53 *1977*

Colours

PETER KELEMEN

In 1971, with seven friends, I walked most of the way from the New York-Connecticut border to Mt. Katahdin in Maine. Not much, when compared to the exploits of stump-legged, iron-lunged trail killers, but enough for scared and inexperienced 14- and 15-year-old kids. The trip affected me deeply. I felt, on finishing, that something fundamental had changed in me, that the summer had been a tremendous success.

Connecticut was the light brown of beaten dust and sunlight hitting dry country tracks. It was indistinct with the haze of fear. The first night I cried myself to sleep in the tent for the weight and the distance and the weakness of my legs. Dreaming, I recalled saying goodbye to my parents, severing my ties with roads, with outside help. The first week stretched ahead, seemingly endless. It had not rained for a long time in Connecticut. Springs were often dry, feet and throats burned. A town of greasy gas stations and smokestacks tempted — a promise of escape. The slow times were worst, hunger and bone weariness became synonymous with aching nostalgia for home. And the trail stretched on, hard baked, the colour of dry leaves, cow dung, or sun-killed grass, winding over, always over, steep-sided knolls. Dull, unvarying woodland opened at the summits of these hills, where we emerged sweaty and caked with dust for a vague view and a short rest. In the valleys, we walked along roads in wavering heat, with the stink of tar and exhaust drilling into minds dazed with sun and step, step, step to the next break, the next dripping, muddy spring.

Feet stopped blistering and bled. However, as we became aware of our capabilities, the fear ebbed slowly. Our progress wasn't funny or enjoyable. It hurt in many ways, yet there was a kind of pride glowing, a defiant hope, not even a hope, a wish that we might, after all, reach Katahdin. We began to laugh. Loudly. The laughter I remember best of all. It was harsh and angry, laced with lonely tears. I remember sleeping on someone's front lawn, at some dump of a resort lake, with the phone ringing worriedly inside the empty house as our cook smoke rose. We laughed. We laughed, sitting on a rusty suspension bridge, waiting for cucumbers from a dirty little store. I remember dinner falling into the fire, and the maps lost on a mountain top, and tents with floors like waterbeds when a thunderstorm filled our gullied campsite, and the National All-time Deerfly Killing Contest (only confirmed kills counted), and refusing a ride from a drunken old lady in a white convertible as darkness fell with miles for us still to go. We laughed.

After that first week, we stopped walking for a while. By-passing some trail, we took a bus trip from Great Barrington, in south-west Massachusetts, to Williamstown in the north-west, where we slept in a sheep shed or a hayfield, depending on the weather. For three days we ate, fished and played tennis while our feet healed and poison ivy disappeared. Bruce, part Indian, invented a rain dance; we joined in under the stars, and watched the morning rain sweep off Mt. Greylock and over the farmlands towards us.

Vermont is green and wet. The Green Mountains. After the rain, we debated the start for hours; now, in a day or two, maybe never. The sun came out and we started at three that afternoon. Enthusiasm marked our first few miles, marked all of our walk through Vermont. Beeches, birches, poplar, spruce and fir of the ridgetops buoyed us up with greens, shiny and rough, light and dark; I loved to watch the popple, junk to the foresters; leaves, translucent like ricepaper, grouped loosely on supple branches, responding like wind chimes to the mountain breezes. I loved the play of sunlight in pine needles, facets of a wilderness emerald, and the silhouette of spruce high up against a storm.

In the valleys, farmland spread around us, regimented like a golf course, with the same clipped, luminous green. There was a mountain, a ridge of white rock, barren with the world open on every side, and gods and ambrosia on the summit; a red dawn on another mountaintop, almost too picture-postcard beautiful. We complained about the 'porkies' (porcupines) like old timers, during the nightly ritual of hanging sweaty boots out of reach, or while pulling quills from a dog's tongue.

A food drop (we used small-town post offices) turned out to be nothing but a locked town hall and empty church. We broke a window by accident and threw in five dollars ("God, don't be mad, please").

Everything worked out in Vermont; the sun was beautiful, the rain seemed gentle. To almost all of us. Jeff had not been sleeping well, had lost touch with the hypnotism of the country and realised, as the rest of us did not, that we were killing ourselves, walking too far, camping too late, waking sluggish and later every morning. Just across the Connecticut River, in Hanover, New Hampshire, Jeff left us to go home, surprising us out of our pleasant dream.

New Hampshire is grey; light grey against the sky on radiant mountain-top days, and sometimes a darker, patchy grey of wet rock and wind-driven rain. Dark grey rain greeted us, tired us. We walked until 9 p.m. one night; and the next day, still behind schedule, we had to run to the post office before closing time or eat no dinner. Exhausted, we rested for a day, but tried to recoup lost mileage on the next 9,000 vertical feet and 13 miles over Mt. Mousilauke and the Kinsman Ridge, with the result that not much of southern New Hampshire was impressed on my tired memory; with the result that diarrhoea hit us one by one in the next few days. We collapsed, and spent three days going six miles, and another week resting and day-tripping. It was a beautiful time, for those no longer bound to the bathroom. Katahdin, a long way off, was forgotten for the moment. We ate spaghetti with tomato paste and bread and milk and cereal as our trail food ran out, and read magazines in the state park headquarters, out of the rain. Not bound to any far-away goal, we spent a day on Mt. Lafayette watching clouds and waterfalls, the legitimate activity of backpackers.

In a holiday spirit, we hitched around to Crawford Notch. A bus trip was again planned to make up for lost time. But we could not miss big, ugly, paradoxical Mt. Washington. Our past experiences associated this mountain — 'highest east of the Mississippi and north of the Smokies' — with thunderstorms and alpine flowers and peaks as much like the fabled West as mountain-hungry Easterners could hope for; with exhaust fumes and hot parking lots and flies and garbage and eroded trails and candy wrappers in the scrub and a cute little train; with the obscenity of a mountain 'developed' by the people and for the people, with liberty and equality for all. I love the Presidentials, but hate the people. In street shoes, sequinned sunglasses and Bermuda shorts they get out of their cars on to sunlit asphalt, and then, if they are lucky, die in arctic weather that hits with the speed of wind, on rock as unyielding and cold as time.

We clambered up Webster Cliffs, at the southern end of the ridge, only to be told that the tundra near the summit was too damaged by our sheeplike kin for us to camp there. We descended, to try again from nearer, undamaged lowland. The 'worst weather in America' blasted us on this second climb, obscuring all but our weary group bent into the wind on piles of rain-black boulders. We lunched at three on top, with coffee in the restuarant as the weather worsened. The wind was gusting to 75 miles per hour, the temperature in the 40s. Probably not a good day to go along the high ridge to Mt. Madison, exposed to gusts and lightning. Down then. We forced open the wind-squeezed door, tried to talk above the roaring gale, retreated inside again for communication, and then out into howling, driven rain and sleet. I was still in shorts. Stupid tourists! The wind picked up as we descended through the boulders, slippery with hail like mothballs in every crevice. Tuckerman's Ravine trail was four inches under water, but it was warm and out of the wind. We smiled, breathed, laughed and had a snowball fight. The best Mt. Washington I've ever seen, a promise of adventures in years to come. We bedded down wetly, and caught a bus the next day.

Going to, or from, or around the wilderness is an experience in itself, a special part of any trip. We viewed everything with detachment; drunken recklessness, a wide-eyed, non-participatory wonder, or silent, haughty disdain. Halfway through our detour, we ate pizza cautiously, talked with the car campers, and wrestled until two or three in the morning on the scratchy mowing of the Skowhegan municipal trailer dump. The bus dropped us in the little crossroads of Caratunk, by the Kennebec River, below Pleasant Pond with its Pleasant Pond Mountain. And, finally, we slept for $2.50 apiece in the

Sterling Hotel, Ned on the floor because the bed was too soft for sleep. Back on the trail, we headed into the flat lake country, with only 150 swampy, meandering lakeshore miles to Katahdin.

Maine is a golden, sunlit and happy place — or maybe it is a time. We were in no hurry, with not far to go: in two weeks we would be done, and no obstacles presented themselves. Neither a climax nor an anticlimax, it was, like the pond and mountain, and all the other ponds and mountains, pleasant — also relaxing, even peaceful. There was swimming, and sunshine, time to fish and read, to stop and listen to a branch fall in the woods, and to go and find it, look at it, feel it; a sort of cosmic duty. Earlier, tied to a far-away destination, a timetable, we had no time for cosmic duties. In Maine we bought fresh food, saw a moose, talked with our fellow travellers, gloried in just being outside and free of roads. Graham was hurt, falling on a rock, and for a while emergency loomed large; long discussions were held. But with courage and self-sufficiency he hobbled on, and we double-packed, rejoicing in the reality of the group, now a baptised entity. The last two days were a haze of activity and little sleep. Having finished our week's worth of food, we gorged ourselves on sardines, peanut butter and cupcakes at a roadside store a few miles from our goal in the middle of a hot, 20-mile day; then stumbled on to steak dinner and Katahdin Streams Campground. We climbed the mountain; the top was cold, covered with fog, trails closed; we took a picture, beat a hasty retreat, and went home.

from MOUNTAIN GAZETTE 42 *1976*

The Spirit of Wildness

What are we trying to preserve?

LAURA and GUY WATERMAN

We have talked about what individual hikers and backpackers are doing to help preserve the backwoods environment. We have explored some of the complex decisions facing managers of wild lands. We haven't suggested many simple answers, but we hope we've shed some light on the questions that we all should be asking ourselves.

Now we come back to certain underlying values which we, as two hikers who love the woods and hills in which we walk, feel should not be forgotten. We are addressing ourselves to the fundamental issues. What is it, in the last analysis, that we go to the backwoods to seek? What are the rare qualities that define an outdoors experience? What, really, are we trying to preserve?

To preserve the mountains themselves, first of all. To preserve the green woods, the pure waters, the quiet valleys, the windswept ridges . . . the moss on the boulder . . . the raven on the cloud . . . the frost feathers on the summit cairn . . . the vari-coloured rocks beneath the clear pool . . . the star flower at the trail's edge.

The physical environment is the *sine qua non* of the backcountry experience. Much of this book has spoken of measures needed to preserve it, and many others have written far more eloquently in its defence — from Bryant and Muir to Colin Fletcher. Safeguarding the vegetation, soils, and watersheds of the backcountry already commands the urgent attention of the managers of wild lands. Eternal vigilance is the price of its preservation.

However, there's a lot more at stake. If all we wanted to do was preserve the land, the obvious solution would be to lock it up and throw away the key. What the game is all about is preserving the right relationship of people to the land.

Hikers have a strong root attachment to something which

the Seattle Mountaineers immortalised in the subtitle of their widely read book *Mountaineering: the Freedom of the Hills.* Freedom, at least as defined by an absence of restraint, is one attraction of the backwoods. It's why people go out there.

Yet, with growing numbers of people and their terrible impact on the resource, freedom has to be limited to a degree. *What* degree is the critical question. As climber Royal Robbins says in *Basic Rockcraft:* "a simple equation exists between freedom and numbers: the more people, the less freedom".

Part of the answer lies in that age-old implication of freedom: responsibility. The sensitive hiker and backpacker of today has come a long way towards this obligation. Obviously, we yet have a way to go.

Where individual responsibility can't do the job well enough or soon enough, land managers can be strongly tempted to impose flat regulations. Many times there is no escaping this necessity. On the other hand, as the Appalachian Mountain Club's Backcountry Management Task Force point out:

> Regulations are one of the least desirable techniques for controlling backcountry use because by restricting the user's freedom, they themselves have a negative impact on the quality of the recreational experience. Before imposing regulations, managers should try other approaches such as information and education programmes.
>
> Regulations are not justified simply to make the manager's job easier or to protect the user from himself.

The issue is broader, though, than one of freedom and responsibility for the resource. Apart from, and deeper than both the policies of managers and the practices of hikers, is the spirit of the hills. We have used the term "the spirit of wildness". Maintaining that spirit more than just preserving trees and flowers, informed freedom and sensible rules — is one of the toughest jobs for all of us. It is also critical to preserving the underlying reason why we go to the hills.

As Rene Dubos expressed it in *So Human an Animal:*

> . . . human beings need primeval nature to re-establish contact now and then with their biological origins; a sense of continuity with the past and with the rest of creation is probably

essential to the long-range sanity of the human species.

When we use the phrase 'the spirit of wildness', we refer to a wide spectrum of loosely connected elements of the back-country experience: to solitude, to difficulty and challenge, to that indefinable but intensely real feeling that grips the hiker buffeted by wind on the rocky heights, or held in fascination by the silence and greenness of deep woods. It is this spirit of wildness which civilisation or man's tailor-made imitations of nature can never replace. It is irreplaceable, and to many it is essential to life's spirit. Frederic Harrison once put it:

> Our present world is a world of remarkable civilisation, but it is not very natural and not very happy. We need yet some snatches of the life of youth . . . to draw sometimes great draughts of simplicity and beauty. We need sometimes that poetry should not be droned into our ears but flashed into our senses. And man, with all his knowledge and his pride, needs sometimes to know nothing and to feel nothing, but that he is a marvellous atom in a marvellous world.

from BACKWOODS ETHICS *1979*

Low Hills

FRANK SMYTHE

There is, doubtless, much to be said for the virtues of walking such-and-such a distance over the hills in such-and-such a time, but I wish somebody could tell me what are these virtues for, lazy fellow that I am, I have never been able to discern them. Because of this laziness I have only once done a long walk; it was some 50 miles in length and the time occupied was in the neighbourhood of 24 hours. And only once have I been over a large number of summits in one day. I am far too lazy ever to want to do anything like it again.

The 50-mile walk was over the Surrey hills a few years ago. It was a still, calm evening when Hugh Slingsby and I left Ashtead and the glow-worms were plain to see on the slopes of Box Hill. Possibly it is due to some hard-bitten prejudice, or possibly to some association with my upbringing, or maybe to some ingrained pride of race and country, but if I had an unlimited choice for the site of my home, I would choose the English countryside. Instinct again; an emotion incapable of a material interpretation or analysis. Home to an Englishman is not only his home, his street, his village or his town, it is the English countryside. To know how much it means you should walk over it as we walked, during a moonlit night in June. Then, whatever your feelings, however much you deplore nationalism, however much of a pacifist you are, you will understand why men have died, and are still ready to die, for England.

We passed over Box Hill, that great close-cropped grassy hump on which the skiing is so good when there is snow, and strolled down to the Burford Bridge Hotel, where we refreshed ourselves and talked Test cricket with the proprietor. Then on, over Ranmore Common, Netley Heath and Albury Downs to the little church of St. Martha's, which stands by the Pilgrim's Way. We stood there and looked across the moonlit hills from Hascombe to Holmbury and Leith Hill, and saw between Hascombe and Hurt Wood the level line of the Weald.

455

Bands of diaphanous vapour lying in the valleys picked out the crests of the ridges, which rose, one after the other, in dark orderly waves. And over all reigned an immense peacefulness. Not silence — there is never absolute silence in a countryside — but peace.

Dawn found us on Blackheath Common. There was nothing dramatic in its advent, no fierce and wild rush of colouring, no bold sallies, nothing to ape the drama and pageantry of an Alpine dawn. It was an opening of dim eyes, a gradual realisation of wakefulness.

We were sleepy; not tired in the sense that our limbs ached or that we were fatigued, but sleepy, so much so that we found it difficult to make a straight course across country, and presently discovered we were going in quite the wrong direction. So we sat down to rest for a moment . . .

We awoke four hours later. The sun was well up and fast drying the dew, the fresh air was full of birdsong, and a light breeze was stirring the gorse and heather.

We ate breakfast, then went on our way and, true to Alpine tradition, ate another and larger breakfast at the first inn we came to.

All that day we lounged among the hills: Hurtwood Hill, Pitch Hill, Holmbury Hill and Leith Hill. It mattered nothing to us how many miles we covered or the time we took to cover them. We walked when we liked and rested when we liked.

There can be few eminences whence the eye can take in more of England's beauty than Holmbury Hill.

From Hampshire the hills stretch ridge on ridge, then comes a long line of Downs crowned in one place by Chanctonbury Ring and broken in another by Brightling Gap. Northwards is the Thames Valley and the Chilterns. Eastwards the long escarpment of the North Downs extends towards Westerham and Sevenoaks, Wrotham and Maidstone — the North Downs of my childhood. Those who love hills need go no higher than Holmbury's summit. They will discover there that height counts for little and that it is the hill that matters. The low hills teach us that height, be it a mere 200 or 300ft. is something precious, something that quickens life to a nobler rhythm. No earth raised on earth can accomplish so subtle a transformation, can bring such joy. There is something greater. It is the spirit of the hills.

from THE SPIRIT OF THE HILLS *1933*

The Conquest of Nature

JOHN HAY

The city I once lived in founded its artificial eyes and its forgetfulness on rock. This glacial deposit I am now perched on rests over deeper deposits that in turn rest on the bedrock of the continental shelf. The granite slopes I climbed as a boy are an inseparable part of me, and lie under all I have since discovered. They have seen me to a new season. Autumn days open to me again, many springs, summers and winters having flowed behind, and I go climbing again in the New Hampshire hills I came from. I pass a thrush in the trees, upright, poised in a scared, wild way, woodbrown with a dark forest eye ringed with white, still carrying spring carrillons in its spirit, a watery advertising, self-struck on a rim of feeling, an edge of knowing that helps keep the forest intact. That thrush is the apple of my eye.

From an open ledge further up, I see three hawks riding down the ridges they follow south, slightly rocking, wheeling and soaring in an easy relationship with the high air. The wind off the ridges carries them down between the lesser and greater hills and mountains of the Appalachians. They glide with only a quivering of their beautifully taut wings, taking the misty blue sky on their feathers. Their wings are sky-bent, hammered and moulded to the uses of the air. So they rock and pass, meeting the wide gaze of distance in their pride. The hawk way is the reliable one that tells me how a continent is measured, mile after electric, blazing mile.

These modest-sized, glaciated, worn, very old mountains are the right size for me. There is a brook pouring down nearby, whose waters carved ages of rock into long fluted channels where, as a boy, I used to 'shoot the chutes' with free and dizzy excitement, landing in deep, cold basins at the bottom. In the side pools and eddies, water striders drift and propel themselves forward with short, thrusting motions, making dimpled reflections on the surface. They meet each other and then spasmodically twitch apart, not unlike birds in flight. The waters of the brook constantly lisp and rustle, rush and whirl over the gracefully accommodating rocks, taking the free way out. Nothing seems to have changed. Even the log shelter where I spent the night on the way up, hearing a porcupine snuffling and chewing on the corner posts, looks much the same as it did. The rocks are in permanent steps and terraces the way they used to be, while the water goes twirling down the long slides. In some places square rocks are perched on larger boulders like the ruins of an ancient civilisation, but this history goes further back; and it is strange to think that I was a part of it and now return, though everything in my life has changed and I live in times that never stop upgrading change. I have had all manner of intermediate, often catastrophic worlds falling or rising around me, and probably the same process will be characteristic of the next thousand years, while the brook keeps rushing down. Its water represents our low allowance, and that it accompanies us puts human impossibility and violence in the frame of fantasy they belong in, at least in the context of abiding room where abysmal fate is taken in its stride. Yes, everything has changed, but all the mountain and these cold, rushing waters have to express is capacity, which, in terms of their patience, must be far greater than it looks to any man, any scientist or engineer, any temporary rider with his foot on the pedal.

The brook makes a wind-like sound as it pours down the rocks, shaded by trees that will soon be sugared with snow. It is going to be much darker in a few weeks, and icy cold, and the blue jay bouncing from the hemlock knows it because it is partly cloaked in darkness already. We know jays for their iridescent feathers, for their mischievous natures and their harshly musical cries. But they have other qualities too, in earth's keeping, as hidden as Mephistopheles. They were

born to the secret masteries of privation, created by the endlessly evolving nature of planetary energy. Their way of
change is as exceptional as ours. Whenever I see them, or
other life forms, in different environments, they present
another vision, which is masterful enough. Jays are great
performers. So it says through the dark evergreens and the
glossy birch that stand over the banks and the perpetually
running water beating in my ears. Everything stands in for
dignity. I feel the total absence of pretence around me, a
power I lack the strength to fully understand. The slow
building of icebergs and their melting back, the restraint in
rocks, the roaring and dying down of the wind, the vast
holding behind all existence, the enormous lag that our
instant perception feels, have given expression to the blue jay
and the trees. They all seem to say, or stridently cry out: "On
time. On time," and though any man or woman might say:
"Not my time," it holds, in the incipience of rainbows, the
darkness in failing light, the sun that ensures that universal
trend toward rising which nothing escapes.

So I go on climbing, thinking that if my own life is any
criterion, the 'Ascent of Man', despite his superior brain, is
no straightforward progress from bottom to top, from lesser
to higher forms. It might in fact go down as well as up, and is
at the very least meandering, facing stubborn resistance all
the way. I think we were held down for a purpose, so that no
matter how far we move out we should return to this monumental gravity, the weight of sea and mountains, the rock
that is the only real leader to the sky. I walk against the wind
and it is in me, a counter force that gives me my direction,
like a fish swimming upcurrent. That my life is full of
dissatisfaction implies promise as much as failure. Incom-
pleteness teases me on, and that was and will be my
beginning, not far from Newfound Lake.

I have no sense of triumph in reaching the top. I have
conquered nothing. I only cry out to the distance: "How
beautiful you are!" The exuberance of giant shadows lies
across it, the waves of a world with all weather on its body,
smouldering red, lavender and dark green, rolling away,
through curtains of mist, with lakes shining below like spots

of glass through a hazy sun. Nothing we can do will defeat that impenetrable unity. There is also no final lifting of the veil to tell you where you are, what entitles you to promises. Heights are climbed not to get away, not to see our lives as the spasms they are, but to join in universal application.

Patches of gray-green lichen cover the bare gray rock of the summit, which is studded by protruding knobs of white quartz. Here and there a lichen of luminous yellow-green overlaps the other variety like so many splashes of paint. The rock leans out with long cracks and crevices, with rounded shoulders, a scoured, bathed, enduring hide. I hear the tinkling twitter of snow buntings close by, and see them rise like a scattering of petals flung up by the wind. They fly out beyond the summit and drop down again. A light brown face patch appears just over the ridge, and then more of the little birds come into view as they explore the rocks for the seeds of the tundra-like plants that shelter there. I walk toward them and they fly ahead of me with airy, gay abandon. I almost follow them out to where the world falls off. Their white underwings shine as they fly, and on the ground they show their wonderfully subtle and delicate blendings of black, white and a cinnamon that contrasts with a still lighter shade of brown verging on orange.

I know them from the ocean shore, where they dip, rise and scatter out like flecks of foam across the dunes. Waves are their medium, the waving open fields, the waves of sand, the tumbling waves of rock from which all sand flows. They belong to thousands of miles of continental shadows and surfaces. All the way down from the arctic barrens where they breed, they know the contours of the earth. They pick out their chosen food and place like a sculptor finding the right marble in the hills, or perfect, water-worn boulders by the shore.

There is an incomparable rightness to things, whose following and transgression were known in us long before the reasonable concept of ecology was born. The directions we take were not only decided through human reckoning. Modern civilisation has not captured the universe as a result of concentrating on its mathematical components. We have not conquered the inherited rhythms of our bodies through engineering. We may spend our lives jumping to the tune of man-made time, but looking into the future is not a modern but a human game. The true adventure lies in waves that I and the snow buntings are aware of in our mutual being.

From the mountain top I see the exuberance and recklessness of theatre everywhere, the ritual of nature fired in its trees. Men are actors, meant for ritual threat and display, greed and extravagance. I am not the apex of evolution, and if there is any lasting value in my presence it is measured by the ceremonials of earth. The mountain is my continuity, waiting for me since I was ten years old, I stand in the axis of its spirit like the red-tailed hawk that hangs in the heights above my head.

On the way back, climbing down through columns of trees, the deeply sparkling pines, the blue-gray beech, the birches in arctic white, the bonfire maples, I meet a nearly immoderate quiet, while scattered yellow leaves fall gently ahead of me. I

"It was most enjoyable, but I think I've had enough of the environment for one day."

know that the human fires down below, out in the cities with the brown haze over them, riding the highways, riding the planet for all it is worth, even now roaring distantly in my head, will consume, flare up, and die down. The nature of peace requires it.

There is exhaustion in the air. The ground is cool and subdued as the hills turn dusky and purple in late afternoon. On the lower slopes there are cleared fields full of lank, dark cornstalks. Milkweeds have split their pods and the white silk lies over browning grass like wisps of cotton, or is concentrated in spots like the downy feathers of a chicken caught by a fox. Now summer is broken for good. There is no certainty except in the spread of evening, royal and wide, and the coming on of a night which all life shares without distinction. Nothing less could equal human desire. Nothing less could reach beyond it.

from NEW ENGLAND REVIEW *1979*

THOU
SHALT
NOT
WRECK
THE
PLACE

WE HAVE RESERVED THIS
LAST PAGE FOR A BIT OF PETTY
MORALIZING....IN TRUTH, NOTHING
THAT CAN BE SAID OR WRITTEN WILL
SAVE OUR WILDS FROM THE DEPREDATIONS
OF THE PLUNDERING HERD, OTHER THAN,
OF COURSE, THE IMMEDIATE AND THOROUGH
ELIMINATION OF THE CHIEF PLUNDERER;
HOWEVER, THIS WOULD CONSTITUTE A CONFLICT
OF INTEREST TO OUR READERSHIP, AS WELL
AS PROVE AN INSURMOUNTABLE HINDRANCE
TO THE FINANCIAL SUCCESS OF THIS BOOK....

Acknowledgements

The following authors and publishers are thanked and acknowledged for use of copyright material:

To B. G. Barfoot for *The Lost Valley* by E. F. Knight
To Alastair Borthwick and John Smith and Son (Glasgow) for *Hunger March* and *Lairig Ghru*, both from *Always a Little Further*
To the Butlins Organisation for *The Big Walk*
To Cassell (London) for *Mountain Dawn* by Seton Gordon, from *Highland Days*·
To Climber and Rambler and (respectively) Malcolm Arney, Roger Smith and Walt Unsworth for *The Long Skye Ridge, More Than Stanes and Watter* and *Rough Shoot*
To Climbing and Michael Tobias for *On Walking Away*
To Constable (London) and John Hillaby for *Departure From Strasbourg* and *The Warm South*, both from *Journey Through Europe*
To David and Charles (Newton Abbot) and Brian le Messurier for *A Dartmoor Mist* from William Crossing's *Amid Devonia's Alps*
To Andre Deutsch (London) and George B. Schaller for *Return to Jumla* from *Stones of Silence*
To Diadem Books (London) and W. H. Murray for *New Year on Ben Nevis* from *Mountaineering in Scotland*
To Victor Gollancz (London) and Showell Styles for *White-out on Foel-goch* and *The Glyders' Ghost* from *The Mountains of North Wales*
To The Great Outdoors and (respectively) Brian Atkin, John T. K. Barr, Tony Foxlow, Chris Godber, Bob Hankinson, Dewi Jones, Cameron McNeish, Graham Newson, Roger Redfern, Kev Reynolds, Frances Slade, Sydney Smith, Showell Styles, Malcolm Gwyn Thomas, Livia Visser-Fuchs, Hugh Westacott and Richard Wilson for *Summer on the South Downs Way* and *Along the Cumbria Way, Quest in a Haunted Glen, A Moorland Mystery, I Know, I Know!, The Pennine Way in Winter, Nantlle to Llanberis, In the Steps of Deirdre, The Art of Coarse Walking, A Very Special Place, The Last Green Valley, Stepper From Whipsiderry, How to Become a Ghost Without Really Trying, Lament for the Roadside Fire, The Conversion of Ol' One-Pocket, North Downs Pilgrimage, Listening to the Silence* and *The Ridgeway, A Pleasant Country Bramble*
To Hodder and Stoughton (London) and The Countess of Essex and Anthony Shiel Associates for *Low Hills* by Frank Smythe from *Spirit of the Hills*
To Moorland Publishing Co. (Ashbourne) for *The Kinder Scout Trespasses* from *Freedom to Roam*
To New England Review and John Hay for *The Conquest of Nature*
To W. W. Norton and Co. Inc. and John Hay for *An Unimagined Frontier*
To Rodale Press (Emmaus, Pennsylvania) and Eric Ryback, James R. Hare and Margaret and Bump Smith for *On the Appalachian Trail, Grandma Gatewood* and *Cold Night in Nantahala*
To Running Press (Philadelphia) for *The Passes of the High Sierra* by John Muir and *Game Regions of the Upper Sacramento* by Joaquin Miller both taken from *West of the Rocky Mountains*
To Dick Sale for *The Wet Welsh Three-thousanders*
To The Scottish Mountaineering Club Journal and (respectively) Robert Aitken,

465

466   ACKNOWLEDGEMENTS

Hamish Brown, Philip Gribbon for *Stravagers and Marauders, Reality Recrudescent* and *Five Times Lucky on Ben Alder*

To The Scots Magazine and Roblu Lloyd Jones for *Beinn Ime by Moonlight*

To Stone Wall Press (Washington, DC) and Laura and Guy Waterman for *Silence and Sounds* and *The Spirit of Wildness* from *Backwoods Ethics*

To Strider (Long Distance Walkers Association) and (respectively) Dick Crawshaw and Dianne Bullard (née Pegg) for *The World's Walking Record* and *Two Dry Feet*

To Showell Styles for *The Art of Walking* from *The Campers' and Trampers' Weekend Book*

To Mountain Gazette (now defunct) and (respectively) Michael Tobias, Randy Thomas and David Joeris for *Sinai, Camping Out* and *From Desert to Pines*

To Backpacker (Ziff-Davis Publishing Co. New York) and (respectively) Nicholas Howe, Les Scharnberg, Dennis Drabelle and Ray Shepherd for *Boots/Roots, Hiking the Great Divide, Peaks and Waves* and *To Bishop Pass and Back*

To Rip Off Press (San Francisco) and Sheridan Anderson for sundry cartoon sketches from *Baron Von Mabel's Backpacking*

Every effort has been made to contact copyright holders for each article included in this anthology, and we apologise to anyone who has been inadvertently omitted.

Notes About the Articles

Vision of the Alps
Hilaire Belloc brilliantly captures the mixture of relief, exultation and humility experienced by the long-distance walker when at last he catches a glimpse of his far-off objective. The extract comes from Belloc's classic work, *The Path to Rome.*

The Ascent of Snowdon
George Borrow at his pompous best. *Wild Wales,* from which this piece is taken, is such a self-important book that I sometimes wonder how Borrow survived to write it — his spouting Welsh verse to a Welshman on Snowdon's summit sums it all up.

Dartmoor Mist
Apart from being an enjoyable example of William Crossing's rumbustious writing, this account shows how even a man who knows the area well can be led astray by the infamous mists that cloak the moor from time to time. Crossing's *Guide to Dartmoor,* first published in 1911, is worth-while reading for anyone visiting Dartmoor for the first time.

A Night among the Pines
Stevenson's story of his travels with Modestine — not the most affable of companions — still makes fascinating reading, even though it was first published over 100 years ago. The route he followed to St Jean du Gard is now a waymarked *sentier de grande randonnée,* traversed by donkeyless modern pilgrims, better equipped physically than R.L.S. — but is our mental approach as good?

The First Gentleman Backpacker
Thomas de Quincey seems an unlikely character to find in an anthology on walking, yet here he is storming through Wales in 1802, with home-made tent and on very short commons for much of the time. Clearly, there's nothing new about self-sufficiency on the trail.

A Walk to Hardraw Force
Wordsworth's letter to Samuel Taylor Coleridge shows how unexceptional such a walk was to the great poet in his younger days. He and his sister, Dorothy, went out in all weathers, with (by modern standards) little protection, and from these experiences sprang the inspiration for some of the finest poetry in the English language.

High Sierra Passes
A sample of American pioneer writing. John Muir, a Scot, explored vast areas of California, including the now-famous Yosemite Valley; through taking President Roosevelt out camping, he was partly responsible for the early establishment of National Parks in the USA.

Stravagers and Marauders
A wry glimpse into the troubled history of rights of way in Scotland: a battle that goes on still. Robert Aitken, a researcher into trends in recreation and tourism, is the author of the official guide to Scotland's first designated long-distance trail, the West Highland Way.

Grandma Gatewood
James Hare was the editor of a monumental two-volume compilation of Appalachian Trail stories. Here he tells the tale of the frail lady who, with minimal equipment, became the first woman to walk the full 2,000 miles of the trail. Grandma Gatewood became a legend in her own lifetime.

The Kinder Scout Trespasses
An episode unlikely to be forgotten while there are ramblers in England. Howard Hill's book, *Freedom to Roam,* tells of the struggle for access to moor and mountain, for which men were prepared to go to prison in the 1930s. Howard Hill died while this anthology was being prepared.

From Nantlle to Llanberis — A Walk From Past to Present
Dewi Jones is a Welshman with a deep feeling for his land and his forebears. This piece is both a description of a fine walk and an evocation of the landscape in the best tradition of historical mountain writing.

In the Steps of Deirdre
Scotland's Highlands are peopled as much with ghosts as with living men and women. Folk memories here are long indeed and the echoes that resound through this tale go back a thousand years. Cameron McNeish, one of the younger generation of Scottish writers, is a man with a passion for his country's hills and traditions.

A Very Special Place
Papadil is on the island of Rhum, off the west coast of Scotland. Roger Redfern, former editor of *Mountain Craft* magazine and author of many books on walking and climbing in Britain, recalls the history of the place and the Bullough family, with whom it is closely associated.

The Ridgeway Path — A Walk Through History
A veritable 'path through history'. No one can say how old this trackway is; it was used as a trade route for thousands of years before it was designated as one of England's long-distance footpaths. Hugh Westacott, author of *The Walker's Handbook,* has a wide knowledge of these ancient trackways, and he catches the mood of the Ridgeway to perfection.

Game Regions of the Upper Sacramento
This piece is written with such a sense of enjoyment that I could not leave it out. I hope the reader will share my pleasure in Joaquin Miller's vivid and refreshing style.

Along the Cumbria Way
Brian Atkin has the gift of capturing the feelings of so many of us in his descriptions of walking long trails. The Cumbria Way passes through the incomparable scenery of the English Lake District, and Atkin's account of climbing Great Gable on a bitter day in what should have been spring is very moving.

Lairig Ghru
We will encounter Alasdair Borthwick again, in more humorous mood. Here, he travels one of the classic walks of Scotland, a brooding mountain pass rising to over 2,700ft.

On the Appalachian Trail
Eric Ryback became famous with his book about the Pacific Crest Trail. In this lesser-known account, he offers a stark description of the loneliness and doubts that can assail those who walk the Appalachian Trail.

Five Times Lucky at Ben Alder
Here is a cautionary tale for all who have made the mistake of supposing some mountains to be easy. They may be, but all too often they are not! It takes a hardy man to return time and again until his goal is achieved.

Mountain Dawn
Seton Gordon lived to be over 90 and published dozens of books on Scotland, all of

them worth reading. This piece is included as a small tribute to the man, and it is a fine example of his more lyrical style of writing.

Cape Cod — An Unimagined Frontier
John Hay is one of America's leading naturalist-writers. Here, he evokes the many moods of a walk around the Cape Cod peninsula — a walk that would now be almost impossible. The sea is never far away, physically or spiritually.

Two Dry Feet
No one can say how many thousands have attempted the Lyke Wake Walk, the notorious 42-mile trudge across North Yorkshire. But it is certain that all who reach the end do so with relief. Diane Bullard, who has completed a number of 100-mile walks, did it twice straight off, and (a rare experience) with two dry feet.

Reality Recrudescent
Hamish Brown is so far the only person to have climbed all 280 Scottish 'Munros' (mountains over 3,000ft.) in a single expedition. This article is a microcosm both of the walk and of the book [Hamish's Mountain Walk] that followed (which has won its author a Scottish Arts Council Award).

The World's Walking Record
Dick Crawshaw, a British Member of Parliament and former soldier, aimed single-mindedly at achieving a world record: the greatest distance walked without lengthy stops by one person. He gives a gripping account of his preparation for this task and its subsequent performance over four days and nights.

The Wet Welsh Three-Thousanders
Another classic expedition — the traverse of the 14 Welsh mountain summits over 3,000ft. This time, though, the party concerned tried very hard *not* to succeed, although eventually they bumbled through in a manner described by Dick Sale with almost too much reality.

More than Stanes and Watter
The Bob Graham Round is a challenge taken up by many fell-walkers and runners: the ascent of 42 Lake District peaks within 24 hours, involving 72 miles of travel and 25,000ft. of ascent. I did it to celebrate my 40th birthday (it seemed as good a reason as any); this account was written two days later.

Sinai
Another dramatic change of mood and location. Michael Tobias sets off into the Sinai Desert, naked in body and soul. The intensity of his experience inspired this piece of exultant, all-out writing.

The Big Walk
The big walk was a very British phenomenon: an organised challenge walk from one end of the land to the other, with substantial cash prizes. The book from which this account is taken was written anonymously by one of the 700 hopeful starters, and it gives an accurate insight into what drives people to such lengths.

The Warm South
John Hillaby's books are all deservedly best-sellers. We have two extracts from *Journey Through Europe;* this short chapter covers the very end of his trek from North Sea to Mediterranean, after months of trials and tribulations.

Extracts from 'The Rucksack Man'
Sebastian Snow went further: he tried to walk from Tierra del Fuego to Alaska, but had to stop in Panama. These two extracts from his book provide an extraordinary contrast: the almost unbelievable unpreparedness of the start and the grim yet never humourless struggle at the end.

Long Skye Ridge
Skye is a mecca for climbers and adventurous walkers. Malcolm Arney put aside the temptations of the better known Cuillin; his ridge is in the north of the island, in Trotternish, and he walked it on a day of almost unbearable heat.

Summer on the South Downs Way
From Skye we move 600 miles south. Brian Atkin's perfect memorandum of the rhythm of a long walk rises and falls with the tides of day, inducing a mood the author is rightly reluctant to break at journey's end.

Peaks and Waves
A different rhythm now — the rhythm that walking close to the sea imposes on the foot-traveller. Dennis Drabelle's walk was in California, but in spirit it could have been almost anywhere.

Departure from Strasbourg
Here we find John Hillaby half way through his European journey, trying to pick up the pace after one of his many memorable encounters with local people.

The Cornish Coastal Path: Stepper from Whipsiderry
It is high summer in Cornwall, in the far south-west of England, and the lyrical mood Frances Slade tries so hard to establish is repeatedly threatened by those who visit the coast, not for walking, but for surfing, sun-soaking or just doing nothing.

To Bishop Pass and Back
Here, Ray Shepherd echoes, almost unconsciously, the writing of John Muir. But it is now a century later and everything has changed — the walker, his equipment, his attitude. Only the landscape remains immutable.

North Downs Pilgrimage
A low key but beautifully balanced observation of the ways of the English by a visitor from Holland. What is not said is almost as important as what *is* said!

From Desert to Pines
David Joeris describes a backpacking trip in the wilderness of the Guadalupe National Park in Texas. The walker crosses the crest of a ridge and finds himself in another country, with no sign of civilisation for a hundred miles.

An Eventful Day
A splendid example of anonymous Victorian Alpine writing. It is a story of a warm day followed by an intensely cold night, a combination which would have led to the death of the writer had it not been for the timely intervention of two monks from the hospice of St. Bernard.

The Pennine Way in Winter
Bob Hankinson discovers that the trail offers a rather more sublime experience in winter than it does in overcrowded summer. The account is brief but has the requisite quality of making the reader wish he was out there walking.

Beinn Ime by Moonlight
A winter moonlight climb is a rare experience, and Robin Lloyd-Jones' account grips the reader as hard as the frost gripped the mountain on that memorable night.

New Year on Ben Nevis
We stay in Scotland to celebrate New Year on Ben Nevis with W. H. Murray. A taut, laconic account of an experience that must have been almost too much to bear.

White-Out on Foel Goch
Showell Styles glimpses unworldly mountains through the driving snow, and imagines briefly that he is dead. Fortunately for us, he is not, though this blizzard might well have defeated lesser men.

I Know! I Know!
Also from North Wales, this is a simply told account of a horrifying mountain accident. What happened to Chris Godber could happen to any of us, and it is no wonder he now believes in guardian angels.

Cold Night in Nantahala
The Appalachian Trail, in November. Margaret and Bump Smith are caught in a

sudden blizzard at 6,000ft. on Standing Indian Mountain, and it is all they can do to keep going until they reach the safety of a cabin.

Return to Jumla
One of the best accounts I have read of walking in the snows of the Himalayas. George Schaller describes in vivid detail the daily battle with the elements as his small party seeks a way out of the mountains.

The Lost Valley
E. F. Knight was a war correspondent for *The Times* (London) in the late nineteenth century, as well as being a fine travel writer. The highly adventurous crossing of the Alps featured here underlines once again man's marvellous ability to survive in a hostile environment.

Notes on Vagrancy
Isabelle Eberhardt reflects on the walker's freedom to wander and concludes that 'leaving is the finest and bravest act of all'.

Boots/Roots
As long as there are walkers, there will be arguments about gear. Nicholas Howe questions some common views on footwear for the hills — his aunt wore sneakers, so why do walkers nowadays need heavy boots? This article will probably encourage many readers to think again about the way they treat their feet.

The Art of Coarse Walking
Graham Newson provides a little light relief for those who find that walkers take themselves a bit too seriously sometimes.

Lament for the Roadside Fire
Showell Styles looks both back and forward. He regrets the passing of the gentlemen of the road and the art they had of coaxing the unlikeliest bundles of sticks into a blaze, and wonders if those days might not return when the oil runs out and the motorways are deserted.

The Art of Walking
The same author considers the walker's art in some depth. There are techniques to be learnt, even in the simple act of putting one foot in front of another; worth thinking about when you do it 36,000 times in the course of a 20-mile walk.

Silence and Sounds
The next two pieces take similar themes: our lack of appreciation of quietness in a noisy, hurried world. Laura and Guy Waterman take to the hills in Vermont, where they find a necessary refreshment of spirit, which they are willing to share with those of like mind.

Listening to the Silence
An art we need to redevelop. Hugh Westacott listens to the silence in Wales. It is perhaps harder to find perfect silence in Britain than in other parts of the world, but that merely makes the effort more worthwhile, and the reward all the greater.

Quest in a Haunted Glen
Strange experiences in the mountains are legion. John Barr and his young companions came across a poltergeist in an abandoned Scottish lodge. This piece describes a later return to the same spot, in the hope of disturbing the ghost.

Hunger March
The hilarious tale of four braw lads who set off on a 30-mile hike across Skye to a distant youth hostel, imagining they could do it in one go. It took them two and a half days, by which time they were delirious with hunger; yet the magic of the Cuillins, which they had come to climb, still exerted itself on their minds.

A Moorland Mystery
A Yorkshire ghost story: an encounter with a headless man on the route of the Lyke Wake Walk. If you have any imagination, read this at home, and not out in a lonely camp somewhere!

How to Become a Ghost Without Really Trying
Sydney Smith created his own ghost, providing three susceptible American girls with a Highland experience they would never forget — and then finds himself overhearing them recounting the tale.

The Glyders' Ghost
Showell Styles' Glyders ghost was formless and seems quite inexplicable: a manifestation of the mountain spirit, perhaps?

Rough Shoot
No ghosts in this story. Walt Unsworth tells of four climbers who took up 'this walking lark'. There is more than a grain of truth for most of us as we follow their uneven progress over the Derbyshire peat hags.

A Pleasant Country Bramble
Richard Wilson details some of the minor hazards likely to be met by the walker in the agricultural country of southern Britain. The author is still walking, despite his 'close encounters' with farmers, jungle-covered paths, and bulls.

Sgor Thuilm and the Corrie of the Birches
The expedition undertaken by W. Kersley Holmes and described here may seem ordinary enough, but it does show how different walking is in Scotland, and how rewarding it is to achieve what you set out to do.

Colours
Peter Kelemen's colours are those of a 15-year-old discovering the wilderness for the first time, on a trip that was too long, too hard, and almost too much for him and his equally young companions. They traversed some of the best and wildest country in New York and Maine, hungry, homesick, yet finally happy.

The Last Green Valley
The valley concerned is in the Spanish Pyrenees, but it could be anywhere. The author makes a sensitive plea for the preservation of the wilderness from man's ravaging advance. Kev Reynolds now lives in England, but his memory of Pyrenean days is acute, and we should all take note of the message he gives us.

Low Hills
The hills described by F. S. Smythe are those of Surrey, far from the usual haunts of this great mountaineer. He tries a long tramp in southern England and is honest enough to admit that it is not entirely to his liking.

Camping Out
This tale is told as much by Randy Thomas's *alter ego* as by himself. He gets lost, climbs and descends a dozen times, loses fear, and ultimately finds a little more of himself.

The Spirit of Wildness
'What are we trying to preserve?' ask Laura and Guy Waterman. What, indeed. It seems at times that we are all seeking to preserve different things, while the quality of wilderness experience fades away. This is an eloquent plea for responsibility.

The Conquest of Nature
Not a conquest at all, in John Hay's poetic description. We climb not to reach a certain physical point, but to get nearer to our inner selves, to shed pretence; not to conquer nature, but to share ourselves with her.

On Walking Away
Finally, irresistibly, Michael Tobias, who provides a good note on which to end an exploration of the world of walking. Tobias is an explorer of every facet of his own walking and climbing experience and at the very end he throws a Zen quotation at us, which will surely strike, as the man says, a deep chord.

Guidebooks and Information

UNITED KINGDOM AND IRELAND

The Walker's Handbook by H. D. Westacott (Penguin Books) gives details of all the guidebooks currently available for Britain's long-distance walks.

A fact sheet on long-distance paths in Britain is published by The Ramblers' Association, 1-5 Wandsworth Road, London SW8 2LJ. Single copies are free (on receipt of an A4 s.a.e.); prices for bulk orders are available on application.

The Ramblers' Association also publish a useful *Bed and Breakfast Guide* (£1 for the 1981 edition) which lists accommodation available on many paths.

Free illustrated leaflets to the officially-designated paths in Britain are available from The Countryside Commission, John Dower House, Crescent Place, Cheltenham, Glos GL50 2RZ. These leaflets also contain details of guides, notably the very high-standard official guides to each path (HMSO).

The Long Distance Walker's Handbook by Alan and Barbara Blatchford (published privately in 1981) is a useful compendium of all the long-distance walks and 'challenge walks' in Britain.

Long Distance Footpaths; An International Directory by H. D. Westacott (Penguin Books), currently under preparation, is likely to be a very useful publication.

Principal publishers of footpath guides and maps in the United Kingdom include the following:
Cicerone Press, Harmony Hall, Milnthorpe, Cumbria LA7 7QE.
Cordee, 249 Knighton Church Road, Leicester LE2 3JQ.
Constable and Co. Ltd., 10 Orange Street, London WC2H 7EG.
Dalesman Publications, Clapham, via Lancaster.
Footpath Publications, Adstock Cottage, Adstock, Buckingham MK18 2HZ.
Her Majesty's Stationery Office, 49 High Holborn, London WC1V 6HB.
Spurbooks, Allander House, 137-141 Leith Walk, Edinburgh EH6 8NS.
Stile Publications, Mercury House, Otley, West Yorkshire.
Thornhill Press, 24 Moorend Road, Cheltenham, Glos.

EUROPE

Maps and guides for many European countries can be obtained from Stanfords International Map Centre, Long Acre, London WC2.

Maps and guides for France can also be obtained from IGN Maps (UK) Ltd., 122 Kings Cross Road, London WC1X 9DS. One map shows all the *Sentier de Grande Randonnee,* the long-distance paths, in France.

The Austrian Alpine Club, 13 Longcroft House, Fretherne Road, Welwyn Garden City, Herts AL8 6PQ, have a comprehensive list of publications covering the Alpine countries of Austria, Italy, and Switzerland, in both English and the native languages.

NORTH AMERICA

The following addresses will be found helpful:
Alpine Club of Canada, PO Box 1026, Banff, Alberta, Canada T0L 0C0.
American Alpine Club, 113 East 90th Street, New York NY 10028, USA.

Appalachian Trail Conference, PO Box 236, Harpers Ferry, West Virginia WV 25425, USA.

American Adventurers Association, Suite 301, 444 NE Ravenna Boulevard, Seattle, Washington WA 98115, USA.

Alaska Discovery Enterprises, PO Box 337, Juneau, Alaska AK 99802, USA, organise treks along the John Muir Trail in Alaska.

The Wilderness Society, 4260 E. Evans Avenue, Denver, Colorado CO 80222, USA, offer backpacking trips in a number of areas.

The Sierra Club, 530 Bush Street, San Francisco, California CA 94108, USA, have an extensive list of publications and also organise trips.

The Mountaineers, 719 Pike Street, Seattle, Washington WA 98101, also produce guidebooks and organise treks.

International Backpackers Association, PO Box 85, Lincoln Center, Maine ME 00458, USA.

National Trails Council, c/o Open Lands Project, 53 West Jackson Boulevard, Chicago, Illinois IL 60604, USA.

American Hiking Society, 1701 18th St. N.W., Washington, D.C. 20009, USA.

Subject Index

476 SUBJECT INDEX

Index of Authors